The Archaeology of Ancient China

The
Archaeology
of
Ancient
China

by Kwang-chih Chang

New Haven and London
Yale University Press
1963

Foreword

I first came to know Dr. Kwang-chih Chang in the fall of 1950, when he enrolled as a freshman in the Department of Archaeology and Anthropology, National Taiwan University. Four years later I saw him graduate, having just completed a bachelor's thesis on the Lungshan Culture, written under my direction. He impressed me then as a most promising young scholar of remarkable industriousness, gifted with a quick mind and abundant natural curiosity which, if duly disciplined, might lead him to scientific achievements of a very high order. And, indeed, it must have taken a considerable amount of mental acuity and applied effort to complete the thesis presented in this book.

The fact that this book contains many hypotheses which are yet to be substantiated perhaps deserves some explanation. There are practical reasons why a book on Chinese prehistoric and protohistoric archaeology, compiled at the present stage of research conditions in this field, has to go beyond the narrow limit of actual data, and be amply interpolated with some hypothetical interpretation. Of these reasons I shall mention only two.

Chang is trained as a specialist in Chinese archaeology. It is in China itself that he should carry on his scientific work in order to contribute his share to the understanding of China's past and test the hypotheses of other scholars as well as his own. This normal course, however, cannot be followed under the present political circumstances. Like many other specialists in Chinese archaeology on this side of the Iron Curtain, Chang is a victim of this tragic state of affairs. His industriousness and imaginative power can be applied only in the study of documentary data supplied to him by others. Fortunately, he has had the opportunity to study in the United States, where he has obtained the best possible training in anthropology at one of America's finest institutions of higher learning, an institution whose standard of discipline makes almost no allowance for the foreign student. In the United States he has been able to read the archaeological literature published in Communist China and, as a specialist with his particular training, to interpret the published material according to a well-planned perspective. As far as I can judge, he has made a good case on the basis of available data. He is naturally handicapped by the inherent weakness of the source materials, over which he has absolutely no control. His interpretations, wherever they are drastically new, must therefore remain hypothetical until they can be tested in the field.

There is certainly a need for new interpretation of Chinese prehistory and early historical archaeology. In the late twenties and early thirties, when my colleagues and I began to undertake scientific excavations in China, the country enjoyed little peace, and field work was frequently carried out in the midst of military campaigns; then followed the Sino-Japanese War and finally the Communist rebellion. I can recall all our difficulties in these years while we were engaged in archaeological investigations. Scientific data were only beginning to be accumulated, and systematic interpretations had scarcely been attempted, when the important archaeological collections, following their custodians, had to be evacuated from the continent.

During the thirteen years since 1949, under a totalitarian regime which has manpower to spare and uses archaeology as an effective political instrument, essentially the same group of trained field workers has been able to accumulate, at an accelerated rate, new archaeological materials, the amount of which has certainly outgrown the interpretative framework conceived before the war years by some of the pioneer workers. The time seems to have arrived when a number of possible new interpretations may be tried. The one chosen in this book is not necessarily the only one, but it provides something that can serve as a basis for further discussion as well as for the planning of future excavations by trained archaeologists like the author himself.

When the Yale University Press agreed to publish his *Archaeology of Ancient China*, the author asked me to write a foreword for this, his first book. I have consented to do it not without some hesitation. But I confess that I was very flattered. So, in concluding this short note, I cannot resist the temptation to quote M. C. Burkitt's Preface, written thirty years ago, for J. G. D. Clark's book, *The Mesolithic Age in Britain*, wherein Burkitt said: "It is true that I have had the privilege of giving him some part of his training in his prehistoric studies. But it is always refreshing when the new generation thinks it worthwhile to make such a request."

Li Chi

Academia Sinica
Nankang, Taiwan, China
November, 1962

Preface

Archaeology in the college curriculum rightfully belongs to both the humanities and the social sciences. In practice, however, Chinese archaeology as it is described and discussed in current scholarly literature too often associates itself unilaterally with technology or the fine arts. Museums exhibit beautifully painted pottery from Pan-shan and masterpieces of the Shang and Chou bronzesmiths; albums record and illustrate ceremonial vessels and jade carvings; textbooks describe the prehistoric and early historic peoples of China as they are characterized by the colors and decoration of potsherds and represented by the names of their rulers and their dynasties. But Chinese archaeologists have yet to describe and interpret the culture and the society of the early Chinese peoples for the edification of anthropologists, or the classification, relationships, and development of ancient cultural groups in China for the knowledge of prehistorians and historians.

Moreover, in the currently written ancient history of China, attention is often focused solely upon the civilizational development of the Yellow River valley, whereas the various local cultures in the rest of ancient China are often lightly dismissed as being either unimportant or archaeologically unknown. It is very true that the North China civilization played a leading role throughout the history of China. It was not, however, the only culture that mattered in the early segments of Chinese history, and the less glamorous cultures in the peripheral regions are often of greater concern to students of Far Eastern prehistory because these cultures extended beyond modern China.

To provide a balanced view of the early history of China according to the archaeological evidence is the immediate aim of the present book. It is intended to be balanced in that, first, it will describe a *history* of cultural development as well as provide a catalogue of archaeological discoveries and, second, it will cover all the areas of China where archaeological remains have been found sufficient for such an undertaking. I have designed this book with two considerations in mind: First, a cultural historical framework is indispensable, not only for understanding and interpreting Chinese prehistory and early history but also for a proper descrip-

ix

tion of data properly placed in time and space. Second, Chinese history is only one part of the world history of man, and in order to compare the patterns of Chinese cultural growth with cultural growth throughout the world, Chinese archaeology must have a general historical framework to serve as a basis for comparison.

For forty years scientific archaeologists have been active in China, and a remarkable amount of data has been accumulated. Insofar as this discipline is a relative newcomer to China, we must certainly expect that working hypotheses are to be constantly offered and the general framework modified, improved upon, and retouched. I intend no more than to offer an up-to-date version of this general framework, grounded upon currently available data; but anyone familiar with the field will realize the difficulty of producing a new conceptual model when the old one has been outdated for some twenty years, while the same twenty years have witnessed a phenomenal increase of new materials needing interpretation. For this reason, as well as the fact that new data is constantly being made available, the results of the present undertaking must be regarded as highly tentative.

I have attempted to offer several things in this volume: to my fellow archaeologists specializing in China, a documented interpretation of the most relevant data now available in the field; to my fellow prehistorians, a cultural historical framework of a major world civilizational center, which might be susceptible to analytical and historical comparisons; to historians and sinologues, information and a structure on the basis of which Chinese history as it is now written might be enriched by archaeological materials; and, finally, to university students, an up-to-date, documented, interpretive textbook on Chinese archaeology. At this juncture, I would like to request the comment and criticism of my readers, since a book of this sort can benefit greatly from the response of its audience.

The field of Chinese archaeology is immense, and the knowledge required for writing the present volume manifold; without the help of many teachers and colleagues, it could not have been written. My thanks are due especially to Professors Li Chi, Tung Tso-pin, Ling Shun-sheng, Shih Chang-ju, Ruey Yih-fu, and Kao Chü-hsün, of the Academia Sinica and National Taiwan University, for their guidance during my college years when I first became interested in the field of Chinese archaeology; to the late Lauristan Ward, the late Professor Clyde Kluckhohn, and Professors Hallam L. Movius, Jr., Gordon R. Willey, and Yang Lien-sheng, of Harvard University, for suggestions and advice on the early drafts of the various chapters in this volume; to Dr. Cheng Te-kun, of Cambridge University, for continuous encouragement through the recent years; to Professor Irving Rouse, of Yale University, and Dr. Kenneth Starr, of the Chicago Natural History Museum, for invaluable suggestions which have been incorporated into the final version; to Professor Cornelius Osgood, of Yale University, for encouragement; to the Concilium on International Studies, Yale University, and Professor Arthur F. Wright, for encouragement and for a grant to cover the expenses of the preparation of the manuscript; to the Harvard-Yenching Institute, Cambridge, Massachusetts, for continuous financial support from 1955–61, the period during which most of the studies in this book were initiated; to Dr. Kai-ming Chiu, Librarian of the Harvard-Yenching Institute, and Warren Tsuneishi, Curator of Far Eastern Collections of the Sterling Memorial Library, Yale University, for assistance in the use of the excellent collections of publications in Chinese archaeology; and, last but not least, to Hwei, my wife, whose assistance in more ways than one cannot be enumerated.

Portions of this book in an earlier form were included in a dissertation presented to the Department of Anthropology, Harvard University, in April 1960, in partial fulfillment of the requirements for the Ph.D. degree. Some of the original hypotheses in Chapters 1 through 4 of this book have been previously published in a number of professional journals (such as *Asian Perspectives, Harvard Journal of Asiatic Studies, Bulletin of the Institute of History and Philology, Academia Sinica,* and *Bulletin of the Institute of Ethnology, Academia Sinica*), but these are for the most part rewritten and greatly expanded in the present context. Christopher F. Carroll, Mrs. Charles Drake, and Mrs. Henry R. Swift have kindly and patiently helped to render the manuscript into readable English. The wise and experienced guidance of Jane V. Olson at the Yale University Press has proved indispensable for transforming the manuscript into a book.

K.C.C.

February 1962
New Haven, Connecticut

Contents

Foreword by Li Chi   v

Preface   ix

Introduction   1

Chapters

1. *Geography and the Palaeolithic Foundations*   21
   Geographic subdivisions of China . . . Human and cultural beginnings in the Pleistocene period

2. *Hunter-Fishers of the Early Recent Period*   35
   Climate in the early postglacial period . . . Mesolithic cultures of North China . . . Mesolithic cultures of South China . . . Recapitulation

3. *First Farmers of the Huangho*   51
   Beginning of food-production in the Huangho . . . The Yangshao farmers . . . Chronological and regional subdivisions

4. *The Lungshanoid Expansion*   77
   The Yangshao-Lungshan relationship and the Proto-Lungshan complex . . . Cultural and social changes among the Lungshanoid farmers . . . Regional Lungshanoid traditions . . . Recapitulation

5. *The Spread of Agriculture and Neolithic Technology*   110
   Northern Shensi, Shansi, and Hopei . . . The Liaoho valley, eastern Mongolia, and southern Manchuria . . . The Sungari valley . . . The Tumen valley . . . Kansu and Chinese Turkestan . . . The Southwest . . . General conclusions

6. *The Emergence of Civilization in North China*   130
   The legendary beginnings . . . From history to archaeology . . . Neolithic foundations of the Shang civilization . . . Shang civilization defined . . . Major cities of the Shang . . . History and culture of the Shang Dynasty

xiii

CONTENTS

Chapters

7. *Further Development of Civilization in North China to 221 B.C.*   175
Chou before the Conquest . . . Development of cities . . . Technology . . . Typology of artifacts and art styles . . . Burial customs . . . General conclusions

8. *Farmers and Nomads of the Northern Frontier*   224
The Pohai cist-grave builders . . . The mounted nomads of the Yin Shan area . . . The "eneolithic" painted pottery tradition of Kansu

9. *Early Civilizations in South China*   246
The Geometric horizon of eastern South China . . . The advent of Shang and Western Chou civilizations in eastern South China . . . Eastern Chou kingdoms in eastern South China . . . Early civilizations in Szechwan . . . Early civilizations in Yünnan . . . General conclusions

Conclusions and Prospect   299

Plates   *opposite page* 308

Appendix—Chinese Characters for Proper Names and Technical Terms   309

Recommendations for Further Reading   321

Index   327

Tables

1. Geographic Contrasts between North China and South China   24
2. Subdivision of the Kansu Yangshao Horizon   74
3. Distribution of Different Wares at the Sites of Miao-ti-kou I, Miao-ti-kou II, and San-li-ch'iao   81
4. Distribution of Different Pottery Forms at the Sites of Miao-ti-kou I, Miao-ti-kou II, and San-li-ch'iao   83

CONTENTS

Tables

5. Yangshao and Lungshanoid Cultural Contrasts 92
6. North China Neolithic—Bronze Age Continuities and Discontinuities 137
7. Shang Dynasty Phases of Cheng-chou 148
8. Characteristic Features of Erh-li-kang and Jen-min Park Phases of the Shang Culture at Cheng-chou 155
9. Old and New Discoveries of Shang and Chou Burial Sites 203
10. Reconstruction of the Shih-chai-shan Culture 290
11. Early Cultural Levels in China: East-West Section 304
12. Early Cultural Levels in China: North-South Section 305

Maps

1. The Geographic Regions and Land Forms of China 23
2. Palaeolithic and Palaeoanthropological Sites in China 27
3. Mesolithic Sites in Northern North China 40
4. Mesolithic Sites in South China 47
5. Distribution of Neolithic Sites of the Yangshao Stage 58
6. The Kansu Profile 72
7. Distribution of Neolithic Sites of the Lungshanoid Stage and Its Regional Traditions 88
8. Important Prehistoric Sites in Inner Mongolia, Sinkiang, and Manchuria 112
9. Shang Dynasty Sites near Cheng-chou 147
10. Shang Dynasty Sites near An-yang 156
11. Location of Some Shang and Chou City Sites and Tombs and the Approximate Boundaries of the Eastern Chou States around 350 B.C. 204
12. Eneolithic Traditions in Kansu 236
13. Early Historic Sites in Szechwan 275
14. Yünnan and Important Cities 288

Figures

1. Teeth of ancient and modern North China inhabitants, showing the persistent occurrence of the shovel-shaped incisors. 31

CONTENTS

Figures

2. Reconstructed house of the Yangshao farmers at the Miao-ti-kou site, western Honan.   63
3. Some painted designs on pottery of the Yangshao stage site at Miao-ti-kou, western Honan.   67
4. Some distinctive decorative designs on pottery of the Yangshao horizon.   71
5. Reconstruction of a Lungshanoid stage house at Miao-ti-kou II, western Honan.   80
6. Some distinctive pottery forms of the Proto-Lungshan complex of Miao-ti-kou II, western Honan.   86
7. The ceremonial complex of the Lungshanoid farmers.   90
8. Two human representations in the Lungshanoid ceramic art.   96
9. Two Lungshanoid *li* tripods excavated from K'o-hsing-chuang, near Sian, Shensi.   101
10. The Tung-pa-chia site near Ch'ih-feng, Inner Mongolia.   115
11. A painted pottery excavated from the Ho-pao-hsi site, near Ta-hsi, in eastern Szechwan.   125
12. The Shang Dynasty site at Hsiao-t'un, An-yang.   158
13. A reconstructed Shang Dynasty ground house at Hsiao-t'un, An-yang.   159
14. Shapes and dimensions of known Eastern Chou cities.   182
15. Incised patterns on a Warring-States bronze vessel, showing one form of platform structure.   192
16. Iron edge blade of plow, excavated from a Warring-States tomb at Ku-wei-ts'un, in Hui Hsien, Honan.   198
17. Common bronze vessel forms in Shang and Chou Dynasties.   199
18. Realistic decorative patterns on a bronze vessel of the Warring-States period excavated from Shan-piao-chen, in Chi Hsien, Honan province.   209
19. Bronze swords of the Eastern Chou period excavated from North and South China.   215
20. Warring-States tombs of the vertical pit type (*above*) and the cave-chamber type (*below*).   216
21. Bronze artifacts discovered from an Eastern Chou tomb at Shih-erh-t'ai-ying-tzu, near Chao-yang, in Liaoning province.   232

xvi

CONTENTS

Figures

22. Geometric designs on pottery from the site at Pei-yin-yang-ying, near Nanking. 248

23. A Ch'u wooden-chambered tomb near Ch'ang-sha, Hunan. 263

24. Ch'u halberd and spears. 265

25. Painted pottery of Ch'u from Ch'ang-sha. 267

26. Some Ch'u pottery of chronological significance; 1) *li*; 2) *tou*; 3) *tui*; 4) *ting*; 5) *hu*. 268

27. Wood carvings from Ch'u tombs near Ch'ang-sha. 269

28. Painted human and animal figures on a lacquered musical instrument discovered from the Ch'u tomb at Hsin-yang, Honan. 270

29. Ceremonial platform at the Yang-tzu-shan site near Ch'eng-tu, western Szechwan. 278

30. A boat coffin in the Eastern Chou and Han cemetery at Pao-lun-yüan, in Chao-hua Hsien, northern Szechwan. 280

31. Designs on spearheads (*above*) and halberds (*below*) discovered from the Eastern Chou and Han burials in the Chialingkiang region of Szechwan. 282

32. Decorated bronze swords and spearheads from the Pai-ma-ssu site, near Ch'eng-tu, western Szechwan. 283

33. An incised decorative band on a bronze vessel excavated from the Tien cemetery at Chin-ning, Yünnan. 293

Plates   *opposite page* 308

I. Two bowls painted with fish figures discovered from the Yangshao stage settlement at Pan-p'o, near Sian, Shensi province.

II. *Above* Potsherd with relief of human face, collected from a Yangshao stage site at Chiang-hsi Ts'un, in Fu-feng Hsien, Shensi. *Below* Two painted jars excavated from the Lungshanoid site at Pao-t'ou-ts'un in Ning-yang Hsien, Shantung.

III. Rice husks found from Lungshanoid sites in Hupei.

IV. Pottery of the Weishui phase of the Lungshanoid Neolithic.

xvii

CONTENTS

Plates

   V. The Lungshanoid sites at Ta-ch'eng-shan, in Hopei (*above*), and Yang-t'ou-wa, in Liaoning (*below*).
  VI. Habitation mounds of the Lungshanoid and Geometric stages in Kiangsu.
 VII. Oracle bones of the Shang Dynasty.
VIII. Pottery of the Hsin-tien B phase.
  IX. Pottery of the T'ang-wang style.
   X. Painted wooden animal figures, excavated from the Ch'u tomb at Hsin-yang, southern Honan.
  XI. Decorated bronze halberds excavated from the Ch'u tombs near Ch'ang-sha.
 XII. Painted and inscribed silk from a Ch'u tomb near Ch'ang-sha.
XIII. Bronze weapons from Pa and Shu tombs of Szechwan.
 XIV. Bronze plow with a section of wooden handle in socket, excavated from a Tien tomb in Yünnan.
  XV. Market scenes cast in the round on the top of a bronze vessel, excavated from a Tien tomb in Yünnan.
 XVI. Scene of a battle cast in the round on the top of a bronze vessel, excavated from a Tien tomb in Yünnan.
XVII. A ritual scene cast in the round on the top of a bronze vessel, excavated from a Tien tomb in Yünnan.

Abbreviations

This list has reference both to the footnotes and to the *Recommendations for Further Reading*. In the footnotes will be found complete data of all works referred to in the text. The *Recommendations for Further Reading*, meant to provide some suggestions for readers of a more advanced level, is, of course, not a complete bibliography.

AA   *American Anthropologist*, Menasha.

AP   *Asian Perspectives* (Bulletin of the Far Eastern Prehistory Association), Hong Kong.

BIE   *Bulletin of the Institute of Ethnology*, Academia Sinica, Taipei.

BIHP   *Bulletin of the Institute of History and Philology*, Academia Sinica, Nanking, Lichuang, and Taipei.

BMFEA   *Bulletin of the Museum of Far Eastern Antiquities*, Stockholm.

GSoC   *Geological Society of China*, Peiping.

GSuC   *Geological Survey of China*, Peiping.

JZ   *Jenruigaku Zasshi*, Tokyo.

KK   *K'ao-ku* (1959–), Peiping.

KKHP   *K'ao-ku-hsüeh-pao*, Peiping.

KKTH   *K'ao-ku-t'ung-hsün* (title changed to KK after 1958), Peiping.

PFEPC   *Proceedings of the Far Eastern Prehistoric Congress* (title changed to AP after 1957).

PS   *Palaeontologia Sinica*, Peiping.

SJA   *Southwestern Journal of Anthropology*, Albuquerque.

TAPS   *Transactions of the American Philosophical Society*, Philadelphia.

TYKKPK   *T'ien-yieh-k'ao-ku-pao-kao* (No. 1 of *KKHP*), Nanking.

VP   *Vertebrata Palasiatica*, Peiping.

WW   *Wen-wu* (1959–), Peiping.

WWTKTL   *Wen-wu-ts'an-k'ao-tzu-liao* (title changed to WW after 1958), Peiping.

Introduction

The following chapters outline a cultural historical framework into which the formative stages of Chinese civilization can be placed and present the necessary data for its documentation. At the outset I must make two things clear: First, much of this structure comes from the results of other scholars' studies, which span several centuries. Second, many of the original parts in this structure are by no means widely accepted by or necessarily acceptable to other archaeologists, and there are a few other hypotheses which a reader may choose in preference to mine. In fairness to the archaeologists who have contributed to the making of the following cultural historical framework and to the reader who prefers to be provided with the opportunity of making his own selections but is not familiar with the historical background against which the present interpretation appears, I must first give a brief summary of the history of archaeological theory, methodology, and field work in China. A full and fair treatment of this subject matter would be possible only in another book-length volume, but even a brief outline of the major trends of archaeology in China will be useful.

Historical studies, as is well known, had an early start and a long history in China, and the study of bygone cultures and civilizations by means of their artifactual remains has never ceased to be a part of the historical method. Even in the Eastern Chou (ca. 770–221 B.C.) and Han (206 B.C.–A.D. 220) Dynasties, when what to us is ancient history was contemporary events and what to us are archaeological specimens of bronze, iron, and stone were still objects of daily use, and when prehistoric cultures were still faintly in the memory of the people in the form of legendary traditions, and their ruins and remains were still exposed on the ground or buried shallowly under the earth, there was already an archaeology of sorts. Han Fei Tzu says in *Shih Kuo*:

> When Yao governed the world, people ate in clay vessels and
>   drank in clay mugs;
> Yü made ritual vessels, painting the interior in black and the
>   exterior in red;

1

> The Yin people . . . engraved their utensils for meals and incised their utensils for drinking wine.

Wei Chü-hsien [1] thinks that Han Fei Tzu, a philosopher of the Warring-States (ca. 450–221 B.C.) period, must have seen some of the prehistoric ceramic remains and Yin bronzes in the ground and tried to identify these with traditional ancient heroes before he could have given such vivid descriptions of ancient artifacts. Ssu-ma Chien of Western Han visited many ancient ruins and relics attributed to various periods before his time before he put the information that he considered verified and thus reliable into his great *Shih Chi, Book of History*. An even more interesting "archaeological" approach to history is seen in Yüan K'ang's *Yüeh Chüeh Shu*. In the chapter on *Swords*, Feng Hu Tzu, an Eastern Chou philosopher, is quoted by Yüan K'ang as saying to a king of Yüeh that:

> In the Age of Hsüan-yüan, Shen-nung, and Hê-hsü, weapons were made of stones for cutting trees and building houses, and were buried with the dead . . . ;
> In the Age of Huang-ti, weapons were made of jade, for cutting trees, building houses, and digging the ground . . . and were buried with the dead;
> In the Age of Yü, weapons were made of bronze, for building canals . . . and houses . . .
> At the present time, weapons are made of iron

In devising the Three Age system, Yüan K'ang's account of Feng Hu Tzu seems to have anticipated C. J. Thomsen of Denmark by about two thousand years, and Yüan K'ang may thus rightfully rank with Lucretius as one of the world's first archaeologists to propose such a classification.[2]

But whatever credits one can give to these Eastern Chou and Han scholars for utilizing material remains of ancient cultures to make historical studies, this "archaeological" foetus was soon

1. Wei Chü-hsien, *Chung-kuo k'ao-ku-hsüeh shih* (Shanghai, Commercial Press, 1937), pp. 50–51.
2. Ibid., p. 58; George G. MacCurdy, *Human Origins* (New York, D. Appleton–Century Co., 1933), 1, 9: "In his poem *De Rerum Natura* Lucretius (about 98–55 B.C.) says: 'The earliest weapons were the hands, nails, and teeth; then came stone and clubs. These were followed by iron and bronze, but bronze came first, the use of iron not being known until later.' "

snowed under during and after the Han Dynasty when the ancient Golden Age of Three Dynasties and their Sage predecessors, systematized by the Confucian political philosophers and blessed by the royal governments, became the ultimate interpretation of ancient Chinese history. Studies of ancient relics, largely confined to bronze vessels and stone tablets—hence the name *Chin Shih Hsüeh,* or the "studies of bronzes and stones,"—continued throughout the Chinese historical periods, but a different attitude prevailed. Bronzes were collected as curios and heirlooms for their intrinsic value, either artistic or fetish, and whatever studies were made of them were largely confined to their inscriptions, from which information was obtained confirming the Golden Age interpretation of ancient history or for paleographic interests. In addition to bronze vessels and stone tablets, bronze weapons, mirrors, chariot and horse fittings, porcelains and ceramics, tiles and eave tiles, jade, seals and so forth, were also studied, and since 1899 oracle bone inscriptions of the Yin Dynasty have been added to this list.

In general, these studies of ancient artifacts, which have appeared throughout the historic period, were either concentrated on the inscriptions, as supplementary data for literary history, or focused upon ancient institutions recorded in existing literary documents which these artifacts confirm or refute. Little attention had ever been given to the historical information these artifacts themselves could provide, or which their cultural contexts, often unknown or neglected anyway, could suggest. In the famous *K'ao-ku-t'u* compiled probably in the Northern Sung Dynasty, Lü Ta-lin recorded 211 bronzes in the palace and private collections and thirteen jade objects, giving illustrations, places of origin if known, and measurements of size, weight, and volume. This is one of the few archaeological books China produced before the modern period that comes close to the modern archaeological method. Such books are rare, and their contributions were never fully taken advantage of by historians. In short, China has had an indigenous tradition of archaeology, but this tradition had never gone much beyond the scope and spirit of antiquarianism before her contacts with the West. The reasons are clear to anyone who is familiar with the development of archaeology in the West and with the cultural and social history of China.

Modern scientific archaeology was born in China in the early twentieth century under the impact of Western civilization and

3

scholarship. The roots of the new inspirations are multiple, and a sheer enumeration of them must necessarily be arbitrary. But the following sources of origin are clear.

First, of course, there was the tradition of antiquarianism and history in China, which represented both a deep-rooted scholarship of past institutions and historical events and an unfailing interest in things ancient, including early inscriptions. For a long period in the early decades of this century this tradition was under heavy fire from the new school of historians and archaeologists, but it nevertheless provided a historic background upon which new methodologies must be shaped, whether in its favor or disfavor. When all things against it are said and done, new archaeologists can never disregard the centuries-long experience of the antiquarians in dealing with objects of the historical period.

Second, with the Nationalist revolution of 1911 and the May Fourth Movement of 1919, the Golden Age interpretation of ancient China fell apart, and a critical school of historical interpretation came into being, symbolized by the publication in 1926 of *Ku Shih Pien*, or *Critical Reviews of Ancient History*, edited by Ku Hsieh-kang.[3] Li Chi states,

> Their slogan, "Show your proof," though destructive in nature, did bring about a more critical spirit in the study of ancient China. Thus, if one wants to pay excessive tribute to the Golden Age of Yao and Shun, well, Show your proof; if one wishes to talk about the engineering miracles of the Great Yü of the third millennium B.C., proofs must also be given. What must be remembered in this connection is that written records alone were no longer accepted as valid proofs.[4]

Ku Hsieh-kang[5] proposed three new approaches to the study of ancient history, now that the traditional doctrines were being rejected and new means needed as substitutes: archaeology, critical reviews of false histories and pseudo histories, and folklore.

In this atmosphere, proofs were sought by the new historians to substantiate the literary records of ancient history, and proofs

3. Ku Hsieh-kang, ed., *Ku-shih pien*, 1, Peiping, P'u-shê, 1926.
4. Li Chi, *The Beginnings of Chinese Civilization* (Seattle, University of Washington Press, 1957), p. 4.
5. Ku Hsieh-kang, ed., *Ku-shih pien*, 1, 57–77.

were at the same time being produced by an assortment of scholars representing Western civilization and the Western methodology of historical study, who *excavated* data from the ground in various parts of China, dated not only to the historical periods but to the prehistoric periods as well. To such data and such new techniques, the new historians of the then enlightening China naturally turned for proof and for new inspirations.

Western scholars came to China, a land of ancient civilization which they had admired in books, soon after the Manchu Dynasty bowed to Western gunboats. To Chinese Turkestan came the Grum-Grzimailo brothers from Russia in 1889, M. Grenard and D. de Rhine from France in 1892, and Sven Hedin from Sweden in 1896. To southern Manchuria from Japan came Torii Ryuzo in 1895. But these were places distant from North China, and what these people produced were either historical documents or studies of apparently insignificant relics from border countries which used to be occupied by "barbarians," thus drawing little attention from the historians of China. With J. Gunnar Andersson, a mining consultant hired by the Peiyang government of Peking in the early years of the Republic, things took a different turn.

In the early decades of the present century, study of the ancient history of China was indeed chaotic. Although Charles Darwin in his *Descent of Man* says that "there is indirect evidence of [flint tools'] former use by the Chinese and ancient Jews," [6] this indirect evidence had never been substantiated, and such Western writers as Jacques de Morgan [7] and such sinologists as Berthold Laufer [8] insisted that Chinese civilization had no prehistory. In China, the critical school of historical studies found no confidence even in the Three Dynasties. But, in 1920, Andersson discovered in Mien-ch'ih Hsien, western Honan, in the heart of Chinese civilization, a Stone Age site near Yang-shao-ts'un, which was to be followed by his discovery of another Painted Pottery site at the cave of Sha-kuo-t'un in Liao-ning in 1922 and many other Painted Pottery Culture sites in Kansu in 1923–24.

6. Charles Darwin, *The Descent of Man* (New York, Crowell, 1874), p. 224.

7. Jacques de Morgan, *Prehistoric Man* (New York, A. A. Knopf, 1925), p. 293.

8. Berthold Laufer, "Jade: A Study in Chinese Archaeology and Religion," *Field Museum of Natural History Publication* 154, Anthropological Ser. 10 (1912), 29, 54–55.

In the meantime, in 1920 two Jesuit missionaries, Emile Licent and Pierre Teilhard de Chardin, found the first Palaeolithic implement at Ch'ing-yang, Kansu, and in the same year Andersson located fossiliferous sites in the Choukoutien limestone hills near Peiping. Bronze Age tombs were opened by farmers in 1923 at Hsin-cheng, in Honan, and at Li-yü-ts'un, in Shansi, and were soon investigated by antiquarians. Thus, within the short period of four years (1920–23), the existence of early man in China during both prehistoric and early historic periods could no longer be doubted. At that time, the authenticity of the oracle bone inscriptions had also been generally accepted as genuine Shang Dynasty writing. Such a sudden appearance of proofs needed by historians for the study of ancient Chinese history deeply impressed Chinese scholars, who thus found in field investigations a new source of historic data.

The greatest contribution made by Western scholarship to the birth of scientific archaeology in China was clearly in demonstrating to Chinese historians an entirely new system of methodology whereby the authenticity of an artifact can be established by digging it out of the ground, its dating can be established by its underground stratigraphic position and relationships, and its historical and cultural significance can be unveiled by the comparative method. The fundamentals of the new discipline also provided the means by which the value of past accomplishments could be reappraised.

The scholarship of the practicing Western scholars in China, however, was not always of the highest quality; along with positive contributions, damage was done which was to take many years of subsequent scientific work to repair. The geologists of the Geological Survey of China apparently did a first-rate job at Choukoutien and in the Ordos in the 1920's and '30's, but their interests were palaeontological first and historical second. Even though their fine field techniques were transmitted to such Chinese scholars as Yang Chung-chien and Pei Wen-chung, their influence on historical studies was relatively slight.

Andersson, on the other hand, whose work and accomplishments were directly involved with the formative stage of Chinese civilization, left a much deeper impression. Chinese archaeology owes to Andersson its present form and content to a considerable extent, but it has also inherited from him many weaknesses, some of which are basic. Chief among these misleading influences are: the use of isolated elements for the characterization of whole complexes or cultures; the tailoring of scientific field work to practical convenience to the point of being unscientific; and the search for data to support preconceived ideas based on prejudice and groundless imagination. These weaknesses were shared to some extent by archaeologists the world over in the early part of the present century. Yet Andersson himself often speaks of his undue haste, and in the following passages shows that his methodology was far from satisfactory according to present standards of field archaeology:

> With the exception of the detailed work at Yang Shao Ts'un all our other excavations in Honan were of the nature of a flying reconnaissance. I was never able to visit the very rich sites in Ho Yin Hsien, and for these important localities I have to rely upon the information given me by my collector Pai.[9]
>
> In the spring of 1923 I started with my native collectors on an expedition to the distant northwest, Kansu and adjacent parts of Mongolia and Tibet. The preconceived plan for this journey was mainly to hunt for fossil mammal vertebrates and to trace the supposed connection of the Yang Shao painted pottery with the painted pottery cultures of the Near East.[10]
>
> The great number of sites revealed through the preliminary reconnaissance carried out by my Chinese assistants forced me to make relatively hurried surveys of some of the most important sites, leaving it to my men to collect test samples of the numerous sites which I could not examine myself . . . As the number of sites were so large when compared with the small number of workers and the short time at our disposal, I was forced to concentrate my detailed surveying activities upon the burial places and individual graves. In the dwelling site deposits my men were left to excavate in small parties, which were visited by me every other day. Only when special stratigraphical structures

9. J. Gunnar Andersson, *BMFEA*, 15 (1943), 15.
10. Ibid., p. 14.

7

were found within these refuse deposits were those spots specially surveyed.[11]

The site of Yang-shao-ts'un, the exception he mentioned above, and the survey which is regarded by him as being "in many respects our most detailed and many-sided investigation of any prehistoric site found by us," [12] was excavated for a total period of only thirty-six days, with the result that a total of seventeen small trenches were dug out of a remarkably large area (approximately 900 x 300 m.). Two things show the quality of that work. First, Andersson reported the finding of *li* tripods at this site. From what is known today for the region of western Honan, *li* tripods could hardly have appeared at that stage of Neolithic development. Second, what "that stage" at Yang-shao-ts'un may be is now a big question, because the Yang-shao-ts'un site now looks more like the stage represented by Miao-ti-kou II than the "Yangshao" stage named after it which is better typified by such sites as Pan-p'o-ts'un and Miao-ti-kou I. Mistakes such as these were probably inevitable, but we must beware of them in utilizing these early archaeological reports.

After the early 1920's when the field method was introduced to China by Western scholars, both a new awareness of China's past, which was even more ancient than the Golden Age traditionally held it to be, and a new historical school came into being in which the new and the traditional were combined to the benefit of both. This new school was symbolized by the founding of the Institute of History and Philology, Academia Sinica, in 1928, but was certainly not confined to this institution. Such scholars as Pei Wen-chung, of the Geological Survey, Hsü Ping-chang, of the National Research Institute of Peiping, and Kuo Pao-chün, of the Research Institute of Honan Antiquities, worked in the same field with Li Chi, Liang Ssu-yung, and Tung Tso-pin, of the Institute of History and Philology, hand in glove in spirit and principle, if not always in sentiment.

Chinese archaeology made considerable strides during the decade from the mid-twenties through the mid-thirties when the outbreak of the Sino-Japanese War wrecked the paths of its further growth. The Palaeolithic sites at Choukoutien were excavated by the Geo-

11. Ibid., p. 16.
12. Ibid., p. 15.

logical Survey and the human remains and artifacts were ably studied by such geologists and palaeontologists as Pierre Teilhard de Chardin, Davidson Black, Franz Weidenreich, Young Chung-chien, and Pei Wen-chung. Although Palaeolithic remains were known only from a few sites at Choukoutien (mainly Locality 13, Locality 1, Locality 15, and the Upper Cave) and in the Ordos area, both Middle and Upper Pleistocene occupations of men were now substantiated, and a comparison of their physical types and cultures with other known Palaeolithic men in East Asia, such as *Pithecanthropus* in Java, threw much light on the human origins in this part of the world. Elsewhere in China, J. H. Edgar collected a few palaeolithic-looking implements from the Yangtze terraces in Szechwan, Russian and Japanese scholars collected Mesolithic implements at Djalai-nor and Ku-hsiang-t'un in Manchuria, the Geological Survey found some Mesolithic industries in limestone caves of Kwangsi, and G. H. R. von Koenigswald collected the giant anthropoid teeth from Hong Kong drugstores which Weidenreich regarded as having belonged to ancestors of *Pithecanthropus* and modern man. These Palaeolithic and Mesolithic data of varying importance, reliability, and quantity were sufficient to give scientists some substantial ideas about man and his culture in China during and immediately after the Pleistocene period. Toward the end of this decade, Helmut de Terra, Hallam L. Movius, Jr., and Pierre Teilhard de Chardin managed to pull together all the bits of information then known to construct a total picture of Chinese Palaeolithic and Mesolithic cultures, and to tie this in with the Himalayan Glacial sequence and with the history of early man in most of the Old World.[13]

In Neolithic archaeology, Li Chi, a Harvard-trained anthropologist, found and excavated another "Painted Pottery" site in southern Shansi in 1926. By this time the existence of a "Painted Pottery Culture" before the dawn of Chinese history in North China had been generally accepted, and the hypothesis had been advanced to identify this culture as that of the legendary Hsia Dynasty. The hypothesis was based on two assumptions: the first, which was beginning to be substantiated archaeologically at that time, was

13. Helmut de Terra, *Pleistocene Formation and Stone Age Man in China*, Peiping, Institut de Géo-Biologie, 1941; P. Teilhard de Chardin, *Early Man in China*, Peiping, Institut de Géo-Biologie, 1941; Hallam L. Movius, Jr., *Papers of the Peabody Museum* (Cambridge), 19, 1944.

that the Painted Pottery Culture preceded the Shang, and thus was apparently the Hsia which preceded the Shang according to legends; the second was that the geographical distribution of the Painted Pottery Culture apparently coincided with the area of activities of the Hsia in the legendary accounts. Furthermore, many scholars, particularly those who were aware of the Painted Pottery cultures in Western Asia, had noted a few similar decorative motifs between the painted ware of North China and that of Western Asia, and it was considered without question by these scholars that the Yangshao Culture was an eastern offshoot of the Neolithic cultures of the West.

It is against this historical background that the importance attached and the interpretations given to the so-called Lungshan or Black Pottery Culture, identified in 1928 with the discovery of its type site, Ch'eng-tzu-yai, near Lung-shan Chen, Li-ch'eng Hsien, Shantung, can be understood. At this site, a different ware was found to prevail, characterized by its black color, thin wall, lustrous surface, and by its having been made on a potter's wheel. Together with this ware were found the *hang-t'u* structure and scapulimancy which were characteristic of the Yin-Shang Culture and apparently quite different from the Yangshao Culture known at that time. The two cultures were known to have different spheres of distribution. Thus the Two Culture Theory gradually became generally accepted; if the Yangshao Culture was to be identified with the Hsia, then why should not the Lungshan Culture be identified with the Eastern Yih, known in historical literatures to have been in the Lower Huangho and along the Pacific seaboard? If the Yangshao Culture was derived from Western Asia, then the Lungshan Culture, in which many Yin-Shang elements were found, could be indigenously Chinese. In 1931, the Hou-kang stratigraphy afforded the first real key to the formative cultural sequence of North China (see p. 78). However, because the Two Culture Theory fit what was then the understanding of ancient Chinese culture too well to be thrown away, and because remains of both cultures were reported from western Honan by Andersson to be from one and the same stratigraphical position, the real significance of the Hou-kang stratigraphy was not fully realized until many years later. What Andersson said about this in 1943 may well sum up the majority opinion during the thirties:

Owing to the Hou Kang section it has been held probable that Yang Shao is the older and Lung Shan the younger of the two. But the occurrence of black pottery with the painted ware at Yang Shao Ts'un, at Hsi Yin, at Sha Kuo T'un and some other sites, even in Kansu, raises the question whether it is not possible that the two are mainly synchronous in that painted and black ceramics occur together in the interior but the black pottery alone rules in the coastal provinces (Shantung and Chekiang?) and has there been given the name Lung Shan.[14]

Further discussion in the present volume will, I believe, make clear the specific reasons that lie behind the insistence that Yangshao and Lungshan were two contemporary cultures of the Neolithic period in North China.

Elsewhere in China, Neolithic and Neolithic-like cultures were found and identified in Manchuria, Mongolia, Sinkiang, and South China. In the former two areas, Lin-hsi (1922), Pi-tzu-wo (1927), Anganghsi (1928–30), Yang-t'ou-wa (1933), and Ch'ih-feng (1935) were among the most important sites excavated during the period. A Microlithic Culture was identified and formulated, and evidence was brought to light of both Yangshao and Lungshan influences. Their exact relationship was not yet clearly understood, however. From 1927 to 1934, Folke Bergman of the Sino-Swedish Expedition located a series of prehistoric sites in Sinkiang, among which the Microlithic and the Painted Pottery Culture sites drew most of the attention. In South China, the first stone implements were collected *in situ* from the Lower Yangtze in 1930, and subsequently a Geometric Pottery Culture was identified from many sites in the southeastern part of China. Stone implements and pottery remains were collected extensively in the Red basin by J. H. Edgar, D. S. Dye, D. C. Graham, and N. C. Nelson from the twenties onward, although the existence of prehistoric remains in this area had been known since 1886 when an Englishman, C. E. Baber, purchased a couple of polished stone implements near Chungking. In the Hong Kong area and the coasts of Kwangtung, Neolithic stone implements and pottery were extensively collected during this period by C. M. Heanley, D. J. Finn, R. Maglioni, and

14. Andersson, *BMFEA* 15 (1943), 292–93.

W. Schofield. These investigations established the human occupation of South China from prehistoric times, but the time-space
framework of prehistoric cultures and their relationships with
North China and other adjacent regions in Southeast Asia was not
at all clear.

Archaeology of the early historical civilizations of China probably made its most significant contribution during this period with
the excavations of the Shang Dynasty site near Anyang, from 1928
through 1937, under the auspices of the Archaeological Section of
the Institute of History and Philology, Academia Sinica, and the
able direction of Li Chi. Aside from the significance of the An-
yang excavations for the study of early Chinese civilization, they
were also important in the history of archaeology in that during
the ten years of excavations many young archaeologists received
their field training at this site, thus participating in one of the
most complicated digs ever undertaken in China. Most, if not
all, Chinese archaeologists now in their early fifties and late forties, such as Yin Ta, now the Director of the Institute of Archaeology of the Communist Chinese Academy of Sciences, Hsia Nai,
now Deputy Director of the same Institute, Yin Huan-chang, of
the Nanking Museum, and Shih Chang-ju and Kao Ch'ü-hsun, of
the Academia Sinica in Taipei, received their training in the field
at An-yang. So did Wu Chin-ting (discoverer of the Cheng-tzu-yai
site), Chi Yen-pei, and Li Ching-tan, who passed away during or
after the war, but who made important contributions to Chinese
archaeology during their lifetimes. Some of these people, such as
Hsia Nai and Wu Chin-ting, subsequently broadened their background in foreign institutions, but it is clear that their An-yang
experiences shaped their professional careers.

Aside from An-yang, Hsiao-t'un-like remains were reported from
Shantung and Anhwei, but otherwise no well-established Shang
Dynasty sites were known. Chou Dynasty sites were excavated here
and there, such as the Hsia-tu of Yen (1929), the Warring-States
burials in Chün Hsien (1932), Chi Hsien (1935), and Hui Hsien
(1935) in Honan, the Ch'u tombs in Shou Hsien (1934), Anhwei,
and Ch'ang-sha, Hunan, and the Kwang-han find of jade artifacts
(1934) in Szechwan. Stray finds of bronzes were reported from
Yünnan and Szechwan, but no cultural contexts were identified.

What I have described so far are some of the most important
discoveries of prehistoric and early historic period remains in China

12

from the mid-twenties to the mid-thirties. Archaeological materials obtained during this period indicate a Palaeolithic and Mesolithic occupation of scattered areas of China, two Neolithic cultures in North China, one along the northern borders (the Microlithic), and another in the southeast (the Geometric), and Bronze Age civilizations in North China and scattered regions elsewhere, which tend to confirm and enrich the literary records of the Shang and the Chou dynasties. The theoretical trends during this period can be characterized as follows: first, an establishment of a scientific discipline of field archaeology; second, a tentative grouping of cultures for the whole of China and for the various periods in her cultural history and a tentative alignment of the relationships among these different cultural groups in space and in time. Archaeological stratigraphy became a generally established principle of chronology, and typological comparison was the basic tool for the reconstruction of cultural sequences.

Looking back, we could criticize the archaeologists working during this period for their overindulgence in single tool and vessel types and their typological classifications. The basic fallacies of the Anderssonian methodology described above were carried over into this period, as shown by the Two Culture Theory of Neolithic development (see Chapter 4). At this time, however, archaeological materials had only begun to accumulate, and cultural groups were being classified only tentatively. Considering the circumstances under which the work was undertaken, these archaeologists fulfilled what was then required of them. Furthermore, Chinese and Western archaeologists did in China what Western archaeologists were then still doing in Europe and North America. The ultimate aim of archaeology in reconstructing prehistoric culture and society was not entirely unrecognized in theory,[15] and in practice, topical studies were not lacking. Many were particularly valuable, such as Kuo Mo-jo's studies of ancient Chinese society according to oracle bone and bronze inscriptions, Bernhard Karlgren's treatises on the stylistic development of Yin and Chou bronzes, and some others. But these scholars, original and brilliant as their works show them to be, utilized for the most part inscriptions and decorative designs on archaeological specimens, the provenance of which

15. Li Chi et al, *Ch'eng-tzu-yai*, trans. Kenneth Starr, *Yale University Publications in Anthropology*, No. 52 (1956), 19; Li Chi, *Bull. Col. Arts, National Taiwan Univ.*, 1, 1950.

13

was often unknown, and frequently based their work upon pre-conceived ideas drawn from disciplines other than archaeology. Full advantage was seldom if ever taken of the underground contexts of ancient cultures excavated by the archaeologists' spades.

During and immediately after World War II, very little field work was done in China. The enforced pause, together with the extremely difficult working conditions for archaeologists—several of whom died or became disabled as a consequence—provided opportunity for a synthesis of past accomplishments and for the formation of programs for the future. Many comprehensive volumes on Chinese prehistory and early historic archaeology appeared, and at the Institute of History and Philology a complete report on the An-yang excavations and several other monographs on relatively minor diggings were completed or underway.

Field work was resumed after the 1949 seizure of the Chinese mainland by the Communist regime, and soon came into full swing with the extensive industrial and commercial constructions. "During the past ten years," says Hsia Nai,[16] "in the course of economic construction . . . there have been discovered at many places ancient dwelling sites and burials, whence many important artifacts were found. Archaeological advances have thus been brought about as a consequence." Quantitatively speaking, archaeological sites of all periods in Chinese prehistory and history increased explosively in the area, and many gaps have been filled or are beginning to be filled. On the other hand, with the sudden increase of activities and the huge amount of accumulated data forced upon the archaeologists, much of the work was inevitably carried out in a hurry and by untrained hands. For China as a whole, planned diggings became a rarity, and the entire archaeological program has become a salvage operation.

On the whole, the historical value of the archaeological data has not been underestimated, and monographic or preliminary reports of excavations are published soon after the field work is completed. An Institute of Archaeology and an Institute of Vertebrate Palaeontology and Palaeoanthropology were established under the Communist Chinese Academy of Sciences, many provincial, county, and municipal museums have been instituted, and in each province, city, and county, a Commission for the Preservation of Ancient Monuments has been set up. The field techniques are in most cases not unreasonably unscrupulous, and the published

16. Hsia Nai, *KK*, 1959:10, 505.

reports are often purely descriptive and usable for reference and study; but there has been a paucity of basic archaeological theory and methodology of interpretation. My three criteria for characterizing the Anderssonian methodology are applicable to many of the published reports, and the reconstruction of ancient culture and society in addition to typological classification and description of artifacts is an ultimate aim still to be achieved.[17] During the last two or three years, however, significant interpretive studies on both analytic and comparative topics have appeared in the literature, as well as many comprehensive and topical studies on the prehistoric and early historic periods.[18] Much of the most important data and many important but still controversial interpretations will be presented and discussed throughout this volume.

In the field of palaeolithic archaeology, one of the most important new discoveries is the Fenho Complex in southern Shansi, which has filled a major gap in our knowledge of the cultural development of North China in the Pleistocene period and has rendered meaningful the whole sequence of Palaeolithic cultures from the Choukoutienian to the Ordosian. Equally important are the new materials on fossil man. A good deal of work remains to be done, however, particularly with reference to the Pleistocene chronology of both North and South China, without a minute subdivision of which the cultural events taking place in China can never be compared with similar events happening elsewhere. In Neolithic archaeology, an influential hypothesis was advanced by Shih Chang-ju in 1952, under which the Neolithic cultures in North China were regarded as being composed of no less than three major traditions, namely, Painted Pottery, Black Pottery, and Gray or Beaten Pottery.[19] Since the discovery of Miao-ti-kou II in western Honan in 1956, this Three Culture Theory, as it is called, has no longer been tenable, and I am inclined to regard Shih's Black and Gray Pottery Cultures as being two contemporary phases of the Lungshanoid stage,[20] a view which has been amply substantiated by new materials from the field.[21]

The Hsia Dynasty remains an unknown period in the early

17. Juo Ku, *KKTH*, 1958:8, 16–17.
18. See: Hsia Nai, *KK*, 1959:10, 505–12.
19. Shih Chang-ju, *Ta-lu-tsa-chih*, 4, 1952.
20. Chang Kwang-chih, *Harvard Journal of Asiatic Studies*, 22 (1959); in *BIHP*, 30, 1959.
21. An Chih-min, *KK*, 1959:10, 559–65; Shih Hsing-pang, *KK*, 1959:10, 566–70; Hsü Shun-chen, *WW*, 1960:5, 36–39.

historic archaeology of China, but during the past decade the archaeology of the Shang Dynasty has made many unprecedented advances, such as the discovery of what are probably pre-An-yang phases in Cheng-chou and the findings of many new Shang sites in northern and western Honan and southern Hopei. Historians have recently been engaged in heated arguments concerning the problem of whether the Western Chou Dynasty was of a stage in social history that is called "slavery," but archaeological evidence is not adequate to solve this problem. For the Eastern Chou, new materials have been sufficient to provide a basis for answering questions about the beginning of iron metallurgy and the cultural groupings of the Eastern Chou China, and in Japan scholars have begun to tackle problems concerning the nature of urbanization in the Eastern Chou period.[22]

Many of these controversial questions of history have been omitted from discussion in this volume, but the basic data on which their answers eventually will have to rely have been presented. It is my conviction that archaeological work, from its beginning in locating a site, through its final stage of making a historical synthesis, is a consistent interpretive process. The historical background against which the archaeological data are brought to light must be inherent in the data themselves, and a library synthesis such as the one I have made in this book is, therefore, handicapped accordingly. I have tried to make a new interpretation in as objective a manner as possible, but I cannot sift out all the prejudices and personal judgments inherent in even the data themselves. For this reason, I have thought it necessary to begin this book with a review of Chinese archaeology. During the last four or five years, several books on Chinese prehistoric and early historic archaeology have appeared in the English language.[23] One might have assumed that, since they are for the most part written by impartial observers, these syntheses would be quite objective, and that their conclusions would essentially converge; but alas, a comparison of these works, and the differences between them and my own, will show that nothing could be farther from the truth.

22. See Oshima Riichi, *Tohogakuho*, 30 (Kyoto, 1959), 39–66, for references.
23. Li Chi, *Chinese Civilization*; Walter A. Fairservis, Jr., *The Origins of Oriental Civilization*, New York, New American Library, 1959; Cheng Te-kun, *Prehistoric China*, Cambridge, W. Heffer, 1959; William Watson, *China, Before the Han Dynasty*, New York, F. A. Praeger, 1961.

This divergence of views, however, is precisely a reason for joy rather than sorrow. Not only because the appearance of competitive theories is a prerequisite for the eventual fruition of the archaeological synthesis of ancient China but also, more significantly, because the different points of view are the results of a number of necessarily different approaches to the same subject matter and the same corpus of data. Some of these recent works aim at summarizing the data without ambitious attempts at interpretation, thus providing invaluable material for study. Others stress the basic unity of human history as a whole and the pool of knowledge shared by the early segments of Chinese and Western culture histories. Still others detail artifacts and their significance to the history of Chinese art and technology.

What has convinced me that a volume like the present one is worth writing even in this recently prolific field of ancient Chinese archaeology is the fact that still another approach, one that has proved capable of bringing about fruitful results elsewhere in the world, has yet to be applied to the Chinese data. By this I mean the method of developmental classification which has been applied with considerable success by V. Gordon Childe and Robert J. Braidwood to the Near East, and also by Gordon R. Willey and Philip Phillips to the New World.[24] This volume does not intend to adopt a monolithic point of view in methodology, and the historical framework it tries to set up is intended to be a balanced one. The reader, however, will not fail to notice that the developmental approach is emphasized somewhat at the expense of all others. I make this attempt with deliberation, believing that in the field of Chinese archaeology there have been sufficient hypotheses on the problems of art, origins, and descriptive analyses of artifacts, whereas the process of cultural and social growth remains to be discussed in a general theoretical fashion.

Archaeological cultures consist of assemblages of artifacts and other artifactual features with recurrent forms and styles. Their forms and styles were shaped both by the selective process of time

24. V. Gordon Childe, *What Happened in History*, New York, Penguin Books, 1942; *New Light on the Most Ancient East*, New York, F. A. Praeger, 1953; Robert J. and Linda Braidwood, *Cahiers d'Histoire mondiale*, 1 (1953), 278–310; R. J. Braidwood and Charles A. Reed, *Cold Spring Harbor Symposia on Quantitative Biology*, 22 (1957), 19–31; Gordon R. Willey and Philip Phillips, *Method and Theory in American Archeology*, Chicago, University of Chicago Press, 1958; Julian H. Steward, *Theory of Culture Change*, Urbana, University of Illinois Press, 1955.

and their peculiar historical experiences, and by the particular functional correlation among ecology, social situation, and actual behavior. As for any individual culture, it developed both as a functioning organism and as a historic isolate, and was accordingly patterned both in substance and in style. Few, if any, cultures could grow in total isolation without external stimulation and exchange of knowledge; on the other hand, few cultures could develop distinctive styles and substantial contents purely as a result of external stimulation, intrusion, or compulsion. In other words, problems of origins and problems of the process of actual growth are equally important for the study of any archaeological unit of culture.

In the following chapters, the archaeological data of ancient China will be interpreted, processed, and arranged with such a perspective in view.[25] Chronological sequences and cultural groups will be formulated for the total area of China and its various regions, and questions will be asked, and answers sought, as to how such sequences and groupings came about, and why such distinctive steps of historical developments were taken in this part of the world. To put this in another way: I wish to describe how civilization rose in China and what course of development it took. To describe is inevitably to interpret, and an interpretation complete in all aspects of this development is not intended. If, for instance, I seem to have treated the Palaeolithic period in an unceremonious and summary manner, it is because, in my opinion, this period is relatively irrelevant to the particular direction and process of Chinese civilizational development except for providing a general foundation of basic cultures and populations. If I seem to have underplayed at times the roles of external influences in shaping the events and the courses of cultural development in ancient China, it is because such influences have been more than adequately dealt with by previous authors, and I wish, instead, to stress the growth process of civilization itself and its formative antecedents which, above all, must be accounted for by what took place *in situ*.

In this respect, I find myself in complete agreement with Cheng Te-kun that "as long as plain archaeological facts are not properly

25. For methodological details, see Chang Kwang-chih, "Prehistoric Settlements in China: A Study in Archaeological Method and Theory," unpublished Ph.D. thesis, Harvard, 1960, pp. 1–74.

18

established in their native contexts, any comparison with distant parallels tends to be farfetched," [26] and with Li Chi that "before we accept this [that the birth of all great civilizations . . . is due to cultural contact] as true of any particular civilization, no effort should be spared to collect all available data in order to examine in detail the process of actual growth." [27] It is precisely around this "process of actual growth" of the Chinese civilization in its "native contexts" that the present study centers.

26. Cheng Te-kun, *Prehistoric China*, p. xix.
27. Li Chi, *Chinese Civilization*, p. 17.

19

Chapter One

Geography

and the

Palaeolithic

Foundations

GEOGRAPHIC SUBDIVISIONS OF CHINA

In discussing the early history of man in China, we must constantly bear in mind that the area known as China is continental in dimensions (ca. 3,700,000 square miles, as against Europe's 3,872,000 square miles and the United States' 2,977,000 square miles). This area contains a great variety of topography, climate, and vegetation, ranging from tropical jungles in the Southwest through subarctic taiga in Manchuria; from the vast Tibetan plateaus through river-dissected hills of the Southeast; and from the deserts and steppes of Chinese Turkestan through the temperate alluvial plains of the lower Huangho valley. In most of these widely differing geographical regions man's progress has been traced in some detail, indicating invariably that human life in each area adapted to its peculiar ecological circumstances.

Largely speaking, the modern subdivision of China into a northern part and a southern part has been a significant demarcation throughout the whole period of man's occupation. Further, in view of the special importance of the Huangho valley in the early cultural history of China, North China can itself be divided in two. Thus, for the purposes of this volume, three ecological zones of the first magnitude are distinguished: the Huangho valley, the southern deciduous zone, and the northern forests and steppes.

The landscape of China is above all dominated by mountains and hills which, in prehistoric times, were presumably covered with

21

thick woods and jungles.[1] The activities of the prehistoric inhabitants, therefore, were largely restricted to the large and small river
valleys. Furthermore, most of the great rivers lie horizontally in a
West-East axis and flow into the Pacific Ocean. This results in a
happy coincidence, in that the great river valleys of concern to us
seldom run through different major climatic and vegetation zones,
and hence can serve as a basis for a cultural as well as a geographical subdivision of China (Map 1).

The Huangho Valley   This region includes the drainage
of the Huangho (Yellow River) and its tributaries, together with
the upper courses of a few tributaries of the Yangtze River and
several small independent drainage systems in the Hopei Plain.
The topography of the Huangho valley is further divisible into
three more or less distinct regions: the loess highlands in the west,
the alluvial plains in the east, and the Shantung Peninsula along
the sea coast. Generally these are all in the temperate climatic
zone, with warm summer and cold winter and with moderate
(400–800 mm.) rainfall. The vegetation cover of the entire area
can be characterized as mixed deciduous-coniferous forests, though
part of the area is now entirely deforested and part of it has become
semiarid.[2]

The Southern Deciduous Zone   The boundary between the
Huangho valley and the Southern Deciduous Zone lies midway
between the Yangtze and the Huangho, near the thirty-third
parallel. In the west, the line corresponds with the crest of the
Tsinling Mountains; farther east it follows the Huai River.[3] This
division between the North and the South is clearly marked by
climate, natural vegetation, soil, and crops, as shown in Table 1.[4]
South China is covered with large and small river systems. These
include the Yangtze River, the Huai River, the Pearl River, and
several smaller but independent drainages in the Southwest and
along the southeastern coast. Topographically, South China is
divisible into three major regions: the hills, which cover most of

1. George B. Cressey, *China's Geographic Foundations* (2d ed., New York,
McGraw-Hill, 1934), p. 37.
2. James Thorp, *Geography of the Soils of China*. Nanking, National
Geological Survey, 1936; George B. Cressey, *Asia's Lands and Peoples*. New
York, McGraw-Hill, 1951.
3. Cressey, *Asia's Lands and Peoples*, p. 99.
4. Simplified after Cressey, *China's Geographic Foundations*, p. 15.

MAP 1. The geographic regions and land forms of China, divisible into three broad ecological zones: (1) the Huangho valley: L (loessland), YP (the Yellow Plain), and SP (the Shantung Peninsula); (2) the northern forests and steppes: MP (the Manchurian plain), KM (the Khingan Mountains), JM (the Jehol Mountains), EMU (Eastern Manchurian Uplands), M (Mongolia), and S (Sinkiang); (3) the southern deciduous zone: YP (the Yangtze plain), SB (the Szechwan basin), CMB (the central mountain belt), SYH (the south Yangtze hills), SC (the southeast coast), CH (the Canton hinterland), and SU (the southwest uplands). Base map by Erwin Raisz, courtesy Harvard-Yenching Institute. Adapted by Rowland Illick in George Cressey's *Asia's Lands and Peoples*, 2d ed., 1951, McGraw-Hill Book Co., Inc., New York.

the area and are drained by all of the river systems mentioned above except the Huai; the Red basin of Szechwan, drained by the Upper Yangtze and its several tributaries; and the Yangtze-Huai Plain, drained by the Lower Yangtze and the Huai. There are two principal lacustrine areas in South China, one among the hills in the Middle Yangtze consisting of the remnants of the ancient Lake Yün-meng, and including such major lakes as Tung-t'ing (Hupei) and Po-yang (Kiangsi); and another situated on the Lower Yangtze-Huai Plain, which includes such major lakes as Hung-tzê and T'ai.

TABLE 1.

Geographic Contrasts between North China and South China

The North	The South
Limited, uncertain rainfall, 400–800 mm.	Abundant rainfall, 800–1600 mm.
Cold winters, hot summers, a little snow	Cold winters, hot, moist summers, snow and ice uncommon
Semiarid climate	Subtropical climate, summer monsoon rains, and typhoons
Unleached calcareous soils	Leached noncalcareous soils
Kaoliang, millet, wheat, beans.	Rice the dominant crop
4–6 months growing seasons, one or two crops	9 months to a year growing season, two or three crops
Mixed deciduous forests and grasslands	Subtropical and tropical forests
Brown and dustblown during the winter	Green landscape at all seasons

The Northern Forests and Steppes   The area immediately to the north of the Huangho valley consists of the modern regions of Inner Mongolia and Manchuria. Topographically, this area may be compared to a horseshoe, opening to the south. The space at the center is the erosion plain of Manchuria, drained by the lower courses of the Liao River and the Sungari River, and originally covered with mixed deciduous-coniferous forests. The eastern branch of the horseshoe is formed by the Eastern Manchurian Uplands, and is drained by the T'u-men and Yalu Rivers and the Lower Amur. The western branch is formed by the Khingan and the Jehol Mountains, and is drained by the upper courses of the

24

Amur, the tributaries of the Sungari, and the Upper Liao. These mountainous areas are covered with coniferous forests or parklands in the east and north, and steppes in the west. The latter landscape extends westward into Mongolia and Sinkiang. Climatically, this entire area is extremely seasonal and continental, with long, severe winters and short, warm summers.

HUMAN AND CULTURAL BEGINNINGS IN THE PLEISTOCENE PERIOD

The geological and palaeontological background on the basis of which modern Chinese geographical features gradually took shape was laid down with the beginning of the Pliocene period when large and small lakes were prevalent in China, tropical and subtropical climate was dominant, and the so-called *Hipparion* fauna appeared.[5] The deposits of the Upper Pliocene beds indicate increased aridity at that time—the lakes became smaller and the fauna included a rich grazing and browsing assemblage.[6] An erosion interval—the Fenho Erosion stage—initiated by a general tectonic movement, then brought an end to the Pliocene period in China and constitutes a well-defined Pliocene-Pleistocene boundary. The beginning phases of the Pleistocene epoch witnessed a series of climatic and sedimentary changes—correlated by Movius with the Himalaya First Glacial and Interglacial stages, the emergence of Villafranchian fauna (*Leptobos, Elephas,* and *Equus*), and the disappearance of the Pontian flora. Toward the end of this stage, the Lower Pleistocene period, there was a general continental uplift to mark a new cycle of sedimentation and the beginning of the Middle Pleistocene period. This led to the widespread deposition in China of the slope-wash red loams (*terra rossa*), the scattered appearances of cave and fissure deposits, and the formation of the modern drainage system of the Huangho River. In the Reddish Clay strata and their corresponding fissure deposits in both North and South China are found typical Middle Pleistocene fauna, with some Upper Pleistocene species appearing toward the end. These faunal remains suggest that during this stage at least

5. Pierre Teilhard de Chardin, *Early Man in China*, pp. 1–2; Hallam L. Movius, Jr., "The Lower Palaeolithic Cultures of Southern and Eastern Asia," *TAPS*, n.s. 38 (1948), 342.
6. Movius, *TAPS*, 38, 342–43.

two main palaeozoological provinces can be distinguished in the Chinese area, North and South. Both geological and palaeontological evidence indicates that at least two cool semiarid phases and a warm and wet interval are discernible within this Reddish Clay stratum in North China, which have been correlated by Movius with the Second Glacial, Second Interglacial, and Third Glacial stages of the Himalaya Glacial sequence. The Reddish Clay stratum then came to an end with another major erosional cycle—the Ch'ing-shui Erosion Stage, which was followed by a cool and semiarid climatic phase. This phase has been correlated with the Fourth Glacial of the Himalayas and was the period when loess and its related deposits were accumulated over the Chinese soil. The loessic stage was the final geological phase of Chinese Pleistocene, and in this stage the fauna drastically changed from the assemblage of the previous Reddish Clay to one which contained many essentially modern forms. Thus, geologically speaking, Pleistocene in China can be subdivided into three main stages: the Villafranchian, starting with the Fenho Erosion; the Reddish Clay, ending with the Ch'ing-shui Erosion; and finally the Loessic.[7] These geological subdivisions can serve as more than chronological yardsticks— for which purpose they are rough indeed. Since these geological changes concurred with climatic fluctuations as well as palaeontological movements and evolution, the shift from one stage to another was also accompanied by changes of the geographical arrangement and ecological background, which bear directly upon the problems of human history (Map 2).

Archaeologists and human palaeontologists now still hold to the view that during the Villafranchian stage China was not occupied by man.[8] There is some evidence to the contrary, however, and archaeological excavations in the near future may yet alter drastically the current picture of the emergence of man in this part of the world. Some forty years ago in the Nihowan beds (generally thought to be Villafranchian) of the Sangkan River valley of Hopei in North China, Emile Licent and Pierre Teilhard de

7. The Pleistocene geology and palaeontology of China have been summarized in the following works: Teilhard de Chardin, *Early Man in China*; Helmut de Terra, *Pleistocene Formation*; Pei Wen-chung, VP, 1 (1957), 9–24; Chang Kwang-chih, AP, 2 (1958), 39–59; Chang Kwang-chih, *Science*, 136 (1962), 749–60.
8. F. Clark Howell, *Science*, 130 (1959), 833.

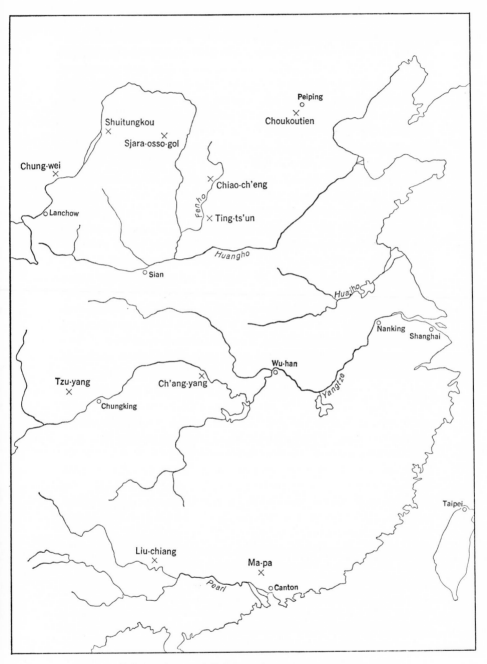

MAP 2. Palaeolithic and Palaeoanthropological sites in China.

Chardin discovered a so-called "faceted stone" and some bone fragments. The Abbé Breuil believed that this stone and some of the bone fragments were modified by human hands, but his view is generally rejected.[9] A new Palaeolithic site was discovered in 1959 and excavated in 1960 and 1961, on the back of a small hill to the northeast of Hsi-hou-tu village, approximately 3 km. to the east of the Yellow River, in Jui-ch'eng county, southern Shansi, where stone implements (bilaterally retouched giant flakes, small scrapers, cores with a small number of flaking scars, and irregularly retouched flakes) of quartzite pebbles were reportedly uncovered from a sandy-gravel layer underneath the Reddish Clay stratum, in direct association with a typical Nihowan fauna. Apparently dating from the First Interglacial period of Lower Pleistocene, this palaeolithic assemblage may prove to be the earliest evidence of human occupation in China; the publication of a full description of the site will be eagerly awaited before we accept unreservedly the artificiality of its stone "implements." [10] Furthermore, there were some anthropoids in China during the Villafranchian stage, including the owner of the so-called *Hemanthropus peii* teeth, and the giant creature, the *Gigantopithecus blacki*. The teeth of the former anthropoid were found by G. H. R. von Koenigswald in Hong Kong drugstores; von Koenigswald believes that they were originally derived from South China Pleistocene deposits, and has compared them morphologically with the *Paranthropus* of South Africa.[11] The latter, *Gigantopithecus blacki*, was first identified shortly before World War II by von Koenigswald on the basis of three gigantic teeth which were also obtained from Chinese drugstores in Hong Kong, where they were used—as were many other palaeontological specimens throughout China as well as the *Hemanthropus peii* teeth—as an ingredient in drug making.[12] Franz Weidenreich thought that the *Gigantopithecus* might have been in the direct lines of descent which led subsequently to the *Pithecanthropus* groups and, finally, to mod-

9. Teilhard de Chardin, *L'Anthropologie*, 45 (1935), 736; Henri Breuil, *L'Anthropologie*, 45 (1935), 746; Movius, TAPS, 38, 345.
10. For a preliminary report, see Chia Lan-po, WW, 1962:4/5, 25–26.
11. G. H. R. von Koenigswald, *Koninkl. Nederl. Akademie van Wetenschappen, Amsterdam, Proceedings*, ser. B, 60 (1957), 153–59.
12. G. H. R. von Koenigswald, *Anthropological Papers, American Museum of Natural History*, 43 (1952), 301–9.

ern man.[13] Weidenreich's hypothesis has been rendered obsolete by advances in the study of the African australopithecines, and the recent discoveries of three mandibles and over a thousand isolated teeth of this species *in situ* in Southwest China have led Pei Wen-chung and Woo Ju-kang to cast further doubts on it, although *Gigantopithecus* is still sometimes regarded as being the anthropoid ape morphologically closest to the hominids of any yet discovered.[14]

When the Middle Pleistocene period started and the Reddish Loam began to accumulate over the eroded river terraces and in the cave and fissure formations, a Middle Pleistocene fauna migrated into the area of China from the south, including the human species known as *Sinanthropus* (or *Pithecanthropus*) *pekinensis* whose skeletal and cultural remains have been recovered from the sites at Choukoutien, southwest of Peiping in North China. In this region a number of fossiliferous localities have been found which contain the cultural remains of Peking Man, but skeletal remains are known only from Locality 1, the Kotsetang Cave. This Cave seems to have been occupied by Peking Man throughout the Reddish Clay stage, while Locality 13 was visited only at the beginning, and Locality 15 occupied toward the end.[15] *Sinanthropus* made tools, hunted game (principally the *Sinomegaceros*), collected nuts, used fire, and was probably cannibalistic. Two stone tool making traditions were favored by *Sinanthropus*: the pebble (or chopper-chopping-tool) tradition, and the flake tradition. The implements were crudely made, and the striking-platform was largely unprepared, though better made scrapers and points and prepared striking-platforms appeared toward the end

13. Franz Weidenreich, *Anthropological Papers, American Museum of Natural History, 40* (1945), Pt. I; Franz Weidenreich, *Apes, Giants, and Man,* Chicago, University of Chicago Press, 1946.

14. Pei Wen-chung, VP, 1 (1957), 2, 65–70; Pei Wen-chung, AA, 59 (1957), 834–38; Pei Wen-chung and Woo Ju-kang, *Acta Palaeontologica Sinica,* 4 (1956), 477–89; Pei Wen-chung and Li Yu-heng, VP, 2 (1958), 193–97.

15. Davidson Black, P. Teilhard de Chardin, C. C. Young, and Pei Wen-chung, "Fossil Man in China," GSuC, Mem., Ser. A, No. 11, 1933; Pei Wen-chung, in GSoC, Bull., 13, (1934), 359–67; Pei Wen-chung, GSoC, Bull., 19 (1939), 147–87; Chia Lan-po, VP, 3 (1959), 41–45; Chao Tze-kui and Li Yen-hsien, VP, 4 (1960), 30–32; H. D. Kahlke and Chou Pen-hsiüng, VP, 1961:3, 212–40; Chao Tze-kui and Tai Erh-chien, VP, 1961:4, 374–78.

of their occupation.[16] Only a very small number of artifacts found at Choukoutien can be said to resemble the bifacially-flaked hand-axes and the Levalloisian flakes which are characteristic of the Lower Palaeolithic cultures of Europe and Africa.[17] Most of the physical characteristics of the Peking Man were primitive and pithecanthropoid: he had a low skull vault, small cranial capacity (average: 1075 cc.), prominent brow ridges, and a receding chin. However, the upper limbs and, to some extent, the lower limbs exhibit almost modern features.[18] Franz Weidenreich,[19] who studied the Peking Man remains, singled out twelve morphological traits, such as the mandibular torus, the shovel-shaped upper incisors (Fig. 1), and the sagittal crest, which he considered as having transmitted into the modern Mongoloid inhabitants of the same area. This is certainly a noteworthy phenomenon, and many other fossil forms in China exhibit similar characteristic features, but few human palaeontologists consider this evidence as being conclusive.[20]

In addition to *Sinanthropus*, human and cultural remains have been found in other parts of China from the same Reddish Clay stratum. From the Fenho valley of Shansi, palaeolithic implements of the Choukoutienian traditions have been uncovered [21] and a maxilla and a skull cap were discovered at Lung-tung, in Ch'ang-yang county in western Hupei,[22] and at Ma-pa, in Ch'ü-chiang county, northern Kwangtung, respectively.[23] These latter human remains are said to show more neanderthaloid features than pithecanthropoid and could possibly be from a later phase within the

16. Cf. Hallam L. Movius, Jr., in *Papers of the Peabody Museum;* Movius, in *TAPS, 38.*

17. Chia Lan-po, KKTH, 1957:1, 1–6; Chia Lan-po, *K'o-hsüeh-t'ung-pao,* 1956:12, 39–41.

18. For a good summary, see E. A. Hooton, *Up From the Ape* (New York, MacMillan, 1949), pp. 298–306.

19. Franz Weidenreich, *Palaeontologia Sinica,* n.s. D, 10 (1943), 253–54.

20. E.g., Woo Ju-kang and N. N. Cheboksarov, *Sovetskaia Etnografiia,* 1959: 4, 3–24.

21. Chia Lan-po, Wang Tsê-yih and Chiu Chung-lang, VP, 4 (1960), 28; Wang Tsê-yih, Chiu Chung-lang, and Pi Chu-chen, *Palaeovertebrata et Paleoanthropologia,* 1 (1959), 88–91; Chia Lan-po, KK, 1959:1, 18–20; Chia Lan-po and Wang Tsê-yih, KKTH, 1957:5, 12–18, Chiu Chung-lang, VP, 2 (1958), 281–87.

22. Chia Lan-po, VP, 1 (1957), 247–52.

23. *Paleovertebrata et Paleoanthropologia,* 1 (1959), 94–96; Woo Ju-kang and Peng Ju-tsê, VP, 3 (1959), 175–82.

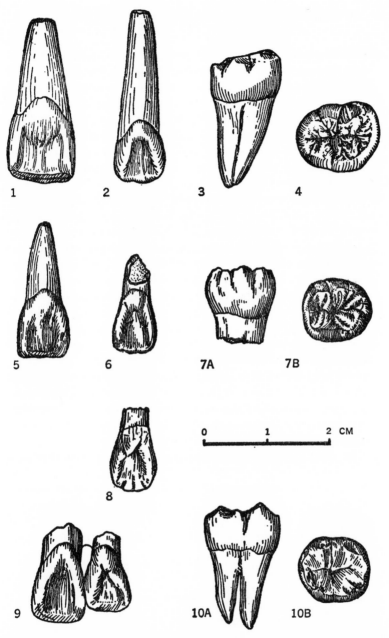

FIG. 1. Teeth of ancient and modern North China inhabitants, showing the persistent occurrence of shovel-shaped incisors. 1–4. *Sinanthropus* (1. left upper median incisor; 2. right upper lateral incisor; 3. right lower second molar; 4. left lower second molar). 5–7. Ting-ts'un Man (5. left upper median incisor; 6. left upper lateral incisor; 7A and 7B. right lower second molar). 8. Ordos Man, left upper lateral incisor. 9–10. Modern northern Chinese (9. right upper incisors; 10A and 10B. right lower second molar). From Kuo Mo-jo, et al., *Chung-kuo jen-lei hua-shih ti fa-hsien yü yen-chiu* (Peiping, Science Press, 1955), p. 44.

Reddish Clay stage. Von Koenigswald collected a hominid tooth, again from a Hong Kong drugstore, which he has termed *Sinanthropus officinalis* and which he believes to have come originally from the Reddish Clay deposits in South China.[24]

From the deposit of Ch'ing-shui Erosion stage, which followed the Reddish Clay and could possibly be correlated with the Third Interglacial of the Himalayas, palaeolithic implements have been discovered in the Ordos area and in the Fenho valley in Shansi.[25] Three human teeth also came to light in 1954 at the Locality 100 of Ting-ts'un, in Hsiang-fen Hsien, southern Shansi (Fig. 1).[26] The teeth, probably all from the same child, are said to exhibit neanderthaloid characteristics but show similarities to the dentition of the Peking Man—two of the three are upper incisors which have pronounced shovel-shaped depressions. The human industries from these deposits indicate considerable advances over those of the Choukoutienian tradition. While the predominant technological traditions remained the pebble and the clactonian flake, the various types of tools included picklike implements, polygonal scrapers, and stone balls, as well as points, scrapers, choppers, and chopping-tools. The techniques were more refined, the number of bifacially flaked core implements increased, the striking platforms and the cores were sometimes both prepared before striking, and most important, there were some finely made parallel-sided flakes which may be regarded as foreshadowing the appearance of blades during the next geological stage.[27]

The next Loessic stage witnessed the appearance of *Homo sapiens* in South China and of industries with mature blades in the North. Human skulls have been found at Tzu-yang in Szechwan[28] and Liu-chiang in Kwangsi[29] from deposits which are regarded as being equivalent to North China's loess. Both of these skulls undoubtedly belonged to the species of *Homo sapiens*, but exhibit

24. G. H. R. von Koenigswald, *Anthropological Papers*, 43, 308.
25. Teilhard de Chardin, *Early Man in China*, p. 68; H. L. Movius, Jr., *Quaternaria*, 3 (1956), 13–26; Pei Wen-chung et al., *Shan-hsi Hsiang-fen-hsien Ting-ts'un chiu-shih-ch'i shih-tai i-chih fa-chüeh pao-kao*, Peiping, Science Press, 1958.
26. Pei Wen-chung et al., ibid.
27. Chang Kwang-chih, AP, 2, 1958; Chia Lan-po, *K'o-hsüeh-t'ung-pao*, 1956:12.
28. Pei Wen-chung and Woo Ju-kang, *Tzu-yang Jen*, Peiping, Science Press, 1957.
29. Woo Ju-kang, VP, 3 (1959), 109–10.

certain features which recall both *Sinanthropus* and the neander-thaloid. Furthermore, the Liu-chiang skull has some morphological features that are comparable with Oceanic Negroid characteristics, and both the Tzu-yang and the Liu-chiang skulls also show pheno-typical similarities to the modern Mongoloids. One may infer that the population in South China during the Loess stage—or proba-bly the Fourth Glacial stage of the Himalaya sequence—may repre-sent an early form of *Homo sapiens* which later differentiated into some of the constituents of the modern Mongoloid and Oceanic Negroid races. But during the same stage the Palaeolithic man in North China, as represented by a parietal, a femur, and a tooth discovered in the Ordos area, appears to have remained neander-thaloid in physical type.[30] His cultural remains, however, show remarkable diversification. In some of the regional facies of the Loess stage in North China—at the Shui-tung-kou site in Ning-hsia, for instance—points and scrapers made on "Mousterian" flakes and burins and end-scrapers on blades were characteristic. In some other regional facies, such as the Sjara-osso-gol site in northern Shensi, where there appeared to be a relatively humid en-vironment, microcores, microflakes, and microblades were manu-factured.[31] The Upper Palaeolithic industry of South China is still inadequately known, but both blades and "Mousterian" flakes ap-pear to be present.[32] Such Loessic industrial traditions seem to have been carried over into the post-Pleistocene assemblages at least in North China after the Panchiao Erosion stage marked the end of the Chinese Pleistocene and Palaeolithic periods.

Modern China in the geological sense began at this point, and the above summary of Palaeolithic man and culture indicates that modern man in China did not grow out of a vacuum. The Pleisto-cene period may have lasted close to a million years. The above survey of the Pleistocene man and culture in China has been of necessity extremely sketchy, yet a number of noteworthy points stand out which can be summarized into the following two ob-servations: 1) There was a continuous development of man, both

30. Wang Yü-ping, WWTKTL, 1957:4, 22–25; Woo Ju-kang, VP, 2, 1958.
31. M. Boule, H. Breuil, E. Licent, and P. Teilhard de Chardin, "Le Paléolithique de la Chine," *Archives de l'Inst. Paléont. Humaine, Mémoire 4*, 1928.
32. See Chap. 2, note 26.

33

in physical types and cultural traditions, which indicates a continuity of genes and traditions in the area of China throughout the Pleistocene period and into the geological modern age; 2) On the other hand, evolutionary changes occurred, both in physical types and cultural traditions, during the various stages of the Chinese Pleistocene and Palaeolithic periods at time intervals comparable geologically to similar changes elsewhere in the Old World. This paradox is readily explicable if we assume neither total autonomy nor successive total replacements for the human and cultural evolution in this part of the world. The mechanisms and precise historic processes which brought about such physical and cultural changes were extremely complicated and involved. We might take great pains and much space to trace and explain some of them, yet never understand the others. There is one thing we can assume, however: the Palaeolithic period was an introduction to modern man in China in a sense that is both chronological and substantive.

Chapter Two

Hunter-Fishers

of the

Early Recent Period

With the retreat of the ice sheets and glaciers in the Himalayas and on other highlands at the end of the stage of the Great Loess, the geological Recent (Holocene) period came to Eastern Asia. Many of the Pleistocene faunal forms became extinct, such as the mammoth and the woolly rhinoceros; while the modern faunal group, which began to appear during the Upper Pleistocene period, came to dominate. There was probably a general rise in temperature and precipitation in the northern regions, together with an increase of vegetation cover, a gradual rising of land, and a stage of erosion. These concurrent geological and palaeontological changes may have occurred in the different regions of Eastern Asia with varying intensity and in different ways, but information from North China indicates that in this region they were sufficiently intense to bring about widespread changes both in landscape and in the human cultures adapting to it.

As described above, the terminal Pleistocene period in North China, which was also the final phase of the Malan Loess stage, was characterized by a cool and semiarid—continental—climate. With the beginning of the Holocene stage, there was probably a general uplift in the mean annual temperature of North China, as indicated by (a) the extinction of the "cool" fauna, such as the mammoth, the woolly rhinoceros, and the *Bos primigenius*; (b) the appearance of many southern species of modern fauna; (c) the apparent thickening of vegetation cover; and (d) the erosion of landscape and the apparent abundance of water. During this warm, moist period Mesolithic and Neolithic cultures began and

35

flourished in North China. The relatively mild and moist climatic condition, however, began to deteriorate after the initial periods of the historic stage, until the climate became cool and the landscape nearly barren, probably as a result of intensive and unrestricted deforestation, on the one hand, and the gradual lowering of temperature, on the other.

With regard to erosion and the abundance of water during the early phases of the Recent period, it is believed that beginning with the Holocene a new sedimentary cycle was initiated by the Panchiao erosion stage. According to Pierre Teilhard de Chardin:

> That a positive movement of the land is today still in process is confirmed by the fact that, since the deposition of the Malan loess, the last remnants of the Pliocene lakes have been largely dessicated in the interior: Sjara-osso-gol depression, Lower Fenho and Taiyuan basins, Sungari Basin, Djalai Nor (and a number of other nors in Mongolia).[1]
>
> During the Late Pleistocene, the distribution and local facies of the modern deserts are fully recognizable. Yet their depressions are abundantly filled with temporary lakes, not so temporary however that they could not feed at places a rich population of Mollusks. Heaps of *Lymnaea* and *Planorbis* occur in the high terraces along the "nors" of East Mongolia . . . The continuation of this regime, or even a somewhat moister period, are necessary for explaining the distribution of human industry during Neolithic times. Since the Neolithic, an increasing aridity is positively indicated by a general extension of the sand dunes, a general reduction of the "nors," and a general deflation of the Late Pleistocene silts. The influence of human agency . . . seems to be, on the whole, insufficient for explaining the main phenomenon.[2]

These "nors" in Mongolia are now largely dessicated, but the wind blown cultural remains in this region "occurred with such regularity in the various basins and hollows, large and small," as to suggest that their formation took place under climatic conditions decidedly different from those of the present day and when these

1. Teilhard de Chardin, GSoC, Bull., 16 (1936/37), 199–200.
2. Ibid., p. 219.

basins were filled with water.[3] Similar climatic peaks during the early post-Pleistocene period are also indicated by peats at Sanho and Chi in Hopei in the Plains area,[4] and by the high water levels near prehistoric sites in Honan,[5] as well as by the literary records of the existence of "nors" in Honan, Shansi, and Shensi in the western loesslands.[6]

Along with the moist climatic conditions in North China went a thick vegetation cover in the areas which are now barren and semiarid, as indicated by a Black Earth horizon at some localities in the North. At Lin-hsi in Jehol, Sha-kang in Hsin-min Hsien, Liaoning, and Ang-ang-hsi in Heilungchiang, cultural deposits were found in a black earth layer, which lies beneath a yellowish, sandy layer of Recent formation and above the loess deposits of Pleistocene origin.[7] This black earth layer, marking the transition from the semiarid Loess stage of the terminal Pleistocene to the semiarid condition of the present day, probably represents an ancient forest cover.[8] The existence of a thick forest cover in North China and on the Manchurian plains is further indicated by cultural remains from prehistoric sites, such as the abundance of charcoal and woodworking implements (axe, adze, chisel, etc.), and by the frequency of bones of wild game.[9] Some of these bones are definitely from forest-dwelling animals such as tigers and deer.

Of even greater importance is the fact that in the woods of that time were certain faunal and floral forms indicative of a climate warmer than that of present-day North China. At the Upper Cave of Choukoutien, which dates from the latest Pleistocene or the earliest Holocene, there appeared such warm animal species as *Cynailurus* cf. *jubatus* and *Paguma larvata*.[10] According to the

3. Nels C. Nelson, *Natural History*, 26 (1926), 250; John Maringer, *Contribution to the Prehistory of Mongolia* (Stockholm, 1950), pp. 207–8.

4. J. G. Andersson, "Essays on the Cenozoic of Northern China," GSuC, *Mem.*, ser. A, 3, 1923.

5. J. G. Andersson, BMFEA, 19 (1947), 20–21.

6. J. G. Andersson, BMFEA, 15 (1943), 40–41; Meng Wen-tung, *Yü-kung*, 1 (Peiping, 1934), 14–15; Hu Hou-hsüan, *Chia-ku-hsüeh Shang-shih lun ts'ung*, 2 vols. Chinan, Chi-lu Univ., 1944 and 1945.

7. Liang Ssu-yung, BIHP, 4 (1932), 5; Liang Ssu-yung, TYKKPK, 1 (1936), 9; Teilhard de Chardin, *Mem. Soc. Géol. France* n.s. 3 (1926), fasc. 3, 24; Wang Tseng-hsin, KKTH, 1958:1, 1.

8. Teilhard de Chardin, *Early Man in China*, pp. 38–39.

9. Andersson, *BMFEA*, 15, 34.

10. Pei Wen-chung, PS, ser. C, 10, 1940.

reports of some early Recent period geological deposits and Neo-lithic and Early Bronze Age archaeological sites,[11] there is evidence of the following "warm" species:

Bamboo rat (*Rhizomys sinensis; Rhizomys troglodytes?*):
Yangshao stage sites, An-yang
Elephant (*Elephas indicus*): An-yang
Rhinoceros: Ma-chia-yao
Bison (*Bos namadicus*): Ma-chia-yao
Tapir (*Tapirus* cf. *indicus*): An-yang
Water buffalo (*Bubalus mephistopheles; Bubalus indicus*):
Sanho
Water deer (*Hydropotes inermis*): An-yang, Sanho
Père David's deer (*Elaphurus davidianus*): Sanho
Menzies' deer (*Elaphurus menziesianus*): An-yang
Porcupine: Peiping
Squirrel (*Tamiops*): Peiping
Warmth-loving molluscs (*Lamprotula tientsiniensis, Lam-protula rochechouarti Lamprotula leai*): Tientsin muds, Ch'eng-tzu-yai
Rice (*Oryza sativa*): Yang-shao-ts'un, Liu-tzu-chen(?)
Bamboo: inferred from the form of pottery and mentioned in early literary records

The existence of rice, bamboo, and elephants is corroborated by the written records,[12] while the presence of elephants and rhinoceri is further confirmed by sculptures and some zoomorphic bronzes from the archaeological site at An-yang.

These bits of evidence together prove beyond reasonable doubt that the beginning of Holocene in North China was marked by a gradual rising of the mean annual temperature, accompanied by an increasing vegetation cover and a corresponding faunal assemblage. This conclusion is extremely broad, but finer characteriza-

11. Andersson, *BMFEA*, 15, 35–40; Carl W. Bishop, *Antiquity*, 28 (1933), 389–404; Arthur de Carle Sowerby, *Jour. North-China Br., Royal Asiatic Soc.*, 53 (1922), 1–20; Gad Rausing, *Bull. de la Soc. de lettres de Lund*, 3 (1956), 191–203; Li Chi et al, *Ch'eng-tzu-yai*, Nanking, Academia Sinica, 1934; Teil-hard de Chardin and C. C. Young, *PS*, ser. C, 12, 1936; Teilhard de Chardin and Pei Wen-chung, *Le Néolithique de la Chine*, Peiping, Inst. de Géo-Biologie, 1944; F. S. Drake, *PFEPC*, 4th, 1 (1956), fasc. 1, 133–49.
12. Chen Meng-chia, *Yen-ching-hsüeh-pao*, 20 (1936), 485–576; Hu Hou-hsuan, *Chia-ku-hsüeh Shang-shih lun ts'ung*, 2, 1945; Meng Wen-tung, *Yü-kung*, 1 (1934).

tions will have to depend upon future investigations. It is perfectly clear, however, that the climatic amelioration in North China during the early Recent period must have had considerable influence upon the human industries previously adapted to the cool and semiarid Loessic conditions, which were now confronted with a changed environment and a widened range of potential for further development. Furthermore, the effect of a high temperature on landscape must have been felt differently in different regions of North China. We may infer that in prehistoric times most of the region which now constitutes the eastern low plains was wet and marshy, while the western high loesslands were clad with forests and dissected by watercourses. If this is true—and the scanty evidence at our disposal leads us to think so—it unquestionably had great bearing on the emergence and distribution of human cultures in post-Pleistocene times.

MESOLITHIC CULTURES OF NORTH CHINA

In the last chapter, it was mentioned that the final Pleistocene cultural traditions in North China can be grouped into two major regional facies: the blade-and-flake tradition of the typical loessic landscape and the microblade tradition of the riverine-lacustrine subcycle. The former facies may have begun slightly earlier, but the latter grew in importance with time. The climate and landscape of the early Recent period, as just described, may properly be regarded as an intensification and spatial expansion of the riverine-lacustrine facies to cover the entire area of North China. To a considerable extent corresponding to this physiographical change, the early Recent human industries underwent adaptive changes also. In other words, if the Recent period brought the riverine-lacustrine landscape to the whole of North China and intensified it by a climatic amelioration, then the Recent period also brought the riverine-lacustrine facies of human industries to the whole of North China and, so to speak, intensified them as well. In the cultural history of North China, we thus find a typological as well as a chronological Mesolithic stage, which is characterized by (a) the predominance of the microblade tradition and the use of composite tools; (b) the use of the pressure-flaking technique; and (c) the growing popularity of projectile points and bone implements. To date, eight Mesolithic or probably Mesolithic sites have been found in North China, Mongolia, and Manchuria: Shabarakh-usu in Outer Mongolia, Ikhen-kung, Gurnai, and Sogho-nor in Inner Mongolia, Djalai-nor and Ku-hsiang-t'un in Manchuria, the Upper Cave of Choukoutien in Hopei, and the Sha-yüan region in Shensi (Map 3). It is significant to note that these Mesolithic sites have so far been found only on the relatively

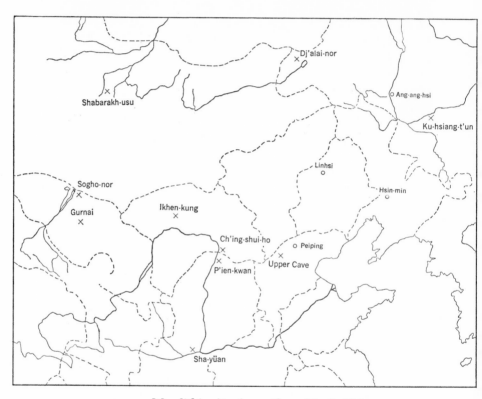

MAP 3. Mesolithic sites in northern North China.

high grounds in the north and in the west, but not on the vast, flat plains in the eastern part of North China—a fact probably accounted for by the physiographical features of North China during that period.

As just mentioned, during prehistoric times the Mongolian steppes formed a vast oasis belt, and the early Recent inhabitants of this area manufactured microcores, microflakes, and micro-

40

blades. Apparently they were engaged in fishing and hunting near the now-dry shallow depressions which were then partially filled with water. The main quest of their hunt seems to have been the ostrich, as shown by many ostrich egg shell rings found at these and later cultural stations. From these sites very few arrowheads have been found, however, which indicates that hunting was probably of secondary importance. This inference is also supported by the scarcity of bone and antler remains and implements from the Mongolian sites, although this can partly be accounted for by the perishability of these remains and the unfavorable conditions for preservation.[13] The Mongolian Mesolithic tradition persisted in this region for a considerable length of time, even when the regions to the south had become farmlands and when neolithic techniques were introduced to give the Mongolian Mesolithic a sub-Neolithic appearance. This will be discussed further in a later chapter.

More is known about the forest dwellers of North China and Manchuria, who were clearly the direct descendants of the Upper Palaeolithic occupants of the area. One of the earliest Mesolithic assemblages in this region was found in the Upper Cave of Choukoutien. Its fauna, still yielding remains of such persisting Pleistocene forms as *Hyaena ultima, Ursus spelaeus, Elephas* sp., and *Paradoxurus,* definitely testifies to the introduction of completely modern forms: *Homo sapiens, Cervus elaphus, Siphneus armandi,* and *Struthio,* as well as the occurrence of some southern warm species: *Cynailurus jubatus* and *Paguma.*[14] The site was probably a burial place, and gives no indication of intensive occupation. The industrial assemblage includes some stone tools (scrapers, flakes, and chopper-chopping-tools), and abundant bone and antler artifacts (worked bone, bone needles, worked antler, perforated teeth of badgers, foxes, deer, wild cats, polecats, and tigers), together with mollusc shells and fish bones. According to W. C. Pei,[15]

> the Upper Cave Man lived in calcareous caves. Nearby there were woods in which tigers, leopards, bears, and wolves

13. N. C. Nelson, AA, 28 (1926), 307; John Maringer, *Prehistory of Mongolia,* pp. 90, 92, 140–43, 151–54, 201, 206. But cf. Chard, AP, 5 (1961), 16.

14. Pei Wen-chung, PS, ser. D, 10, 1940; Pei Wen-chung, VP, 1 (1957), 9–24.

15. Pei Wen-chung, *Chung-kuo shih-ch'ien shih-ch'i chih yen-chiu,* (Shanghai, Commercial Press, 1948), pp. 72–73.

dwelt; there were steppes on which the Chinese deer, the red deer, and gazella roamed about; and plains and lakes in which gigantic fish swam. The man hunted in the woods and fished by the lakes, and made abundant bone and shell artifacts.

The marine shells found in this site, furthermore, indicate either extensive trade connections or long-distance seasonal migrations. From the cave were also found skeletal remains of men, apparently belonging to seven individuals. Since skulls or skull fragments and lower jaws are preserved, Franz Weidenreich has been able to determine that this population of seven was composed of an adult male over sixty, a relatively young male adult, two young adult females, one adolescent, and two children. It is interesting to note that all of the skullcaps which have been preserved show depressions, fractures, or holes, which according to Weidenreich, "apparently have been caused by heavy blows with sharp and blunt implements delivered at a time when the scalp still covered the bones." Weidenreich thus infers that these skeletal remains belonged to a single family who, being "victims of a sudden attack and dismembered, were thrown into the cave." [16] This suggestion is certainly plausible, but other explanations cannot be ruled out. The earth which surrounded the skeletons was partly covered with hematite, indicating that funeral rites probably took place. The depressions, fractures, or holes in the skulls, as W. C. Pei has suggested, could have been caused by rockfalls from the cave ceiling. It is, therefore, entirely possible that the family, if it was one, fell victim to a local epidemic and was buried in the cave by kinsfolk or companions.

Another intriguing fact concerning the Upper Cave skulls concerns their racial characteristics. The morphological analysis of the three best-preserved adult skulls by Weidenreich has convinced him that "they typify three different racial elements, best to be classified as primitive Mongoloid, Melanesoid, and Eskimoid types." [17] This conclusion has led the late Ernest A. Hooton to discuss the Upper Cave population in his *Up From the Ape* under the heading "The Old Man of China who Married an Eskimo

16. Franz Weidenreich, *Bulletin of the Natural History Society of Peking*, 13 (1938/39), 163.
17. Ibid., p. 170.

and a Melanesian." [18] Recent findings of Upper Palaeolithic men in South China as mentioned in the last chapter has shed much new light on this problem. If Wu is right in identifying the Upper Cave specimens as altogether Mongoloid according to recent studies of casts,[19] it then seems that by the beginning of the Recent period the population in North China and that in the Southwest and in Indochina had become sufficiently differentiated to be designated under the names Mongoloid and Oceanic Negroid races respectively, even though both of them may have evolved out of a common Upper Pleistocene substratum as represented by the Tzu-yang and the Liu-chiang skulls. If, on the other hand, the original racial determination of the Upper Cave specimens made by Weidenreich is upheld, then the appearance of a Melanesoid skull in North China is not at all surprising, for a certain amount of intermixture between two contemporary populations is to be expected.

It is quite possible that Manchuria in the Early Holocene period was covered by woods, and its climate was probably a cool one. Here also several surviving Pleistocene faunal forms are found in association with Mesolithic industries. From the Mesolithic sites at Ku-hsiang-t'un and Ta-kou, near Harbin, stone (scrapers, willowleaves, microliths), bone (knives, spearheads, and barbed points), and antler implements were found, indicating that the Mesolithic inhabitants of this region lived in woods and hunted game.[20] Further to the north, at Djalai-nor, implements of stone, bone, and antler, and willow basketwork have been found in direct association with remains of woolly rhinoceros, bison, and mammoth, indicating a similar ecology and culture.[21]

The Sha-yüan assemblage of Shensi is of uncertain age, but it is believed to date from early post-Pleistocene times. Cultural remains from no less than fifteen localities were collected during 1955 and 1956 in the area of Chao-yih Hsien and Ta-li Hsien in the central part of Eastern Shensi, an area in the western portion of a sand-dune region (referred to as Sha-yüan by the local inhabit-

18. E. A. Hooton, *Up From the Ape*, p. 401.

19. Wu Hsin-chih, VP, 1961:3, 181–203.

20. Tokunaga Shigeyasu and Naora Nabus, JZ, 48 (1933), 12; Tokunaga and Naora, *Manshuteiko Kitsurinsho Ku-hsiang-t'un kaiikkai hakkutsu butsu kenkyu hobun*, Tokyo, Waseda University, 1934.

21. V. J. Tolmatchov, *Eurasia Septentrionalis Antiqua*, 4 (1929), 1–9; Teilhard de Chardin, *Early Man in China*, p. 78.

ants) of considerable dimensions.[22] Many of the flakes, stone implements, and bone fragments that were collected are badly rolled, and no habitation layers have been recognized, indicating that the original cultural deposits have been destroyed by the strong sand-bearing winds blowing through centuries. The frequent movements of the sand dunes may also have disturbed the original distribution. The fifteen localities, therefore, are really nothing more than fifteen spots where cultural remains happen to have been concentrated.

A total of 519 specimens, all found on the surface, were singled out as being representative by the investigators of the Institute of Archaeology, Academia Sinica. Most of these consist of chipped flakes and implements, of which only a small portion were secondarily retouched. The rest include two polished stone arrowheads—presumably later intrusions—a bone bead, a mollusc shell ornament, and a fragment of a stone ornament. The chipped stones fall into two major categories. One, the microliths, consists of small flakes and blades made of flint, quartzite-silicate sandstone, agate, opal, jade, and light-colored siliceous pebble by means of indirect percussion and pressure flaking. Retouching, when it occurs, is in most cases limited to a single surface. In typology, these microliths include cores, leaf-shaped points, microblades, points, arrowheads, and scrapers. The other category consists of flakes of quartzite silicate sandstone and light-colored siliceous pebbles; agate also occurs occasionally. These flakes as a rule are larger than the microliths, but their maximum length is still less than 9 cm. According to the investigators, direct percussion was the principal technique for making this series of flakes and implements, which include such types as points and scrapers.

Although more precise dating of the Sha-yüan assemblage is needed, nevertheless it is one of the most significant discoveries in the prehistoric archaeology of North China in recent years. It is the first evidence in North China proper of a microlithic industry (probably of the early post-Pleistocene period) which shows affinities with the Microlithic horizon in Manchuria, Mongolia, and Soviet Siberia, and thus indicates a widespread cultural substratum in North China on which later cultural developments might have been built. On the other hand, the "Mousterianlike" flakes of this assemblage indicate an unmistakable linkage with

22. An Chih-min and Wu Ju-tso, *KKHP*, 1957:3, 1–12; Chang Shen-shui, *VP*, 3 (1959), 47–56.

the Ordosian industries of the Upper Pleistocene period in the same region. In a way, this new finding has thrown a great deal of light upon the problem of Palaeolithic-Neolithic continuities in North China, a problem which deserves close observation by archaeologists.

These Mesolithic sites in North China, Manchuria, and Mongolia indicate a series of closely similar hunter-fisher industries, featuring microblades and pressure-flaking. Considering the ecological characteristics of the areas in which these sites have been found, it is tempting to infer that there might have been at least two regional facies of the Mesolithic cultures in North China, Mongolia, and Manchuria: 1) the Mongolian dune- or oasis-dwellers, and 2) the North China and Manchuria forest-dwellers. The facts that remains of projectile points have been found in the Manchurian sites and the Sha-yüan assemblage of North China but not in Mongolia, and that the ostrich shell rings occur widely in the Mongolian sites but not elsewhere seem to give some support to this inference, although a good deal more data are necessary before we may regard this or other subdivisions as being probable. In any case, the woodland Mesolithic may be regarded as related to the Siberian Palaeolithic and even the European Mesolithic, on the one hand, and to the woodland cultures in Japan and North America, on the other.[23] Furthermore, this woodland Mesolithic may well have been the forerunner of the type of Neolithic culture which subsequently emerged in North China, as indicated by the following facts: (a) in the Neolithic assemblages of the Huangho valley, chipped stone implements and microblades have been found in considerable quantity; (b) Neolithic semisubterranean dwellings could represent a continuation of the Upper Palaeolithic tradition; (c) the distinctively North China Neolithic semilunar and rectangular stone sickle-scrapers may have been foreshadowed by the Mesolithic scrapers; (d) the characteristic Neolithic prismatic arrowheads, which Andersson regards as having been influenced by metal prototypes, seem indeed to be at least remotely related to the prismatic arrowheads of the northern Eurasiatic woodlands;[24] and (e) as described above, the environment of this period was sufficiently favorable

23. Teilhard de Chardin, *GSoC, Bull.*, 19 (1939), 333–39.
24. J. G. Andersson, *Children of the Yellow Earth* (London, Kegan Paul, Trench, and Trubner, 1934), p. 216; C. J. Becker, *Acta Archaeologica*, 27 (1956), 137–48.

45

so that a settled life and the development of agriculture on the part of these hunter-fishers is not at all improbable.

MESOLITHIC CULTURES OF SOUTH CHINA

A different situation prevailed in the early post-glacial periods south of the Tsinling Shan and the Huaiho valley. During Late Pleistocene times, the only well-known human industry in mainland Southeast Asia was the Late Anyathian of the Irrawaddy valley in Upper Burma which, except for a brief intrusion of a blade assemblage, represents a persistence of the Lower Palaeolithic chopper-chopping-tool tradition.[25] In South China, the cultural equipment of Upper Pleistocene man is only beginning to be discovered, and Indo-China offers few substantial clues in this respect.[26]

During the Recent period in Southeast Asia, there was widespread expression of the old pebble-tool technological tradition, generally known as the Hoabinhian pebble-tool complex. This can be characterized by (a) chipped pebble tools, reminiscent of the older chopper-chopping-tool tradition, including "hand-axes" and scrapers; (b) the absence of blades, "Mousterian" flakes, and the microlithic industry; and (c) the association of "Negroid" skeletons, in contrast to the North where, as shown previously, a "Mongoloid" population seems to have prevailed throughout. This general Southeast Asiatic pattern manifests itself regionally in South China in the widespread finds of chipped stone implements in Szechwan,[27] Kwangsi,[28] Yünnan[29] and in the western part of

25. Hallam L. Movius, Jr., "The Stone Age of Burma," TAPS, 32 (1943), 372–74; Movius, Cahiers d'Histoire Mondiale, 2 (1955), 269–70.
26. For Palaeolithic discoveries in South China prior to the Second World War, see: Movius, TAPS, 38, 406–7; Teilhard de Chardin, Early Man in China, pp. 84–85. For recent findings, see: Chiu Chung-lang, VP, 2 (1958), 157–63 (eastern Tibet); Pei Wen-chung and Chou Ming-chen, VP, 1961:2, 139–41; Li Yen-hsien and Huang Wei-wen, VP, 1962:2, 182–89 (Yünnan); and Yang Ling, in VP, 1961:4, 353–59 (Szechwan). For Indo-China, see: Teilhard de Chardin, L'Anthropologie, 47 (1937), 23–33; L'Anthropologie, 48 (1938), 449–56; Movius, TAPS, 38, 406.
27. Cheng Te-kun, Archaeological Studies in Szechwan, Cambridge, Cambridge Univ. Press, 1957.
28. Pei Wen-chung, GSoC, Bull., 14 (1935), 393–412; Chia Lan-po and Chiu Chung-lang, VP, 4 (1960), 39; Ku Yü-min, VP, 1962:2, 193–99.
29. Bien Mei-nien and Chia Lan-po, GSoC, Bull., 18 (1938), 327–48.

Kwangtung as far as the Pearl River delta [30] (Map 4). Paucity of reliable data still makes a classification of regional facies extremely difficult, but some significant assemblages from this area offer clues. In the Red basin of Szechwan, the antiquity of the chipped axes is suggested by their geographical distribution,[31] but is supported by scanty stratigraphical evidence at Tai-hsi. Little is known about the cultural associations of these chipped axes in

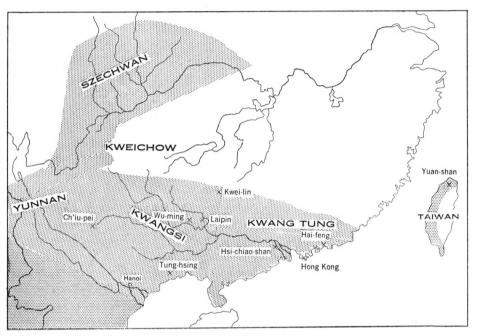

Map 4. Mesolithic sites in South China. Shaded area shows the approximate distribution of the Hoabinhian Mesolithic and sub-Neolithic industries.

a preceramic context. More is known about Yünnan and Kwangsi, however, where chipped stone tools, shell middens, and charred animal bones have been found in limestone caves and under rock shelters. From a cave at Ch'i-lin-shan, in Lai-pin Hsien, Kwangsi province, cultural debris, charred bones, two quartzite flakes, one

30. VP, 4 (1960), 38; W. Schofield, *Hongkong Naturalist*, 5 (1935), 272–75; Mo Chih, KKHP, 1959:4, 1–15; Peng Ju-tzê and Wang Wei, WW, 1959:5, 75; R. Maglioni, *Hongkong Naturalist*, 8 (1938), 211.
31. Cheng Te-kun, *Archaeological Studies in Szechwan*, p. 130.

chopper made of a quartzite pebble, and parts of a human skull were discovered in 1956 in a yellowish breccia stratum in association with bones of deer, wild boar, and a large number of mollusc shells. The human skull fragments include a large part of the upper jaw, the hard palate, the right zygomatic bone, and the occipital bone; it is reportedly the skull of a male individual of advanced age. Its morphological features certainly indicate characteristics of *Homo sapiens,* but the flat malar bone and a well-marked ridge at the entrance to the nasal floor are said to separate this skull from the Mongoloid pattern.[32] A rock-shelter site at Hei-ching-lung, near Ch'iu-pei, in Yünnan, has yielded, in addition to charcoal and ash layers and two pieces of flint flakes, many seeds of *Celtis* and bones of *Canis gray,* Ursidae indet., Felinae indet., *Cervus* sp., Bovidae indet., and *Macacus* sp.[33] Similar assemblages were found in 1959 at Ya-p'u-shan near Hsi-chiao Ts'un and Ma-lang-ch'uan-shan near Ma-lang-chi Ts'un, both in Tung-hsing Hsien, western Kwangtung. Four strata are excavated at these two sites: (a) top soil; (b) shell bed with pottery and neolithic implements; (c) bed with shells and concretions with abundant chipped implements; and (d) red sandstone basement rocks. The cultural remains from layer (c) are characterized by core implements including hand axes, choppers, and so forth, most of which retain the original cortex of the pebbles. The associated fauna, all of modern species, is distinguished by such forms as *Rusa, Bubalus,* and various molluscs.[34]

Around the Pearl River delta area, open sites have been discovered where chipped stone implements were found in a pre-ceramic context. In addition to the somewhat dubious finds in the Hong Kong area,[35] a highly important assemblage has been brought to light since 1955 at Hsi-chiao-shan in Nan-hai county, Kwangtung.[36] An inactive volcano called the Hsi-chiao-shan hill, approximately twelve square kilometers in area, and surrounded by creeks and dried-up ponds, is situated about seventy kilometers to the southwest of Canton. Around the hill have been discovered fourteen prehistoric localities which can be grouped into three classes:

32. Chia Lan-po and Woo Ju-kang, VP, 3 (1959), 37–39.
33. Bien Mei-nien and Chia Lan-po, GSoC, Bull., 18 (1938), 345–46.
34. VP, 4 (1960), 38.
35. W. Schofield, *Hongkong Naturalist,* 5 (1935); W. Schofield, *PFEPC,* 3 (1940), 243.
36. Mo Chih, *KKHP,* 1959:4; Peng Ju-tsê and Wang Wei, WW, 1959: 5.

preceramic, sub-Neolithic, and Neolithic. The latter two classes will be discussed in a later chapter, but it should be remarked here that these three groups of localities repesent a common culture substratum characterized by chipped stone implements. The implements found in a nonceramic context, as well as those in association with pottery and polished stone tools, include both flake and core implements made of flint and sandstone. The core implements apparently resemble the familiar chopper-chopping-tool varieties, but some of the flakes bear faceted platforms and many of them fall into the categories of endscrapers, points, and flake-blades. The occurrence of this flake assemblage in an area predominantly characterized by pebble tools is difficult to explain. Predominantly flake industries are not entirely lacking in the Upper Pleistocene of the Southeast Asiatic regions, and they are found widely during the early Recent period of the Archipaelago area. The flake elements at Hsi-chiao-shan could either be regarded as in some manner related to these assemblages, or rather as a local variation of the continental Hoabinhian complex which took a different manifestation here because of the nature of the raw materials. A final answer must await further discoveries of such assemblages.

It is clear that the majority of archaeological discoveries of the early Recent period in South China indicate a culture confined to the southwestern part of the area, characterized by chipped stone implements of the archaic chopper-chopping-tool tradition of the Palaeolithic, by the hunting of small game animals, and by the collecting of wild plants and molluscs. The single finding of physical remains for this period seems to group the population with the Negroid elements widely substantiated for this stage in the rest of Southeast Asia,[37] and apart from the contemporary Mongoloid inhabitants to the north.

37. P. V. van Stein Callenfels, *Bulletin of the Raffles Museum*, ser. B, 1 (1936), 41–51; H. D. Collings, *Bull. Raffles Mus.*, ser. B, 2 (1938), 122–23; I. H. N. Evans, *Bull. Raffles Mus.*, ser. B, 2 (1938), 141–46; D. A. Hooijer, *SJA*, 6 (1950), 416–22, 8 (1952), 472–77; G. H. R. von Koenigswald, *SJA*, 8 (1952), 92–96; M. W. F. Tweedie, *Jour. Malayan Br., Royal Asiatic Soc.*, 26 (1953), pt. 2, no. 1; Chang Kwang-chih, *Bull. Ethnol. Soc. China*, 2 (1958), 53–133; Joseph B. Birdsell, "The Problem of the Early Peopling of the Americas as Viewed from Asia," in *Papers on the Physical Anthropology of the American Indian*, W. S. Laughlin, ed., New York, Viking Fund, Inc., 1951.

RECAPITULATION

Thus during the early Recent period there were no less than two major cultural traditions discernible in the archaeological record of the area which is modern China. One, distributed in the northern part of the area, but seemingly confined to the woods, parklands, and oases of the western highland regions, is characterized by marked adaptive changes to the changing post-Pleistocene environment, by a predominantly microblade industrial tradition, and by a hunting-fishing subsistence, and may possibly be related to a population Mongoloid in racial affiliations. The other, confined to the southwestern part of South China, is characterized by a stubborn persistence of the Upper Palaeolithic hunting-gathering subsistence and chopper-chopping-tool technology, and appears to be related to a Negroid population which continued on southward into a large part of Southeast Asia. Subsequently, as the archaeological materials now indicate, the Mesolithic hunter-fishers of the North began to cultivate plants and to domesticate animals, entering the food-producing stage in cultural history, and laying a foundation for the North China Neolithic and post-Neolithic cultures to appear and prosper. The Hoabinhian cultures, on the other hand, into which some neolithic techniques such as ceramics and polished stone were subsequently brought, transforming the cultural inventories of these peoples into a sub-Neolithic type, gradually diminished in size and importance and eventually perished to make room for the oncoming immigrant farmers from the North. Details of the agriculturization of South China will be described elsewhere in this book, but first we might begin by focusing our attention upon the Nuclear Area in North China.

Chapter Three

First Farmers

of the

Huangho

Throughout the modern landscape of the Huangho valley there are thousands of Neolithic sites, characterized by the remains of pottery, bones of domesticated animals, polished stone implements, and a general absence of metal tools. These sites also show evidence of agriculture as well as village self-sufficiency and autonomy. As mentioned above, on the basis of the characteristic features of potsherds from these sites, students of Chinese archaeology have long classified these sites into two major cultures, the Yangshao, or Painted Pottery, and the Lungshan, or Black Pottery.[1] It is maintained that the Yangshao Culture occupied the western part of North China and that the Lungshan, slightly later and of a distinctive cultural strain, occupied the eastern part; also that a third culture, subsequent to them both and the forerunner of the historic Shang, intruded from origins unknown.

With the advancement of more intensive and holistic interpretive theories and the increase of knowledge about the Neolithic cultures in North China, this long-held view is gradually being challenged and even rejected in favor of new classifications. The current view, still tentatively constructed, is that the Neolithic culture of the Yellow River valley, emerging from the foundations of the Mesolithic hunter-fisher cultures, first achieved a level of "primary village-farming efficiency," to borrow Robert J. Braidwood's term for the self-sufficient food-producers living in

1. P. Teilhard de Chardin and Pei Wen-chung, *Le Néolithique de la Chine;* Pei, *Chung-kuo shih-ch'ien shih-ch'i;* Yin Ta, *Chung-kuo hsin-shih-ch'i shih-tai,* Peiping, San-lien, 1955; Li Chi, *Chinese Civilization;* Cheng Te-kun, *Prehistoric China,* pp. 73–95; W. Watson, *China,* p. 48; M. Loehr, *Saeculum,* 3 (1952), 15–55.

village settlements, then expanded to become "stratified village-farmers," a term coined by myself for the Neolithic farmers who remained living in village settlements but produced enough food to sustain specialized upper classes, and eventually gave rise to the first civilization in the area.[2] The stratified village-farmers stage and the civilizations which developed out of it are topics of subsequent chapters. But first we should see how this Neolithic culture emerged and how a full-fledged Neolithic village-efficiency was achieved.

The cultural inventory of the first farmers in the Huangho valley and the means by which they emerged to a food-producing way of life unfortunately remain unknown. Theoretically, there are two alternatives: either the Neolithic culture of the Huangho was brought in by immigrants from other regions (e.g. the Near East, where agriculture began about ten thousand years ago), or else the Neolithic population was a continuation from the Mesolithic substratum which had switched to the food-producing way of life. Practically all archaeologists would unhesitatingly rule out the first alternative on the basis of the available materials. According to physical anthropological studies [3] the earliest known farmers in North China were physically "Mongoloid" beyond any doubt. Since the Mongoloid occupation of the northern part of the Far East can be traced back into the Mesolithic, if not the Palaeolithic,[4] a continuity of inhabitants can be assumed as highly probable. As pointed out in the last chapter, in the Neolithic cultures of North China there were several noticeable features that may have been inherited from the local Mesolithic and Upper Palaeolithic. These considerations point to the likelihood that the Mesolithic dwellers of the Huangho valley adopted the cultivation of plants, and that a cultural transformation from forest hunting-fishing into the full-fledged village farming communities took place among them. If we assume this as likely, then there is again the question of independent invention vs. stimulus diffusion. In other words, such questions arise as to whether the Mesolithic hunter-fishers in

2. Robert J. Braidwood, "Levels in Prehistory," in *Evolution of Man after Darwin*, Sol Tax, ed. (3 vols. Chicago, Univ. of Chicago Press, 1960), vol. 2, p. 149; Chang Kwang-chih, BIE, 13, 1962.

3. Davidson Black, PS, ser. D. 1 (1925); D. Black, PS, ser. D, 6 (1928); Yen Yen, Liu Chang-chi, and Ku Yu-min, VP, 4 (1960), 103–11.

4. Li Chi, *Chinese Civilization*, pp. 10–11; but see Joseph Birdsell, "Early Peopling of the Americas," and Chaps. 1 and 2 of this volume.

this region entered the food-producing way of life on their own initiative, or as a result of the ideas and/or actual knowledge of food-production from the Near East. I think that it is still too early to ask these questions. To know the cultural contacts between East and West during this early period we must (a) have a valid absolute chronology for the Chinese Neolithic stage; (b) have some evidence in the intervening regions to substantiate the route of diffusion; and/or (c) make an extensive comparison of the Chinese and the Near Eastern Neolithic cultural traditions to demonstrate the cultural affiliations, if any. None of these approaches are feasible at present. It is all well and good to assume that the idea diffused from one region to another, but this assumption is as difficult to prove as it is to disprove when substantial evidence is totally lacking. Some food plants such as wheat, which seem to have been cultivated alongside the millet, in North China during the Neolithic period, and some domestic animals, such as cattle and sheep, apparently had a Near Eastern origin. Furthermore the East-West cultural contacts during the duration of the Neolithic cultures cannot be denied. But this is far from conclusive evidence for proving that the first idea of plant and animal domestication was carried over with these plants and animals, for we know nothing about the time when these items first appeared in China in relation to various other, native plants and animals. There has been much controversy over this problem, much of which has been charged with bias and emotion. For the present it is best, I think, to concentrate our efforts on knowing more about the Neolithic culture in China itself before making any farfetched conclusions.

As soon as attention is focused upon the Yellow River valley itself and to the problem of the earliest evidence of Neolithic culture in this region, several facts become instantly clear and instructive. First, it is highly probable that the Neolithic culture first emerged in the central region of the Yellow River valley, which we call the North China Nuclear Area, and subsequently radiated toward both east and west. Second, a distinctive Chinese way of life in cultural terms came into being with the earliest available archaeological record of the Neolithic stage. Third, a distinctive ceramic horizon can probably be assumed to antedate the earliest available Neolithic evidence, continuing into the known Neolithic stage and into the historical period as a persistent and

53

predominant ceramic tradition. Thus it is evident that the so-called East-West relationship problem concerns itself mainly with the first spark of food-producing ideas which transformed the Mesolithic culture into the Neolithic. This point, for the time being, is purely academic.

What we have called the Nuclear Area of North China refers to the region around the confluences of the three great rivers in North China: the Huangho, the Fenho, and the Weishui. This area is also the approximate joining place of the three modern provinces of Honan, Shansi, and Shensi.[5] It is in fact a small basin encircled in the north, west, and south by the Shansi Plateau, the Shensi-Kansu Loessic Plateau, and the Tsinling Mountains, but open to the eastern plains. The possible role of this region in cradling the food-producing cultures of North China is based on a number of considerations. In the first place, as described in the previous chapter, during the "climatic optimum," the Nuclear Area was located on the border between the wooded western highlands and the swampy eastern lowlands, and thus provided both the "hilly flanks" and the habitat for the sedentary waterside fishermen that Robert J. Braidwood [6] and Carl Sauer,[7] respectively, believe to be the birthplace of farmers and herders. It had enough rain and enough warmth to be suited to agriculture and enough herds of game and fish shoals to sustain its inhabitants. It was also conveniently located at the intersection of natural avenues of communication. Secondly, it is in the Nuclear Area—in the Shayüan region of Chao-yih and Ta-li counties in eastern Shensi of the lower Weishui valley—that the only Huangho basin Mesolithic assemblage was found. Thirdly, the only stratigraphically suggested pre-Yangshao Neolithic evidence—which will be mentioned presently—was found in Pao-chi Hsien in the middle Weishui valley, peripheral to the Nuclear Area. In the fourth place, the importance of fishing, as shown during the subsequent Yangshao stage in this same region, is a highly suggestive fact. In the fifth place, archaeological evidence demonstrates that the Nuclear Area played a leading role in the transition from the Yangshao to

5. Chang Kwang-chih, *BIHP*, 30 (1959), 302.
6. Robert J. Braidwood, *The Near East and the Foundation for Civilization* (Eugene, Oregon State System of Higher Education, 1952), p. 11.
7. Carl O. Sauer, *Proc. Amer. Phil. Soc.*, 92 (1948), 65–77.

the Lungshan, the significance of which will be made clear with
the description of that crucial event in the next chapter. Finally,[8]
during most of the four thousand years of historic China, the
Nuclear Area has been one of the strategically vital regions that
to a considerable extent have controlled the destiny of the entire
Empire.

It is thus conceivable that a few millennia B.C. the terminal
food-gatherers in the Nuclear Area, possibly already settled down
with a well-developed culture, switched to food-production by
inventing or adopting plant cultivation and animal domestication.
From what we know of it, Chinese Neolithic culture assumed from
the very beginning a distinctive pattern that shows configurational
independence and originality. The following traits, singly or totally considered, have been enumerated as characteristic of Chinese
Neolithic culture tradition: [9]

(1) The cultivation of millet and rice (and possibly kaoliang and the soy bean);

(2) The domestication of pigs, cattle, sheep, dogs, chickens, and possibly horses;

(3) The construction of *hang-t'u* (stamped-earth) and
wattle-and-daub structures, and the use of a white limy
substance for house floor and wall plaster;

(4) The domestication of silkworms and the possible loom
weaving of silk and hemp;

(5) Probable use of tailored garments;

(6) Pottery with cord-mat-basket designs;

(7) Pottery tripods (especially *ting* and *li*), steamers
(*tseng* and *yen*), and the possible use of chopsticks,
perhaps indicating a distinctive cooking style;

(8) Semilunar and rectangular stone sickle-scrapers
(knives);

(9) The extensive development of ceremonial vessels;

(10) Elaborate complex of jade artifacts; possible wood-
carving complex;

(11) Scapulimancy.

8. Cf. Owen Lattimore, *Inner Asian Frontiers of China* (New York, American Geographical Society, 1951), pp. 27–33.

9. Chang Kwang-chih, *BIHP*, 30, 266.

In addition, the presumably distinctive Chinese language which was to be recorded during subsequent stages by the Chinese system of writing must have had a Neolithic basis. In village planning, the location of the kiln quarter in a separate area within the village also appears to be quite distinctive. Other stylistically distinctive socioeconomic and ceremonial features, such as the localization of corporate kinship groups, the pre-eminence of ancestor cult, and the mythology, which are known to be characteristic of the immediately following phases, could also be enumerated as probably having a Neolithic basis. The items listed above could be seen directly in the archaeological materials. All of them did not emerge from the very beginning, nor are all considered to have been invented in China. These, and others, are the cultural constituents of a cultural tradition distinguished from other comparable cultural centers in the rest of the world.

Above and beyond the available archaeological record, cord-marked pottery appears to be among the very first cultural elements that occurred during the initial emergence of the Neolithic stage in North China. Among all the kinds of ceramic wares of a prehistoric nature, cord-marked pottery had the widest distribution and the longest temporal duration in the area of China. Under the term "cord-marked pottery" are included a wide variety of colors, pastes, techniques of manufacture, forms, and surface treatments. The predominant colors are red, brown, and gray; the paste may be coarse or fine, but usually contains a great deal of temper; the ware is molded or hand-made (mostly coiled) and sometimes finished with paddle-and-anvil; the form of the ware ranges from the point-bottomed cooking ware and storage jars to tripods, ring-footed vessels, and flat-bottomed bowls; the surface of the ware was by definition impressed with cord marks, which were applied with cord-marked molds, cord-wrapped sticks, or paddles carved with cord designs, and the marks were either left intact or partially smeared smooth. All of these varieties can be regarded as the product of a single pottery tradition, since they had an uninterrupted geographical distribution and an uninterrupted temporal duration, were similarly made and probably served for similar purposes, and were associated with similar coexistents in the Chinese Neolithic context.

Whether or not this significant pottery tradition constituted a distinctive horizon at one time remains a problem to be explored.

There are four basic facts, however, that point to the possibility that this was the case. First, stratigraphic evidence at one site (in Pao-chi Hsien, Shensi) indicated the possible existence of cord-marked pottery alone in a pre-Yangshao horizon context.[10] Secondly, the age-area concept gives a great antiquity to this widely distributed pottery tradition.[11] Thirdly, in the subsequent horizons the cord-marked pottery tradition is still the predominant component insofar as the record goes [12] which implies, among other things, that the cord-marked pottery tradition was a kind of main course, so to speak, of Chinese ceramic history, while other traditions were but successively incorporated tributaries. And, finally, it has been stratigraphically established that in South China the cord-marked pottery tradition represents the oldest stylistic horizon in that area. I have proposed, therefore, to set up a more or less hypothetical horizon characterized by cord-marked and other kinds of textile-impressed pottery to antedate and initiate known Chinese Neolithic history, and have given it the name of Sheng-wen horizon, literally the horizon of the cord-marked designs.[13] Evidence has yet to come to light, however, for the subsistence and settlement patterns of this hypothetical ceramic horizon.

THE YANGSHAO FARMERS

The earliest well-established cultural stage of the Northern Chinese farmers has been named the Yangshao stage, after the site of Yang-shao-ts'un, in Mien-ch'ih Hsien, western Honan, where in 1921 the Swedish geologist J. G. Andersson excavated the first assemblage characterized by the painted pottery which has been regarded as one of the diagnostic features of this whole stage. Recently, students of early China have begun to realize that the Yangshao stage might much better be typified by other sites, and that the site at Yang-shao-ts'un was probably inhabited toward the very end of the Yangshao stage if not at the beginning of the next

10. Hsü Ping-chang, *Bull. Nat. Acad. of Peiping*, 7 (1930), 201–8.
11. Cf. Lauristan Ward, "The Relative Chronology of China Through the Han Period," in *Relative Chronologies in Old World Archaeology*, R. W. Ehrich, ed. (Chicago, Univ. of Chicago Press, 1954), p. 133.
12. E.g., Shih Hsing-pang, *KKTH*, 1955:3, 12; Li Chi, *Hsiao-t'un T'ao-ch'i* (Taipei, Academia Sinica, 1956), p. 117.
13. Chang Kwang-chih, *BIHP*, 30, 280. For a definition of "horizon," see p. 246, below.

—or Lungshan—stage. For the sake of convenience, the name Yangshao is retained in this book for this whole cultural stage which may or may not include the site at Yang-shao-ts'un.

The criteria for dating the Neolithic settlement sites to the Yangshao stage are both stratigraphical and typological. Stratigraphically, the Yangshao sites or phases of sites lie above the

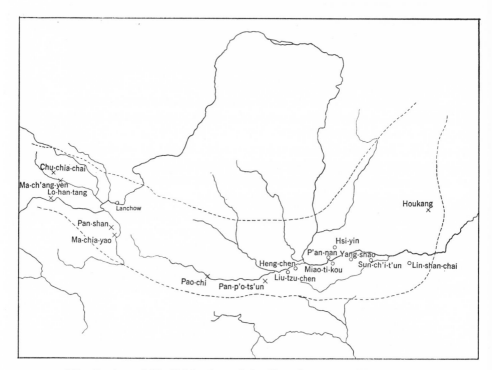

MAP 5. Distribution of Neolithic sites of the Yangshao stage. Named sites in Shansi, Honan, and eastern Shensi belong to the Proto-Lungshan Complex.

Palaeolithic and Mesolithic strata but beneath the remains of the Lungshan stage of the Neolithic and of various later historic periods, depending on the area where these several cultural phases were distributed. Typologically, the Yangshao stage sites exhibit definite sociocultural and stylistic characteristics, as will be described. The prehistoric sites attributable to this cultural stage are found widely in North China, but are largely confined to the Nuclear Area and its immediate neighborhood (Map 5). Earlier

58

phases of the Yangshao stage are seen in southern Shansi, western Honan, and central-eastern Shensi, mainly in the valleys of the Huangho, Fenho, and Weishui Rivers in that area. Later phases probably expanded into eastern Kansu, central Shansi, and northern Honan. Throughout the entire span of this stage, however, the Yangshao settlements are largely confined to the river valleys and small basins in the western highlands of North China. It appears likely that the earliest Chinese farmers, after their first emergence in the Nuclear Area, developed only gradually and slowly in the vicinity of the natural habitat of the plants and animals they had come to domesticate and slowly came to establish the so-called "primary village-efficiency" in this region. It was not until the following Lungshan stage that these early farmers began to expand, somewhat explosively, outside this area into the humid low country to the east and south.

The Yangshao stage farmers cultivated a variety of crops which, as archaeologists have determined from their remains, consisted of such cereals as foxtail millet (*Setaria italica* Beauv. var. *germanica* Trin.) from Pan-p'o-ts'un,[14] Liu-tzu-chen,[15] and Tou-chi-t'ai [16] in central Shensi and Ching-ts'un in southern Shansi; [17] Broom corn millet (*Panicum miliaceum* L.) from Ching-ts'un; grand millet, or kaoliang (*Andropogon sorghum* Brot.) also from Ching-ts'un; [18] rice (*Oryza sativa* L.) from Yang-shao-ts'un [19] and Liu-tzu-chen; [20] and, possibly, wheat from Wang-chia-wan, Pao-tê Hsien, Shansi.[21] It is possible that the sites at Yang-shao-ts'un and Liu-tzu-chen could be placed toward the end of the Yangshao stage, in which case the cultivation of rice in North China may not be as early as the above enumeration would seem to imply. I personally believe that the natural habitat of wild and cultivable rice was in South China rather than North China, and that rice was one of the plants newly cultivated by the Lungshanoid immigrants in South China. This problem will be further discussed in Chapter 4. By

14. Shih Hsing-pang, KKTH, 1955:3, 15–16.
15. KK, 1959:2, 73.
16. Amano Motonosuke, *Shigaku Kenkyu*, 62 (1956), 15–16.
17. An Chih-min, *Yenching Social Sciences*, 2 (1949), 39.
18. Bishop, *Antiquity*, 28 (1933). For *kaoliang*, compare Ho Ping-ti, *Pacific Affairs*, 34 (1961), 291–97.
19. Andersson, BMFEA, 19, 21–22.
20. KK, 1959:2, 73.
21. An Chih-min, *Yenching Social Sciences*, 2, 40.

and large, millet of one kind or another was without question the main staple of these early farmers in the Nuclear Area. Remains of cultivating implements include hoes, spades, and possibly digging sticks. Perforated stone discs, possibly the weights of digging sticks, have been found in considerable quantity. Other relevant implements are polished stone celts, often oval in cross-section and presumably effective tools for field clearance, and polished or chipped rectangular and semilunar stone sickle-scrapers which were probably fastened to the hand with string or leather ropes through a hole or around two side notches for cutting, scraping, weeding, and harvesting. Some of the pottery jars found widely in the Yangshao context were presumably used for storing grains, the remains and impressions of which are sometimes found therein. Some of the harvest must have been prepared and preserved in the form of flour, for grinding stones have also been discovered.

The most important domesticated animals in this stage were dogs and pigs, whose bones have been unearthed from countless sites. Much less common were cattle (Ching-ts'un, Kao-tui [Southern Shansi], and Kwang-wu [Northern Honan]), and sheep/goats (Ching-ts'un and Lo-han-t'ang).[22] Hemp was probably cultivated,[23] and silkworms (*Bombyx mori*) were raised. A half-cut cocoon of the latter was found at Hsi-yin-ts'un in Southern Shansi.[24] Stone and pottery spindle whorls and eyed needles of bone, which have been discovered extensively, were probably used with hemp, silk, and other fabrics.

Wild grain collecting, hunting, and fishing supplemented the diet. Remains of a kind of foxtail weed (*Setaria lutescens*) were found at Ching-ts'un.[25] Bones of a variety of wild animals were recovered from the middens of the Yangshao settlements: horse, leopard, water deer, wild cattle, deer, rhinoceros, bamboo rat, antelope, hare, and marmot. The hunters must have used bow and arrow and spear, for remains of stone and bone points and arrowheads are numerous. Some round-headed arrowheads were probably employed for shooting birds. Stone balls have been found occasionally, perhaps sling stones for the hunt. The importance of

22. Andersson, BMFEA, 15, 43; Margit Bylin-Althin, BMFEA, 18 (1946), 458; Tung Chu-chen, KKHP, 1957:2, 9.
23. Andersson, GSuC, Bull., 5 (1923), 26: KK, 1959:2, 73.
24. Li Chi, *Hsi-yin-ts'un shih-ch'ien ti yih-ts'un* (Peiping, Tsing-hua Research Institute, 1927), pp. 22–23.
25. Bishop, Antiquity, 28, 395.

fishing is indicated by the abundance of bone fish spears, harpoons, and fish hooks, as well as grooved pottery and stone net-
sinkers, fish designs on pottery, and the bones of fish. The decorative fish motif on pottery is particularly abundant in the Weishui
valley sites [26] (Pl. I).

These early cultivators lived in villages. There are several indications that their village settlements shifted from one locale to another after a short period of occupancy, that some favorable locales
were repeatedly occupied, and that the shifting and repetitive
settlement pattern probably resulted from the slash-and-burn technique of cultivations. First of all, careful and intensive excavations
of the village sites have disclosed that these villages were of moderate size and short duration. Pan-p'o-ts'un, near Sian, in eastern
Shensi, for instance, one of the few Yangshao stage sites that have
been excavated completely, is only one hundred by two hundred
meters in dimension. Other village measurements, those of Lo-
han-t'ang, Hou-kang, Chu-chia-chai, Ma-chia-yao, and the Lo-ning
Hsien sites, for example, do not as a rule exceed two hundred
thousand square meters. Secondly, the deposits of the villages,
often very thick, usually consist of multioccupational remains,
which seems to indicate that these localities were occupied dis-
continuously but repetitively. In the third place, we find that in
the same general neighborhood, the Yangshao stage sites were
widely distributed over a vast area, and each component consists
of remains that show no marked changes in typology through
time. In 1952 and 1953 twenty-one Yangshao sites were located
in the vicinity of Sian, Shensi. As regards these sites, the surveyors
made the following remarks:

> The Yangshao sites are many and widely distributed. Re-
> mains at a single locality are chronologically simple and
> neighboring localities can easily be given a relative dating
> on their respective cultural inventories.[27]

At Miao-ti-kou, Shan Hsien, Honan, similar phenomena have also
been recorded.[28] And finally, the general cultural configuration
gives similar indications which, taken together, convincingly point

---

26. See, e.g., Chao Hsüeh-chien, *KK*, 1959:11, 589.
27. Su Ping-chi and Wu Ju-tso, *KKTH*, 1956:2, 37; cf. also Chao Hsüeh-
chien, *KK*, 1959:11, 588–89.
28. *KKTH*, 1958:11, 68.

61

to the conclusion that the pattern of settlements was characterized by shifting and repetitive occupations. This conclusion is not in agreement with the former general impression of most scholars, who considered the "Yangshao" villages as having been large, sedentary communities.[29] We are now able to suggest that this impression is erroneous, and that there are at least two sources of error. In the first place, most of the large Yangshao stage sites were measured in a preliminary manner during a survey or survey excavations. Thus it seems likely that the large volume of Yang-shao remains represent discontinuous occupations which the surveyors or the excavators failed to recognize. Furthermore, granted that the measured village site represents one component, that is, a single occupation village, these sites were probably of the very latest Yangshao stage, which had already begun to show changes toward the next stage, e.g., the Yang-shao-ts'un site itself.

The physical layout of the Yangshao villages is known only where the sites were extensively excavated and the results given in published accounts. The Pan-p'o-ts'un settlement, for instance, is one of these. It is situated on a river terrace about 800 meters to the east of the River Ch'an, a tributary of the Weishui, and about 9 meters above the riverbed. Two hundred meters long (N-S) by 100 meters wide (W-E), the site has 3 meters of cultural debris, which may have been left during no less than four successive occupations. Houses of fairly permanent nature were constructed, however. The most common kind of house was about 3–5 meters in diameter, and was square, rectangular, or round, with plastered floors, semisubterranean or ground level, wattle-and-daub wall foundations, and upper walls and roofs supported by large and small wooden posts. Some forty of these houses have been discovered. During a later occupation, a huge (over 20 meters long and 12.5 meters wide) rectangular ground house was constructed, separated inside into a number of compartments by partition walls. It appears that during this stage the communal house was located at the center of the village plaza, whereas the small houses were constructed to encircle the plaza, with their doors facing the center. Each individual house and each compartment of the long house was equipped with a hearth (a burned surface in the earlier occupations and a gourd-shaped pit in the later occupations). These houses were grouped in the western part of the site to form the

29. E.g., Cheng Te-kun, *Prehistoric China*, pp. 69–72.

dwelling area. Some of these houses were separated from one another by narrow ditches. East of the dwelling area was probably the pottery-making center, which had no less than six pottery kilns, in one of which were found some unfired pots. North of the dwelling area was the village cemetery, in which were over a hundred and thirty adult burials, mostly found singly—with two exceptions, one double, the other quadruple—lying face upwards and stretched. Infants and children were buried in urns between the dwelling houses. A long, wide ditch had been dug along the

FIG. 2. Reconstructed house of the Yangshao farmers at the Miao-ti-kou site, western Honan. From An Chih-min, Cheng Nai-wu, and Hsieh Tuan-chü, *Miao-ti-kou yü San-li-ch'iao* (Peiping, Science Press, 1959), Fig. 5.

northeastern edge of the dwelling area, possibly to separate it from the cemetery and the pottery-making center and to serve as the foundation for an impermanent village wall.[30]

This Pan-p'o-ts'un pattern in subdividing a village into a dwelling area, a kiln center, and a cemetery recurs throughout the Yangshao stage settlements that have been extensively excavated, such as those near Pao-chi [31] and Hua Hsien [32] in Shensi, and

30. Shih Hsing-pang, *KKTH*, 1955:3, 7–16; *KKTH*, 1956:2, 23–30; Hsia Nai, *Archaeology*, 10 (1957), 181–87; Shih Hsing-pang, *Revue archéologique*, 2 (1959), 1–14.
31. *KK*, 1959:2, 229–30, 241.
32. *KK*, 1959:2, 71–75; *KK*, 1959:11, 585–87, 591.

Lin-shan-chai [33] and Miao-ti-kou [34] in Honan. More detailed information on small houses is known from the Miao-ti-kou site (Fig. 2); another huge communal building was found at Liu-tzu-chen; and the cemetery at Pao-chi has yielded more extensive and richer findings. But the general pattern repeats itself throughout, with such exceptions as that at Liu-tzu-chen where the Yangshao village did not in itself incorporate a cemetery, but seems to have shared a large cemetery some distance away with neighboring residential villages. This is a very notable exception nevertheless, considering that the Liu-tzu-chen site belongs chronologically to a late phase of the Yangshao stage, for this may indicate a tendency on the part of the farming villages near the end of this stage toward growth and fission. This tendency is made clear by J. G. Andersson's discovery in 1923–24, of a cemetery area on the Pan-shan Hills, in the T'ao River valley in eastern Kansu. The prehistoric cultures in eastern Kansu of the Yangshao stage, as will be described presently, are generally of a later phase than the Yangshao sites in the Nuclear Area. The location of the Pan-shan sites is best described in Andersson's own words:

> On both sides of the broad flat river-plain [of the River T'ao] the hill-sides rise in terraces up to 400 m. above the river-valley, where we stand upon a dissected peneplane, which, at a level of 2200 m. above the sea, extends far to both sides of the T'ao valley. The Pan Shan hills occupy a small area of this elevated plateau.[35]

Five burial areas have been located in the Pan-shan Hills: Pan-shan, Wa-kuan-tsui, Pien-chia-kou, Wang-chia-kou, and another unnamed site. Each is within a short distance (ca. 1000-1800 meters) of the others.

> Each of the five grave sites is situated on one of the highest hills in the district, surrounded by steep and deep ravines, 400 meters above the floor of the neighboring T'ao valley . . . These cemeteries must have belonged to the habitations of the same period down on the valley terraces. It

33. An Chin-huai, *WWTKTL*, 1957:8, 16–20; Chao Ching-yün, *KKTH*, 1958:9, 54–57; Mao Pao-liang, *KKTH*, 1958:2, 1–5.
34. An Chih-min, Cheng Nai-wu, and Hsieh Tuan-chü, *Miao-ti-kou yü San-li-ch'iao*, Peiping, Science Press, 1959.
35. Andersson, *BMFEA*, 15, 116.

then became clear that the settlers in the T'ao valley of that age carried their dead 10 km. or more from the villages up steep paths to hill-tops situated fully 400 meters above the dwellings of the living to resting places from which they could behold in a wide circle the place where they had grown up, worked, grown grey and at last found a grave swept by the winds and bathed in sunshine.[36]

The custom of sharing common cemeteries during the later phases of the Yangshao stage carries important social implications. It shows that toward the end of this stage the population pressure had caused the fission of residential villages, which probability has important bearings upon the further development of the North China Neolithic culture into the next Lungshan stage. They also show that a strong lineage consciousness must have been behind the custom of sending the dead to rest in the common ancestral grounds. This latter inference is substantiated by the community patterns of the Yangshao stage farmers. The long houses at Pan-p'o-ts'un and Liu-tzu-chen, and the planned layout of the Pan-p'o-ts'un and the Lin-shan-chai villages, as well as the clustered pit houses at Sun-ch'i-t'un, near Lo-yang in Honan,[37] suggest planned and segmented village layouts, and on these grounds and others, lineage and clan types of kinship groupings could be postulated. The graveyards were presumably burial places of kin groups as well as of village residents.

The dead were inhumed in extended or flexed posture, singly or in groups, in amorphous pits in the village cemetery. A belief in the afterlife is indicated by the utensils and stored foods buried with the dead. In the Kansu area, pottery painted with red, the color of blood, and decorated with so-called "death patterns," was found, particularly in funerary association.[38] Considering the probable lineage alignment of the village cemetery and the regularity of arrangement of individual burials within the cemetery in many cases, it is highly probable that the cult of ancestors to symbolize lineage solidarity may already have been initiated during the Yangshao stage, although it was not until the Lungshan stage that the evidence of this cult became remarkable in the archaeological record. On the other hand, the Yangshao stage farmers may have

36. Ibid., p. 112.
37. WWTKTL, 1955:9, 58–64.
38. Andersson, *Children of the Yellow Earth*, p. 315.

performed in their villages some kind of fertility rite for the sake of crop harvests and fishing and hunting gains. This is implied by their burials of deer,[39] the frequent occurrence of female symbols among their ceramic decorative designs, and a painted bowl discovered at Pan-p'o-ts'un on the inner surface of which was depicted a tattooed face, possibly that of a priest, wearing a fish-shaped headdress (Pl. I, upper). Some of the beautifully painted bowls and miniature vessels also may have been used in this connection. Andersson, on the basis of some incised parallel lines on bone artifacts from Lo-han-t'ang,[40] has also postulated a sort of "cryptic magic."

Turning to the Yangshao farmers' technological achievements, we have considerable data on their ceramics, and on their stone, bone, and antler industries. Stone implements were polished, pecked and chipped. The most frequently found types are axes and adzes, with cylindrical bodies or an oval or lentoid cross-section,[41] used for cutting down trees and for carpentry; hoes and spades, with flat bodies and often with a hafting portion, for cultivation; chisels, for carpentry and possibly woodcarving; rectangular knives, with central holes or two side notches, for weeding, harvesting, skinning, and scraping; and arrowheads. Other stone-made artifacts are net sinkers, mealing, grinding, and polishing stones, spindle whorls, etc. Ornaments such as rings and beads were made often of semiprecious stones, including jade.

Bone and antler constitute another class of materials used for implements: needles, awls, fish hooks, arrowheads, spearheads, chisels, hoes, points, polishers, beads, etc.

Their pottery was handmade and molded, and indications of coiling techniques were observed at Liang-ts'un, in Ch'i Hsien, Shansi, at Pai-tao-kou-p'ing, near Lanchow in Kansu, at Yang-shao-ts'un in Honan, and at several localities near Sian, Shensi.[42] A turning table may have been used for the finishing of the rim in Shansi-Shensi regions.[43] Pottery-making implements recovered in-

39. Andersson, *BMFEA*, 15, 130.
40. Ibid., pp. 252–55.
41. Tung Chu-chen, *KKHP*, 1957:2, 19; Andersson, *BMFEA*, 15, 48; Chang Kwang-chih, *Chung-kuo tung-hai-an shih-ch'ien wen-hua chih fen-pu yü i-tung*, Taipei, 1954; An Chih-min, *KKHP*, 10 (1955).
42. Yang Fu-tou and Chao Chi, *KKTH*, 1956:2, 42; Ho Lo-fu, *KKHP*, 15 (1957), 5; Andersson, *BMFEA*, 19, 54; Su Ping-chi and Wu Ju-tso, *KKTH*, 1956:2, 35; Shih Hsing-pang, *KKTH*, 1955:3, 12.
43. An Chih-min, *KKTH*, 1956:5, 5.

FIG. 3. Some painted designs on pottery of the Yangshao stage site at Miao-ti-kou, western Honan. From An Chih-min, et al., *Miao-ti-kou*, Fig. 15.

clude bone scrapers, stone polishers, paint-grinding stones, and paint containers. Kilns were discovered at many settlements. Several classes of pottery were made for various purposes. For cooking there were red or gray-brown thick-walled pointed-bottomed jars, containing a noticeable amount of sand or mica tempers and decorated with thick and thin cord-mat-basket impressions; for storage, coarse or fine red and gray pottery in the form of thin-necked, big-bellied jars were manufactured; red and gray cups and canteens of a variety of pastes were made for drinking; and beautifully polished red and black bowls and basins, sometimes painted with black or red designs (Fig. 3), were made of fine paste to serve at meals or for rituals. In addition to these receptacles, spindle whorls, knives, sling balls, and net sinkers were also made of baked clay.

CHRONOLOGICAL AND REGIONAL SUBDIVISIONS

The above generalizations about the eco-social life of the Yang-shao farmers, despite brevity and necessary incompleteness, are sufficient to show that each of such villages was a self-sufficient "little community." [44] Such small communities during the earlier stages of the Neolithic dotted the North China landscape in the river valleys and on river terraces. Several factors in their lives, however, have led archaeologists to tie them together for the sake of synchronization, chronological alignment, and a regional subdivision of cultural phases. In the first place, close social ties apparently existed among neighboring communities as the result of lineage and village fission, as mentioned above. In the second place, trade connections with places near and far are indicated by the remains of seashells and stone materials of foreign origin (such as jade). And, lastly but not the least, the ceramic decorative art of the Yangshao farmers throughout North China constitutes a well-established horizon-style of considerable overall uniformity. This style consists of plastic art and painting. The former is represented by only a handful of human figurines discovered at scattered and isolated places (Pl. II, upper), but ceramic painting is universal and can be given an analytic treatment because of its infinite variety. All the painted pottery of this period in North China has

44. Robert Redfield, *The Little Community*, Chicago, Univ. of Chicago Press, 1955.

a brick-red or yellowish brown base, which is then burnished or polished and painted with red or black pigment. Regional variations are to be expected. In some regions, white slips were applied before painting (western and northern Honan and, occasionally, central Shensi), and in other areas (Kansu and Chinghai, southern Shansi and western Hopei) pigment was directly applied on the red or brown surface; black was used as paint in all areas, but red is more restricted; and painted decor was applied on the inner surface of the pottery only in some of the areas (Kansu, Chinghai, and central Shensi).[45] However, a major contrast is seen between the painted pottery of Kansu (including Chinghai for the sake of convenience) and that of Chungyüan (the Central Plains, including western Honan and vicinity):

> In a very striking way the painted motifs of the Kansu group are different from those of the other groups. The colours are red and black, but the red is seldom so fresh and bright as it is in western Honan. Except at Hsin-Tien, the painting seems to have been done with the intention of covering the surface as much as possible, and not leaving any blank space, contrary to what is found in the Shansi and Honan groups . . . The painted decoration, unlike that of the other groups, is intended to be viewed from the top, instead of from the side. The motifs are very complicated, though there are a number of stock designs, which frequently occur.[46]

Admitting the differences in decorative motif and form between the painted pottery of Kansu (represented by Ma-chia-yao) and Honan (represented by Yang-shao-ts'un), Andersson nevertheless considers these two phases as "strictly contemporary" regional variations.[47] In other words, according to Andersson and his followers, the Yangshao horizon of the North China Neolithic contains no less than two parallel regional pottery traditions. Recent investigations in the intermediate areas (especially southeastern Kansu), however, tend to disprove this view. It can now be sug-

45. Wu Chin-ting, *Prehistoric Pottery in China* (London, Kegan Paul, Trench, and Trubner, 1938), pp. 145–47; An Chih-min, *WWTKTL*, 1956:8, 41–49; An Chih-min, *KKTH*, 1956:5, 1–11; Shih Hsing-pang, *KKTH*, 1955:1, 28–30; Tung Chu-chen, *KKHP*, 1957:2.
46. Wu Chin-ting, *Prehistoric Pottery in China*, p. 146.
47. Andersson, *BMFEA*, 15, 104.

69

gested that within the Yangshao horizon, there are at least two separate subhorizons, the Chungyüan subhorizon and the Kansu subhorizon, with the former earlier in time than the latter. G. D. Wu, in fact, has already initiated this thesis on the basis that the decorative designs of the Kansu group are more complicated and mature than the Honan group.[48]

The Chungyüan Subhorizon, insofar as ceramic painting is concerned, is characterized by a wide band of black patterns on the upper part of the vessel body, consisting of relatively simple but vividly varying motifs. The lines composing the motifs are few in number, curve and widen or narrow smoothly, with large blank spaces in the background. Discs, rectangles, net patterns, spirals, and whirls and spirals are some of the common motifs (Fig. 4). The rims of bowls and beakers are sometimes painted, but the designs tend to be simple, and consist of a few wide solid lines. The inner surface of the vessels is only occasionally painted.

The Kansu Subhorizon is also characterized by bands painted on the upper part of the exterior surface of the body, but the rim is often painted with complicated designs of thin lines, and interior decorations are common. The band on the exterior surface, in contrast to the Chungyüan custom, consists of recurrent motifs (such as the teeth pattern, the drapery or garland pattern, parallel wavy thin lines, thin and complicated spirals, and diamonds) of thin black and red lines which fill much of the space, leaving little blank background exposed. The lines and the exposed background usually form the constituent elements of the design (see Fig. 4). This Kansu subhorizon can be subdivided into two major stages, Pan-shan, characterized by bands of gourd-shaped designs, and Ma-ch'ang, characterized by medallions and bands of human or frog figures, in the same chronological order. Stratigraphical, geographical, and typological evidence have established the following stylistic sequence in the Kansu area:

3. Kansu subhorizon: Ma-ch'ang stage (the latest)
2. Kansu subhorizon: Pan-shan stage
1. Chungyüan subhorizon (the earliest)

To explain this sequence, the following profile cutting across the entire region will prove helpful (Map 6): Kui-tê Basin (Lo-han-t'ang)—the Middle Huangshui (Chu-chia-chai and Ma-ch'ang-

48. Wu Chin-ting, *Prehistoric Pottery in China*, pp. 168–69.

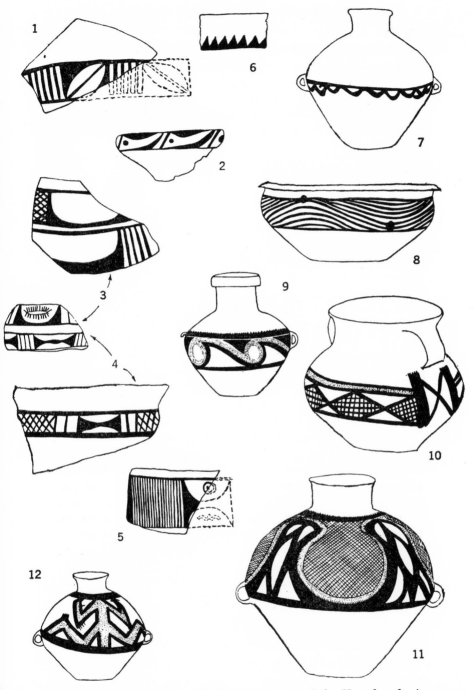

FIG. 4. Some distinctive decorative designs on pottery of the Yangshao horizon. 1–5. Markers of the Chungyüan subhorizon [1, Ch'in-wang-chai; 2, Liu-tzu-chen; 3 (*above*), Niu-k'ou-yü; 3 (*below*) and 4 (*above*), Ch'in-wang-chai; 5, Hou-chia-chuang] 6–12. Markers of the Kansu subhorizon [6, Pan-shan-ch'ü; 7, Pan-shan-ch'ü; 8, Ma-chia-yao; 9, Yü-chung Hsien; 10, Kansu; 11, Lanchow; 12, Lanchow]. From Chang Kwang-chih, *Prehistoric Settlements in China*, Cambridge, Harvard University, unpublished Ph.D. thesis, 1960, Pl. VI.

yen)—Lanchow—the T'ao valley (Pan-shan-ch'ü and Ma-chia-yao) —the Upper Wei. Going into the Kansu area from Chungyüan along the River Wei, we see a continuation of the Chungyüan subhorizon along the way into the T'ao valley, especially at the sites in T'ien-shui Hsien, Kan-ku Hsien, Wu-shan Hsien, and Lung-hsi Hsien. However, starting from T'ien-shui Hsien in the Upper

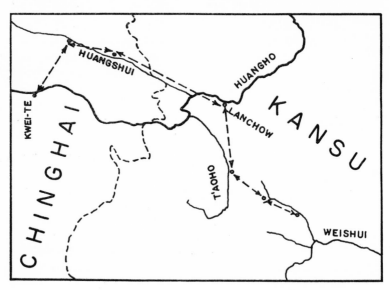

MAP 6. The Kansu Profile.

Wei, remains of painted pottery of the Kansu subhorizon begin to occur and become increasingly dominant going into the T'ao valley and further northwest. In the Upper Wei and the T'ao valleys the two subhorizons overlap.[49] A key stratified site was found in 1957 at Ma-chia-yao in Lin-t'ao Hsien, where sherds of the Kansu subhorizon were found overlying sherds of the Chungyüan subhorizon:

> On the First Terrace (10–30 meters) at the northern bank of the Ma-yü ravine, south of Ma-chia-yao, the cultural deposits are fairly deep. A clear section is seen on an exposed surface. The uppermost layer is a stratum of disturbed

49. Kuo Tê-yüng, KKTH, 1958:9, 72–73; Chang Hsüeh-cheng, KKTH, 1958:9, 41; An Chih-min, KKTH, 1956:6, 13.

modern humus. Beneath the humus, about one meter in thickness, is a layer of prehistoric cultural deposits, about 3.5 meters thick. The upper meter and a half of this layer is composed of loose ashes, from which were derived a great number of potsherds. These are of fine or coarse paste, tempered or not tempered, some with painted designs. The paint was applied in black pigment. The designs are in most cases composed of thick lines, and include many parallel lines and black dots. Sherds painted on the inner surface, and rim sherds with complicated painted patterns are also found. The forms of the painted sherds include bowls, jars, basins, and pots. The unpainted, fine-pasted red or gray sherds are mostly parts of bowls. The sand-tempered sherds are mostly cord-marked, and are in the forms of pots and basins with out-curving, flaring mouths. These types are similar to the Ma-chia-yao types excavated from Yen-erh-wan, near Lanchow. The ashy layers below this stratum consist of compact earth, about two meters thick. Cultural remains from this lower layer include polished stone chisels, bone artifacts, gray rings of baked clay, and potsherds. Some of the sherds are painted in black pigment in the designs of wavy triangles, hooked dots, thin parallel lines, thick bands, and net patterns. There are also some rim sherds with simple painted patterns, sherds of basins with inwardly curved mouths, plain fine-pasted red and gray sherds, and a great number of cord-marked pointed-bottomed jars and thick-rimmed basins and pots. In short, this lower cultural stratum is similar to the Yangshao types of the Upper Wei.[50]

According to such distributional and stratigraphic evidence, it appears clear that the Yangshao horizon of the Chungyüan sub-division expanded westward as far as the T'ao River valley, where it developed into the Kansu subdivision. The Pan-shan-ch'ü, Ma-chia-yao, and Lanchow sites of the Yangshao horizon, in the lower T'ao River valley and the Huangho valley, have yielded decorative assemblages of both the Pan-shan and the Ma-ch'ang stages. If we consider that the Pan-shan stage and the Chungyüan sub-horizon are chronologically consecutive, as shown by the Ma-chia-

50. Chang Hsüeh-cheng, *KKTH*, 1958:9, 38–39.

yao stratigraphy, then we must conclude that the Huangshui valley and Kui-tê sites (Ma-ch'ang-yen, Chu-chia-chai, and Lo-han-t'ang) are chronologically later than the Pan-shan. For two reasons, Andersson places Lo-han-t'ang as antedating Chu-chia-chai, which in turn antedates Ma-ch'ang-yen: (a) stylistic counterparts for the pottery at Ch'i-chia-p'ing, which he considers earlier than all

TABLE 2.

Subdivision of the Kansu Yangshao Horizon

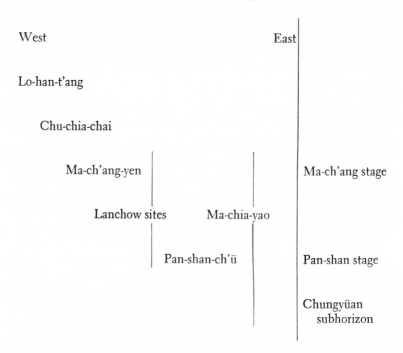

three, cannot be found at Ma-ch'ang-yen; and (b) the decorative art at Ma-ch'ang-yen has achieved greater maturity and is more conventionalized than that at the other two sites.[51] The first reason can now no longer stand, for the chronological position of Ch'i-chia-p'ing has now been established as postdating the entire Kansu Yangshao horizon, as will be described in Chapter 5. The

51. Andersson, "Preliminary Report on Archaeological Research in Kansu," *GSuC, Mem.*, ser. A, 5 (1925), 21.

second reason—the relative artistic maturity—can never stand alone without solid historical support. Thus, the abovementioned profile results in the subdivision of the Kansu subhorizon as shown in Table 2.

The implications for the cultural history of North China of the above stylistic studies of Yangshao stage ceramics are manifold, but two in particular are worth mentioning at this juncture. First, it is clear that the primary village farmers of the Chinese Neolithic are grouped together by a uniform cultural style. Second, regional variations that are discernible are primarily of chronological significance and indicate the nuclearity of the Nuclear Area and the marginality of Kansu. Whether or not stimulus diffusion from the Near East can be held responsible for the emergence of food-production in the North China Nuclear Area, the available archaeological evidence from the area of Kansu and regions west of Kansu (the latter to be discussed later on in the book) does not substantiate any such cultural contact, despite the fact that Kansu is situated intermediately between the Nuclear Area and the West. A recent publication by my friend Walter Fairservis, Jr. on the early cultural history of China, contains the following statements:

> Kansu presents one of the most provocative of all archaeological problems. Here should be found the tangible links between East and West during prehistoric times that are hardly suggested by the present evidence . . . It may well be that places such as the Hsi-ning or T'ao River valley were the easternmost seats of Western civilization that evolved into the form which later moved to the Yellow River basin and there, in combination with what had gone on before, produced the beginning of historical China. We have little evidence for this idea as yet. Future excavation in these places is the course Chinese scientists must set for themselves if they are to know more about their civilization's origins.[52]

When J. G. Andersson and Carl Bishop made similar statements some decades ago, when Chinese Neolithic archaeology was still in its early infancy, Kansu was indeed a *terra incognita* where scholars with preconceived "ideas" could indulge in farfetched speculations. However, excavations "in these places" conducted by

52. Fairservis, *The Origins of Oriental Civilization*, pp. 113–14.

75

scientists after Andersson's time have turned up plenty of cultural materials marginal to the Huangho basin, but none at all marginal to the so-called "Western civilization" to serve as the "tangible links between East and West during prehistoric times" that "should be found." Perhaps it would be more fruitful for anyone interested in the early history of Chinese civilization to set aside his ideas for the time being and take a hard look at the available facts.

Another equally pertinent problem regarding the time depth of the Yangshao stage concerns the chronological subdivision of the Chungyüan horizon. The cultural growth of the Yangshao farmers in the Nuclear Area was relatively slow, but the distinct changes through time in this area have not been clearly defined. Two major regional types, however, are distinguishable. One is typified by the Pan-p'o-ts'un site near Sian in central Shensi, characterized by a smaller amount of painted pottery among the ceramic wares, by the relative simplicity and realism of the painted designs, and by the abundance of round-bottomed bowls. The other is typified by the Miao-ti-kou site in Shan Hsien, western Honan, characterized by a larger amount of painted pottery, a complexity and variety of painted decors, and high, curved-walled bowls and beakers instead of round-bottomed bowls.[53]

> The reliable stratigraphical evidence at the Pan-p'o site proves that the Pan-p'o type of site was earlier in time. One can, therefore, state that the Weishui valley was probably where the Yangshao culture early developed, which then gradually expanded toward other regions.[54]

Again it is in the Nuclear Area that the major transition toward the following Lungshan stage probably took place.

53. An Chih-min, KK, 1959:10, 561. See also the discussions in KK, 1961:1, 29–30.
54. Shih Hsing-pang, KK, 1959:10, 567. This conclusion has been given added support by recent stratigraphical findings at the Yangshao site near Hsia-meng-ts'un, in Pin Hsien, Shensi; see KK, 1962:6, 292–95.

Chapter Four
The
Lungshanoid
Expansion

THE YANGSHAO-LUNGSHAN RELATIONSHIP AND THE PROTO-LUNGSHAN COMPLEX

During the Yangshao stage of the Neolithic in North China, the cultural distribution in the rest of China can be summarized as follows: Mesolithic hunter-fishers inhabited the forests and the steppe of the northern frontiers in Sinkiang, Mongolia, and Manchuria; the alluvial plains of the Lower Huangho and the Huaiho and the Shantung Uplands were but sparsely populated, if at all, for no early Recent remains have been discovered; the whole area of the eastern part of South China, including the Lower Yangtze, the hill region to the south, and the southeastern coast, also lacks substantial evidence of human occupation; and hunter-collectors of the Hoabinhian cultural tradition still occupied the Southwest. To be sure, these Mesolithic hunting-fishing cultures must have had cultural contacts with the Yangshao farmers, as shown by the diffusion of some neolithic techniques among these peoples—a topic to be described in the next chapter. The wide spread of food-production, however, did not take place until the Lungshan stage evolved in the Nuclear Area, and a whole sheet of Lungshanoid cultures began to appear in the hitherto underexplored areas of the Pacific seaboard.

Remains of the new stage of culture were first found in 1928 by G. D. Wu at the site of Ch'eng-tzu-yai in the heart of Shantung near Lung-shan-chen, from which the name Lungshan Culture was derived.[1] Excavations at this site conducted by the Academia Sinica revealed an assemblage of cultural remains showing wide differ-

1. Wu Chin-ting, *BIHP*, 1 (1930), 471–86.

ences from and sharp contrasts to the Neolithic cultures to the west, known at that time as the Yangshao Culture. Instead of painted pottery and oval stone axes, this new culture is characterized by thin, lustrous, black pottery, and rectangular axes and adzes, in addition to such new cultural features as scapulimancy, the *kui* type of pottery tripods, and *hang-t'u* village wall constructions. Archaeologists then began to come to the conclusion that the Yangshao and the Lungshan were two Neolithic cultures in North China, and that the former, probably derived from Western Asia, occupied the western part of North China, whereas the latter, an indigenous Chinese culture, was confined to the eastern lowlands. In 1931, Liang Ssu-yung of the Academia Sinica excavated the site at Hou-kang near An-yang, in northern Honan, and established the first stratigraphical sequence of early Chinese cultures in the Huangho valley. At this site, Yangshao cultural remains were found at the bottom, Lungshan cultural remains were in the middle, and the historic Yin-Shang remains on the top.[2] Nevertheless, this sequence was considered only locally applicable, and the two prehistoric cultures were regarded as largely concurrent. This is explained by no less than three factors in the Neolithic archaeology of North China: (a) The geographical distribution of these two cultures had been found, prior to the Second World War, to be mutually supplementary rather than to coincide, for Yangshao culture remains failed to appear in Shantung, and Lungshan culture remains had not been identified west of Honan. (b) The northern Honan stratigraphy did not repeat itself in the western part of Honan where remains of both cultures were reportedly found mixed together, thus implying contemporaneity. (c) Scholars of ancient history in the thirties favored an interpretation of the late Fu Ssu-nien, Director of the Institute of History and Philology, Academia Sinica, for the distribution of ancient ethnic groups in North China, in which he distinguished an Eastern Yih domain in the East and a Western Hsia territory in the West.[3] Thus, the subdivision of the Yangshao culture and the Lungshan culture somewhat substantiated the ethnic distribution

2. Liang Ssu-yung, "Hou-kang fa-chüeh hsiao-chi," *An-yang Fa-chüeh Pao-kao*, 4 (1933), 609–25.
3. Fu Ssu-nien, "Yih Hsia tung hsi shuo," *Ch'ing-chu Ts'ai Yüan-p'ei Hsien-sheng liu-shih-wu-sui lun-wen chi*, Pt. 2, Peiping, Inst. Hist. Phil., Academia Sinica, 1933.

as worked out by Fu on the basis of literary records. It is because of these and other factors (such as the paucity of pertinent data in many key regions and the theoretical slant of the investigators) that the Two Culture Theory dominated North China Neolithic archaeology during the thirties and forties. This theory has survived to appear in a number of recent publications.[4]

Archaeological investigations during the last decade in North China have rendered obsolete such an interpretation, however, due to a combination of factors. First and foremost are the recent discoveries of remains of the Lungshan type in the western part of North China where the Hou-kang stratigraphy is repeated. Such findings have made the mutually exclusive distribution thesis no longer tenable, and have compelled archaeologists to re-examine the differences between the so-called two cultures—differences that have turned out to be more developmental than cultural. Archaeologists then began to suspect that the Lungshan type of remains might represent a later stage of Neolithic culture evolved on the basis of the Yangshao stage. Such new hypotheses have been confirmed by the discovery in the Nuclear Area during the past three or four years of a proto-Lungshan cultural complex which may be regarded as transitional.

The proto-Lungshan complex was first recognized in 1956-57 during salvage excavations conducted by the Yellow River Reservoir Archaeological Team of the Institute of Archaeology, Academia Sinica, at the site of Miao-ti-kou, near Shan Hsien, in western Honan, where a proto-Lungshan type of cultural assemblage was identified in a layer overlying the Yangshao stage remains. Similar cultural assemblages have been discovered before this in the neighboring areas, but their significance as an early type of the Lungshan stage cultures was not recognized until after the Miao-ti-kou II discovery. It is now known that the Miao-ti-kou II type of Lungshan stage is exemplified at the following sites (see Map 5): Miao-ti-kou in Shan Hsien, Sun-ch'i-t'un near Lo-yang, Yang-shao-ts'un in Mien-ch'ieh Hsien, and Lin-shan-chai near Cheng-chou, in western and northern Honan; Ching-ts'un in Wan-ch'üan Hsien and P'an-nan-ts'un in P'ing-lu Hsien, in southern Shansi; and Liu-tzu-chen in Hua Hsien, and Heng-chen-ts'un in Hua-yin Hsien, in

4. Li Chi, *Chinese Civilization*; Cheng Te-kun, *Prehistoric China*; William Watson, *China*.

79

central eastern Shensi.[5] Stratigraphical evidence at Miao-ti-kou, Sun-ch'i-t'un, Yang-shao-ts'un, and Liu-tzu-chen shows conclusively that this Miao-ti-kou II type of assemblage is later than the Yang-shao remains but earlier than the Lungshanoid remains that subsequently became widespread in Honan. Typologically, its "transitional" nature is clear.

At the Miao-ti-kou II settlement, a round semisubterranean house floor was found, with an entrance ramp and wattle-and-daub and lime-plastered floor and stairs. The post-hole pattern seems to suggest a conical roof (Fig. 5). Ruins of pottery kilns and storage

FIG. 5. Reconstruction of a Lungshanoid stage house at Miao-ti-kou II, western Honan. From *Miao-ti-kou yü San-li-ch'iao*, Fig. 9.

pits are said to exhibit "advanced" features compared with the Yangshao stage structures. The ceramic change from the previous stage is shown by a tabulation of ceramic features and forms among three sites: Miao-ti-kou I (Yangshao), Miao-ti-kou II (proto-Lungshan), and San-li-ch'iao (Lungshan). San-li-ch'iao is a site near Miao-ti-kou, also in Shan Hsien, western Honan, where a typical Honan Lungshan assemblage was found and can serve to typify a later stage of the Lungshan.[6]

The quantitative figures tabulated in Tables 3 and 4 from the

5. An Chih-min, *KKTH*, 1957:4, 4; An Chih-min, *WW*, 1959:10, 20–21; An Chih-min et al., *Miao-ti-kou yü San-li-ch'iao*, pp. 108–12.
6. An Chih-min et al., *Miao-ti-kou yü San-li-ch'iao*, pp. 25, 64, 93.

TABLE 3.

Distribution of Different Wares at the Sites of Miao-ti-kou I,
Miao-ti-kou II, and San-li-ch'iao

Ware	Surface Treatment and Decoration	Miao-ti-kou I (Pits 5, 10, 363, 387)		Miao-ti-kou II (Pits 551, 567, 568)		San-li-ch'iao (Pit 3)	
		No.*	%	No.*	%	No.*	%
Fine Red	Coil marks	4741	29.48				
	Coil marks and basket	76	0.48				
	Cloth impression	3	0.02				
	Painted	2254	14.02	36	0.91		
	Plain	2095	13.03	34	0.87	10	0.3
	Basket			11	0.26	38	1.13
	Total	9169	57.02	81	2.05	48	1.43
Coarse Red	Coil marks	3441	21.4				
	Coil marks and incision	168	1.05				
	String	23	0.15				
	Appliqué	146	0.91				
	Plain	1468	9.13			208	6.19
	Cord					95	2.83
	Total	5246	32.62			303	9.02
Coarse Gray	Cord			120	3.05	1138	33.86
	Basket			1779	45.14	327	9.73
	Checker			55	1.39	34	1.02
	Appliqué			125	3.17	21	0.63
	Incision			36	0.91		
	Plain			502	12.72	188	5.6
	Total			2617	66.45	1708	50.82
Fine Gray	Plain	1651	10.27	620	15.73	205	6.1
	Appliqué	12	0.08	78	1.97		
	Incision			41	1.04		
	Cord			65	1.65	527	15.68
	Basket			404	10.31	273	8.13
	Checker					20	0.6
	Cut-out					6	0.18
	Total	1663	10.34	1208	30.62	1031	30.69

81

TABLE 3. (continued)

Distribution of Different Wares at the Sites of Miao-ti-kou I,
Miao-ti-kou II, and San-li-ch'iao

	Surface Treatment and Decoration	Miao-ti-kou I (Pits 5, 10, 363, 387)		Miai-ti-kou II (Pits 551, 567, 568)		San-li-ch'iao (Pit 3)	
		No.*	%	No.*	%	No.*	%
Fine Black	Plain	4	0.03	30	0.76	240	7.14
	String			5	0.12		
	Incision					31	0.93
	Total	4	0.03	35	0.88	271	8.07

* Number of sherds.

three types of sites—Yangshao, proto-Lungshan, and Lungshan—
suggests both changes and continuities in ceramic features. In the
manufacture of pottery, essentially the same traditions cut through
all stages, although a major change is noted from the Miao-ti-kou
II strata in the techniques of firing which led to the predominance
of the gray color during the Lungshan phases. Even the fine gray
and black wares that are considered typical of Lungshan occupy
as much as 10.37 percent of the total Yangshao stage sherds at
Miao-ti-kou I. There are, however, some other notable changes.
The painted decoration of pottery, which is of considerable importance (14.02 percent of the total sherds are painted) at Miao-
ti-kou I, drops to 0.91 percent at Miao-ti-kou II and disappears
altogether at San-li-ch'iao. The coiling marks and the use of ap-
pliqué are also more typical of the Yangshao stage than of the
Lungshan. On the other hand, the Lungshan stage witnessed a
marked increase of incised sherds and the appearance of checker
impressions. The latter may be due to the emergence of the paddle-
and-anvil technique of manufacture. Generally speaking, the majority of Yangshao wares was of a fine paste, whereas the Lungshan
wares were characterized by a predominance of sand-tempered
coarse wares, either gray or red. This may indicate that the functions served by the fine wares during the Yangshao stage were
partially taken over by artifacts made of some other materials than
clay during the Lungshan stage. This is made more apparent by
a consideration of forms and functions. The Lungshan cooking

TABLE 4.

Distribution of Different Pottery Forms at the Sites of Miao-ti-kou I, Miao-ti-kou II, and San-li-ch'iao

Form	Ware	Miao-ti-kou I		Miao-ti-kou II		San-li-ch'iao	
		No. of Sherds	%	No. of Sherds	%	No. of Sherds	%
SHERDS OF COOKING WARE							
Pot	Coarse red	3	0.03				
Stove	Coarse red	3	0.03				
	Coarse gray			3	0.35		
Steamer	Fine red	3	0.03			17	1.32
	Fine gray						
ting	Coarse gray			32	3.74		
chia	Coarse gray			10	1.16	19	1.47
li	Coarse gray					196	15.16
kui	Fine red					2	0.16
SHERDS OF RECEPTACLES							
Bowl	Fine red	521	3.75				
	Coarse red	87	0.63				
	Fine gray	92	0.67	3	0.35	35	2.71
	Fine black			1	0.12		
Basin-	Coarse red	1027	7.39	5	0.59		
beaker	Fine red	3126	22.48	12	1.41		
	Coarse gray			16	1.89		
	Fine gray	924	6.65			59	4.57

TABLE 4. (continued)

Distribution of Different Pottery Forms at the Sites of Miao-ti-kou I, Miao-ti-kou II, and San-li-ch'iao

Form	Ware	Miao-ti-kou I No. of Sherds	Miao-ti-kou I %	Miao-ti-kou II No. of Sherds	Miao-ti-kou II %	San-li-ch'iao No. of Sherds	San-li-ch'iao %
Jar	Fine red	3125	22.48			37	2.87
	Fine red	1089	7.84			84	6.50
	Coarse red	3754	27.00			154	11.91
Pot	Fine gray	119	0.86	198	23.18	87	6.73
	Fine black	4	0.03	6	0.7		
	Coarse gray			496	58.08	525	40.61
Cup	Coarse red	12	0.09				
	Fine red			9	1.05		
	Fine gray			2	0.23	37	2.87
tou	Fine gray			3	0.35		
	Fine black					41	3.64
SHERDS OF ACCESSORIES	Fine red	11	0.08				
	Coarse red	4	0.03				
Lid	Coarse gray			3	0.35		
	Fine gray			35	4.08		
	Fine black			1	0.12		
Handle fragments	Coarse gray			19	0.23		
Pedestal	Fine gray	2	0.02				

ware is more complicated and of greater variety than the Yang-shao, suggesting a more elaborate cuisine. Particularly noteworthy is the appearance of tripods during the Lungshan stage—*ting, chia, li,* and *kui* (Fig. 6). On the other hand, bowls and basin-beakers decrease in quantity, suggesting that other materials than clay grew more important in making the dinnerware. Also during the Lungshan stage appeared the *tou* or fruit stand, generally considered more ceremonial than utilitarian. All of these changes are illustrated by the comparison of the total cultural configuration of the Yangshao and Lungshan stages which will be made presently. The significance of the Miao-ti-kou II, on the other hand, is that during this stage a cultural transition appears to have taken place. Although many essential Lungshan stage characteristics had already appeared, many continuities from the previous cultural phase still existed.

> Many pottery forms seem to have evolved out of the Yang-shao forms, particularly the cup, pot, pointed-bottomed jar, and the *ting* tripod. The pointed-bottomed jars are typical of the Yangshao culture; this type of jar, similar to the finds at Miao-ti-kou II, is also found in Yang-shao-ts'un, Mien-ch'ih Hsien, and at Heng-chen-ts'un in Hua-yin Hsien, Shensi, all closely related to but different from the Yang-shao stage forms. The small cups slipped in red pigment are typical of this site, but possibly related to the coarse small cups of the Yangshao stage. . . . In short, the ceramics of Miao-ti-kou II exhibit features transitional from the Yangshao to the Lungshan.[7]

Similar conclusions can be drawn from an inventory of stone, bone, and antler artifacts. Axes and stone knives of the Yangshao types remained, but semilunar knives and stone sickles of the Lungshan types also appeared at Miao-ti-kou II. Bone artifacts are more abundant and better made, including such new types as hairpins and combs. Mollusc shell artifacts also began to appear. This may be accounted for in part by the growing importance of animal domestication. In addition to pigs and dogs, which still predominated, cattle and sheep-goats grew more substantial in quantity, and chicken bones have also been discovered.

Thus, it is becoming clear that the Yangshao farmers in the

7. Ibid., pp. 110–11.

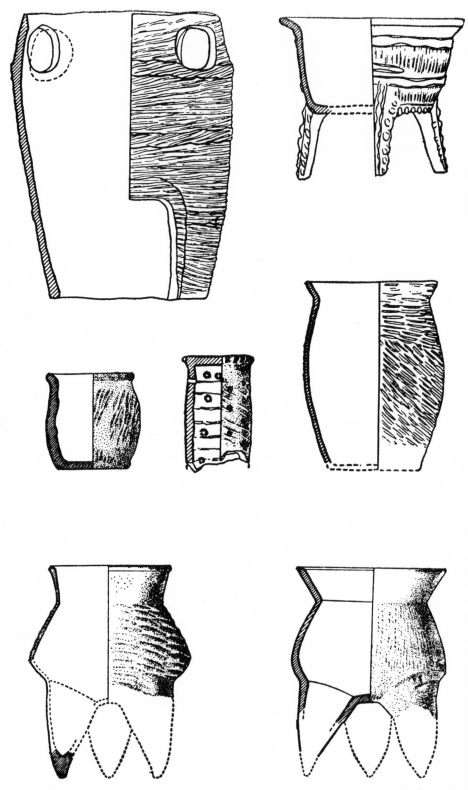

FIG. 6. Some distinctive pottery forms of the Proto-Lungshan complex of Miao-ti-kou II, western Honan. The solid-foot tripod is a *ting* tripod, and the hollow-foot ones *chia* tripods. From *Miao-ti-kou yü San-li-ch'iao*.

Nuclear Area began to take the lead in evolving into a new form of culture, as represented by the proto-Lungshan complex recognized in eastern Shensi, western Honan, and southwestern Shansi, which rapidly developed into the mature form of the Lungshan stage in the Nuclear Area and expanded into other areas of North China and beyond.

CULTURAL AND SOCIAL CHANGES AMONG THE LUNGSHANOID FARMERS

Ruins of settlements and cultural remains of the second known stage of the North China Neolithic, including both the proto-Lungshan complex and the Lungshan phases, for which the term "Lungshanoid" has been proposed to underscore both the horizon-wide cultural similarity and the regional variations,[8] have been uncovered from a much wider area than the previous Yangshao remains in North China, and similar assemblages extended far beyond the Yellow River valley. As of now, the Lungshanoid assemblages have been identified in Shensi, Shansi, Honan, Shantung, Hopei, Liaoning, Hupei, Anhwei, Kiangsu, Chekiang, Fukien, Taiwan, and Kwangtung; in fact, they have been found throughout the entire middle and lower Huangho valley, the northern coasts of the Pohai Bay, the entire middle and lower Yangtze, and much of the southeastern coast. Furthermore, Lungshanoid influences appear to have reached even beyond these territories, and food-production and neolithic technology radiated into the peripheral hunting-fishing-collecting populations. It was during the Lungshanoid stage that much of China began to be populated by village farmers (Map 7).

It is not surprising, then, that the Lungshanoid assemblages of the various regions exhibit marked local characteristics, as will be described presently. These regional phases, however, are unified under the Lungshanoid banner, so to speak, by the following three factors: a similar stratigraphical position, common stylistic characteristics, and the same developmental level. These phenomena apparently resulted from a series of related historical events generated by cultural and social dynamics taking place in the Nuclear Area.

With the identification of the proto-Lungshan complex, the

8. Chang Kwang-chih, *BIHP*, 30, 269.

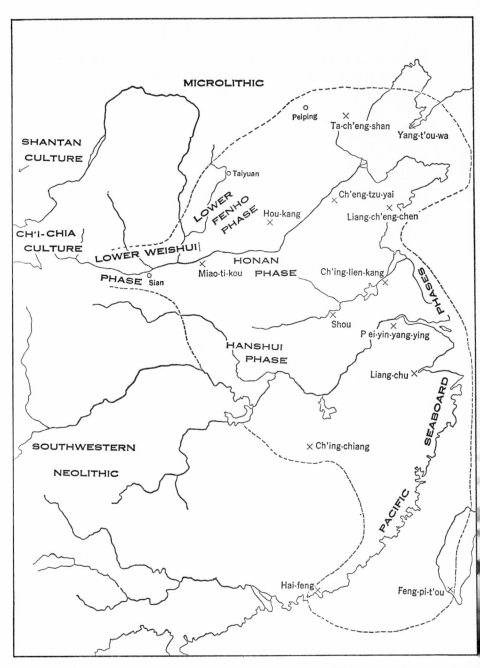

MAP 7. Distribution of Neolithic sites of the Lungshanoid stage and its regional traditions.

stratigraphical "mixture" of Yangshao and Lungshan elements in western Honan, long considered an obstacle to making generalizations about the Hou-kang sequence, is not only explained but made significant in providing the necessary stage during which a major cultural transformation took place. Within and beyond the Nuclear Area, a sufficient number of stratified sites have been found to show that the Lungshanoid assemblages invariably lie above the Yangshao remains, if and when these two are encountered at the same site, and that the former, in turn, is overlain by historical strata, either Shang or Chou as the case may be in the various parts of China. The "transitional" stratigraphy has been observed at the following sites: Yang-shao-ts'un,[9] Sun-ch'i-t'un near Lo-yang,[10] the Lo-ning Hsien sites,[11] Shang-tien in Yih-yang Hsien,[12] Ch'ing-t'ai and Tien-chün-t'ai in Kwang-wu Hsien,[13] all in western Honan; Kao-tui in Lin-fen Hsien, and other sites in southwestern Shansi; [14] and Feng-hao-ts'un near Sian [15] and Liu-tzu-chen in Hua Hsien, in central-eastern Shensi. In some sites in this same neighborhood and areas beyond this nuclear cluster, a stratigraphic break between the two cultural phases seems to be the rule. This kind of stratigraphic evidence—Lungshanoid over Yangshao—has been brought to light in the following areas in North China where the Yangshao phase was confined. *Honan:* Hou-kang, Kao-ching-t'ai-tzu, T'ung-lo-chai, all in the An-yang area; Liu-chuang, Ta-lai-tien, Ts'ao-tien, Feng-huang-t'ai, Lu-t'ai, in Chün Hsien; Hui-tsui in Yen-shih Hsien; and Miao-ti-kou in Shan Hsien; *Shensi and Shansi:* a series of localities in the Ching and Wei valleys; K'ai-jui-chuang near Sian; Sanmen Gorge Reservoir sites; and several localities in southern Shansi.[16]

The following stylistic features may serve as the few interareal horizon markers for the Lungshanoid stage of North China and beyond:

9. Andersson, *BMFEA*, 15, 30–31.
10. Tung Chu-chen, *KKHP*, 1957:2, 13.
11. Li Chien-yüng, Pei Chi, and Chia Eh, *KKTH*, 1956:2, 53.
12. Chia Eh, *KKTH*, 1958:1, 5.
13. Hsia Nai, *K'o-hsüeh-t'ung-pao*, 2 (1951), 725–28.
14. Tung Chu-chen, *KKHP*, 1957:2, 9; Chang Tê-kwang, *WWTKTL*, 1956:9, 53.
15. Shih Chang-ju, *BIHP*, 27 (1956), 237–40.
16. Tung Chu-chen, *KKHP*, 1957:2; Chou Tao, *KKTH*, 1957:1; An Chih-min, *KKTH*, 1957:4; An Chih-min, *KKTH*, 1956:5; An Chih-min, *KKTH*, 1956:6; Shih Chang-ju, *BIHP*, 27 (1956); Ku Tieh-fu, *WWTKTL*, 1956:10.

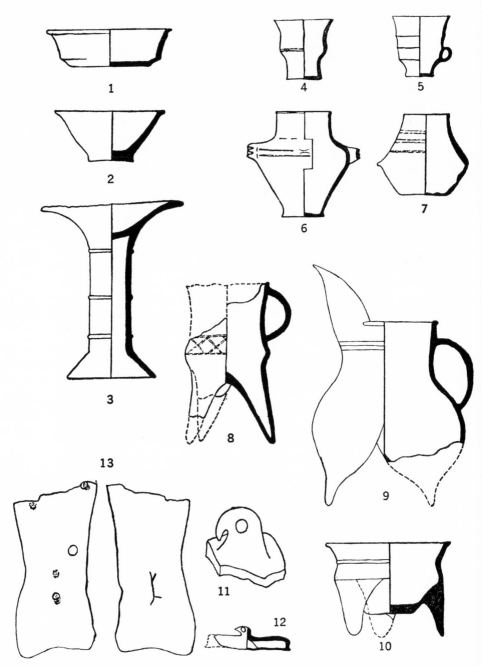

FIG. 7. The ceremonial complex of the Lungshanoid farmers. 1–10. Pottery vessels probably used primarily for ceremonial purposes (1–4, 7–10, from Ch'eng-tzu-yai; 5, 6, from Liang-ch'eng-chen). 11–12. Pottery lids, probably for ceremonial vessels. The bird motif might have had particular ritual significance. (11, Ch'eng-tzu-yai; 12, Liang-ch'eng-chen). 13. A piece of oracle bone of deer shoulder blade, grooved, burned, and cracked. (From Yang-t'ou-wa). From Chang, *Prehistoric Settlements*, Pl. VII.

(1) A great variety of pottery forms, including tripods (*li, ting, chia, kui*) and ring-footed vessels (*tsun, p'o,* and *tou* or fruit stands), characterizes the Lungshanoid horizon, and may, together with scapulimancy, suggest the complexity of rituals in this stage (Fig. 7).

(2) One of the most striking features of the Lungshanoid pottery is the sharpness of the curves on every part of the body. This is a significant contrast with the general roundness of the pottery shapes of the Yangshao stage. As pointed out above, a considerable number of containers during the Lungshan stage may have been made of materials other than clay: possibly wood, bamboo, and/or metal. This may at least partially account for the sharp curves of the pottery vessels of this stage.

(3) Another important stylistic marker of the Lungshan horizon is the cut-out ring-feet of fruit stands and other forms of vessels.

(4) A fourth marker is the decline of the art of pottery painting, the increase of incisions and combed marks, and the appearance of checker impressions. The color of the pottery is predominantly gray. Wheel marks and fine, lustrous, black pottery appear in this horizon in considerable quantity in some regions, but are far from universal.

These horizon markers can apparently be explained in terms of eco-social development during this stage, for Chinese farmers now began to establish permanent settlements, on the one hand, and, on the other, to expand outside the natural habitat of domesticated plants and animals—two of a complex of related events that were taking place. The core of this complex is probably the progress of agricultural techniques and the resultant population increase. A number of related eco-social and stylistic changes may be seen in the comparison of the Yangshao and the Lungshanoid stages in Table 5.

This comparison shows (a) that these two complexes were two "stages" of a single developmental sequence rather than, as originally hypothesized, two "cultures" of different origins, since the differences are more developmental than cultural, and (b) that this development involves the total cultural and social configuration rather than minor modifications in single "cultural traits." To be sure, the above generalizations are not all applicable to all regions, but the patterns of change are well-defined. It is shown that Chinese farmers were now emancipated from a low-level pri-

91

TABLE 5.

Yangshao and Lungshanoid Cultural Contrasts

Yangshao	Lungshanoid
Shifting settlement; repetitive occupation	Permanent settlement; relatively permanent occupation
Slash-and-burn cultivation	Irrigation? Fertilizer? Fallow fields?
Largely confined to the Nuclear Area; indicative of stable population density?	Far-reaching expansions into the eastern plains, Manchuria, and Central and South China; indicative of population pressure resulting from permanence of settlement and great productivity?
Interareal uniformity of style	Emergence of a variety of regional styles
More symmetrical edges than asymmetrical on all edged tools; more circular and oval cross-sections; indicative of extensive use of the wood-felling complex for field clearance	More asymmetrical edges than symmetrical; more rectangular cross-sections; indicative of extensive use of carpenters' tools (adzes, chisels, antler wedges)
Rectangular, single-holed or double-notched stone knives characteristic; indicative of more game-hunting and the use of longitudinal cutting tools	Semilunar and double-holed, or sickle-shaped stone knives and shell sickles characteristic; indicative of more extensive use of harvesting tools
Pottery handmade	Beginning of wheel-made pottery; indicative of intensified crafts specialization
None	Scapulimancy; indicative of intensified occupational specialization
No defensive works; few artifacts exclusively for fighting	Appearance of *hang-t'u* village walls and weapons; indicative of the necessity for fortification and means for offensive action
Burial practice showing age and sex differentiation	Growing number of otherwise differentiated burials; possibly indicative of more rigidly constituted classes

92

Yangshao	Lungshanoid
Community patterns showing little evidence of major social stratification	Concentration of jade artifacts at isolated spots in one site; indicative of more intensive status differentiation
Art associated with domestic crafts (ceramics)	Art not conspicuously associated with domestic crafts; possible association with theocratic crafts (?)
Utility wares (cord-mat-basket pattern) characteristic	Ceremonial wares (eggshell forms and fine, well-made cups, fruit stands and shallow dishes) characteristic
"Fertility cult" characteristic	Evidence of institutionalized ancestor cult; ceremonials far beyond merely agricultural; possibly associated with specialized groups of people

mary village efficiency and from the small confines of the Nuclear Area and had developed a relatively sophisticated society to pave the way for the eventual emergence of civilization in this area.

The basis of economy of the Lungshanoid stage is, of course, agricultural. Hoes, spades, and sickles were again the principal cultivating implements. The farmers grew rice and wheat in addition to millet, which presumably continued to be the leading staple in the North. Remains of wheat have been found at Tiao-yü-t'ai in Po Hsien, northern Anhwei,[17] and remains of rice at Yang-shao-ts'un in western Honan, Liu-tzu-chen in central Shensi, at a great number of sites in the Hanshui valley in northern Hupei (Pl. III), the Huaiho valley in Anhwei, and the Lower Yangtzu region in Kiangsu.[18] Considered by most botanists to have been first domesticated in Southeast Asia, rice may have been one of the new crops successfully cultivated by the Lungshanoid farmers in South China and brought back to the North.

17. Hu Yüeh-chien, *KKHP*, 1957:1, 26.
18. Ting Yih, *KKHP*, 1959:4; Hu Yüeh-chien, *KKHP*, 1957:1, 27; Hsieh Chun-chu, *WWTKTL*, 1955:8, 50–51. In addition to rice (*Oryza sativa*), the Ch'ien-shan-yang site of the Lungshanoid stage in Wu-hsing Hsien, southern Kiangsu, has yielded remains of certain species of peach (*Prunus persica*), melon (*Cocumis melo*), water chestnut (*Trapa natans* or *T. bispinosa*), peanuts (*Arachis hypogaea*), possibly sesame (*Sesamum indicum* or *S. orientale*), and possibly beans (*Vicia faba*). See *KKHP*, 1960:2, 84–85.

Pigs and dogs remained the principal domestic animals, and a great quantity of their bony remains has been encountered at the Lungshanoid sites. Other varieties increased in importance, such as cattle, sheep/goats, and possibly horses. The growing importance of poultry is also attested to at many sites, ranging from Yang-t'ou-wa in the Liaotung Peninsula in the north [19] to the Hanshui sites in the south.[20] Wild game, such as bamboo rat, hare, horse, wild boar, water deer, and deer, still appear among the remains. Fishing is again indicated by numerous remains of fish hooks, net sinkers, and bone harpoons. Spindle whorls, bodkins, and eyed needles show the presence of fabric weaving.

In the Nuclear Area and its immediate neighborhood at least, the slash-and-burn method of cultivation had given way to some other sort of planting technique by means of which relatively permanent settlement was made possible. Irrigation, fallow field, and the use of fertilizer are some possible innovations, though actual evidence is lacking for any of these. In some regions at least, wells were dug.[21] Observations at Lo-ning Hsien, Hou-kang, and Ta-lai-tien [22] in Honan have established the fact that all of the Lungshanoid occupations were larger in area and longer in duration than the former Yangshao occupations at the same sites or nearby. The sedentary nature of the Lungshanoid villages is further indicated by the permanent village walls of Ch'eng-tzu-yai and Hou-kang [23] and the abundance of asymmetrically-edged tools, which served more for carpentry than for felling trees. The village wall also indicates the need for fortification, and during the Lungshan stage warfare must have been common. A site of this stage in Hantan, Hopei, has yielded many skeletons in a well, presumably thrown there after a village raid.[24]

The community was again of the village pattern, but of its architecture we know relatively little. Around the whole village there was, in some cases, a mud wall, constructed of stamped earth

19. T. Kanazeki, S. Miyake, and S. Mizuno, "Yang-t'ou-wa," *Archaeologia Orientalis*, ser. B, 3 (1942), 95.

20. Chang Yün-peng, KKTH, 1956:3, 15–16.

21. KK, 1959:10, 531; Mei Fu-ken, KKHP, 1960:2, 95.

22. Li Chien-yüng, Pei Chi, and Chia Eh, KKTH, 1956:2, 52–53; Liang Ssu-yüng, "Hou-kang fa-chüeh hsiao-chi," pp. 614–16; Liu Yao, TYKKPK, 1 (1936), 75.

23. Shih Chang-ju, "Ho-nan An-yang Hou-kang ti Yin mu," *Liu-t'ung pieh-lu*, 1 (1945), Li-chuang, Inst. Hist. Phil., Academia Sinica, 3.

24. KK, 1959:10, 531–32.

layers. Inside the wall were semisubterranean dwelling houses, square or circular in plan, with clay- or lime-plastered floors, each with a hearth at the center. Huge communal dwelling houses, carrying on a Yangshao tradition, have also been found. Near the dwelling houses are semisubterranean granaries constructed similarly to the circular houses. In the settlement were also found burials. The dead were inhumed in simple rectangular pits in an extended posture, lying on their backs or facing downward. A few pots or cups and sometimes stone tools accompanied the dead.[25] The prone burials, together with the ceremonial wares, the wheel-making of pottery, and other indications mentioned above, suggest the intensification of the internal differentiation of individual status and industrial specialization.

A belief in the afterlife, a fecundity cult and an agricultural rite, a deer ceremony, and the use of miniature vessels may be considered to have continued from the preceding stage, but here there is definite evidence of institutionalized ancestor worship.[26] There is also the important addition of scapulimancy. Scraped and burned shoulder blades of cattle, deer, and occasionally sheep were found at many Lungshanoid sites in Honan, Shansi, Shensi, Hopei, Liaoning, Shantung, Anhwei, and Kiangsu.[27]

As for artistic activities, the making of figurines (Fig. 8) and the production of some masterpieces of eggshell pottery carried on the great Yangshao artistic tradition, but the remarkable ceramic painting drastically diminished or was gone altogether. The sphere of decorative art may have shifted from domestic utensils to ceremonial crafts. An advanced wood-carving tradition, however, may have developed, as shown by the abundance of tools or carpentry (adzes, gauges, chisels, and antler wedges).

The Lungshanoid farmers had mastered the art of manufacturing pottery: chemical analysis of Lungshan sherds has revealed that its paste had become standardized,[28] and evidence of the use of the potter's wheel is plentiful. Yet handmade pieces still pre-

25. Cf. Wang Ssu-li, *KKHP*, 1959:4, 17–29.
26. Chang Kwang-chih, *BIE*, 9, 1960.
27. Shih Chang-ju, *Ta-lu-tsa-chih*, 8 (1954), 265–69, gives a complete list of pre-1950 findings of oracle bones at Lungshanoid sites in China; for new discoveries, see: Chen Hui, Tang Yün-ming, and Sun Tê-hai, *KKHP*, 1959:3, 32–33; Shou Tien, *WWTKTL*, 1957:1; Chou Tao, *KK*, 1959:9; Chao Ching-fang, *KKHP*, 1958:1, 14.
28. Li Chi, *Hsiao-t'un T'ao-ch'i*, p. 24.

dominated, and the introduction of paddle-and-anvil techniques accounts for the growing number of pots impressed with geometric patterns. Stone polishers and stone balls, possibly used as anvils, and stone paddles have been unearthed. In form, the Lungshanoid pottery is characterized by the ring-footed pots and the abundance of tripods. Gray is the predominant color, black and red come next, and yellow is characteristic of scattered regions.

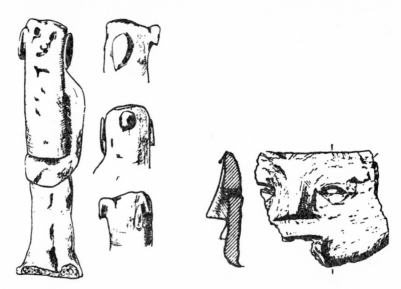

FIG. 8. Two human representations in the Lungshanoid ceramic art. *Left:* from Pu-chao-ch'ai, after Andersson, *BMFEA*, 15 (1943), Pl. 180, No. 2; *Right:* from Ch'i-li-p'u, in Shan Hsien, Honan, from *KK*, 1959:4, 179.

Stone implements were mostly polished, and again included such common types as axes, adzes, hoes, spades, chisels, knives, and arrowheads. Differing from those of the Yangshao farmers, however, these are characteristically asymmetrically edged and rectangularly cross-sectioned. Bone, antler, and mollusc shell implements were abundant. The use of metal may have begun toward the end of the stage, for traces of a metal saw were observed on some antler fragments, and some of the pottery styles resemble metallic fashions. Actual findings of metals are scarce and of dubious date, as will be described below.

Although the above description of the Lungshanoid stage serves to suggest that we are dealing with a widespread horizon style and a common developmental stage in the prehistory of China, it must be stressed that within this broad outline there are a number of regional stylistic variations. In 1939, eleven years after the discovery of the Lungshan site at Ch'eng-tzu-yai, when Liang Ssu-yüng presented his synthesis of this stage of Chinese prehistory, he already recognized that the "relics, especially the potsherds, collected from these sites exhibit definite local differences which cannot very well be ignored" and proposed a "tentative division into three areas": [29]

(a) *Coastal Shantung area.* This area includes sites of the Jih-chao region. The pottery of this area is characterized by the very large number of tripod pots, tripod basins, spouted hollow-footed tripod jugs (*kuei*), a type of collared small-footed pots with two, four, or twelve small handles, squat jars, tapering-collared jugs, and a special type of steamer (*hsien*). The stone artifacts of all types show a predominating number with asymmetrically placed cutting edge.

(b) *North Honan area.* The sites of North Honan are included in this area. The pottery of the area is characterized by the numerous ovoid jars which are sometimes elongated in proportion but never as squat as jars of the Coastal Shantung Area, wide-mouthed shallow pots, collared pots with three perpendicularly attached hollow feet, tripods of the *li* type, steamers (*hsien*) with raised chainlike belt around the waist, and the use of "bat-and-pad method," which leaves on the surface of the vessels marks that resemble, in a general way, impressions of mat, basket, and net. Sherds with similar bat marks are met with in the Coastal Shantung Area, but so few in number that they may be regarded as intruders from North Honan. The maximum dimension achieved by the potters of this area is larger than that of the Shantung Coast. The proportion of finest ware is much lower. The cylindrical prismatic ar-

---

29. Liang Ssu-yüng, *Proc. 6th Pacif. Sci. Cong.,* 4 (1939), 69–79.

rowheads of stone and bone, plastered floors, and multiflued stoves are typical of this area and unknown in the Coastal Shantung Area. The cutting implements show a smaller proportion of asymmetrically placed cutting edge.

(c) *Hangchow Bay area.* Sites of the Hang Hsien region are included in this area. The pottery shapes characteristic of this area are dishes and basins with ring foot of various length, ring-footed beakers, short-collared vases with or without ring foot, and tripod pots with solid legs of special shapes. But it is the large proportion of round bottoms, ring feet, and horizontal parallel decorative ridges which marks this area off from the other two regions. The round bottoms are also indicative of an important technical divergence.

The site at Ch'eng-tzu-yai is considered by Liang as intermediate between Area (a) and Area (b), and the sites in the Huai River drainage a blend of three areas. The temporal relation of the several facies, according to Liang, could not be determined, though the Hangchow Bay phase was possibly later than the others. Subsequent efforts [30] to subdivide the "Lungshan Culture" into various stages and to make the Coastal Shantung Area the earliest and the Honan group the latest seem to be derived from little more than the notion that this "culture" originated from the east and spread westward into Honan, a notion that has since been rendered obsolete. In the last two decades since Liang's synthesis, Lungshanoid assemblages have been unearthed from a much wider area and with much greater intensity within the regions he has considered, and a reassessment of the regional classification of the Lungshanoid facies is certainly called for. The relationships among these various regional facies will be discussed below, but first we will describe each of them in turn, in geographical order (see Map 7).

The Lower Weishui Valley An archaeological survey in the Weishui valley and its tributaries (Ching and Yüng) undertaken by Shih Chang-ju in 1943 brought to light sixty-six prehistoric and early historic sites, which he has grouped into seven stages.[31]

30. Yin Ta, *Chung-kuo hsin-shih-ch'i-shih-tai*, pp. 48–49; Cheng Te-kun, *Prehistoric China*, pp. 93–95.
31. Shih Chang-ju, BIHP, 27, 315–17.

(a) Lung-ma stage: Red ware, some painted sherds.

(b) Pin Hsien stage: Red and gray wares, painted and incised; this is equated by Shih to Andersson's Yangshao stage.

(c) Feng-hao stage: More gray than red ware. "None of the red sherds are painted; these are coarse and thin, showing signs of retrogression in typology. Brown sand-tempered jugs are the most numerous and characteristic of this stage. The gray ware contains mostly *li* tripods and jugs, decorated by basket and thin-cord patterns. It has some Lungshan stage characteristics. Possibly a transitional phase from the Painted Pottery to the Paddle-and-Pad Pottery."

(d) Hu-hsi stage: Neither painted nor red ware is present. It is characterized exclusively by the gray ware.

(e) Tou-men stage: Characterized by cord-marked and incised gray ware, similar to the ceramics of Hsiao-t'un of Shang Dynasty.

(f) Chang-chia stage: Characterized by gray ware, *li* tripods.

(g) Ming-yü stage: Same as (f).

In this sequence, the Lung-ma and Pin Hsien stages could probably be correlated to the Yangshao stage, whereas the Tou-men, Chang-chia, and Ming-yü stages could correspond to the historical Western Chou period. It is the Feng-hao and Hu-hsi stages in between that are significant: these are the first cultural stages formulated in Shensi which occupy, stratigraphically as well as stylistically, a similar position to the "Lungshan Culture" in Honan, as noted by Shih.[32] This stage was further looked into after the Communist occupation by archaeologists of the Institute of Archaeology, Academia Sinica, during the excavations of the K'ai-jui-chuang (K'o-hsing-chuang) site in 1951 and the A-ti-ts'un site in 1953. They noted many similarities in the remains of these sites to the "Lungshan Culture" of Honan, but, because of the absence here of some features heretofore regarded as diagnostic of Lungshan, the archaeologists have proposed the term Shensi Lungshan Culture for the assemblages uncovered in this region;[33] some would prefer to use another term for it, the K'ai-jui-chuang Culture.[34]

It appears to the present author that the K'ai-jui-chuang Culture

32. Ibid.

33. Shih Hsing-pang, *KKTH*, 1955:1, 30; Tung Chu-chen, *KKHP*, 1957:2, 12; An Chih-min, *KKTH*, 1956:5, 6.

34. Su Ping-chi and Wu Ju-tso, *KKTH*, 1956:2, 32–36.

of the Lower Weishui valley was undoubtedly a regional phase of the Lungshanoid horizon-stage described above. In the first place, stratigraphical evidence from K'ai-jui-chuang has established that the Weishui Lungshanoid phase came after the Yangshao but before the earliest historical period of the region, that of Western Chou.[35] Sites of this stage, as mentioned earlier, are topographically lower than the Yangshao sites in the same neighborhood, represent concentrated occupation, and contain cultural remains left during a relatively long duration and exhibiting a great complexity.[36] The dwelling houses at K'ai-jui-chuang, near Sian, are rectangular or round semisubterranean structures, consisting of one or two rooms.[37] Those at Mi-chia-yai, near Sian [38] and at Liu-tzu-chen in Hua Hsien [39] were plastered with white lime. Near the houses are deep pocket-shaped storage pits with small openings.[40] Pottery kilns were also found at the K'ai-jui-chuang site.[41]

The practice of scapulimancy is evidenced by remains of burned scapulae of sheep at K'ai-jui-chuang.[42] The inventory of stone and bone artifacts is similar to the local Yangshao stage, but rectangular axes and sickles of stone are more characteristic.[43] Pottery is predominantly handmade, using the coiling or molding technique, but wheel-made pieces are not totally lacking.[44] The color of the ceramics is predominantly gray, and red and black pieces are rare. According to Wang, Chung, and Chang,[45] 80 percent of the sherds collected at K'ai-jui-chuang in 1955–57 are gray, 18 percent of them are red, and only 1 percent black. Li (Fig. 9) and chia tripods are the most characteristic forms, but kui, tou, ting, ho, and other Lunshanoid forms also occur alongside the common

35. Ibid.
36. Ibid., p. 38.
37. Wang Po-hung, Chung Shao-lin, and Chang Chang-shou, KK, 1959:10, 517.
38. Yih Ting, KKTH, 1956:6, 31–32.
39. KK, 1959:11, 587.
40. Su Ping-chi and Wu Ju-tso, KKTH, 1956:2, 38; Wang Po-hung, Chung Shao-lin, and Chang Chang-shou, KK, 1959:10, 518; KK, 1959:11, 587.
41. Wang Po-hung, Chung Shao-lin, and Chang Chang-shou, KK, 1959:10, 518.
42. Ibid., p. 520.
43. Ibid.; An Chih-min, KKTH, 1956:5, 7.
44. An Chih-min, KKTH, 1956:5, 6; Tung Chu-chen, KKHP, 1957:2, 12; Wang Po-hung, Chung Shao-lin, and Chang Chang-shou, KK, 1959:10, 520.
45. Wang Po-hung, Chung Shao-lin, and Chang Chang-shou, KK, 1959:10, 520.

jugs and pots [46] (Pl. IV). In surface treatment, cord and basket patterns are predominant, but the cut-out ring feet and the checker impressions are also found, as is evidence for the use of paddle-and-anvil.[47]

The Weishui Lungshanoid phase, then, has in common with the Lungshanoid phase in Honan its settlement patterns, house

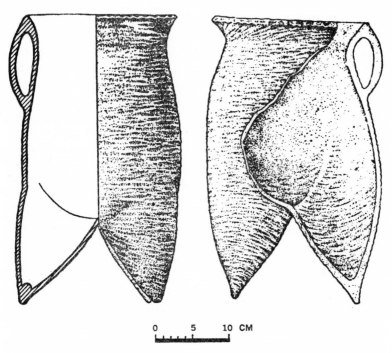

0   5   10 CM

FIG. 9. Two Lungshanoid *li* tripods excavated from K'o-hsing-chuang, near Sian, Shensi. From *KK*, 1959:10, 521.

construction, stone axes and sickles, the predominance of gray in ceramic color, the appearance of tripods and ring-footed forms of pottery, the use of paddle-and-anvil technique in pottery manu-facture, the cut-out ring foot and the checker impressions of pot-

46. Su Ping-chi and Wu Ju-tso, *KKTH*, 1956:2, 35; Yih Ting, *KKTH*, 1956:6, 35; Shih Hsing-pang, *KKTH*, 1955:1, 30; Tung Chu-chen, *KKHP*, 1957:2, 12; Wang Po-hung, Chung Shao-lin, and Chang Chang-shou, *KK*, 1959:10, 520.

47. An Chih-min, *KKTH*, 1956:5, 6–7; Wang Po-hung, Chung Shao-lin, and Chang Chang-shou, *KK*, 1959:10, 520; *KK*, 1959:11, 587.

tery, and the practice of scapulimancy. It differs from the latter, however, in that wheel-made pottery is rare, black ware is inconspicuous, li and chia tripods predominate over all other ceramic forms, and checker impressions are relatively rare. It also shows connections with the contemporary Ch'i-chia Culture of Kansu in the presence of the double-loop-handled jars.[48]

The Fenho Valley At some of the Yangshao stage sites in the Fenho valley in southern Shansi, in contrast to the Yangshao stage of western Honan, gray ware with cord and basket patterns predominated in the ceramic industry. This is true, for instance, of the two well-known Yangshao Culture sites, Hsi-yints'un in Hsia Hsien and Ching-ts'un in Wan-ch'üan Hsien.[49] At the site of Kao-tui in Lin-fen Hsien, corded and basket-impressed gray ware accounts for no less than 60 percent of the total number of potsherds collected, whereas there are 20 percent painted sherds, 19 percent red ware, and 1 percent "white ware."[50] At the Pei-kao-ts'un site, in Hsiang-fen Hsien, painted sherds, incised red potsherds, and pointed-bottomed jars were found in the same stratum from which a typical Lungshanoid assemblage was brought to light, consisting of cord-marked gray li tripods and hsien steamers of the same paste.[51] It is thus probable that the so-called proto-Lungshan complex was extended into the Lower Fenho valley, although its complete inventory remains to be explored.

During the last few years, several sites have been discovered where gray and black pottery predominated and where the cultural inventories suggest a Lungshanoid classification. The most important of these are "Tung-pai-chung and Tung-hu of Ch'ü-wo, Liu-ch'üan of Wen-hsi, and Ko-ta-ts'un of Hsia Hsien. There Lungshan type sherds (burnished and lustrous black or plain, corded, and basket-impressed gray wares) were found . . . According to the form and decoration of pottery, these probably constitute a regional phase of the Lungshan Culture."[52] Stratigraphical evidence serves to establish, again, that the gray ware

48. An Chih-min, KKTH, 1956:5, 7; Wang Po-hung, Chung Shao-lin, and Chang Chang-shou, KK, 1959:10, 517.
49. Tung Chu-chen, KKHP, 1957:2, 9.
50. Chang Tê-kwang, WWTKTL, 1956:9, 55.
51. Yang Fu-tou, KK, 1959:2, 107.
52. Ku Tieh-fu, WWTKTL, 1956:10, 22. See also: Chang Yen-huang, et al., KK, 1962:9, 461–63.

phase in the Lower Fenho was chronologically later than the Yang-shao phases.[53] Other Lungshanoid characteristics, such as the lime-plastered floor, checker impressions on pottery, and wheel-made pottery, are also represented.[54]

The proto-Lungshan–Lungshanoid sequence can be traced upstream along the Fenho as far as the neighborhood of T'ai-yüan. Yih-ching, near T'ai-yüan in central Shansi, can be regarded as a "mixed" site, where painted pottery occurs alongside Lungshanoid gray and black wares.[55] A "pure" Lungshanoid site has been located at Kuang-shê, near T'ai-yüan, on a loessic terrace of the Fen River. Here lime-plastered house floors and wattle-and-daub remains, bones of cattle, horses, sheep/goats, pigs, and deer, and polished stone axes, chisels, spades, sickles, adzes, knives, and shouldered hoes were found. The burned oracle bones of cattle's shoulder blades and the Lungshanoid pottery are particularly characteristic. The latter is mostly corded gray ware, but lustrous black pottery, basket-impressed red and gray ware, and impressed red ware are also present. Tripods, cups, *tou* fruit stands, and *hsien* steamers occur in addition to jugs, bowls, and basins. No wheel-made pieces, however, have been found.[56]

On the whole, the Fenho valley phase of the Lungshanoid seems closer to the Weishui phase than to the Honan phase, but more exact characterization remains to be made.

Western and Northern Honan With the significance of the so-called "mixed" sites in western Honan now being recognized with the formulation of a proto-Lungshan complex, the Lungshanoid sites in the Huangho valley in western and northern Honan can be grouped under a single heading, for common stylistic features can be discerned which are characteristic for the entire region. An examination of the topography of this neighborhood shows that the Yellow River valley in western and northern Honan forms a narrow strip of flat land, flanked in the north and the south by highlands, but open to the west (the Weishui valley) and the east (the vast alluvial plains of the Lower Huangho and the Huaiho). It therefore forms a unit in itself, but at the same

53. Ibid.
54. Chang Tê-kwang, *WWTKTL*, 1956:9, 56.
55. Tung Chu-chen, *KKHP*, 1957:2, 9; Tai Tsun-tê, *KK*, 1961:4, 203–6.
56. Shou Tien, *WWTKTL*, 1957:1, 57–58.

time, it is connected with both the Weishui and the eastern lowlands, particularly the latter.

Liang Ssu-yüng's characterization of the northern Honan area of the Lungshan culture is largely true of this entire region.[57] The stratigraphical position of the Lungshanoid between Yangshao and Shang can now be considered as established. All of the Lungshanoid characteristics enumerated above can be found here, such as the scapulimancy, the earthen village wall, and the lime-plastered house floors. Gray ware still predominates in the ceramics, but red ware is rare and black pottery markedly increased. The thin, lustrous, and fine-pasted black pottery that is said to characterize the sites of the Lungshanoid in Shantung is found in this area, some approaching, by all standards, the so-called eggshell pottery. Tripods and ring-footed vessels are characteristic, but the abundance of *ting* tripods at the expense of *chia* tripods and the large number of ring-footed vessels set this region apart from the Weishui phase of the Lungshanoid. Checker impressions on pottery and the paddle-and-pad technique which was responsible for most of the checker and cord-basket-mat impressions are characteristic of this area, and, together with the comparative rarity of *kui* tripods and wheel-made pottery, set it apart from the Shantung phase of the Lungshanoid. In many respects, the western and northern Honan phase of the Lungshanoid can be said to be situated between the Weishui and the Fenho phases of the Lungshanoid and the Shantung and Huaiho phases. This may have some chronological significance, as will be discussed presently.

The Hanshui Valley The Upper Hanshui valley in southwestern Honan and northern Hupei was easily accessible from western Honan along the eastern slopes of the Fu-niu Mountains, and the prehistoric remains of this area show distinct connections with the western and northern Honan phase of the Lungshanoid, closer to the proto-Lungshan complex than to the late Honan Lungshanoid phase.

The only relatively well-known site in the upper reaches of the Hanshui in Honan is the Erh-lang-kang site in Nan-chao Hsien. It is located on a small hill, 300 by 200 meters in dimensions, surrounded by the Paiho River, a tributary of the Hanshui. The

57. Andersson, BMFEA, 19; Liang Ssu-yung, Proc. 6th Pacif. Sci. Cong. 4; Chang Kwang-chih, COWA Survey, Area 17, No. 1 (1959), p. 3.

dwellings and burials are found on the southern part of the hill, and the northern part served as a trash area. Eight houses, mostly rectangular, were excavated, and wattle-and-daub construction was discovered in both the floor and the wall foundations. Amidst the dwellings, thirteen burials and twenty-two urn burials were found, the latter exclusively for children. Bones of cattle, sheep, pigs, and deer were unearthed, as well as stone hoes, axes, arrowheads, and mollusc shell sickles. The ceramics show close affinities to the proto-Lungshan complex of the Nuclear Area, and are characterized by gray, red, and black wares, mostly plain but with some incised, corded, and painted decorative patterns. The pots were handmade (in many cases, coiled) and wheel-made, and include *ting* tripods, pointed-bottomed jars, jugs, bowls, shallow and deep dishes and basins, and *tou* fruit stands.[58]

Similar assemblages have been discovered in the Lower Hanshui valley in northern Hupei province, but detailed reports are lacking. The Ch'ü-chia-ling assemblage in Ching-shan Hsien consists of gray, buff, and red eggshell-thin potsherds with painted designs and wheel marks in association with black pottery of the ring-footed type, red ware cups, and gray ware bowls with high, cut-out pedestal stands.[59] At Shih-chia-ho in T'ien-men Hsien, painted spindle whorls, pottery figurines of domestic and wild animals and fowls, and pottery kilns were found, possibly in that chronological order according to stratigraphic evidence. In association with the painted spindle whorls were painted bowls, cups, and small jugs, gray ware with high and cut-out pedestals, and other ring-footed wares and *kui* tripods. The pottery figurines depicted sheep, dogs, ducks, geese, turtle, fish, and several wild animals and birds, and were found in association with *ting* tripods, *kui* tripods, high cut-out pedestals, and other forms of pottery in gray, black, and red. Potsherds of checker impressions and cord marks and paddy husks and straws were found together with the pottery kilns. This sequence, the validity of which remains to be confirmed, seems to repeat the cultural succession seen in the Nuclear Area.[60] Other sites, where black pottery—some approaching the so-called typical black pottery of Shantung—red pottery, and gray ware, of tripod and ring-footed forms were recovered, are distributed

58. WW, 1959:7, 55–59.
59. Chang Yün-peng, *KKTH*, 1956:3, 11–21.
60. Ibid.

105

widely in northeastern Hupei, but a clear and complete account of them has not yet been made.[61]

The Pacific Seaboard The regions enumerated above are either within or peripheral to the Nuclear Area where the Yang-shao farmers first established "primary village-efficiency" and then evolved into a more advanced stage of cultural development. The Lungshanoid stage, however, witnessed the emancipation of the North China farmers from the natural confines of the Nuclear Area and their expansion into the vast alluvial plains of the eastern Pacific seaboard, extending from the Pohai Bay coasts of the north to the Yangtze delta and the coastal valleys of the south. In this vast area of distribution, the Lungshanoid assemblages exhibit marked regional variations. A regional characterization, however, cannot be made on the existing evidence, because the Lungshanoid distribution in this area is tangled with the problem of chronology; we are not yet able to distinguish chronological phases from regional variations. In the present volume, the entire Pacific seaboard is treated as a unit. Certain chronological generalizations are possible, however. First, there seems to have been an explosive expansion of the proto-Lungshan phase of the Nuclear Area into the Huaiho, the Yangtze delta, and the southeast coast. Subsequently, the later phrase of the Honan Lungshanoid probably penetrated only into northern Anhwei and western Shantung, regions close to the Honan area, whereas the rest of the eastern low country underwent developments of its own, only to be influenced by successive historical radiations from the Nuclear Area until the establishment of the Geometric Kingdoms in the East and the South (see Chapter 9), and the eventual sinicization under the Ch'in and Han empires.

The first phase of the eastern Lungshanoid, which can definitely be linked with the proto-Lungshan complex of western and northern Honan, is characterized by gray, red, and black wares, wheel-making of pottery, *ting* and *kui* tripods, and the absence or extreme rarity of *li* tripods, ceramic painting (Pl. II, lower), high and cut-out ring feet of *tou*, and other concurrent stone and bone indus-

61. Hsia Tun, KK, 1960:5, 1–6; Wang Chin, KK, 1960:4, 38–40; Kao Ying-chin, WWTKTL, 1957:12, 81–82; Hsü Sung-chün, KKTH, 1958:5, 32; Hsiao Mao, Chen An-yih, and Chen Te-hua, WWTKTL, 1956:6, 80; WWTKTL, 1956:1, 65–66; Kao Ying-chin and Chou Pao-chuan, WWTKTL, 1956:12, 49–52; Chang Yun-peng, KK, 1962:7, 339–44.

tries. It is best documented by Tz'u-ts'un (Kang-shang-ts'un) in T'eng Hsien [62] and Yü-chia-lin in P'ing-yin Hsien [63] in southwestern Shantung; Ch'ing-lien-kang in Huai-an Hsien,[64] and Hua-t'ing-ts'un in Hsin-yih Hsien [65] in northern Kiangsu (where the term "Ch'ing-lien-kang Culture" has been proposed for it); the burial site at Pei-yin-yang-ying near Nanking; [66] the so-called Lungshan phase in Shou Hsien [67] in northern Anhwei; Liang-chu [68] and Lao-ho-shan [69] near Hangchow in Chekiang; and the lower layer of Pei-ch'iu in Hsin-yang in southeastern Honan.[70] The elements of this phase can be found as far south as Formosa [71] and the Hai-feng region in coastal Kwangtung.[72] It undoubtedly represents a farming culture, and remains of both rice and millet have been unearthed from its sites. Architectural features as well as the practice of scapulimancy also link it with the proto-Lungshan in the north, although the habitations are in most cases located on hills or mounds because of the wet environment [73] (Pls. V, VI).

This widespread early Lungshanoid phase in the eastern low country may have been followed by three later cultural phases in the different regions. In northern Anhwei, southeastern Honan, and western Shantung, it was followed by the Honan phase of the

62. Liu Tun-yüan, *WWTKTL*, 1958:1, 50–52.
63. *KK*, 1959:6, 315–16.
64. Chao Ching-fang, *KKHP*, 9 (1955), 13–23.
65. Sung Po-ying, *WWTKTL*, 1956:7, 23–26.
66. Chao Ching-fang, *KKHP*, 1958:1, 7–23.
67. Wang Hsiang, *KKHP*, 2 (1947), 179–250.
68. Ho Tien-hsing, *Hang-hsien Liang-chu-chen chih shih-ch'i yü hei-t'ao*, Shanghai, Wu-yüeh Shih-ti Yen-chiu Hui, 1937; Shih Hsin-keng, *Liang-chu—Hang-hsien Ti-erh-ch'ü Hei-t'ao wei-hua i-chih ch'u-pu pao-kao*, Hangchow, Hsi hu Museum, 1938; S. S. Beath, *China Journal*, 31, 1939; S. Kaplan, *Archives of the Chinese Art Society of America*, 3 (1948/49), 13–42; Wang Chi-ying, *WWTKTL*, 1956:2, 25–28.
69. Wei Chü-hsien, ed., *Ku-tang hsin-shih-ch'i-shih-tai i-chih shih-chüeh pao-kao*, Shanghai, Soc. for the Study of Wu Yüeh History and Geography, 1936; Chiang Tsuan-chu, *KKHP*, 1958:2, 5–15; Tang Hua, *WWTKTL*, 1955:8, 69.
70. An Chin-huai, *KKHP*, 1959:1, 1–11; *WWTKTL*, 1954:6, 25–31.
71. Kanazeki Takeo, in *Symposia of Taiwan Cultures*, 1 (Taipei, 1943), 1–16; Kanazeki Takeo and Kokubu Naoichi, *Taiwan Wenhua*, 5, Taipei, 1949; Chang Kwang-chih, *SJA*, 12 (1956), 383.
72. Raphael Maglioni, *Hongkong Naturalist*, 8 (1938), 213–16, passim.
73. Chang Kwang-chih, *Chung-kuo tung-hai-an shih-ch'ien wen-hua chih fen-pu yü i-tung*; Yin Huang-chang, *Hua-tung hsin-shih-ch'i-shih-tai i-chih*, Shanghai, Hsüen-hsi-sheng-huo Press, 1955; Wang Chih-min, *KKTH*, 1955:1, 32–33; Tung Chu-chen, *KKHP*, 1957:2; Chiang Tsuan-chu, *KKHP*, 1959:4.

Lungshanoid, and in turn by the Shang civilization; this later Lungshanoid phase is indicated by the appearance of checker impressions on pottery and the abundance of *li* tripods.[74] In the Pohai Bay area, the early Lungshanoid seems to have evolved into the mature coastal Lungshan culture represented by Liang-ch'eng-chen, Ch'eng-tzu-yai, Ta-ch'eng-shan, and, possibly Yang-t'ou-wa, where cultural sophistication developed to a considerable extent and metallurgy may have been introduced from the already civilized western part of this region.[75] In the southern Huaiho drainage and in the Lower Yangtze, the Lungshanoid was followed by the cultural remains of the Geometric Kingdoms, which also probably came into being as a result of cultural contact.[76]

RECAPITULATION

The brief picture given above of the Lungshanoid stage of Chinese Neolithic may serve to show that the farmers of this stage still lived in village communities but, due to agricultural growth and population pressure, were beginning to expand into a vast area in the east and south hitherto underpopulated or unpopulated by men. As far as we can see from the available archaeological material, the Huaiho and the middle and lower Yangtze valleys can not be considered to have been a birthplace of farmers. The earliest farming cultures in this region were but elements of a widespread Lungshanoid horizon which centered in the Nuclear Area of North China and spread into these regions through pioneer farmers and settlers. It is true that these farmers may have found in the subtropical jungles and valleys in South China a habitat widely different from the one they were accustomed to, and that as a result they had to carry out new experiments in domesticating plants and animals. Rice, for instance, appeared in the various regions of China simultaneously about the beginning of this Lungshanoid horizon, and probably is one of the innovations of the

74. Li Ching-tan, *KKHP*, 2 (1947), 83–120; An Chin-huai, *KKHP*, 1959:1, 1–11. For the stratigraphical relation between the "Ch'ing-lien-kang culture" and the Lungshan, see Wang and Yü, *KK*, 1962:3, 111–16.
75. Li Chi et al., *Ch'eng-tzu-yai*; Liu Tun-yüan, *KKHP*, 1958:1, 25–42; Yüan Ming, *WWTKTL*, 1955:12, 20–41; Kanazeki, Miyake, and Mizuno, "Yang-t'ou-wa," *Archaeologia Orientalis*, 3; Chen Hui, Tang Yün-ming, and Sun Tê-hai, *KKHP*, 1959:3, 17–34.
76. Lo Tsung-chen, *KK*, 1962:3, 117–24.

northern farmers in the southern environment. But, as far as the first ideas and knowledge of plant cultivation and animal domestication are concerned, these areas of South China were not independent centers of the first inventions of agriculture. This is true for the rest of South China too, as will be discussed in the next chapter.

In the vast area in which the Lungshanoid farmers were distributed, regional cultural styles developed, such as those described above. A chronology of the whole Lungshanoid horizon should also be considered carefully. It seems to me that at least two cultural strata must be distinguished—two that have different regions of geographical distribution and contain divergent local styles. The first, to which the name of proto-Lungshan has been given for one of its regional facies, is generally characterized by *ting* and *kui* tripods, some ceramic painting, high and cut-out pedestals in the form of ring feet, and other concurrent features. It is distributed in the Weishui valley, the Lower Fenho valley, the Huangho valley in western and northern Honan, the Hanshui valley, the Huaiho valley, the Yangtze delta, and the southeastern coastal valleys. Subsequent development of this Lungshanoid horizon followed diverse paths in the various regions. In the Weishui and the Fenho valleys, distinctive local phases evolved to antedate the local historical periods. In western, northern, and southeastern Honan, western Shantung, and northern Anhwei, and possibly in northern Hupei and northern Kiangsu also, a later phase developed, characterized by the total disappearance of ceramic painting, the great development of *li* as well as *ting* tripods, the popularity of the paddle-and-anvil technique of pottery manufacture, and the checker pattern of ceramic impressed designs. In the Pohai Bay area, the earlier Lungshanoid phase moved in and evolved into the well-known Ch'eng-tzu-yai and Liang-ch'eng-chen assemblages. In the southern Huai-ho drainage and in the Yangtze delta, the early Lungshanoid phase continued until the impact was felt of metallurgy from the North China civilizations. This chronological alignment is a far cry from the current understanding of the Lungshan culture, but I think it is worthy of a test in further investigations.

Chapter Five

The Spread
of Agriculture
and Neolithic
Technology

Efforts have been made in the last two chapters to trace the development of the Neolithic farmers in North China and their expansion into East and South China. In other areas, a basically hunting-fishing subsistence persisted; during various periods in some regions, the hunter-fishers were exposed to the advanced farming cultures of the Huangho valley, and adopted for local use many neolithic technological elements such as polished stone tools and pottery, thus giving rise to cultural phases that can be described as "sub-Neolithic." [1] In other regions the hunter-fishers adopted the new ways of life and became part-time or full-time farmers. Such cultural transformations took place from the time that Yangshao farmers first appeared in the Nuclear Area through the subsequent Lungshanoid expansion and early historic periods. The discussion of such transformations is placed here—between the description of the Lungshanoid and the discussion of the emergence of historical civilization in North China—because the cultures in question are classified as "Neolithic." Actually, farming was not introduced into some regions until after the historical civilizations had already started in North China. This will become clear in the following sections, each dealing with a separate historical region.

1. Marija Gimbutas, "The Prehistory of Eastern Europe," *American School of Prehistoric Research Bulletin,* 20 (1956), 11.

SPREAD OF AGRICULTURE, TECHNOLOGY

Since the provincial boundaries have shifted back and forth several times during the present century, a geographical clarification of the title of this section is in order. In general terms, the area referred to is simply the northern part of North China proper and the southern fringes of Inner Mongolia, a region of relatively high altitude, with a steppe vegetation and drained by the northernmost section of the Huangho River, its many small tributaries, and the upper reaches of several rivers in the alluvial plains in the northwestern part of the Pohai Bay area. It is a relatively arid and barren area at the present, though oases, parklands, and large and small basins with stable water supplies may have characterized the landscape during the prehistoric period (Map 8).

The Ordos area in northern Shensi and southern Suiyüan is famous for its Upper Palaeolithic industries, and recent discoveries in the neighborhood of P'ien-kuan Hsien in northwestern Shansi and Ch'ing-shui-ho Hsien in southern Suiyüan appear to indicate Mesolithic assemblages characterized by microblade artifacts and points and scrapers made on "Mousterian" flakes, features resembling the Sha-yüan assemblage of the Lower Weishui valley in central Shensi.[2] Small arrowheads, small elongated scrapers, and microblades have been found in the Hei-liu-t'u-ho valley in Hengshan Hsien, in what may be a nonceramic context.[3] Ceramic assemblages, with and without evidence of agriculture, have been unearthed widely in Ch'ing-shui-ho, Chün-wang-ch'i, and Pao-t'ou.[4] The pottery is red, brown, or gray, of a fine or coarse paste; the red ware is often painted in black pigment, but cord-marking is characteristic of the red pottery. Bowls, jugs, and basins are common forms, but *li* tripods also occur occasionally. The stone industries contain two clearcut traditions: chipped microliths, in the form of blades, flakes, arrowheads, scrapers, and awls; and polished stone implements, including such agricultural implements

---

2. Chang Shen-shui, VP, 3 (1959), 47–56; An Chih-min, KK, 1959:10, 560.

3. Tung Chu-chen, KKHP, 1957:2, 11.

4. Egami and Mizuno, "Inner Mongolia and the Region of the Great Wall," *Archaeologia Orientalis*, ser. B, 1, 1935; J. Maringer, *Contribution to the Prehistory of Mongolia*; Wang Yu-ping, KKTH, 1955:5, 9–13; KKHP, 1957:1, 9–20; Li Yih-yu, WWTKTL, 1957:4, 26–28; Li Yih-yu, KKHP, 1959:2, 1–13; WW, 1961:9, 6, 12, 13; Lü Tsun-eh, KKHP, 1960:1.

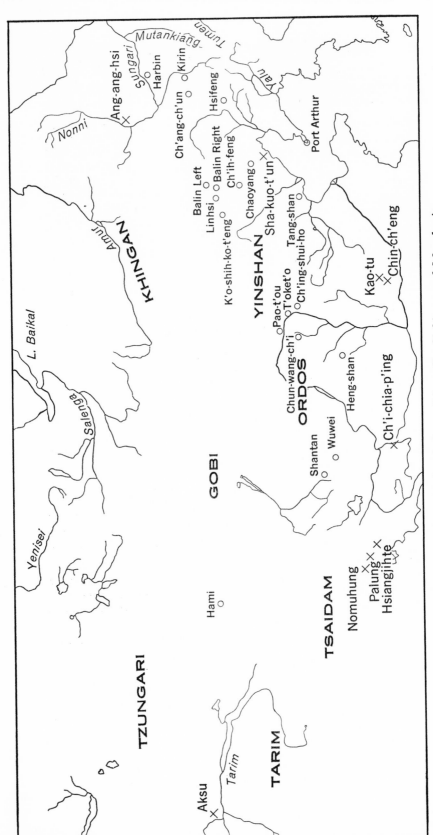

MAP 8. Important prehistoric sites in Inner Mongolia, Sinkiang, and Manchuria.

as mortars and pestles, hoes, knives, and sickles, in addition to axes and adzes. It is apparent that the Yangshao technology and sub-sistence patterns must have been introduced among the Micro-lithic hunter-fishers of this area, and the neolithic ways of life may have persisted here well into the historic periods. Subsequent arid conditions apparently did not favor the growth of civilization in the Ordos, and these Neolithic cultures were followed by steppe nomads.

To the east of the Ordos, in northern Shansi and northern Hopei, preceramic assemblages have not been found. Microlithic finds in a ceramic context have been discovered as far south as Chin-ch'eng Hsien and Kao-tu Hsien in southeastern Shansi.[5] But Yangshao types of sherds have been found in southeastern Shansi [6] and western Hopei,[7] and Microlithic assemblages mixed with the Yangshao type of red sherds have been uncovered in Shansi and Hopei.[8] Microlithic elements were still very conspicu-ously present in the Lungshanoid assemblages at Ta-ch'eng-shan in northern Hopei.[9] It seems likely, therefore, that this area had a Microlithic substratum into which Yangshao and Lungshanoid elements were introduced, with or without agriculture.

THE LIAOHO VALLEY, EASTERN MONGOLIA, AND SOUTHERN MANCHURIA

The Liaoho drainage is divided into two well-defined sections: the upper Liaoho valley in eastern Inner Mongolia and Jehol, consist-ing of two major tributaries, Hsi-liao or Sharamurun and Lao-ha, which drain the eastern fringes of the Mongolian plateau; and the lower Liaoho valley of the southern Manchurian erosion plain, immediately to the north of the Pohai Bay (See Map 8). The known cultural history of this region can be summarized as fol-lows: no preceramic industries have been found; there are cultural assemblages characterized by microlithic industries mixed with

5. Kuo Yüng, *KK*, 1959:2, 63.
6. Ibid.
7. Chao Yin-tang and Yang Chien-hao, *KKTH*, 1955:1, 45–46; Meng Chao-lin, *WWTKTL*, 1955:11, 73–76.
8. *KK*, 1959:7, 332–37; Li Chieh-min and Meng Chao-lin, *KKTH*, 1958:6, 45–46; Kuo Yüng, *KK*, 1959:2, 63; An Chih-min, *WWTKTL*, 1953:5/6, 143–52.
9. Chen Hui, Tang Yun-ming, and Sun Te-hai, *KKHP*, 1959:3, 21–22.

Yangshao and non-Yangshao ceramic features, some of which definitely show, while others conspicuously lack, evidence of agriculture and animal domestication; following these sub-Neolithic and Neolithic phases in a large part of this area, there were occupations of a nomadic kind of culture similar to the nomadic assemblages on the Ordosian steppe.

The best known prehistoric site in the Lao-ha River valley is the Hung-shan-hou site near Ch'ih-feng, discovered by Torii Ryuzo in 1908 and investigated by other scholars in 1924, 1930, and 1935.[10] Two phases of occupation have been distinguished here, the Painted Ware and the Red Ware. The Red Ware phase contains bronze artifacts and other Eastern Chou affinities, and the Painted Ware phase has been synchronized with the Yangshao Stage in North China. This Painted Ware phase undoubtedly has a northern Microlithic and sub-Neolithic cultural base, as indicated by microliths and brownish coarse pottery with loop and lug handles and combed, dentated, and rocker-stamped designs. Yangshao influence is strongly suggested by remains of thin-walled, handmade orange-red pottery of a fine texture, characterized by bowl and small-necked jar forms, and painted in geometric patterns of dark red and black pigment. The practice of agriculture is indicated by the remains of stone hoes, spades, knives, and pestles and mortars. Remains of cattle, sheep, pig, and horse bones were also found, as well as many spindle whorls of clay and artifacts of shell, bone, antler, and teeth. In 1943, what was probably a later settlement was found in the nearby village of Tung-pa-chia, also in Ch'ih-feng Hsien.[11] Stone and ceramic remains again indicate a northern Microlithic and sub-Neolithic base, but black pottery and *ting* tripods are found, possibly indicating Lungshanoid or later influences from North China rather than the Yangshao. The most significant feature of this site is that the whole village was surrounded by a wall of rocks. The village fortification and the arrangement of houses inside the compound (Fig. 10), which indicates the existence of a paramount chief in the village, seem to suggest that a tightened social organization also came into being in this part of China following the stage of the first farmers, as was the case in North China proper.

10. Hamada Kosaku and Mizuno Seiichi, "Ch'ih-feng: Hung-shan-hou," *Archaeologia Orientalis* ser. A, 6 (1938); Lü Tsun-eh, KKHP, 1958:3, 25–40.
11. Tung Chu-chen, KKTH, 1957:6, 15–22.

Sites in the Sharamurun River valley have been widely found in Lin-hsi Hsien, K'o-shih-k'o-t'eng Banner, Balin Left Banner, and Balin Right Banner.[12] Microlithic implements were found in most of the cultural assemblages, and the predominant pottery is brownish-gray or red in color, coarse in texture, and characterized by

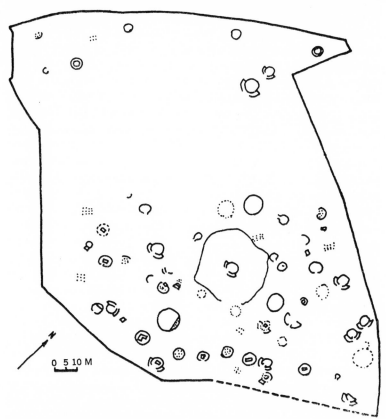

FIG. 10. The Tung-pa-chia site near Ch'ih-feng, Inner Mongolia. From Tung Chu-chen, *KKTH*, 1957:6, Fig. 2.

combed and dentated decorative designs. Evidence of contact with North China consists of rare painted sherds and a number of *li* tripods, probably introduced at different times. Remains of polished stone hoes and spades and large pestles and mortars at most of the sites suggest the prevalence of agriculture.

12. See note 4, above.

115

In the lower Liaoho valley on the southern Manchurian plains, a cultural sequence similar to that of the upper Liaoho can be postulated. Cultural assemblages found here show a mixture of microlithic implements, combed ware, painted pottery, polished stone axes, knives, and sickles, black pottery, checker-impressed sherds, and *li* tripods.[13] A northern sub-Neolithic base characterized by microliths and combed pottery can be assumed, and Huangho Neolithic influences seem to have reached this area in successive waves, as indicated by the predominantly Yangshao elements in the Sha-kuo-t'un site [14] and the predominantly Lungshanoid features at Shao-hu-ying-tzu-shan in Chao-yang Hsien.[15] The Liaotung Peninsula also seems to have a similar cultural sequence, although it does not appear to have been exposed to the Yangshao influence but to have been heavily influenced by the Lungshanoid horizon, as shown at the site of Yang-t'ou-wa.[16]

It is still too early to say whether this Liaoho valley was populated during Mesolithic periods, evidence of which is completely lacking. It is possible to say, however, that a significant population of this area was achieved by the Microlithic hunter-fishers of the northern part of China whose culture was enriched by the introduction of North Chinese neolithic technology and/or agriculture. A neolithic way of life prevailed in this area until the Eastern Chou and Han periods, when nomadic tribes roamed on the upper Liaoho steppes and Han-Chinese settlements began to penetrate this region from North China.

THE SUNGARI VALLEY

The sub-Neolithic and Neolithic cultures of the Sungari valley in central Manchuria [17] (See Map 8) are representative of the entire northern peripheries in that the native cultural substratum in this region is well established by excavated materials and can be clearly distinguished from the Neolithic influences from the

13. Liu Chien, *KKTH*, 1955:6, 13–16; Liu Chien, *KKTH*, 1956:6, 19–25; Wang Tseng-hsin, *KKTH*, 1958:1, 1–4.

14. Andersson, *PS*, ser. D, 1, 1923.

15. Liu Chien, *KKTH*, 1956:6, 19–25.

16. Burnished red potsherds similar to sherds of the Yangshao stage in North China were reported from Wen-chia-t'un in the Port Arthur region of southern Liaotung Peninsula, but these were uncovered from a Lungshanoid context; see Kanazeki et al, "Yang-t'ou-wa." *Archaeologia Orientalis*, 3, 81, note 6.

17. Chang Kwang-chih, *SJA*, 17 (1961), 56–74.

Huangho valley. This native cultural base is represented by the microlithic and nonceramic assemblages in the Harbin area (see p. 43), apparently a continuation of the Upper Palaeolithic in the North, and by the microlithic and ceramic assemblages at the Ang-ang-hsi site in the Lower Nonni valley [18] and a series of sites in the Lower Mutankiang.[19] The ceramic features as well as stone and bone inventories, characterized by flat-bottomed pottery and bone harpoons and needle cases, are definitely linked with the sub-Neolithic cultures on the Pacific coast.

Distinct Huangho Neolithic influences upon the native sub-Neolithic substratum are found in the southwestern part of this area, around the cities of Kirin and Ch'ang-ch'un, where agriculture (millet) and pig domestication, as well as pottery tripods, polished stone knives, and stone sickles have been found.[20] The same cultural traditions continued in this area even when The Han Dynasty and later civilizations became firmly established in the Liaoho valley and Chinese cultural elements appeared in the native artifactual inventories.[21]

THE TUMEN VALLEY

The Tumen valley of southeastern Manchuria has an early cultural history similar to that of the northern and eastern Sungari in that the native, northern sub-Neolithic cultural substratum is strongly marked, and that, although the impact of Huangho civilization is evidenced by occasional import items, hunting-fishing continued to be the principal mode of subsistence during most of its cultural history.[22] The Tumen valley can best be described as a phase of the Pacific cultural tradition of northeastern Asia.

18. Liang Ssu-yung, BIHP, 4 (1932), 1–44; A. S. Loukashkin, GSoC, Bull. 11 (1931), 171–81; Loukashkin, China Journal, 15 (1931), 198–99; Lü Tsun-lu, KK, 1960:4, 15–17.

19. Chao Shan-tung, KK, 1960:4, 20–22; Komai Kazuchika, Kōkogaku Zasshi, 24 (1934), 11–16; Komai Kazuchika and Mikami Tsuguo, Kōkogaku Zasshi, 26 (1936), 487–96; Li Wen-hsin, KKHP, 7 (1954), 61–75; Okuda Naoshige, Jenruigaku Zasshi, 54 (1939), 459–63; V. V. Ponosov, Bull. Inst. Sci. Res., Manchukuo, 2 (1938), 23–30; Tan Hua-sha and Sun Hsiu-jen, KK, 1960:4, 23–30.

20. Tung Chu-chen, KKTH, 1955:2, 5–12; Tung Chu-chen, KKHP, 1957:3, 31–39; Wang Ya-lou, KK, 1960:4, 31–34.

21. Li Wen-hsin, KKHP, 7 (1954), 61–75; Wen Chung-yih, BIE, 5 (1958), 115–210. chen, KKHP, 1957:3, 31–39; Kang Chia-hsing, KKTH, 1956:6, 25–30.

22. An Chi-min, Hsüeh-yüan, 2 (Nanking, 1948), 26–36; Tung Chu-

Geographically, western Kansu, Chinghai, and Sinkiang are but parts of a huge steppe, desert, and oasis belt extending from the Caspian and Black Seas in the west to the Upper Huangho valley in the east. This has proved to be a frequently-used corridor for the transmission of cultural ideas and for trade between the East and the West during historical periods. Therefore, scholars had some grounds for speculating that there may have been a similar route of cultural diffusion during an earlier period, whereby the first ideas of agriculture and the first ideas of civilization could have been transmitted from the Near East and Central Asia to the Huangho valley.[23] This conjecture, however, remains to be borne out by actual archaeological findings in the area.

From a Huangho terrace near Chung-wei in Ninghsia province, Teilhard de Chardin and C. C. Young in 1930 discovered remains of chipped implements which they regarded as Upper Palaeolithic, and probably of the Ordosian tradition.[24] Nonceramic assemblages which may be of relatively recent periods have been located by the same scholars near Hami in eastern Sinkiang, apparently of the Microlithic horizon.[25] Inasmuch as these sites remain unexcavated, the Mesolithic stratum has yet to be established. But microlithic implements in association with pottery have been collected widely in southern Ninghsia, Chinghai, and Sinkiang, and even pebble tools predominate in one or two known assemblages in a ceramic context, such as the site of Aksu.[26] The pottery found in some of the sites has no definitely discernible counterpart in the rest of China, for it is of a generally nondescript kind and may actually be quite late. But painted sherds have been collected from many parts of the Chinese Northwest, and in the eastern fringes of this region they occur in whole Neolithic assemblages.[27] As far as the

23. E.g., Carl W. Bishop, *Antiquity*, 28 (1933), 389–404; Bishop, *Origin of the Far Eastern Civilization*, Washington, D.C., Smithsonian Institution, 1942.

24. Teilhard de Chardin and Young Chung-chien, GSoC, Bull., 12 (1932), 103–4.

25. Ibid.

26. Folke Bergman, *Archaeological Researches in Sinkiang* (Stockholm, Bokförlags aktiebolaget Thule, 1939), pp. 13–37; Ning Tu-hsüeh, KK, 1959:7, 329–31; Shih Shu-ching, WW, 1960:6, 22–31; Li Yü-chun, KK, 1959:3, 153–54; Teilhard de Chardin and Young, GSoC, Bull., 12, 1932.

27. See Bergman, Li, and Teilhard de Chardin and Young in note 26, above.

available archaeological record goes, we are sure of the following three facts: (a) archaeological assemblages that can be considered Neolithic are confined to the eastern part of Kansu east of Chiu-ch'üan Hsien and the eastern part of Chinghai in the Huangshui valley, and these are definitely extensions of the Kansu-Yangshao horizon; (b) the ceramic assemblages in Sinkiang and western Chinghai contain elements which indicate that a native Microlithic and sub-Neolithic substratum may have persisted in this region into early historical times; and (c) those ceramic assemblages that contain the so-called "painted pottery" in Sinkiang and western Chinghai are probably late in time, in most cases considerably later than the Neolithic of North China, as indicated by the metal objects sometimes associated with them. Andersson declared in 1943 that "as far as the Yang Shao time is concerned, Sinkiang remains an unknown quantity." [28] Extensive investigations in Sinkiang since 1943 have failed to make any significant changes in this view, except by suggesting the probability that during the Yangshao stage of North China Neolithic, Sinkiang played little if any role in the shaping of cultural history in areas to the east of it.

But the Yangshao farmers definitely brought the food-producing way of life into eastern Kansu and the Huangshui valley in eastern Chinghai. After the Lungshanoid farmers evolved in the Nuclear Area to the east, the Yangshao stage in Kansu and eastern Chinghai seems to have been gradually replaced by several new cultural phases whose origins remain unclear but which seem to have some sort of connection with the sub-Neolithic and possibly Neolithic peoples to the north and west in the steppe regions. Three such phases can now be defined, namely, the Ch'i-chia phase, the Shan-tan (or Ssu-pa) phase, and the Tsaidam (or Nomuhung) phase (see Maps 7 and 8).

The Ch'i-chia phase, so named after its type site at Ch'i-chia-p'ing in Ning-ting Hsien in the T'ao-ho valley of eastern Kansu, was discovered in 1923 by Andersson and was regarded by him as the earliest Neolithic Culture in Kansu, from which the Yangshao Culture in Kansu and Honan was ultimately derived.[29] This thesis,

---

28. Andersson, BMFEA, 15, 280.
29. Andersson, "Preliminary Report on Archaeological Research in Kansu," GSuC, ser. A, 5; Andersson, Children of the Yellow Earth; Andersson, BMFEA, 15.

to which some people still subscribe, is—let it be made completely clear once and for all—completely fallacious. Stratigraphical evidence in the entire area of its distribution has shown that the Ch'i-chia phase followed the Kansu Yangshao horizon, but preceded the Chou strata in the Upper Weishui and several other contemporary local eneolithic cultures to the west.[30] Its area of distribution is confined to the valleys of the T'ao, the Upper Weishui, and the Upper Hsi-han-shui, all in the eastern part of Kansu. Its pottery is characterized by yellow and buff ware with combed or incised decorative designs and especially by a kind of flat-bottomed jar with a constricted neck, flaring mouth, and two large vertical loop handles on the shoulder. Painted pots are seen occasionally, and cord-marking is another surface feature. Remains of millet were found at the Ta-ho-chuang site in Lin-hsia Hsien, oracle bones of sheep scapula at Ta-ho-chuang and Ch'in-wei-chia in Lin-hsia Hsien, oracle bones of cattle, sheep, and pig scapula at the Huang-niang-t'ai site in Wu-wei Hsien, and copper ornaments and small objects at all three of the last named sites.[31] Bones of pigs, cattle, and sheep and remains of hemp have also been found.[32] At the Ta-ho-chuang site were also discovered rings of small rocks on the ground, possibly a religious construction, nearby which were the burials of sacrificed animals. Without question, the Ch'i-chia phase represents the culture of farmers, and their farming tradition was probably introduced from the Yangshao horizon. But there is plenty of room for dispute as to its cultural affiliations. Its similarities to the Yangshao, the Weishui phase of the Lungshanoid, and Western Chou civilizations have been noted,[33] but these could easily be accounted for by cultural contacts during various time periods. It is possible that in this area, which is adjacent to the dry steppes of Northwest China and Inner

30. The stratigraphical position of the Ch'i-chia tradition over the Kansu Yangshao layers has been observed in a number of sites in the T'ao-ho valley and the upper Weishui; see: Hsia Nai, KKHP, 3 (1948), 101–17; An Chih-min, KKTH, 1956:6, 9–19; Chang Hsüeh-cheng, KKTH, 1958:5, 1–5; Chang Hsüeh-cheng, KKTH, 1958:9, 36–49; Kuo Tê-yüng, KKTH, 1958:7, 6–16; Kuo Tê-yüng, KKTH, 1959:3, 138–42, 146.

31. Cheng Nai-wu and Hsieh Tuan-chü, KK, 1960:3, 9–12; Kuo Tê-yüng, KKTH, 1958:7, 6–16; Shih Tao, KK, 1961:1, 6; Kuo Tê-yüng, KKHP, 1960:2, 59–60.

32. Bylin-Althin, BMFEA, 18, 457–58.

33. Wang Po-hung, Chung Shao-lin, and Chang Chang-shou, KK, 1959:10, 517; Jen Pu-yün, KK, 1959:7, 323–25, 345; Kuo Tê-yüng, KK, 1959:3, 138–42, 146; Shih Tao, KK, 1961:1, 10.

Mongolia, and where the climatic conditions of the present time tend to be on the arid side, the Yangshao farming culture was not well adapted, and was replaced by cultural phases having a native sub-Neolithic base but receiving considerable cultural influence from the Yangshao farmers. The nature of its contemporary cultural phases and the many local cultural traditions which followed the Ch'i-chia seem to indicate this possibility.

In Shan-tan, Min-lo, Yüng-ch'ang, and Chiu-ch'üan counties of central Kansu, immediately to the northwest of the Ch'i-chia phase area, there was probably another cultural phase contemporary with and possibly related to the Ch'i-chia. This could be named the Shan-tan phase, after its type site, discovered in 1948, at Ssu-pa-t'an in Shan-tan Hsien. This phase is characterized by agriculture, stone phallus models, and a distinctive kind of pottery. The pottery is of a coarse texture and often painted in pigment of very thick consistency which makes the designs project out from the ceramic surface. The basic form of pottery is again the double-handled jar. This phase may very well be a regional branch of the Ch'i-chia, but its distinctive pottery painting and the large number of phallus models seem to warrant considering it as a separate cultural tradition.[34]

The Tsaidam phase is thus far represented by three sites in Nomuhung, Palung, and Hsiangjihte counties of northwestern Chinghai, south of the Tsaidam basin.[35] These were discovered in 1959, and are characterized by *tells* as habitation sites, wool fabrics, plain pottery jugs and basins with straight walls, and tent rings of sand bags. Copper objects were found at one of the sites. These remains apparently indicate a food-producing culture leaning toward animal domestication and nomadic life, but the rarity of metal objects seems to provide grounds for synchronizing this cultural phase with the Ch'i-chia to the east. It may very well be one of the cultural phases ancestral to the later Neolithic and metal age nomads on the steppes, but we are still far from knowing enough about it to make further historical inferences.

Stratigraphical evidence in eastern Kansu and eastern Chinghai shows that the Ch'i-chia phase was followed by several small, local cultural phases possessing metallurgy, with some inclining toward

34. An Chih-min, *KKHP*, 1959:3, 7–15.
35. Chao Sheng-shen and Wu Ju-tso, *WW*, 1960:6, 37–40; Wu Ju-tso, *KK*, 1961:1, 16.

animal domestication, and carrying on the painted pottery tradition; such include the well-known phases of Andersson's Hsin-tien, Ssu-wa, and Sha-ching "cultures" and the newly identified "T'ang-wang Culture," all of which will be discussed further in a later chapter.

THE SOUTHWEST

The Greater Chinese Southwest includes the Red basin of Szechwan and the hills and plateaus of Kwangsi, Yünnan, Kweichou, and western Kwangtung, on the upper reaches of the Pearl River, the Mekong, the Menam, and the Irrawaddy (see Map 4). When farmers began to appear in North China and while a good deal of "revolutionary" activity was going on there, the Mesolithic population in the Southwest described in Chapter 2 apparently continued their old ways of life. During the later phases of their occupation, however, polished stone implements and pottery gradually made an appearance in the industrial assemblages which have been unearthed in this area.[36] The ceramic phases at the site at Hsi-chiao-shan in Kwangtung, which was mentioned earlier, show conclusively that they were continuations from the preceding non-ceramic stratum,[37] a conclusion which is in complete agreement with evidence from Indo-China.[38] The life and society of these peoples are little known archaeologically, but apparently they continued to have a hunting-fishing-collecting existence and made great use of mollusc shells and the small game of the forest. Partially polished (the so-called proto-neoliths) and totally ground stone tools must have increased the efficiency of their implement kits, and pottery of reddish color and with corded and basketed surface treatment was made and used widely. Evidence of their occupation, however, is still largely confined to their former habitat, though traces of chipped stone implements and corded pottery

36. Cheng Te-kun, *Archaeological Studies in Szechwan*; Liu Chi-yih, *WWTKTL*, 1958:3, 69–71; R. Maglioni, *Hongkong Naturalist*, 8 (1938), 211; W. Schofield, *PFEPC*, 3d (1940), 259; D. J. Finn, *Hongkong Naturalist*, 7 (1936), 258; Chang Kwang-chih, *Ta-lu-tsa-chih*, 9 (1954), 4–8.
37. Mo Chih, *KKHP*, 1959:4, 1–15.
38. Henri Mansuy, "Stations préhistoriques dans les cavernes du massif calcaire de Bac-Son (Tonkin)," *Mémoirs du Service Géologique de l'Indochine*, 11, fasc. 2, 1924; H. Mansuy, "Nouvelles découvertes dans les cavernes du massif calcaire de Bac-Son (Tonkin)," *Mem. Serv. Geol. l'Indochine*, 12, fasc. 1, 1925.

have been found along the Kwangtung coast as far as Hong Kong, and on the island of Taiwan.[39]

Agriculture and a fully neolithic industry and culture did, nevertheless, enter the Southwest before the later Chinese historical civilizations made their full impact felt in this region. We cannot be certain whether agriculture was brought in by immigrants from North China, as was the case in the rest of South China. The possibility cannot be ruled out that the Mesolithic and sub-Neolithic populations in the Southwest adopted agriculture as a result of intensified cultural contacts. For the time being, only the following can be said for certain: (a) Agriculture did not originate in this region independently. (b) The Chinese Southwest was accessible from the Nuclear Area of North China by no less than two main routes: the Upper Chialingkiang which connects the Red basin with eastern Kansu, and the Yangtze valley around Yih-ch'ang in Hupei, which opens into the Red basin from the Hanshui valley. The latter route, significantly, is dotted with prehistoric sites of a neolithic character, which indicate that it may actually have been so employed. (c) The Neolithic assemblages in the Southwest show distinctive local characteristics, but at the same time unmistakable elements that are attributable to cultural influences from the Nuclear Area during Yangshao and Lungshanoid stages. Evidence of agriculture notwithstanding, most of the Southwestern Neolithic sites show the great importance of fishing and/or mollusc shell collecting, but hunting does not appear highly significant, for stone arrowheads and other hunting implements are as a rule rare. The stone inventories include the highly characteristic shouldered axes, remains of which have been unearthed from Ya-an in Sikang in the west, to the island of Hainan in the east.[40] The ceramics are characterized by a predominantly yellowish hue, the long persistence of corded red ware, the abundance of flat-bottomed and concave-bottomed forms, and

39. Schofield, Finn, and Chang, in note 36, above.
40. The shouldered axe has been discovered widely in the Chinese Southwest: Szechwan (Cheng Te-kun, *Archaeological Studies in Szechwan*, p. 60), Yünnan (Huang Chan-yüeh and Chao Hsüeh-chien, *KK*, 1959:4, 175; Wu Chin-ting et al., *Yünnan Ts'ang Erh ching k'ao-ku pao-kao*, Lichuang, National Museum, 1942, p. 37), Kweichou (*KKTH*, 1956:3, 48–50; *WWTKTL*, 1955: 9, 67–69), Sikang (Wei Ta-yih, *WWTKTL*, 1958:9, 48–49;) Kwangsi (Jung Kuan-hsiung, *WWTKTL*, 1956:6, 58–59), Kwangtung (Mo Chih, *WWTKTL*, 1956:11, 42; Mo Chih, *KKTH*, 1957:6, 9–12; Mo Chih, *KKTH*, 1956:4, 5–6), and Hainan (Jung Kuan-hsiung, *KKTH*, 1956:2, 38–41).

123

the general use of shell and grit as temper. Painted pottery, black pottery, stone knives and sickles, and pottery tripods, which may be indicative of North China influences, are all present at various sites, but are relatively rare. Geometric ware similar to that of the Southeast is seen only along the eastern fringes of this region, while the characteristic southeastern stone implement, the stepped adze, is not present at all. Aside from these generalizations, well-documented excavated materials are available for only eastern Szechwan in the Yangtze valley, and in the regions around Lakes Erh-hai and Tien-ch'ih in the province of Yünnan.

Neolithic remains have been located in an area approximately one kilometer in length on the terraces of both banks of the Han-ching-kou River near Chung Hsien, in eastern Szechwan.[41] These remains, investigated by the Szechwan Museum in the middle fifties, were concentrated in six clusters on the western bank and another on the eastern. The sites on the western bank, apparently residential settlements, have yielded a large number of sand-tempered, corded ceramics of the *li* tripod and round-bottomed jug forms, together with small numbers of gray and black sherds. Basket impression and checker stamping are both evidenced on some sherds, and some of the rim sherds are painted in black pigment. Stone axes, adzes, chisels, hoes, and pestles, chipped, chipped /polished, and totally ground, have been discovered, together with remains of horses, sheep, pigs, and deer, a human skull, a large number of fish bones, and many mollusc shells. The site on the eastern bank, 100 by 50 meters in size, has produced a large number of pebbles, blanks, and finished stone tools from what was possibly a workshop site, near which was a dwelling house. Seen as a whole, the Chung Hsien sites show significant similarities to the late Yangshao and early Lungshanoid stages in southwestern Honan and Hupei, the regions just to the east of eastern Szechwan. Painted pottery sherds have been unearthed in several sites near Wu-shan Hsien, further down the Yangtze, and such cultural remains continue into Hupei, concentrating in the Yih-tu and Kui-chou territories [42] (Fig. 11).

No less than nine Neolithic sites have been located on the

41. Yüan Ming-shen, *KK*, 1959:8, 393–97; Yüan Ming-shen and Pang Yu-lin, *KKTH*, 1958:5, 31–32.

42. Cheng Te-kun, *Archaeological Studies in Szechwan*, p. 105; Chen Pei-hsü, *WW*, 1959:5, 75; *WW*, 1961:11, 15.

eastern shore of the Lake Tien-ch'ih in central eastern Yünnan [43] (see Map 14). Most of these sites can be described as shell mounds or kitchen middens, consisting of compact layers of molluscan shells (most of which have been knocked open) mixed with a large number of potsherds, some stone implements, and a few shell artifacts. The stone implements consist of shouldered axes, net sinkers with a constricted waist, perforators, and grinding stones. Potsherds from these kitchen middens have been grouped

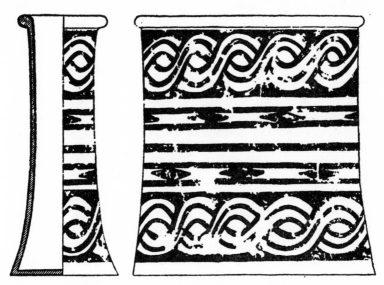

FIG. 11. A painted pottery excavated from the Ho-pao-hsi site, near Ta-hsi, in eastern Szechwan. From KK, 1959:8, 400.

into four classes: (a) Red ware of fine texture, predominantly handmade (coiled), tempered with paddy husks. This pottery is generally of small size, with a plain surface, and in the form of cups, small bowls, and shallow dishes with a flat or concave base. This ware makes up a large percentage of the sherds uncovered from such sites. (b) Gray ware with grit or shell temper, made on wheels and sometimes slipped and then burnished. Pottery of this class, generally larger in size, includes jugs with straight or flaring mouths, basins with two handles, and concave-based cups, and its

43. Huang Chan-yüeh and Chao Hsüeh-chien, KK, 1959:4, 173–75, 184; Sun Tai-chu, WWTKTL, 1957:11, 47. For more recent work in the Tien-ch'ih area, see KK, 1961:1, 46–49.

incised or impressed decoration includes feather patterns, lozenges, wavy parallel lines, cross-hatches, basket designs, and rows of dots. (c) Yellow-slipped ware with grit or shell temper, wheel- or mold-made, in the forms of basins, cups, and ring-footed vessels. (d) Orange-yellowish ware with grit or shell tempers, sometimes decorated with cord marks and checker impressions. Stone arrowheads were found here, but the remains of rice grains and husks imprinted or imbedded in the pottery of the first class suggest the importance of rice farming.

Farming terrace fields were identified by Wu Chin-ting in the Ta-li region near Erh-hai Lake during the late thirties at the sites of Ma-lung and Fo-ting on the slopes of the Tien-ts'ang Mountains.[44] Natural creeks must have been utilized here for irrigation purposes, and semisubterranean houses have been excavated. Differing from the Tien-ch'ih region, however, the Ta-li pottery is characterized by spouted jars, *ting* tripods, and stamped designs. Stone sickles and the absence of kitchen middens in the Ta-li area further distinguish it from the Tien-ch'ih phase, and some archaeologists contend that the latter might have been slightly earlier in time.

Satisfactory stratigraphic evidence indicates that such neolithic farming settlements appeared in the Southwest after the sub-Neolithic phase, but prior to the metal civilizations to be described in a later chapter. The origins of pottery and agriculture in this area are unquestionably to be found in North China, as is indicated by the stone inventories and the stylistic similarities in ceramics, by the crops planted in both of these regions, and by the continued importance of fishing and collecting in the Southwest. Such Neolithic cultures provided a background for the appearance of the subsequent indigenous civilizations in the middle of the first millennium B.C. under the strong influence of the Eastern Chou civilization in the areas to the north and the east.

GENERAL CONCLUSIONS

The above brief descriptions of the emergence of pottery and agriculture in areas peripheral to the Nuclear Area culture and its direct derivatives in Central and South China may serve to demonstrate the pattern of cultural growth in these regions. It is clear that the hunting-fishing Mesolithic populations continued

44. Wu Chin-ting et al., *Yünnan Ts'ang Erh ching k'ao-ku pao-kao.*

to occupy their original habitat after the neolithic ways of life began in the Nuclear Area of North China, but that they gradually adopted the technology of ceramic making and stone polishing from the Huangho Neolithic and from other Neolithic sources outside of China. It is also clear, then, that their remains are best described as sub-Neolithic. Agriculture and animal domestication, furthermore, were introduced into some of these regions, and the Neolithic transformation process took place gradually. The whole process and pattern of cultural assimilations can be elaborated and clearly understood when some of the early cultural history of the regions adjacent to China is taken into consideration. While a lengthy discussion of these adjacent regions is not possible in this volume, some general remarks will prove helpful.

The northern Asiatic regions to the west and north of the Huangho valley and immediately adjacent to it can be grouped on the basis of vegetation and topography into three groups: the steppe-desert zone of Central Asia, Sinkiang, Mongolia, and southwestern Siberia; the taiga zone around Lake Baikal and the Upper Lena, the Selenga, and the Amur; and the Pacific coast from the Okhotsk down to the coasts of Korea. Sub-Neolithic and Neolithic cultures in these regions more or less follow similar subdivisions. The taiga culture may be omitted from discussion for the present, for the reason that the region directly adjacent to it, northernmost Manchuria, which is separated from Lake Baikal by the Khingan Mountains, is archaeologically unexplored. The available archaeological evidence from central Manchuria in the Sungari valley, as mentioned above, indicates more direct affiliations with the Pacific coast than with the taiga zone to the north.

The northwestern part of China, extending from eastern Mongolia through Sinkiang, is the eastern portion of the steppe-desert belt that consists of Russian Turkestan and eastern European steppes as well as Northwest China, and the Microlithic cultural assemblages from the latter region resemble the Kelteminar complex to the west. This complex is characterized by microblade implements which show considerable elaboration but which are rarely retouched bifacially, and seems to suggest a whole series of local cultures adapted to a similar natural environment. According to A. A. Formozov, the "best witness for the ethnic diversity of this large culture area is the variation of pottery types found within it." [45] In the Chinese peripheries, pottery elements in association

45. A. A. Formozov, *American Antiquity*, 27 (1961), 87.

with microlithic implements can be classified into three groups: those that show connections with the Huangho valley, such as some of the painted pottery and the *li* and *ting* tripods; those that show connections with the Kelteminar complexes in southwestern Siberia and Khazakstan, such as the combed and some of the incised pottery; and those that show affiliations with neither, such as the brownish and plain-surfaced wares of eastern Mongolia. This may lead to the conclusion that the Microlithic assemblages in the northern frontiers of China, instead of belonging to a single cultural complex (such as the so-called "Gobi Culture"),[46] may represent a series of local survivals of the Upper Palaeolithic hunting-fishing cultures, which adopted ceramic and other neolithic technological traits compatible with their local environment and cultural ecology from China and from their northern and western neighbors. Some of these groups in more favorable environments had even adopted agriculture and animal domestications. This process as observed in northern frontiers of China is parallel, for example, to that seen in the eastern Caspian areas where pottery and food-production were introduced from the Nuclear Area of Iran, leading to a series of food-producing assemblages such as the Jeitun Culture of Jeitun-Tepe and Anau near Ashkabad.[47] The steppe zone undoubtedly also served as a route of cultural movement and diffusion between the high cultural centers in the East and in the West. In the current archaeological record, we see two radiating centers, one in the Iraq-Iran area and the other in the Huangho, which spread their influence across the intervening steppes from opposite directions and made scattered contacts. We do not see, however, that the steppe zone during the sub-Neolithic and the Neolithic stages served as route of cultural transmission from one of the high culture centers to the other.

The influence of the steppe culture phase tapers off toward the east and is only weakly felt in southern and central Manchuria, which may legitimately be classed, during the sub-Neolithic and Neolithic stages, with the Pacific coast traditions. During the several millennia before the Christian era, the regions in north-eastern Asia in Manchuria, Korea, and the Maritime Province of the U.S.S.R. can probably be said to belong to a single culture area characterized by flat-bottomed and straight-walled pottery, shell collecting, fishing, and sea-mammal hunting, as well as a distinctive

46. Cheng Te-kun, *Prehistoric China*, p. 52.
47. M. E. and V. M. Masson, *Cahiers d'histoire mondiale*, 5, 1959.

complex of bone artifacts such as barbed and (occasionally) toggle harpoons, bone armors, and needle cases made of bird bones.[48] This phase of culture is of considerable antiquity on the islands off the coast and in scattered areas on the coast. The sub-Neolithic cultures in the Sungari and in the Tumen valley appear to be the interior phases of this same cultural tradition. It is upon such a tradition of culture that the Neolithic farmers' cultural influences were imposed from the Huangho valley to the southwest. Farming, however, seems to have been introduced only into the Upper Sungari, where ecology was permissible, while elsewhere in central and eastern Manchuria the archaic hunting-fishing cultures persisted into historic periods.

In South China, the early Recent period hunter-fishers were apparently part of the widespread population whose cultural remains, discovered throughout all of mainland Southeast Asia, bear striking resemblances from region to region, and which have been named the Hoabinhian after their type region. It has been suggested that in northern Indo-China the Hoabinhian horizon, characterized by crude pebble choppers, was followed by a Bacsonian horizon, a continuation of the previous Hoabinhian but with the addition of ceramics and partially polished stone implements. Skeletal remains from Hoabinhian and Bacsonian strata, similar to those found in southwest China, bear Oceanic Negroid features. Lungshanoid farmers coming down from the Huangho valley not only assimilated or replaced the hunting-fishing-collecting population of Southwest China, but also may very well have been responsible for the emergence of agriculture in a large part of Southeast Asia.[49] Furthermore, the Neolithic cultural distributions in Southeast Asia suggest further extensions into the South Seas, following the subdivision of Neolithic cultures of South China. Shouldered axes and corded ware are characteristic of the Indo-Chinese Neolithic as well as the Chinese Southwest, whereas rectangular stone axes, stepped adzes, and many other cultural traits are common to both southeastern China and the eastern part of Malaysia and some parts of Oceania.[50]

48. A. P. Okladnikov, *Proc. 32d Internatl. Cong. Amer.*, 1958, pp. 545–56.

49. See the special issue on Sa-huynh pottery relationships in Southeast Asia of *AP*, 3, 1959.

50. Robert von Heine-Geldern, *Anthropos*, 27, 1932; H. O. Beyer, "Philippine and East Asian Archaeology and Its Relation to the Origin of the Pacific Islands Population," *Bull. Natl. Res. Counc. Phil.*, 29, 1948.

Chapter Six

The Emergence

of Civilization

in North China

THE LEGENDARY BEGINNINGS

Before the advent of scientific archaeology in China, the traditional historians had all the earliest parts of Chinese history accounted for—with myths, legends, and pseudo histories. There were accounts of the creation of the universe, often attributed to P'an-ku, its catastrophic destruction together with the deluge, which is considered to be the deed of Kung-kung, and its reconstruction by Nü-wa, who is sometimes said to have also created human beings. Later in the sequence came legendary monarchs and cultural heroes, sometimes schematized as the Three Sovereigns (San Huang) and the Five Emperors (Wu Ti), who invented dwellings, fire, agriculture, writing, and social and political institutions. These were followed by the Three Dynasties, Hsia, Shang, and Chou, considered even by scholars to initiate the historical period.

Historian-critics of early twentieth century China, who demanded proof other than documentary records for these early historic events, accepted the existence of the Chou Dynasty, the last of the Three Dynasties, which is solidly established beyond any doubt, but were skeptical of everything before the Chou. All of the pre-Chou legendary data, according to such historian-critics as Ku Hsieh-kang, were probably fabricated by scholars during and after the Han Dynasty for philosophic and political purposes. The archaeological excavations conducted by the Academia Sinica during the late twenties and early thirties at An-yang in northern Honan, believed to be the last capital city of the Shang Dynasty, have established the existence of this ancient dynasty with scien-

130

tific "proof" acceptable even to the historian-critics. This has led many historians to consider favorably the possibility that the literary account on the Hsia Dynasty in Ssu-ma Chien's *Shih Chi*, whose description of the Shang history and the royal genealogy has been borne out almost completely by the archaeological findings of An-yang, may also have a great deal of truth in it. There may have been, they contend, a Hsia Dynasty after all, which the archaeologist's spade may eventually uncover. But then what about the creation, the cultural heroes, and the pre-Hsia legendary figures?

The schematic sequence in which these events and figures appeared, worked out by Han and subsequent scholars, may be totally unacceptable, but the mythical units that began to be recorded during the Eastern Chou period (771–221 B.C.) relating to the pre-Three Dynasties history may be regarded as elements of an oral tradition of that time and can be studied as such. The pre-Shang cultures in North China disclosed by archaeology and described in the previous chapters of this volume must then serve as the known factual background of this portion of Chinese history against which the mythical data can be checked.

The most pertinent data for the present purposes are the myths about the origin of institutions, which indicate clearly a change from village societies to state organizations. Most of these myths cluster around two important heroes, Shen-nung and Huang-ti, who mark two stages in the earliest legendary history.

The Age of Shen-nung is characterized by the "peaceful co-existence" of self-contained village communities, and with this hero are associated the invention of agriculture, the manufacture of pottery, and the system of market exchange.

> Shen-nung cultivated plants and made pottery (*Chou-shu,* as quoted in *T'ai-p'ing-yü-lan*).
> Shen-nung invented wooden agricultural implements (*lei* and *ssu*) and taught the whole world his inventions . . .
> He instituted the market held at noon. He administered all the peoples of the world and gathered their produce in the markets. The people went back to their homes after exchange and rested contented (*Hsi-tz'u,* in *Yih*).
> During the Age of Shen-nung, people rested at ease and acted with vigor. They cared for their mothers, but not for

131

their fathers. They lived among deer. They ate what they cultivated and wore what they wove. They did not think of harming one another (Chapter "Tao-t'o," in *Chuang-tzu*).

These passages are sufficient to show that as late as the second half of the first millennium B.C., when the above were supposedly written, vivid recollections of the Neolithic life of their ancestors were still in the mind of the Chinese in North China. Concerning the invention of agriculture by Shen-nung, there are some stories of special interest. Some relate that the first plant cultivation was the result of necessity:

> The ancient people ate meat of animals and birds. At the time of Shen-nung, there were so many people that the animals and birds became inadequate for people's wants, and therefore Shen-nung taught the people to cultivate (*Pai-hu-t'ung*).

In some other stories, the cultivated plants were given by divine forces:

> At the time of Shen-nung, millet rained from the Heaven. Shen-nung collected the grains and cultivated them (*Chou-shu*, as quoted by *Yih-shih*).
> [At the time of Shen-nung], there was a red bird holding in its mouth a cereal stalk with nine ears. Some of the grains fell onto the ground. Shen-nung picked them up and cultivated them in the field. Those who ate the grains lived long and did not die (*Shih-yih-chi*, by Wang Chia of the Chin Dynasty).

Whether plant cultivation was independently invented in China and, if so, how the process was first established, we do not know. It is significant, however, that Shen-nung, besides being the inventor of agriculture, was in the meantime the first and greatest herbalist. It is said that Shen-nung "whipped," or tasted, a "hundred varieties of grasses" and knew the nature of them all. According to one folktale of the people at Szechwan, it was a highly poisonous grass that killed Shen-nung. Even today, Shen-nung, among his numerous other characteristics, is the patron divinity of the Chinese druggist and herbalist. Anthropologists have proposed many theories about the origin of agriculture, but to my knowledge none have suggested that the first cultivation of plants in

132

some parts of the world might have been the deed of a (or *the*) herbalist in the hunting-fishing stage of culture. The tale of Shennung the Herbalist implies this, and opens an interesting line of study.

Subsequent to the Age of Shen-nung was the Age of Huang-ti, or the celebrated Yellow Emperor, who marks the emergence of the state and the urban way of life:

> During the Age of Shen-nung, men cultivated food and women wove clothing. People were administered without a criminal law and prestige was built without the use of force. After Shen-nung, however, the strong began to rule over the weak and the many over the few. Therefore, Huang-ti administered internally with penalties and externally with armed forces (Chapter "Hua-ts'ê," in *Shang Chün Shu*).

Huang-ti is also attributed with the invention of metallurgy, writing, the chariot, and the palace, all the essential elements of a civilization. In these two ages of legendary Chinese history one finds the memory of a major transition of the Chinese society from self-contained, peaceful villages to warlike states with centralized government.[1]

FROM HISTORY TO ARCHAEOLOGY

In the archaeological record, this major societal transformation is clearly defined. As discussed above, the stage of primary village-farming efficiency is known in North China as the Yangshao, and, following it, the Lungshanoid stage represents stratified village-farmers. The Shang, which follows the Lungshanoid in Honan, marks the earliest stage of Chinese civilization that is known archaeologically. Figuratively speaking, the Shen-nung Age is similar to the Yangshao stage, and the Age of Huang-ti comes to a

---

1. For mythology in ancient China, see: Marcel Granet, *Danses et légendes de la Chine ancienne*, Paris, Libraire Félix Alcan, 1926; Henri Maspero, *Journal Asiatique*, 204 (1924), 1–100; Bernhard Karlgren, *BMFEA*, 18, 1946; Derk Borde, "China," in *Mythologies of the Ancient World*, New York, Doubleday and Co., 1961; Chang Kwang-chih, *BIE*, 8, 1959; Chang Kwang-chih, "Kingship, Myths, and Animal Style Art in the Shang and Chou," mimeographed in New Haven, 1962; Yang Kuan, *Ku Shih Pien*, 7, 1941; Hsüan Chu, *Chung-kuo Shen-hua yen-chiu ABC*, Shanghai, Shih-chieh Book Co., 1929.

peak with the beginning of the Shang. In legendary history, however, Shang was not the first dynasty of the Huang-ti Age, which
was initiated by Huang-ti himself and passed through several legendary epochs and a major dynasty, the Hsia, before arriving at the
Shang. The problems encountered by one who tries to tie legendary
accounts and archaeological sequence together center around these
questions: Should the epochs of Huang-ti and other legendary
heroes and the Hsia Dynasty be sought in an initial Bronze Age
antedating the Shang and as yet undiscovered, or should they be
looked for among remains of the Lungshanoid stage? Or are some
of them attributable to the former and some others to the latter?

To a volume such as this, which is archaeologically oriented,
these problems are somewhat irrelevant. But an archaeologist has
to face them sooner or later, and I do not think that the legendary
history should be completely ignored. Archaeology and history
merge at these points, and if they should be complementary
when doing so it would prove mutually beneficial. In any case,
several points regarding these problems are self-evident. In the
first place, the archaeological sequence in the northern Honan area
is reasonably complete in showing that the Shang civilization in
that region was derived from the Lungshanoid culture, and that
there was no major break in the sequence. Unless this is a strictly
local phenomenon (which is not at all impossible, considering
that for other areas the record for this stage is incomplete), it is
likely that the legendary history from Huang-ti through the Hsia
Dynasty is included in the time span of the Lungshanoid. Secondly,
the Lungshanoid stage of Chinese Neolithic cannot be considered
to have achieved the kind of civilization that has been attributed to
Huang-ti through Hsia. This need not, however, worry us particularly, for a strong political organization certainly appeared
during the Lungshanoid stage, probably along with some other
items of civilization such as incipient metallurgy, intensified industrial specialization, and intensified status differentiation. On the
other hand, we need not regard the Huang-ti through Hsia interval
as necessarily having achieved a full-fledged civilization, as recorded in the traditional history, for this part of the tradition
must have been tempered considerably in accordance with the
historical perspectives of these early times. It is possible, therefore,
that the Hsia Dynasty was one of the local cultural groups immediately preceding the Shang Dynasty. Finally, this identification

134

may never be certain unless and until some archaeological finds belonging to the late Lungshanoid stage are identified by means of written records as having been left during the Hsia Dynasty. Since we are still uncertain about the early history of Chinese writing, it is impossible to say at this stage whether or not this is a likely prospect.[2]

In any case, prior to the Shang Dynasty there are two kinds of prehistories of the Chinese, namely, archaeological sequence and legendary history. The former is certainly the more reliable of the two, but an archaeologist must also bear the latter in mind constantly for future reference and clarification which will undoubtedly prove useful to the study of both kinds of prehistories. With the emergence of the Shang civilization, there is a fusion of archaeology and history. In order to describe the formation of Chinese civilization, and to discuss the pertinent problems both within and beyond North China during the formative stages of civilization—a prerequisite for an understanding of the following chapters—I will attempt to give a brief account of the early history of North China from the beginning of the Shang until the unification under the Ch'in Empire, as seen from the archaeological evidence. Literary sources, of course, have to be consulted from time to time to amplify some of the archaeological materials and to supplement others. But in the present chapter and the next, a full account of Chinese ancient history is not intended.

NEOLITHIC FOUNDATIONS OF THE SHANG CIVILIZATION

With the coming of the Shang Dynasty, the absolute chronology of the cultural history of early China can, for the first time, be determined in terms of centuries and even decades, if not years. Traditional sources place the founding of the dynasty by T'ang in 1766 B.C. This may not be quite reliable, but Tung Tso-pin of the Academia Sinica, a student of oracle bone inscriptions for more than thirty years, is convinced that P'an-keng moved his capital city to An-yang in 1384 B.C. and that the last Yin king, Ti-hsin (or Chou), was overthrown by the invading Chou in 1111 B.C.[3] Tung's An-yang chronology is not accepted by all authorities, some of

2. Hsü Chung-shu, *An-yang Fa-chüeh Pao-kao*, 3, 1931; Hsü Liang-chih, *Chung-kuo shih-ch'ien-shih hua*, Hong Kong, Asia Press, 1954, pp. 197–230.
3. Tung Tso-pin, *Yin li p'u*, Li-chuang, Academia Sinica, 1945.

whom prefer to place the downfall of the Yin at as late a date as 1027 B.C. But this argument, in my opinion, has little relevance to the major trends of Chinese cultural growth.

Whichever chronological scheme we may choose, the fact is that the known beginning of civilization in China is approximately a millennium and a half later than the initial phases of Near Eastern civilization. We can also take note of the fact that many essential elements of Chinese civilization, such as bronze metallurgy, writing, the horse chariot, human sacrifice, and so forth, had appeared earlier in Mesopotamia. Here, then, is the problem of East-West relationships all over again. And again, the problem must be resolved in two parts. First, did some of the civilizational elements of the Shang Dynasty originate in North China or did they come from the Near East? Second, were these, if coming from the West, responsible for the emergence of civilization in North China? The first question must obviously be answered piecemeal, and for many of the elements, there is no definite evidence one way or the other. As to the second question, many scholars argue that civilization came to China as a result of stimulus diffusion from the Near East, principally because they think it came suddenly and without previous foundation.[4]

Descriptions of the Lungshanoid stage of Chinese Neolithic in Chapter 4 have shown that the Shang civilization did not evolve out of a vacuum. As I have pointed out, a number of Lungshanoid elements foreshadowed the subsequent birth of civilization in the Huangho valley: (a) The permanent settlement and the large area of the farming villages, and the advancement of agriculture. (b) The specialization of industries which had been considerably developed, as shown by the appearance of wheel-made pottery in some of the areas. (c) The village fortifications indicating the need for defense, and hence the frequency of warfare between settlements. (d) The oracle bone, the prone burial, and the concentration of jade objects in certain places within the village, which may imply an intensification of the differentiation of individual status. (e) The regional variation of styles and the possible importance of the residential group at the community-aggregate level which foreshadowed, if it did not indicate, the formation of urban

4. Max Loehr, *Amer. Jour. Arch.*, 53 (1949), 126–44; Bishop, *Origin of the Far Eastern Civilization*; Li Chi, in *Ch'ing-chu Ts'ai Yüan-p'ei hsien-sheng liu-shih-wu-sui chi-nien lun-wen chi*, Pt. 1, 1933.

networks and the beginning of regional states. One of these local states eventually succeeded in expansion and conquest, and is subsequently known as the Yin-Shang.

TABLE 6.

North China Neolithic—Bronze Age Continuities and Discontinuities

Continuities	*Discontinuities*
A. Formation of village-aggregate	a. Mature urbanism and related institutions (especially the formation of settlement groups)
B. Raid and warfare	
C. Industrial specialization	
D. Differentiation of status and prone burials	b. Class differentiation
E. The elaborate ceremonial complex (more lineage-ancestral than community-agricultural)	c. New government and economic patterns (conquest, tribute, redistribution, etc.)
	d. Wider trade, currency
F. Cultivation of millet, rice. kaoliang, wheat, hemp	e. New war patterns (capture of slaves and use of chariots)
G. Domestication of dog, pig, cattle, sheep, horse, chicken	f. Chamber burials and human sacrifices
H. Stamped-earth structures	g. Domestication of water buffalo
I. Semisubterranean houses and lime-plastered floors	h. Highly developed bronze metallurgy
J. Scapulimancy	i. Writing
K. Some pottery forms (especially ritual forms with ring feet and lids)	j. Advanced stone carvings
	k. New pottery forms
L. Some decorative motifs	
M. Some stone implements and weapons (especially semilunar knife, sickle, arrowhead, adze, axe, hoe, spade, perforated axe, halberd)	
N. Shell and bone craft	
O. The cord-marked pottery tradition	
P. Silk	
Q. The jade complex	

The Yin-Shang civilization was indeed a new phenomenon in the Huangho valley, an outcome of a quantum change, which put a full stop to the Neolithic way of life in the area of Shang's dis-

137

tribution, and in doing so prefaced a new book which has the title of Chinese history instead of prehistory. But the main stream of this new civilization was evidently handed down from the previous Neolithic substratum. There were, in the Shang culture, new elements of culture and new systems of organization for new and old elements of culture, but this does not necessarily mean that the Shang civilization was not a native growth. Table 6 shows, in a preliminary fashion, the Neolithic heritage of the Yin-Shang Bronze Age culture and its innovations. From this enumeration it becomes apparent that the "suddenness" of the emergence of the Yin-Shang civilization has been unduly exaggerated by past scholarly writing. In fact, few Yin-Shang eco-social and stylistic elements did not have a Neolithic basis. Thus, one thing can be considered as settled, namely, that the Chinese civilization, on the whole, was built upon the Chinese Neolithic foundation. With this basic question out of the way, three problems still confront us: (a) the origins of the cultural elements that appeared during the Shang Dynasty for the first time, and the extent to which these new elements can be considered responsible for the appearance of the civilization; (b) the new structure and configuration of the Shang civilization which distinguish it from the Neolithic, continuities in cultural elements notwithstanding; and (c) the regional phase of the Lungshanoid stage that is directly ancestral to the Shang. The second problem will be discussed at length in subsequent sections of this chapter. Evidence pertaining to the first and the third problems is still meager, but the following remarks may be of some help.

Most of the new features that appeared during the Shang Dynasty and serve to mark it off from the Neolithic are largely developmental and functional in nature. Urbanism, class distinctions, political systems, and the like are poor indications of historical relationships; the use of currency, patterns of warfare, and many ceremonial practices can apparently be said to be concomitant with particular functional contexts. Only bronze metallurgy, the use of writing, and the horse chariot are, therefore, of possible historical significance. Unfortunately, the history of these elements and their occurrence in China has yet to be studied. As mentioned in Chapter 4, horse bones have been found from some of the Lungshanoid sites. It is widely accepted that during the Shang Dynasty, horses were used only for drawing chariots, and were neither ridden nor used for food.[5] There is no reason to suppose that horses during the Lungshanoid stage, if domesticated, were employed for purposes other than warfare. Since the riding of horses during the Lungshanoid is highly unlikely, we might even be tempted to conclude that the horse chariot appeared during that period, but the ground for this conclusion is dangerously thin. In the first place, horse bones have been found only rarely at Lungshanoid sites, and the zoological characteristics of those that have been found remain to be specified. Secondly, chariot warfare does not seem to fit the Lungshanoid context satisfactorily. Thirdly, remains of chariots have never been found at Lungshanoid sites. A great number of excavations and comparative studies of horse and chariot remains in China and in Mesopotamia must be made before we can be certain about the origin of the horse chariot in the Shang Dynasty.[6]

The history of writing in China is another unknown factor. Palaeographers are agreed that a stage of writing existed in China prior to the period of the Shang Dynasty when An-yang was the capital. The scripts during this pre-An-yang stage were supposedly more representational and elaborate than the An-yang oracle bone inscriptions which were highly simplified and conventionalized. Such archaic characters have been found on An-yang bronzes and oracle bones, along with the simplified and conventionalized form, probably for artistic and ceremonial usage.[7] Archaeologically, however, this archaic writing has not been found from a stratigraphic context demonstrably earlier than the An-yang period.[8] Past efforts to link the early Chinese writing to ancient Sumerian and Egyptian writing have proved to be futile. Chinese writing was probably an independent invention, but its early history is still unknown.

The history of bronze metallurgy in China is now better known than previously, although it is not yet a solved problem. In 1949, Max Loehr states that:

5. Shih Chang-ju, Bull. College of Arts, Natl. Taiwan Univ., 5 (1953), 6–7; Hayashi Minano, Minzokugaku-Kenkyu, 23 (1959), 39–40.

6. Cf. Hayashi Minano, Minzokugaku-Zasshi, 23 (1959), 39–40; 24 (1960), 33–57; Hayashi Minano, Tohogakuho, 29 (Kyoto, 1959), 155–284.

7. Tung Tso-pin, Ta-lu-tsa-chih, 9 (1952), 348–58; Tang Lan, KKHP, 1957:2, 7–22.

8. In Paideuma, 4 (1950), 81–99, Robert von Heine-Geldern erroneously stated that writing appeared during the Lungshanoid stage.

An-yang represents, according to our present knowledge, the oldest Chinese metal age site, taking us back to ca. 1300 B.C. It displays no signs of a primitive stage of metal working but utter refinement. Primitive stages have, in fact, nowhere been discovered in China up to the present moment. Metallurgy seems to have been brought to China from outside.[9]

Regardless of its apparent validity at the time, this statement has been rendered obsolete by findings in China since 1949. Based on these findings, the following points can be made: (a) An-yang does not represent the oldest Chinese metal age site; the existence of bronze metallurgy during the Shang Dynasty before the period of An-yang has been established. Even the possibility that metallurgy began to appear in North China toward the end of the Lungshanoid stage of the Neolithic cannot be ruled out, as mentioned in Chapter 4. (b) At Cheng-chou, where bronze artifacts have been unearthed from a pre-An-yang stratigraphic context, bronzes are few and less refined than those at An-yang, although metallurigcal details are not yet available. It is not impossible that this marks one of the "primitive stages" that Loehr spoke of as lacking. (c) An intensive investigation into the metallurgical techniques of the Chinese Bronze Age has convinced Noel Barnard [10] that, showing little similarity to Western bronze metallurgy, bronze foundry in China was invented independently *in situ*. (d) Deposits of copper and tin ores, according to the studies of Amano Motonosuke [11] and Shih Chang-ju,[12] are abundant in North China, and were easily accessible from northern Honan. This indicates that, given appropriate necessity and stimulus, the opportunity for independent metallurgical invention was available to the first Chinese bronze workers. (e) It is generally agreed that the Shang craftsmen used bronze as a new medium for working the traditional artifactual forms; in other words, the Shang bronzes manifested the traditional forms and functions by means of a new kind of raw material and technology. Considering all of these points, we could say that much new light has been thrown upon the

9. Max Loehr, *Amer. Jour. Arch.*, 53 (1949), 129.
10. Noel Barnard, *Bronze Casting and Bronze Alloys in Ancient China* (Tokyo, Australian National Univ., 1961), p. 108.
11. Amano Motonosuke, *Tohogakuho*, 23 (1953), 231–58.
12. Shih Chang-ju, *BIHP*, 26, 1955.

problem of the origin of bronze metallurgy in China, which renders likely the possibility of independent invention of this new technology in China. Much more information, to be sure, is required to transform this possibility into certainty, but the trend of available data is clear, and we are more sure of the various areas in which intelligent questions can be asked.

Furthermore, some new light has also been thrown upon the problem pertaining to the transition from the Lungshanoid to the Shang. The fact that the Lungshanoid culture was the forerunner of the Shang civilization is certain. But as yet we have to pin down the exact region where this transition took place, and—still more difficult—to determine the exact process of how it took place. Cheng-chou in northern Honan offers the first tangible clue toward the solution of these problems. As will be discussed presently, a long stratigraphical sequence has been established for the area of Cheng-chou, ranging from an early phase of the Shang when metallurgy was poorly represented, if at all, to the final phase of the Shang. The earliest phase, represented by the sites at Shang-chieh, Nan-kuan-wai, and the lower strata of Lo-ta-miao, Tung-chai, and Ko-ta-wang, is, actually, on the borderline between the Lungshanoid and the Shang. It has many ceramic, stone, and bone features characteristic of the later phases of the Shang, but its many artifacts and pottery forms are indistinguishable from the inventory of the Lungshanoid sites in the same area. It still has some pocket-shaped storage pits, typical of the Lungshanoid, a large number of shell artifacts, which diminished subsequently, oracle scapulae with little trace of advanced preparation, and no actual remains of bronze artifacts.[13] At the Ko-ta-wang site, this early Shang phase lies stratigraphically above a Lungshanoid stratum, and the culture was apparently continuous from one layer to the next.[14] We might be tempted to conclude that the transition from the Lungshanoid to the Shang took place principally in the Cheng-chou area. But since similar early Shang phases have not yet been found widely in other areas in Honan, much more work remains to be done before we can be sure that what took place in Cheng-chou was not simply a local manifestation of a widely occurring phenomenon, nor the result of cultural assimilation, with the major centers of cultural radiation being located elsewhere. Furthermore,

13. KK, 1960:6, 11–12; Chao Hsia-kwang, KKTH, 1958:2, 6–9.
14. Chao Ching-yün and Liu Tung-chin, KKHP, 1958:3, 41–62.

Lungshanoid-Shang similarities have been noted in western Honan and southwestern Shansi,[15] and allegedly early Shang bronzes have been turned up in the Hanshui valley in Hupei.[16] It is likely that the Shang civilization was derived directly from the Honan phase of the Lungshanoid horizon, but it will probably be some time before we can rule out other possibilities, and before we can pin down an exact location, if there was one, where the actual cultural transformation took place.

SHANG CIVILIZATION DEFINED

As stated in Chapter 3, a distinctive North China cultural tradition was initiated with the beginning of village agriculture in the Nuclear Area of the Huangho valley. In a broad sense, this cultural tradition was carried on into historical periods. The Shang civilization, no doubt, was within this cultural tradition. On the other hand, a new stylistic horizon appeared with the spread of the Lungshanoid, and the emergence of the Shang marked another stylistic horizon of the same magnitude. In terms of society and development, this new horizon resulted from a quantum transformation of Chinese society, as, to a lesser extent, did the previous Lungshanoid. The new society of the Shang will be described below, but first there are important questions to be answered: What are the horizon markers of the Shang? What kind of archaeological sites should be called Shang, and what was the geographical distribution of these sites? These questions are important because the Shang civilization did not extend throughout all of North China. During at least part of the period when Shang cities were established in some regions in North China, Lungshanoid cultures persisted in others. They are particularly difficult to answer because up to the present time archaeologists have more or less taken the Shang for granted, and have made no specific attempts to define the period as a whole in stylistic terms.

In attempting to define the Shang civilization, we must take a number of points into serious consideration. In the first place, An-yang does not fully represent Shang, nor does any other single site. Information concerning the Shang has in the past been de-

15. An Chih-min, *KKTH*, 1956:5, 6.
16. See Chapter 9 for discussion on the Shang influence in the Hanshui valley.

rived exclusively from An-yang, and archaeologists have tended to use An-yang as a cultural yardstick, and to describe the An-yang culture as if describing the Shang civilization. It is now clear that An-yang was but one of many Shang Dynasty sites, and that the An-yang culture represents only a portion of the Shang as a whole. In the second place, in defining the Shang civilization, we should define a total culture rather than individual cultural traits. The occurrence of a few isolated cultural traits characteristic of the Shang civilization does not necessarily mean the occurrence of a Shang cultural totality. In tracing the distribution of the Shang civilization, for instance, many archaeologists have been led to believe that "Shang sites" have been found in Shensi, Szechwan, and the Lower Yangtze delta. It is probably true that Shang traits have been found in these regions, but the predominant cultures of the sites there at which the Shang traits were found were more likely than not local Neolithic cultures, either Lungshanoid or some other. Shang sites where the Shang culture is found in configurational terms are much more restricted geographically, and outside of the area of their distribution the occurrence of Shang traits is apparently the result of cultural contact. To meet these and other requirements the following conceptual characterization of the Shang civilization is suggested:

(1) Shang sites can easily and effectively be recognized according to the pattern of settlement. Village or hamlet sites tend to cluster and form settlement groups. Single villages within a group tend to specialize in function. Some were residential farming villages, exhibiting little difference from neolithic sites, but within the same settlement group were sites devoted to specialized activities, such as administration, religion, aristocratic burials, and handicrafts.

(2) At one or a few of the sites within the same settlement group, an aristocratic complex of artifacts and architecture can easily be recognized. In architecture, this includes ceremonial altars, rectangular house structures with stamped earth (hang-t'u) floors, stone pillar foundations, and in some cases, stone sculptures used as pillar-rests. Such sites have a complex system of graves, including tombs of gigantic dimension and sophisticated structure, evidence of human sacrifice and accompanying burials of animal victims and horse chariots. This aristocratic complex is often associated with a sophisticated ritual complex, manifested by such

archaeological remains as human sacrifice, animal sacrifice, scapulimancy, and ceremonial vessels of pottery (e.g., white pottery) and bronze. Horse and chariot fittings and other apparatus for ritual use help to mark the distinction of status, along with such artifacts as prepared and inscribed oracle bones, white, hard, and glazed pottery, elaborately carved bone hairpins, jade weapons, and bronze ceremonial and household utensils. Remains of cowry shells, probably used as media of exchange, may also be significant. Writing is apparently associated with the aristocracy, and so is the highly developed decorative art such as the *t'ao-t'ieh* style, mosaic designs, and stone and bone sculptures and engravings. Discovery of such artifacts points to a strongly consolidated aristocracy that had definitely been lacking prior to the Shang.

(3) As a part of the above complex, both bronzes and writing deserve separate status as horizons markers; particularly the bronze vessels, which include forms not previously represented in stone or ceramics, such as square-shaped containers (*yih* and *yu*) and vessels in the shape of animal effigies.

(4) Scapulimancy had appeared during the Lungshanoid stage, but the Shang oracle bones were often elaborately prepared by hollowing out cavities and scraping thin the opposite surface before the application of heat (Pl. VII). The use of turtle shells for similar oracle purposes was apparently also a Shang Dynasty innovation.

(5) Deep pit houses and storage pits with long stairways or footrests on the wall were probably features of the Shang Dynasty.

(6) A large number of stone sickles is found at every known Shang site. Stone sickles are abundant at some Lungshanoid sites, but only with the Shang civilization was there such a heavy concentration of stone sickle remains in proportion to other stone implements at single localities.

(7) Although many of the pottery forms were carryovers from the Lungshanoid stage, a great number of new forms appeared during the Shang. The following forms are particularly characteristic: cord-marked gray *li* tripods with relatively short feet; round-bottomed jugs with in-turned rims and cord marks; beakers with markedly out-turned rims and large mouths; flat-bottomed and small-mouthed jars with short and rounded shoulders (*lei*); ring-footed, round-bottomed, and small-mouthed jars (*p'o*). White

pottery, hard pottery, and glazed pottery are known to occur only with the Shang.

(8) The Shang pottery, furthermore, presents a complicated series of geometric decorative motifs, incised or stamped. Some of these motifs have parallels in Shang bronze art.

Undoubtedly this list will be expanded when the excavated data from many Shang sites are made available. It can serve for the time being as a preliminary checklist for the discussion of the geographic distribution of the Shang sites. So far, the Shang civilization as defined has been found from only a limited number of sites. An-yang and Cheng-chou in northern Honan are the only sites where a fairly complete picture of the Shang cities can be reconstructed. Lo-yang and Shan Hsien in western Honan, Hui Hsien in northern Honan, and Hsing-t'ai in southern Hopei, though far from containing all the elements listed, have furnished enough materials to indicate the existence of Shang sites at these localities. On the other hand, some sites where Shang traits occur in a local cultural context, in Szechwan, Kiangsi, Hunan, Anhwei, Shantung, Shansi, and Hopei, when considered configurationally, are apparently *not* Shang sites. Between these two extremes are a number of sites in Honan, Shensi, Shansi, Anhwei, Hopei, and Shantung, which are reported and described as Shang sites in the literature but which have not furnished sufficient data to warrant a classification one way or the other. For the present, therefore, on the basis of archaeological evidence, we can say with certainty only that the Shang civilization was distributed in western and northern Honan, southern Hopei, and probably the western end of Shantung (see Map 11). Literary sources and some plausible archaeological materials could extend the Shang territory to southeastern Honan. Shang traits found outside this area must have resulted from cultural contacts between the Shang and the native populations. There is absolutely no evidence to show, as some authorities seem to indicate, that the Shang civilization was established in a wide area stretching from the Shantung coast in the east to the Lower Weishui in the west, and from northern Hopei and Shansi in the north to the Huaiho valley or even the Yangtze valley in the south.[17] Local cultures prevailed in these regions, as

17. Cheng Te-kun, Asia Major, n.s. 6 (1957), map; Cheng Te-kun, *Shang China* (Cambridge, W. Heffer & Sons, 1961), map 2.

will be discussed in subsequent chapters, although evidence pointing to cultural influences from the Shang territory is abundant
and serves as an indispensable time indicator.

MAJOR CITIES OF THE SHANG

With the exact boundaries of the Shang territory still unsettled,
it would be as impractical to speak of the Shang civilization *in
toto* as it is fallacious to describe only the culture at An-yang as
representing the whole civilization of the dynasty. We must first
describe the culture and society at certain major cities of the
Shang Dynasty that are known archaeologically.

These, for the present, are Cheng-chou, An-yang, and to some
extent, Hsing-t'ai. The sites at Cheng-chou have provided a complete chronological sequence of Shang development, according to
which the sites at An-yang, Hsing-t'ai, and a few others have been
synchronized by some students into a framework for all of North
China.

Cheng-chou Discovered in 1950, the Shang Dynasty remains (Map 9) in the vicinity of Cheng-chou, northern Honan,
are still being excavated and studied. Enough has been discovered,
however, for An Chin-huai to conclude that the "Shang Dynasty
remains, except for those found in scattered spots in the western
suburbs of Cheng-chou, are mostly concentrated within the ancient
city site of Cheng-chou and its vicinity. Shang settlements spread
continuously in an area of about forty square kilometers east from
Feng-huang-t'ai west to Hsi-ch'eng-chuang, and south from Erh-li-
kang to the north of Tzu-ching-shan." [18] Prior to the Shang, the
area of Cheng-chou was occupied by both Yangshao and Lungshanoid farmers, whose remains have been unearthed at Lin-shan-
chai, Niu-chai, Ko-ta-wang, and other sites. Immediately subsequent to, and apparently evolving out of, the Lungshanoid Honan
phase were strata of the earlier stages of the Shang. The Shang
history of settlement seems to be divisible, according to available
evidence, into no less than five stratigraphical phases,[19] as shown
in Table 7.

18. An Chin-huai, *WWTKTL*, 1957:8, 17.
19. Cheng Te-kun, *Shang China*, p. 28; Tsou Heng, *KKHP*, 1956:3;
Honan Wenhuachü, *Cheng-chou Erh-li-kang*, Peiping, Science Press, 1959;
Chao Ching-yün, *KKTH*, 1958:9, 54–57; *KK*, 1960:6, 11–12; An Chin-huai,
WW, 1961:4/5, 79–80.

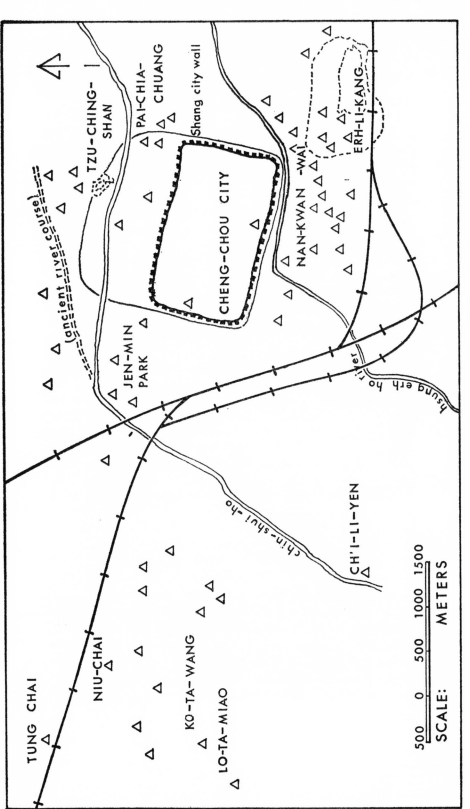

MAP 9. Shang Dynasty sites near Cheng-chou. After *WW*, 1961:4/5, 73.

The Shang-chieh phase, thus far represented only by the site at Shang-chieh, is on the very borderline between the Lungshanoid and the Shang. At the site nine house floors were found, all but one rectangular in shape. Fifteen storage pits, mostly with oval-shaped openings, were excavated. Among the artifactual discoveries, polished stone spades and the multi-perforated knives particularly recall the Lungshanoid forms. In ceramics, jugs, *tou* fruitstands,

TABLE 7.

Shang Dynasty Phases of Cheng-chou

Jen-min Park Phase	Jen-min Park III Ko-ta-wang III
Upper Erh-li-kang Phase	Erh-li-kang II Jen-min Park II Pai-chia-chuang II Nan-kuan-wai III Tung-chai III
Lower Erh-li-kang Phase	Erh-li-kang I Jen-min Park I Pai-chia-chuang I Nan-kuan-wai II Tung-chai II Ko-ta-wang II
Lo-ta-miao Phase	Lo-ta-miao Nan-kuan-wai I Tung-chai I Ko-ta-wang I
Shang-chieh Phase	Shang-chieh

bowls, basins, *li* tripods, and wide-mouthed jars are characteristically Shang items, but the flat-bottomed jugs with checker impressions and cord marks and the round-bottomed jugs with a high body resemble the Lungshanoid forms. No metal artifacts have been unearthed here. Pig bones were found which had been utilized for oracle purposes, but evidence of preparation before heat application is completely lacking.[20] Discovery of more sites of this phase

20. *KK*, 1960:6, 11–12.

is eagerly awaited to throw light upon the crucial stage of Lung-shanoid–Shang transitions.

Four sites have been located so far that can be grouped into the second, or Lo-ta-miao, phase. These all seem to have been residential villages, but pottery kilns were also uncovered from the site at Ko-ta-wang. Stratigraphic evidence shows conclusively that this phase was chronologically situated between the Lung-shanoid and the Lower Erh-li-kang phase, although the relative dating between the Lo-ta-miao and the Shang-chieh phases is still typologically based. Metal objects are lacking in the cultural remains of this phase, perhaps indicating that they were still rare. In the cultural inventory, typical Shang traits increased, but many traits still strongly resemble Lungshanoid features, such as the great number of shell artifacts, the bone hairpins with awl-shaped heads, the pocket-shaped storage pits (which had become rare, however), and the generally unprepared oracle bones. Some diagnostic ceramic features are the round-bottomed and cord-marked jugs with high and nearly vertical bodies, vessels with large mouth openings, small basins and jars, and jugs with checker impressions. This stage is again known only imperfectly, but there is no question of its existence.[21]

Cheng-chou of the Lower Erh-li-kang phase seems to have stepped suddenly into increased activities, and expanded the size of its settlement. Sites of this phase contain dwelling houses, burials, workshops, and a city wall.[22] It has been suggested that during this stage dwelling quarters and burials were located inside the city wall, and that the city itself was the center of living and administration, but that the nonaristocrats' residences, cemetery, craft shops, and farming fields were outside the wall. According to literary records, the ancient Shang kings changed their capital sites several times before finally settling at Yin, the site of the present city of An-yang. One of these earlier capitals, two capitals before An-yang, is said to have been the city of Ao or Hsiao, probably in the vicinity of the present town of Ying-tsê, about 15 km.

21. Chao Chüan-ku et al., KKHP, 1957:1, 56–58; Hsia Nai, China Reconstructs, 6 (1957), 20; An Chin-huai, KKTH, 1955:3, 18; Chao Hsia-kwang, KKTH, 1958:2, 6–8; Chen Chia-hsiang, WWTKTL, 1957:10, 48–51; Chao Ching-yün, KKTH, 1958:9, 54–57; Chao Ching-yün and Liu Tung-chin, KKHP, 1958:3, 41–62.

22. Honan Wenhuachü, Cheng-chou Erh-li-kang; An Chin-huai, WW, 1961:4/5, 73–80; Chao Chüan-ku et al, KKHP, 1957:1, 53–73.

to the northwest of Cheng-chou. Intensive investigations were undertaken during the fifties in the neighborhood of Ying-tsê, but they failed to turn up any Shang Dynasty remains. In Cheng-chou, however, a full-fledged city site has been located, dating to the Lower Erh-li-kang phase, which, as will be shown, is considerably earlier than the dynastic phase of An-yang stratigraphy. Some scholars have suggested, therefore, that Cheng-chou may have been the site of the ancient capital of Ao.[23]

The Shang city wall was roughly rectangular in shape, with a total perimeter of 7195 meters and an enclosed area of 3.2 square km. The maximum height of the surviving wall is 9.1 meters, and the maximum width at the base of the wall, 36 meters. The wall was built in successive compressed layers, each of which has an average thickness of 8 to 10 centimeters. On the surface of each layer are clear depressions made by the pestles used for the compressing work, and the soil making up the wall is hard and compact. The inner structure of the wall shows that it was built at two different periods, both within the time of the Shang, possibly corresponding to the Lower and the Upper Erh-li-kang phases. This Shang city wall was apparently used and mended during the subsequent historic periods, but a new wall was built during the Han Dynasty to make a smaller enclosure.[24] The above description of the Shang wall shows that the city of Cheng-chou during the Shang Dynasty was of considerable importance and was constructed only with major effort. An Chin-huai [25] estimates the original wall to have been 10 meters in average height, with an average width of 20 meters, which, multiplied by the total length of 7195 meters, required no less than 1,439,000 m.[3] of compressed soil or (using a ratio of 1:2) 2,878,000 m.[3] of loose soil. Experiments carried out by archaeologists show that an average worker produced per hour 0.03 m.[3] of earth by means of a bronze pick of 0.02 m.[2] by means of a stone hoe. An concludes that to build the whole city wall of Cheng-chou, including earth digging, transporting, and compressing, required no less than eighteen years, with ten thousand workers working three hundred and thirty days a year. This impressive figure, even though roughly

23. An Chin-huai, WW, 1961:4/5, 73; but see Liu Chi-yih, WW, 1961:10, 39–40.
24. An Chin-huai, WW, 1961:4/5, 73–74; Hsia Nai, *China Reconstructs*, 6 (1957), 18–19; Chao Chüan-ku et al., *KKHP*, 1957:1, 58–59.
25. An Chin-huai, WW, 1961:4/5, 77.

calculated, indicates that Cheng-chou of the Shang Dynasty was no ordinary town.

The enclosure apparently marks the center of administration and ceremony. Since it overlaps in area the present city site of Cheng-chou and has therefore been only spottily excavated, the layout of this city site is not completely understood. But enough has been found to provide some ground for speculation about this layout. A large house floor has been identified at the northwestern corner of the city site, with a compressed, burned-hard, and lime-plastered floor, with post holes 14 to 35 cm. deep and 19 to 34 cm. across. Such large buildings have not been found outside the city area. North of this large building was found a platform of compressed earth, with an incomplete length of 25.5 m. east to west, and an incomplete width of 8.8 m. north to south. This reminds us of the earth altar at the center of Hsiao-t'un in the An-yang area. From a test trench in the northern part of the enclosure, south of the Tzu-ching-shan Hill, archaeologists found, in addition to potsherds, bone artifacts, stone implements and scores of jade hairpins of excellent workmanship. Only two or three hairpins of this kind have ever been found in the vast area outside the enclosure.[26]

Outside the city enclosure there were a number of residential sites and handicraft workshops, which can be attributed chronologically to the Lower and Upper Erh-li-kang stage. Two bronze foundry sites have been found thus far, one, north of the Tzu-ching-shan Hill, is approximately 100 meters north of the city wall, and the other about 500 meters south of the wall at the point of the present South Gate (Nan-kuan). The workshop to the south covers an area of 1050 square meters and has yielded crucibles of pottery, clay molds for both vessels and weapons, bronzes, debris of melted ocher, charcoal, and other stone and pottery remains. They are assigned to the Lower Erh-li-kang phase.[27] The bronze foundry remains to the north are significantly connected with one of four stamped-earth house foundations: (a) On the floor of the house is a layer of fine-grained and hardened light green earth containing copper, and on this layer are some dozen conical depressions. In each of the depressions a layer of

26. An Chin-huai, WW, 1961:4/5, 78–79.
27. Chao Chüan-ku et al, KKHP, 1957:1, 56; Hsia Nai, *China Reconstructs*, 6 (1957), 20.

melted copper is attached to the interior. (b) Outside the house is another area of verdigris about 0.1 to 0.15 meters thick. (c) A heap of clay molds and relics of crucibles was placed beside a door connecting two rooms inside the house. (d) A big lump of copper ocher was found ten meters to the west of the house. This site belonged to the Upper Erh-li-kang phase.[28] The latter find is especially interesting, indicating that the bronzesmiths of the Shang Dynasty lived in stamped-earth houses and thus seem to have enjoyed a higher privilege than the common folk who were satisfied with residing in semisubterranean houses.

Approximately 50 meters to the north of the Tzu-ching-shan bronze foundry was a bone workshop. It is a good-sized pit, possibly of the Lower Erh-li-kang phase, containing a large number (over a thousand pieces) of sawed and polished finished bone artifacts (arrowheads and hairpins), half-finished bone pieces, bone fragments used as raw materials, rejected pieces of bone, and eleven grinding stones. The bones are recognizable as those of human beings (about 50 percent), cattle, deer, and pigs.[29]

A pottery kiln site of the Erh-li-kang phases has been located on the west side of the Ming-kung Road, about 1200 meters to the west of the Shang city wall. In an area of 1250 square meters, archaeologists have located fourteen kilns, near which are storage pits containing unfired pottery, misfired pottery, pottery-making paddles and anvils, and stamps. Among the kilns are stamped-earth house foundations, which may have been the houses of the potters.[30] Since all of the pottery found at this site is of fine clay texture, there were presumably other kiln quarters for the manufacture of sand-tempered culinary wares, hard pottery, glazed pottery, and/or white pottery.

At the site of Erh-li-kang, a large number of big coarse-textured pottery jars were found, on the inner surface of which is left a layer of white substance which may indicate that these jars were containers for a kind of alcoholic beverage. The possibility that this was a wine-making industrial quarter has been suggested.[31]

28. Liao Yüng-min, WWTKTL, 1957:6, 73–74.

29. Chao Chüan-ku et al, KKHP, 1957:1, 58; Hsia Nai, China Reconstructs, 6 (1957), 21.

30. Chao Chüan-ku et al., KKHP, 1957:1, 57; Hsia Nai, China Reconstructs, 6 (1957), 19; Ma Chüan, WWTKTL, 1956:10, 50–51; Chou Chao-lin and Mou Yüng-hang, WWTKTL, 1955:9, 64–66.

31. An Chin-huai, WW, 1961:4/5, 78. For a suggested origin of wine making in the Neolithic period of North China, see Li Yang-sung, KK, 1962:1, 41–44.

Besides those listed above, a large quantity of other kinds of remains has been unearthed both inside and outside the city enclosure. House foundations have been located at Pai-chia-chuang.[32] Scattered water ditches have been found at Erh-li-kang, Pai-chia-chuang, Nan-kuan-wai, and the region on the west side of the Ming-kung-lu.[33] These ditches average 1.5 to 2.5 meters in width and 1.5 meters in depth. Those near Pai-chia-chuang have rows of small round depressions along both sides of the bottom. More than two hundred storage pits have been located throughout the area. Besides cultural debris and occasional pig and human skeletons, some of the pits contain large numbers of dog or cattle burials and apparently had some ceremonial significance.[34] Burials have been located at Erh-li-kang, Tzu-ching-shan, Pai-chia-chuang, and the Jen-min Park, and are particularly numerous at the two latter sites.[35] Some of the burials found at Pai-chia-chuang (Upper Erh-li-kang phase) are described as Large Graves, with grave furnishings and (in two cases) human sacrifices, and the others are Small Graves, which are numerous at the sites above named, and contain little or no grave furnishing.

These remains indicate that during the Erh-li-kang phases the city at Cheng-chou was a major political and ceremonial center. The population was apparently very large, in view of the extent of cultural distribution, the nature of settlement, and the depth of deposits (1 meter in average and with a maximum depth of 3 meters). The artifacts found here include not only stone, bone, shell, and bronze implements and vessels, as well as pottery, but also bronze ceremonial vessels, glazed pottery, hard pottery, white pottery, jade, ivory artifacts, and three pieces of inscribed oracle bones. The dating of the inscribed bones is uncertain, but it has been suggested that they might have been intrusive from later strata and do not antedate the An-yang sequence of oracle records. The city enclosure was apparently occupied by a ruling aristocracy, while the craftsmen and farmers inhabited the suburbs surrounding the city site. It is indeed highly probable that the traditional Shang capital of Ao was located here.

32. Tung Hung, WWTKTL, 1956:4, 3–5; Chao Chüan-ku et al., KKHP, 1957:1, 57.
33. Chao Chüan-ku et al., KKHP, 1957:1, 58.
34. An Chin-huai, WWTKTL, 1957:8, 19; Chao Chüan-ku, et al., KKHP, 1957:1, 58.
35. An Chin-huai, WWTKTL, 1957:8, 19; Chao Chüan-ku et al., KKHP, 1957:1, 70–71.

The Shang city life apparently continued into the final, Jen-min Park phase of the Cheng-chou sequence, for Large Graves of the Jen-min Park phase have been located in the park, a short distance to the west of the Shang city wall.[36] Aside from the findings here, however, Jen-min Park phase remains have thus far been found only in the upper stratum of the Ko-ta-wang site.[37] Whether this results from imperfect exploration in the whole area or indicates diminishing activities during this final phase of the Shang Dynasty, when the political center of the aristocracy had shifted away from the city of Ao, is a problem awaiting solution.

Some characteristic features of the Lower and Upper Erh-li-kang and the Jen-min Park phases are listed in Table 8.[38]

An-yang   The ruins of the last capital of the Shang Dynasty, known in history as Yin, are situated on both banks of the Huan River near An-yang, northern Honan. They have been known to historians for ages past, and were referred to as Yin-hsü, the "Ruins of the Yin," by Ssu-ma Chien (2d century B.C.) in the *Biography of Hsiang Yü* volume of his *Book of History* (*Shih Chi*). But it was not until 1899 when the remains of inscribed oracle bones were known to have been found in this area that the Ruins of the Yin were brought to the attention of scholars.[39] From 1928 to 1937, fifteen seasons of scientific excavation were undertaken in this region by the National Research Institute of History and Philology. Small-scale diggings were resumed after 1950. Remains of the Yin settlements of this group have been uncovered in the following localities: (southern bank of the River Huan, from east to west) Hou-kang, Hsüeh-chia-chuang, Hsiao-t'un, Hsiao-chuang, Wang-yü-k'ou, Ssu-p'an-mo, Fan-chuang, (northern bank, from east to west) Ta-ssu-k'ung-ts'un, Hsiao-ssu-k'ung-ts'un (Ssu-mien-pei), Nan-pa-t'ai, Hou-chia-chuang-nan-ti, Hsi-pei-kang (and the adjacent Wu-kuan-ts'un), Kao-ching-t'ai-tzu, and T'ung-lo-chai. These sites cover an area of approximately fifteen square kilometers (Map 10).

36. An Chin-huai, *KKTH*, 1955:3, 16–19; An Chih-min, *WWTKTL*, 1954:6, 32–37; Chao Chüan-ku et al., *KKHP*, 1957:1, 70–71.

37. Chao Ching-yüan and Liu Tung-chin, *KKHP*, 1958:3, 41–62.

38. Honan Wenhuachü, *Cheng-chou Erh-li-kang*; Chao Chüan-ku et al., *KKHP*, 1957:1; Tsou Heng, *KKHP*, 1956:3.

39. Cf. Tung Tso-pin, *Chia-ku-hsüeh wu-shih nien*, Taipei, Yih-wen, 1955; Kaizuka Shigeki, *Kodai Yin tegaku*, Tokyo, Misuzu Shobo, 1957.

TABLE 8.

Characteristic Features of Erh-li-kang and Jen-min Park Phases of the Shang Culture at Cheng-chou

Lower Erh-li-kang phase: The pottery has relatively thin walls, fine tempering materials, fine cord marks, and is generally well made; the characteristic ceramic forms are *li* tripods with elongated bodies, rounded rims curving outward and downward, high feet with long conical ends; *hsien* tripods with fine tempering materials and breast-shaped feet; *chia* tripods with out-turned rims; *kuan* jugs with fine cord marks and thin bodies; *tsun* beakers with squat bodies and short collars; *ting* tripods with basin- or bowl-like bodies; *tou* fruit stands with shallow dishlike bodies. Oracle bones are similar to the Lo-ta-miao forms, and bone hairpins are of the conical-head type.

Upper Erh-li-kang phase: Pottery of this phase is similar to the previous phase, but the tempering materials are generally coarser, the bodies thicker, and the cord marks made of thicker strands. Many of the Lower Erh-li-kang ceramic forms continued into this phase, but some of the forms that were only initiated during the previous phase now became prevalent, such as the *li* tripods with angular and up-turned rims, *hsien* tripods with coarser cord marks and conical feet, *chia* tripods with in-turned rims, *ting* tripods imitating bronze forms, *tou* with bottoms considerably higher than indicated by the external contours (false-bodied *tou*), and *tsun* beakers with elongated bodies and long collars. Oracle bones and bone hairpins are similar to the previous phase.

Jen-min Park phase: The ceramic style has changed markedly, and the pottery is largely of coarse tempering material, thick bodies, large-stranded cord marks, and crude workmanship. Few Erh-li-kang phase forms remain, while squat and short-footed *li* tripods, *tou* with low pedestals, *p'o*, *yü*, and *yu* vessels appeared. There also appeared bone hairpins with carved heads. Most of the oracle bones are turtle shells, and the preparation was elaborate. The large graves containing human victims and rich furnishings which appeared in the Upper Erh-li-kang phase continued into this phase.

The importance of the An-yang excavations in the history of archaeology in China cannot be exaggerated. The scale of the work, the time, money, and manpower devoted to the excavations, and the scientific precision of the digging are still unsurpassed in China, and it was the An-yang excavation, that settled, once and

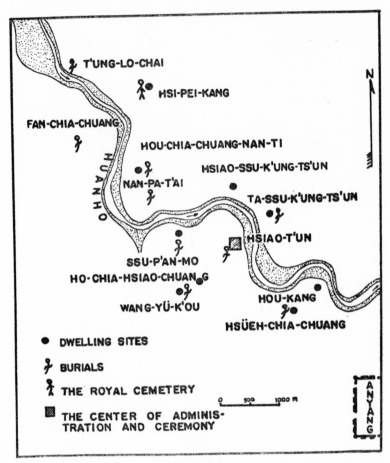

MAP 10. Shang Dynasty sites near An-yang. After KKHP, 2 (1947), 76.

for all, the controversial problem of the existence of this dynasty, previously founded exclusively on legendary history. It was also the first site given a date in the earliest segment of the Chinese written history, and thus ties written history with the prehistoric Neolithic cultures. At present, however, the importance of this site must remain qualified by the facts that the excavation work was interrupted by the Sino-Japanese War, leaving many sites in the An-yang group only partially excavated, and that the results have yet to be completely published. The center of Shang

156

studies has tended to shift from An-yang to Cheng-chou, where a longer sequence has been uncovered and a series of preliminary and final reports have been made available. An-yang's fundamental importance, however, can never be doubted. Among other things, the oracle bone inscriptions found from this area furnish much indispensable information concerning Shang culture and society that other Shang Dynasty sites may never be able to match.

According to the available data, it is clear that every known settlement in the An-yang group was a unit fairly selfsufficient in subsistence and domestic activities. Dwelling areas, pottery kilns, bronze foundries, stone workshops, bone workshops, and cemeteries have been found at most settlements. The inhabitants of each settlement probably engaged in farming and handicrafts in their own neighborhood. However, in terms of administration, economic redistribution, and religious and ceremonial affairs, each of these settlements was apparently not an autonomous and self-contained unit. In these aspects, the entire An-yang group formed a tightly organized unit, and the presence of the Royal House in this group is symbolized by the administrative and ceremonial center near Hsiao-t'un and the "Royal Cemetery" at Hsi-pei-kang.

The excavated part of the site at Hsiao-t'un (Fig. 12) is divided into three sections, A, B, and C. Section A, the northernmost, consists of fifteen parallel rectangular houses built on stamped-earth foundations. Section B, in the middle, includes twenty-one large houses, rectangular or square, built on stamped-earth foundations, and accompanied by a number of burials. These houses are arranged in three rows on a North–South axis, the central row consisting of three large houses and five gates. Section A and Section B are separated by a square-shaped stamped-earth foundation (of pure loess), which is interpreted as being a ceremonial altar. Section C, at the southwestern corner of the site, consists of seventeen stamped-earth foundations, arranged according to a preconceived plan and again accompanied by burials. Under the foundations in Section B is a complicated system of underground water ditches. The entire area of the Hsiao-t'un settlement includes about ten thousand square meters. According to the interpretation of Shih Chang-ju, Section A was probably the dwelling area of the settlement, Section B the Royal Temples, and Section C a ceremonial quarter. It is noteworthy, however, that these three

157

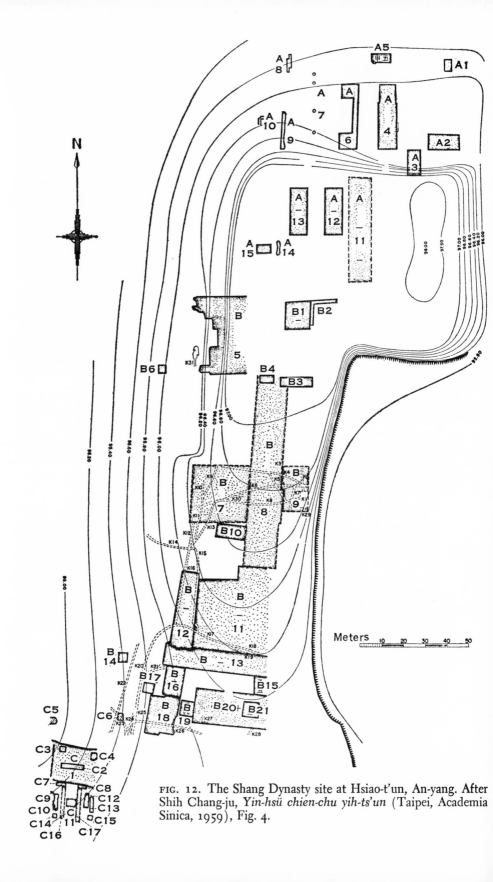

FIG. 12. The Shang Dynasty site at Hsiao-t'un, An-yang. After Shih Chang-ju, *Yin-hsü chien-chu yih-ts'un* (Taipei, Academia Sinica, 1959), Fig. 4.

sections seem to have been constructed during different time intervals, in the order of A, B, and C.[40] Considering the large scale of the construction, the elaborate planning of the houses, the extensive employment of sacrificial victims for the construction of the temples and the ceremonial altar, the fact that innumerable inscribed oracle bones were found at the site, and the mode of construction in stamped earth in contrast to the ordinary semisubterranean dwellings, it appears reasonable to assume that this settlement was the center of the Royal House of the Yin Dynasty. These "palaces" and "temples," as Tung Tso-pin describes them,

> were all above-ground houses with stamped-earth foundations and stone pillar supporters. Although they were constructed of wattle-and-daub, these structures looked glorious and solemn enough [Fig. 13]. Nearby these foundations are often semisubterranean pit houses, about four meters in diameter and same in depth. These were presumably the service area of the Royal House's subordinates. Inside the pit houses are round or rectangular bins, several meters deep and possibly places of storage.[41]

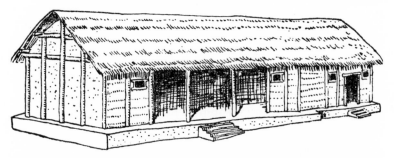

FIG. 13. A reconstructed Shang Dynasty ground house at Hsiao-t'un, An-yang. From Shih Chang-ju, *Annals*, Academia Sinica, no. 1 (1954), Fig. 2, no. 4.

These "service areas" included bronze foundries, stone and bone workshops, and pottery kilns. But some of these pit houses must have also served as domiciles. It is apparent that this Hsiao-t'un site assumed the role played by the city enclosure of Cheng-chou,

40. Shih Chang-ju, *Yin-hsü chien-chu yih-ts'un*, Taipei, Academia Sinica, 1959.
41. Tung Tso-pin, *Ta-lu-tsa-chih*, 5 (1950), 12.

but remains of a city wall have not been found. Nevertheless, it must be remembered that the Hsiao-t'un site was not completely excavated and that the excavators presumably did not look specifically for a city wall. Considering that the construction of city walls appeared at Cheng-chou before the Hsiao-t'un phase, and continued into later historical periods, I would not be surprised if future, more intensive investigations find that this site also had a walled enclosure.

Hsi-pei-kang, near Hou-chia-chuang, and the contiguous Wu-kuan-ts'un area, is best known for its "Royal Cemetery," although commoners' dwellings, workshops, and small burials have also been found here. The "Royal Cemetery" has eleven large tombs, happily coinciding in number with the eleven monarchs from P'an-keng, founder of the capital, to Ti-yih, the next to last ruler (the last king, Ti-hsin, was burned to death when the capital fell to the Chou invaders). Although it may never be fully established that these were the kings' graves, we know that they were constructed on a large scale, with elaborate ceremonial procedures.[42] According to the estimates of Li Chi,[43] the earth digging alone required no less than seven thousand working days for each of the large graves of Hsi-pei-kang.

Little is known concerning settlements at An-yang other than Hsiao-t'un and Hsi-pei-kang. Those that have been partially described include Hou-chia-chuang-nan-ti, Hou-kang, Ta-ssu-k'ung-ts'un, and Hsüeh-chia-chuang. At Hou-chia-chuang-nan-ti were found two rectangular stamped-earth foundations, each of which was accompanied by round storage pits. In the storage pits were potsherds, bone artifacts, and inscribed oracle bones, but remains of bronze foundry have not been discovered. The inscriptions on the oracle bones include questions as to the well-being of the coming ten days and of the coming evening, rituals to be performed, weather, and journey schedules.[44] These remains suggest that the Hou-chia-chuang-nan-ti settlement may have been a kind of resort palace of the kings. The Yin remains at Hou-kang con-

42. Kao Chü-hsün, *Bull. Dept. Arch. Anth., Natl. Taiwan Univ.*, 13/14 (1959), 1–9; Paul Pelliot, "The Royal Tombs of An-yang," in *Independence, Convergence, and Borrowing in Institutions, Thought, and Art*, Cambridge, Harvard Univ. Press, 1937; Tung Tso-pin, *Ta-lu-tsa-chih*, 1 (1950), 15–18; Kuo Pao-chün, *KKHP*, 5, 1951.
43. Li Chi's "Preface" to Shih Chang-ju, *Yin-hsü chien-chu yih-ts'un*, p. iii.
44. Tung Tso-pin, *TYKKPK*, 1 (1936), 91–166.

sist of dwellings and burials. The latter include one large grave and some smaller tombs. The large grave consists of a square pit, a southern and a northern ramp, a cross-shaped wooden chamber, and a central sacrificial pit (or "waist pit"). In the southern ramp were found one hundred and forty-eight bone fragments, and in the chamber were twenty-eight human skulls. This large grave may have belonged to the royal family.[45] The Ta-ssu-k'ung-ts'un remains also consist of domiciliary structures and burials. The graves are smaller than those of Hsi-pei-kang and Hou-kang, but are also accompanied by one or two sacrificial human victims, wooden structures, and bronze and jade artifacts.[46] The site at Hsüeh-chia-chuang again consists of dwelling structures and burials. In the dwelling quarter were found remains of storage pits, bronze foundries, pottery kilns, and bone workshops. The graves are both large and small, the larger ones being accompanied by bronzes and jades and the waist pits with dog sacrifices.[47]

The Yin settlement at An-yang may be summarized as follows: prior to the time of P'an-keng (1384 B.C., according to T. P. Tung's chronology), who made An-yang his capital, Yin people had already occupied the An-yang area. At any rate, at Hsiao-t'un [48] and Hsüeh-chia-chuang [49] remains were found that are similar to the Erh-li-kang phases of Cheng-chou. These are mostly of a domiciliary nature, but a bronze industry had already been established here.[50] Whether the other settlements had been occupied cannot be established at present because of the lack of stratigraphic evidence. From the time of P'an-keng (so says the traditional history, which is supported by oracle bone records), the An-yang area was the capital of the Royal House of the Shang Dynasty. Most of the settlements of the An-yang group were probably occupied by the people of Yin and by nobility connected with the Royal House. Royal palaces and ceremonial centers were constructed at Hsiao-t'un and Hou-chia-chuang-nan-ti, and the cemeteries of the royal family were constructed at Hsi-pei-kang (and Wu-kuan-

45. Shih Chang-ju, *Liu-t'ung-pieh-lu*, 1 (1945), 1–26.
46. Ma Te-chih, Chou Yüng-chen, and Chang Yün-peng, *KKHP*, 9 (1955), 25–90.
47. Chao Hsia-kwang, *WWTKTL*, 1958:12, 31; Liu Tung-chin, *KKTH*, 1958:8, 23–26.
48. Li Chi, *Chinese Civilization*, p. 45; Tsou Heng, *KKHP*, 1956:3.
49. Liu Tung-chin, *KKTH*, 1958:8, 23–26.
50. Shih Chang-ju, *Yin-hsü chien-chu yih-ts'un*.

ts'un) and Hou-kang. The individual settlements were probably more or less self-sufficient in terms of basic subsistence and handicrafts, but as far as the control of economy, political administration, and religious and ceremonial affairs are concerned, the entire An-yang settlement group appears to have formed but a single unit.

Hsing-t'ai Since 1954, Shang Dynasty sites have been located widely in the neighborhood of Hsing-t'ai, in southern Hopei, directly to the north of An-yang. Neither literary tradition nor archaeological evidence itself gives this group of Shang sites a royal capital status, but this site is all the more important in the picture it gives of Shang Dynasty civilization outside of the settlement groups which were politically prominent. Archaeological work in this area is still going on, and only preliminary reports have been published on the excavated sites. Some socioeconomic characteristics of these sites, however, are of immediate interest.

Over ten Shang Dynasty sites have thus far been located in the regions north and west of the Hsing-t'ai city, in an area approximately ten kilometers N–S and seven kilometers E–W.[51] The cultural deposits at some of the sites attain a maximum depth of three meters, testifying to the permanent nature of the settlement and the considerable duration of its habitation. Three cultural phases have been distinguished for the Yin-kuo-ts'un site, which correlate with other stratified sites in this region as follows: [52]

> Upper Yin-kuo-ts'un phase: Upper Ts'ao-yen-chuang, Upper Nan-ta-kuo-ts'un.
> Middle Yin-kuo-ts'un phase: Lower Ts'ao-yen-chuang, Lower Nan-ta-kuo-ts'un.
> Lower Yin-kuo-ts'un phase.

Cultural remains from these Shang Dynasty phases of Hsing-t'ai include many of the diagnostic Shang traits, such as oracle bones, bone hairpins, and some characteristic pottery forms and decorative motifs. Pottery kilns were found at some of the sites, whereas a bone workshop was discovered at only one settlement,

---

51. *WWTKTL*, 1956:9, 70; *WWTKTL*, 1956:12, 53–54; *WWTKTL*, 1957:3, 61–63; *WWTKTL*, 1958:10, 29–31; *KKHP*, 1958:4, 43–50; *KK*, 1959:2, 108–09; *WW*, 1960:4, 42–45, 60.
52. Tang Yün-ming, *WW*, 1960:4, 42–45.

indicating that these settlements were tied together in terms of handicraft specialization, as was the case with An-yang or Cheng-chou. *Hang-t'u* house structures, inscriptions, and bronze foundries have not been unearthed, however. Stone constituted the raw material for all of the implements, though bronze arrowheads, awls, adzes, and ornaments appear occasionally in the remains. Further investigations in the Hsing-t'ai area will undoubtedly throw much more light upon this settlement group, but the available data suggests that here in Hsing-t'ai the Shang people had an urban network similar to those at An-yang and Cheng-chou, even though there may not have been an outstanding aristocratic complex.

Other Shang Dynasty Sites Other sites of the Shang Dynasty where information is sufficient to warrant classification of Shang civilization status include Ch'i-li-p'u in Shan Hsien,[53] a series of sites in the neighborhood of Lo-yang,[54] Lu-wang-fen in Hsin-hsiang,[55] several sites in Hui Hsien,[56] Chao-ko in T'ang-yin Hsien,[57] and Shih-li-p'u in Nan-yang Hsien,[58] all in Honan province; Ta-hsin-chuang in Chi-nan, Shantung province;[59] and Feng-chia-an in Ch'ü-yang, Hopei province.[60] The sites in Lo-yang and Hui Hsien approach Cheng-chou and An-yang in extent, yielding large graves with human victims and bronze foundries. Bronze foundries have also been found at the site in Nan-yang. The other sites, however, are like the Hsing-t'ai group, yielding networks that were probably economic, yet lacking a clearly defined aristocratic complex. A typological classification of the Shang Dynasty sites as they are known at the present also has a geographical significance: Shang Dynasty sites with aristocratic complexes are confined to northern Honan, extending as far west as Lo-yang;

53. Yang Chi-chang, *KKHP*, 1960:1, 25–47.
54. Kuo Pao-chün and Lin Shou-chin, *KKHP*, 9 (1955), 91–116; Kuo Pao-chün et al., *KKHP*, 1956:1, 11–28; An Chih-min and Lin Shou-chin, *KKTH*, 1955:5, 26; *KK*, 1959:10, 537–40.
55. Wang Ming-jui and Chin Shih-hsin, *KKHP*, 1960:1, 51–60.
56. Kuo Pao-chün, Hsia Nai, et al., *Hui Hsien fa-chüeh pao-kao*, Peiping, Science Press, 1956; Li Te-pao, *KKTH*, 1957:2, 32–35.
57. An Chin-huai, *WWTKTL*, 1957:5, 86.
58. Yu Ching-chüan, *KK*, 1959:7, 370.
59. F. S. Drake, *China Journal*, 31 (1939), 77–80; 33 (1940), 8–10; Yang Tzu-fan, *WW*, 1959:11, 8–9; Li Pu-ching, *KK*, 1959:4, 185–87.
60. An Chih-min, *KKTH*, 1955:1, 39–44.

those showing a similar urbanized structure but without concentrated aristocratic complex are extended to western Honan as far as Shan Hsien, southern Hopei as far as Ch'ü-yang, and Shantung as far as Chi-nan. Shang culture traits are also found outside of this circle, but in primarily Neolithic contexts, such as those in easternmost Shensi, southeastern Honan, and northern Anhwei. These facts are indispensable in delineating the cultural and societal boundaries of the Shang civilization.

HISTORY AND CULTURE OF THE SHANG DYNASTY

Before the Shang sites at Cheng-chou were excavated, the An-yang culture was the sole representative of the Shang civilization, and our understanding of the latter was accordingly restricted and conditioned.[61] Since those excavations, however, the Cheng-chou sequence, by virtue of its long and seemingly complete stratigraphy, has been used by archaeologists as the yardstick with which the other Shang Dynasty sites are measured. Tsou Heng, for instance, has classified the cultural remains at Hsiao-t'un of the An-yang group into three stages: pre-Hang-t'u, Hang-t'u, and post-Hang-t'u. The Hang-t'u phase of An-yang, according to Tsou, can be synchronized with the Jen-min Park phase of Cheng-chou, whereas the pre-Hang-t'u was earlier than the Jen-min Park phase but later than the Upper Erh-li-kang phase, and the post-Hang-t'u phase later than the Jen-min Park phase of Cheng-chou.[62] The earliest phase at Hsing-t'ai, according to Tang Yün-ming, was probably earlier than the Erh-li-kang phases, and the later phases correspond to the latter.[63] For other sites, the terms of Erh-li-kang and Hsiao-t'un are used freely for similar chronological and classificatory purposes. Carrying this scheme to the extreme, Cheng Te-kun boldly attempts to synchronize all of the Shang Dynasty sites, which he divides into five groups: Proto Shang, Early Shang, Middle Shang, Late Shang, and Post Shang.[64]

It is true that cultural remains similar to this or that phase of the Cheng-chou sequence are found elsewhere, and this may have chronological significance. Until a number of sites other than

61. E.g., H. G. Creel, *The Birth of China*, London and New York, Reynal and Hitchcock, 1937; Li Chi, *Chinese Civilization*.
62. Tsou Heng, *KKHP*, 1956:3.
63. E.g., Cheng Te-kun, *Shang China*, p. 27.
64. Cheng Te-kun, *Shang China*, p. 37.

Cheng-chou and An-yang are excavated intensively, however, it would be impossible for us to claim that the five-fold subdivision of the Shang sequence at Cheng-chou, as it is known at a certain period in the history of Shang archaeology, is universally valid. The Shang-chieh phase of Cheng-chou, for instance, may possibly be earlier than the Proto Shang phase of Cheng Te-kun. What, then, should it be called? Cheng's Middle Shang includes both Upper Erh-li-kang of Cheng-chou and Hsiao-t'un I of An-yang, the two phases that are regarded by Tsou Heng as being chronologically successive rather than concurrent. Cheng's grouping them together apparently employs one set of criteria, then, whereas Tsou's setting them apart must use another. In the future, when a number of such long sequences will presumably be determined for a number of Shang Dynasty sites that are not as yet extensively excavated, the Cheng-chou sequence may or may not prove to be serviceable as the basic yardstick. Before we have further knowledge of the other sequences, any synchronization of all the Shang sites in North China according to the Cheng-chou sequence would seem to be dubious at best. For the time being, I believe that we are better off to confine discussion of the chronological development of the Shang culture to the few sites whose stratigraphy is reasonably well established.

The earliest strata of the Shang civilization known at present appeared in the northern part of Honan province at such sites as Ch'i-li-p'u of Shan Hsien, Tung-kan-kou of Loyang, Shang-chieh, Lo-ta-miao, and a few other sites in Cheng-chou. By this time the Neolithic economy had already begun to give way to the formation of settlement groups as self-contained units. Bronze metallurgy does not seem to have fully developed, and at the sites one does not yet see a highly intensified and sophisticated aristocratic complex. This stage seems to be a transitional phase between the Neolithic and the climactic Shang civilization. We must, nevertheless, confess that our knowledge in this stage is far from complete as yet. Available archaeological materials do not warrant the assumption that a fully-developed Shang aristocracy did not yet exist, nor are they sufficient to say that the Shang civilization came into being in the northern Honan area.

By the time the city wall was constructed at Cheng-chou, however, the socioeconomic nature of the Shang civilization and the beginning of the urbanization in North China were becoming clear. Because the term "urbanization" is somewhat arbitrarily defined in the archaeological literature,[65] we must carefully characterize the nature of city life of the Shang Dynasty in North China. The first and foremost feature of the Shang sites is that individual villages were organized into intervillage networks in economy, administration, and religion. Each in the group depended upon others for specialized services, and offered in kind in return. There was a political and ceremonial center, (a walled enclosure in the case of Cheng-chou), where the royal family and the nobles resided. It apparently served as the nerval nucleus of the entire group and, when the capital of the dynasty was located there, as the center of political and economic control of the whole kingdom. Surrounding and centripetal to this nucleus were industrial quarters, with a high degree of specialization, and farming villages. Goods apparently circulated among the various villages, with the administrative center serving also as the center for redistribution. The population size of the entire settlement group was considerable, as indicated by the spatial dimensions of the group and by the quantity and complexity of the cultural remains, and the social stratification and industrial specialization of the populace were highly intensified. We find in Shang Dynasty China no physical counterparts to such large population and architectural configurations as Ur of Mesopotamia, Mohenjo Daro of the Indus, and Teotihuacan of Mexico, yet the Shang capital sites performed all of the essential functions of a city, indicating a definite break from the Neolithic community pattern. This basic Shang city pattern continued on into later historic periods. During the Eastern Chou period the capital sites grew into large commercial and political urban centers, as will be described in the next chapter.

Purely from an archaeological perspective, the populace of a Shang city seems to have been divided into three major groups: the aristocracy, the craftsmen, and the farmers.

The Aristocracy Archaeological excavations, oracle bone inscriptions, and historic records have jointly established the fact that the Shang capitals at Cheng-chou and An-yang were seats of a powerful centralized government in control of a number of settle-

65. V. Gordon Childe, *Town Planning Review*, 21 (Liverpool, 1950), 3–17; but see R. J. Braidwood and G. R. Willey, eds., "Courses Toward Urban Life," *Viking Fund Publications in Anthropology*, 32, 1962.

ment groups scattered over a part of North China. From the oracle inscriptions and the historic records, a little is known about the Royal House, the rule of succession to the throne, and the political relationships among the various settlement groups. Mythological sources relate that the Royal House of the Shang Dynasty was a grand lineage by the name of Tzu, attributed to a divine birth in Ssu-ma Chien's *Shih Chi*, vol. 3:

> The mother of Ch'i, founder of the Yin Dynasty, was called Chien-ti, a daughter of the tribe Yu-jung and second concubine of Emperor Kao. Basking with two companions, Chien-ti saw an egg fallen from a black bird (swallow or phoenix) and swallowed it. She then became pregnant and gave birth to Ch'i.

As will be discussed below, the grand lineage occupied a central position in the state's political, economic, and ceremonial structures, which were expressed and maintained with elaborate and solemn ancestor worship rites. There is little question as to the relationship between the ancestor worship rites performed by and for the grand lineages and the origin myths of the descent of the grand lineages. According to the ancestor cult calendar worked out from the oracle inscriptions, Li Hsüeh-chin [66] has been able to generalize that among thirty-five kings of the Shang Dynasty, whose rules of succession are relatively clear, the throne was assumed by sons for eighteen generations, and for seven generations (ten kings) it was taken over by brothers.

The settlement groups that were not under the direct rule of the monarch were administered by lords appointed by the central government. The lords were relatives of the monarch (sometimes junior sons), high officials who made great contributions to the cause of the Royal House, and the *de facto* rulers of regions that paid tributes to the central government but were out of the reach of the royal forces, and whose administrative status had to be recognized.[67]

The central government and the local governments thus formed a tightly organized hierarchy, with the king at the top, assisted by officials of a royal court and priests who practiced scapulimancy, among other duties. Communications between the various settle-

66. Li Hsüeh-chin, *Wen-shih-chê*, 1957:2, 31–37.
67. Hu Hou-hsüan, *Chia-ku-hsüeh Shang-shih lun ts'ung*, 1, 1944.

ment groups and the central administration were possible with the aid of a highly developed system of writing and standardized currency. Raids and warfare between states were frequent, as judged by the war records in the inscriptions, the abundant remains of weapons, the sacrificial use of what were apparently war captives, and the use of chariots. The centralized power of government is most clearly indicated by the centralized control of manpower. As we shall see, some of the agricultural production may have been under a centralized management. In addition, public works began to appear to a significant extent. The *hang-t'u* structures at Hsiao-t'un and Cheng-chou, such as the walled enclosure and the temples and altars, were probably built by large groups of people, organized and directed by administrative powers. The construction of the big royal tombs at Hsi-pei-kang, An-yang, is of particular interest in this connection.

The social institutions that governed the aristocracy and its auxiliary groups, as indicated by the archaeological evidence and the oracle bone inscriptions, were as follows: (a) Marriage in the royal family was as a rule monogamous; the families of the Royal House, the nobility, and some of the craftsmen were of the extended family type, probably patrilineal. (b) Beyond the family, unilinear lineages may have been prevalent among the nobility and some of the craftsmen; these were possibly ramagelike kin groups based on patrilineality and primogeniture (see below). (c) The ramagelike kin groups may have been related to a part of the class structure. (d) The kinship terminology of the royal family was possibly of the generation type.

The organization of the royal family is relatively clear. According to the Yin calendar of rituals, as recorded in the oracle bone inscriptions, each king had one particular spouse.

> *P'i* (grandmothers and female ancestors) was partnered to *tsu* (grandfathers and male ancestors), *mu* (mothers) partnered to *fu* (fathers), and *fu* (daughters-in-law) partnered to *tzu* (sons). Each man usually had only one official spouse. Among all the fathers, one, and one only, had a specially supreme status, and his spouse also had a supreme status. The family descent and the calendar of rituals were both based on patrilineality.[68]

68. Li Hsüeh-chin, *Wen-shih-chê*, 1957:2, 36.

The families of the nobility seem to be of the extended type. Their domiciliary house can be represented by the foundation A4 at Hsiao-t'un, which is 28.4 meters long and 8 meters wide, and is divided into two large halls and eleven small rooms, all connected by doors.[69]

There is little question as to the existence of lineages during the Yin Dynasty. But what kind of lineage organization it was is a baffling matter. It is clear that in Yin times the principle of primogeniture played an important role, and that the order of seniority of birth was duly symbolized in the order of rituals and the classification of temples and altars into grand and lesser lines.[70] It is therefore possible that the so-called *tsung-fa* system of kinship, well known to be characteristic of the Chou Dynasty, had already started in the Yin stage, and that the Yin lineages were somewhat like the ramage system characterized by Raymond Firth and Marshall Sahlins, or the "stratified lineage" named by Morton Fried.[71] This system is characterized above all by the close correlation of political status with kinship descent, i.e., an individual's rank within the clan is determined by his consanguineal proximity to the alleged main line of descent. This being so, the class differentiation of the Yin royal famly and the local lords can at least be partially accounted for.

The highly organized ceremonial patterns of the Yin Dynasty essentially carried on the Neolithic heritage, as indicated by an institutionalized ancestor worship, the practice of scapulimancy, and the elaboration of ceremonial objects, especially vessels. But by Yin times, the ceremonial structure of society had been very much intensified and was unmistakably tied up with the aristocracy. Priests, whose main duty was probably to divine and foretell future events, served the royal court; the elaborate and sophisticated ceremonial bronze vessels were apparently used for rituals performed for the Royal House according to an annual calendar, mainly rituals of ancestor worship; the ceremonial center of the An-yang settlement group was spatially identified with the administrative center (Hsiao-t'un); and large-scale human and animal sacrifice was made for no other than the royal family.

69. Shih Chang-ju, *Annals*, Academia Sinica, 1 (1954), 267–80.
70. Hu Hou-hsüan, *Chia-ku-hsüeh Shang-shih lun ts'ung*, 1 (1944), 16.
71. Raymond Firth, *We, the Tikopia*, London, Allen and Unwin, 1936; Marshall D. Sahlins, *Social Stratification in Polynesia*, Seattle, Am. Ethnol. Soc., 1958; Morton H. Fried, *Jour. Royal Anth. Inst.*, 87 (1957), 1–29; Li Hwei, *BIE*, 4, 1957.

In this manner, the ceremonial structure was possibly correlated with the kinship structure on the one hand and with the economic system on the other. Ancestral worship was stressed and the calendar of ancestral worship rituals was carefully scheduled, reminding of and reinforcing the rules of primogeniture, the supremacy of the grand lineages, and the ramification of the lesser lineages, which became more and more degraded with each succeeding generation. The King, at the top of the hierarchal clan, was not only the supreme ruler of the kingdom and of the clan, but also the focus of attention for all rituals. The relationship among the various settlement groups of the Yin Kingdom was thus not only economically based (concentration and redistribution) but also accounted for in terms of kinship, and sanctioned and reinforced by rituals.

The Craftsmen At the Shang cities, craftsmen were physically identified with farmers rather than with the aristocracy, since the industrial quarters were distributed among the farming villages in the suburbs. Our knowledge about these men is rather limited; we know that industry was a minutely specialized affair, that each settlement group had a number of industrial centers at the service of the aristocracy to provide for the whole settlement group, that the craftsmen probably enjoyed a higher status than the ordinary farmers by virtue of their special skill and knowledge, and that various handicrafts may have been tied together with the kin group. It is mentioned in the "Chronicle of the Fourth Year of Ting Kung" (of Lu State in the Spring-Autumn Period) in *Tso Chuan* that:

> after King Wu conquered the Shang, King Ch'eng established the regime and selected men of wisdom and virtue and made them feudal lords to protect the Chou. Therefore, Chou Kung assisted the Royal House . . . and gave Lu Kung . . . six lineages of the Yin people, namely, the T'iao lineage, the Hsu Lineage, the Hsiao Lineage, the Suo Lineage, the Ch'ang-shao (a kind of drinking utensil) Lineage. And he gave K'ang Shu . . . seven lineages of the Yin people, namely, the T'ao (pottery) Lineage, the Shih (flag) Lineage, the Fan Lineage, the Ch'i (pots and pans) Lineage, the Fan Lineage, the Chi Lineage, and Chung-k'ui Lineage.

170

This passage shows that during the Yin Dynasty handicraft work was possibly a kin group affair. Some of the lineages were specialized in particular branches of handicrafts, either part time as a supplement to agriculture, or full time. The Cheng-chou potters, as mentioned above, seem to have devoted full time to a special kind of pottery, whereas other kinds of ceramics probably were the business of other groups. The skills and special technical knowledge were probably passed down within the kin groups and, due to this, the members of the group may have enjoyed certain privileges that the ordinary farmers did not have. As described above, at Cheng-chou the bronzesmiths and potters lived in aboveground stamped-earth houses which were usually associated with the nobility. The bronzesmiths' dwellings found in the region north of Tzu-ching-shan in Cheng-chou consist of four houses.

> Each house is partitioned by walls into two rooms. The two rooms are connected by a door in between. The two rooms may both have had a door to communicate with the outside, or only one of them may have had. Each room has an earth-platform by the door, and a fireplace.[72]

Furthermore, these four houses are arranged according to a definite plan, and each is separated from the next by a distance of ten to eleven meters. These facts may indicate that the bronzesmiths' families were of the extended type, and that their households belonged to one and the same patrilineage, a conclusion in complete agreement with the historic records concerning the lineage–occupation linkage.

Archaeologically substantiated handicrafts include bronze foundry, pottery manufacture, stone artifact manufacture, bone manufacture, and possibly wine making. Other professions that can be inferred from archaeological remains or have been mentioned in the oracle bone inscriptions include carpentry, sculpture, earth construction, masonry, drinking utensil manufacture, chariot manufacture, weapon manufacture, tailoring, fabric making, and flag manufacture.[73]

72. Liao Yüng-min, WWTKTL, 1957:6, 73.
73. Li Chi, *Chinese Civilization*; Li Ya-nung, *Yin-tai shê-hui sheng-huo*, Shanghai, Jenmin Press, 1955; Amano Motonosuke, *Tohogakuho*, 23, 1953; Shih Chang-ju, *BIHP*, 26, 1955; Hsia Nai, *China Reconstructs*, 1957:12; Li Chi, *BIHP*, 23 (1951), 523–619; Li Chi, *Hsiao-t'un T'ao-ch'i*; Yü Yü, *WWTKTL*, 1958:10, 26–28.

The metallurgy of the Yin Dynasty was very highly developed, as evidenced by the great variety of molding techniques, the finely cast decorations, and the huge size of some of the vessels (an extreme case being a square *ting* from An-yang, 137 cm. high, 110 cm. long, 77 cm. wide, and 700 kilograms in weight). Presumably there was minute specialization and large-scale cooperation between various specialists. However, the bronze artifacts seem to have been the monopoly of the upper classes, made for the most part for such exclusive purposes as ceremonies, warfare, and hunting. On the other hand, practically all of the tools for basic subsistence purposes, such as agricultural implements, and the utensils for domestic utilities, such as containers, continued to be made of wood, stone, clay, and bone. Thus we find that the industrial specialization during the Yin Dynasty was tightly correlated with status differentiation.

The Farmers The Yin subsistence was based on agriculture and supplemented by hunting and fishing. Remains of crops of the Yin Dynasty have been found at Cheng-chou, An-yang, and Hsing-t'ai, but have not been specified. From the oracle bone inscriptions, it can be determined that millet (probably both *Setaria* and *Panicum*), rice, and wheat were planted.[74] Little is known about the cultivation techniques except that stone hoes, spades, and sickles were used, as well as a kind of large, wooden, digging stick which may have been pushed by men or pulled by cattle and dogs, and was possibly a prototype of the plow.[75] Two crops of millet and rice were harvested each year, and irrigation was probably employed,[76] although the connection of the water ditches discovered at An-yang and Cheng-chou with irrigation has not been satisfactorily demonstrated. Those at Hsiao-t'un, at least, are not likely to have been connected with irrigation. Fertilizers may have been used, but this again is by no means certain.[77] An elaborate agricultural calendar was developed.[78] Other archaeological finds connected with farming include pestles and mortars.

74. Hu Hou-hsüan, *Chia-ku-hsüeh Shang-shih lun ts'ung*, 2 (1945), 134.
75. Ibid.
76. Ibid.
77. Hu Hou-hsüan, *Li-shih Yen-chiu*, Peiping, 1955:1.
78. Tung Tso-pin, *Yin Li P'u.*

Among the cultivated materials for fabrics were hemp [79] and silk.[80] In the domestication of animals the Yin carried on the Neolithic heritage (pigs, dogs, cattle, sheep, horses, and chickens), with some additions (water buffalo) and modifications (as the use of dogs, cattle, and sheep for sacrifice).[81]

Fishing is indicated by fish bones,[82] fishhooks, and the scripts for fish nets and fish tangles. Hunting is indicated by the large quantity of wild animal bone remains (e.g., tiger, leopard, bear, rhinoceros, deer, water deer, hare, etc.), by the remains of stone and bronze arrowheads, by the hunting records in the oracle bone inscriptions, and by the animal designs in the decorative art. However, the part played by hunting in the basic subsistence may not have been very significant. According to Li Chi, the "game huntings mentioned in the ancient inscriptions were evidently pursued for pleasure and excitement rather than for economic necessities . . . Such pursuits were the monopolies of a privileged class." [83]

There is no question that agriculture was the basis of Shang subsistence, or that the techniques were highly developed and the yield considerable. In the suburbs of Cheng-chou and An-yang, the many residential hamlets were presumably occupied by farmers who tilled the fields nearby and in the neighborhood. One controversial point among Shang specialists is whether the direct participants in agricultural production were free farmers or slaves. It is known that live slaves suffering from malnutrition, possibly war captives,[84] were sacrificed for the construction of palaces, temples, and royal tombs, were buried dead or alive with the royal body in the royal tomb, and that their bones were used as raw material for the manufacture of bone artifacts. But whether or not slaves were the sole laborers in the farming fields is not known. At Hsiao-t'un was found in one storage pit a horde of no less than four hundred stone sickles, bearing signs of usage. It has been

79. Li Chi, *An-yang Fa-chüeh Pao-kao*, 3 (1931), 466; Iwama, *Manshu Gakuho*, 4 (1936), 1–7.

80. Amano Motonosuke, *Tohogaku*, 1 (1955); Vivi Sylwan, BMFEA, 9 (1937), 119–26.

81. Shih Chang-ju, *Bull. Col. Arts, Natl. Taiwan Univ.*, 5, 1953.

82. Chao Chüan-ku et al, KKHP, 1957:1, 63; Wu Hsien-wen, KKHP, 4 (1949), 139–43.

83. Li Chi, *Bull. Dept. Arch. Anth., Natl. Taiwan Univ.*, 9/10 (1957), 12.

84. Mao Hsieh-chün and Yen Yen, VP, 3 (1959), 79–80.

suggested that this find indicates the centralized management of agricultural laborers and, this being so, that free farmers probably did not exist. Generalizations should perhaps not be made too hastily about this find, however. Amano suggests that during the Yin Dynasty there were two kinds of fields: the royal field, cultivated by slaves under a centralized management; and the clan fields, cultivated by the lower classes of the clan members.[85] This theory may have some truth in it, but no thorough general conclusion is yet in sight.

85. Amano Motonosuke, *Shigaku Kenkyu*, 62 (1956), 11.

174

Chapter Seven

Further Development

of Civilization

in North China

to 221 B.C.

The nucleus of the Shang civilization, as outlined above, was probably confined to the northern third of Honan and some of its immediate surrounding areas. While the Shang civilization flourished in this area, Neolithic and sub-Neolithic cultures apparently continued in most of the rest of China. Shang, however, was such a consolidated and vigorous power that its influence was widely felt, and archaeological evidence shows that Shang traits had probably penetrated into such far-reaching places as the Liao-tung Peninsula in the northeast, Chinese Turkestan in the west, and the South China coast in the south. Whether the Shang civilization elements played consequential roles among these Neolithic and sub-Neolithic peoples is a question for discussion in subsequent chapters; at this juncture it can be said that in areas immediately adjacent to the Shang territory the Shang influence was significant enough to have stimulated societal changes in the native cultures. Two such areas where the archaeological record shows this effect are the Huai River valley in northern Kiangsu and Anhwei, and the Lower Weishui valley in Shensi. The former, where the so-called Geometric States developed under the impact of the Shang civilization, will be described in Chapter 9. The latter, the Weishui valley civilization, must be discussed here, for this civilization, later known as the Chou, replaced the Shang when the Shang was weakened by long and exhaustive military involvement with the Huai valley powers. Until the unification of China under Shih

175

Huang Ti of the Ch'in Dynasty in 221 B.C., the historical platform of North China was occupied by the Chou civilization.

The literary records for the Shang are meager aside from the oracle bone inscriptions. Those for the Chou before the Conquest are even poorer; literary documents on the Chou civilization after the Conquest were not much more abundant until the Eastern Chou Dynasty, when literacy became relatively widespread and historical documents began to speak for a large portion of the political events. For the earlier periods of the Chou, archaeology and the study of bronze inscriptions still provide the principal sources of historical information.[1] This is one of the reasons for including in this volume the historic periods which are rightfully in the domain of historians rather than archaeologists. We have also to deal with the early historical periods here, however, for a much more pressing reason. In the next two chapters we shall discuss the emergence of civilizations and states in other parts of China which took place largely as a result of the expansion of the civilizations in North China. Without a brief description of the happenings in the North during the Shang and Chou Dynasties, contemporary events elsewhere in China become difficult to understand; nor could we even engage in a chronological study of these peripheral civilizations, which during the initial phases were mostly illiterate.

A few historical dates are of importance for this chapter. According to the traditional Chinese chronology, the Conquest, which caused the fall of the Shang and raised the Chou to the center of North China's historical stage, took place in the year 1122 B.C. Historians are not in agreement on this date, however, and no less than nine other dates have been suggested for this important historical event: 1116, 1111, 1070, 1067, 1066, 1050, 1047, 1030, and 1027.[2] Since the ancient Chinese calindrical system

---

1. The most important text in the Shang and Chou history, aside from the oracle bone and the bronze inscriptions, is Ssu-ma Chien's *Shih Chi*, compiled in the beginning of the first century B.C. *Tso Chuan* is also indispensable. Some other useful works of literature are: *Shih Ching*, *Shu Ching*, *Chu Shu Chi Nien*, *Kuo Yü*, *Kuo Ts'ê*, *Shih Pen*, and *Chou Shu*, most of which were compiled during the Eastern Chou period. For standard translations in the Western languages, with or without annotations, see: Edouard Chavannes, trans., *Les Mémoires historiques de Se-ma Ts'ien*, 5 vols. Paris, E. Leroux, 1895–1905; James Legge, trans., *The Chinese Classics*, 2d ed., 5 vols., Oxford, Clarendon Press, 1893–95.

2. Tung Tso-pin, *Bull. Col. Arts, Natl. Taiwan Univ.*, 3 (1951), 178.

is still imperfectly known, the selection among these ten different dates is more or less a matter of convenience—depending upon which date suits best each author for any particular historical problem. For the purpose of discussing civilizational and societal trends at a macroscopic scale, a precise dating of the Conquest is of secondary importance; the traditional chronology therefore will suffice.

The Chou Dynasty is ordinarily divided into two segments, Western Chou and Eastern Chou. The former designates the period during which the royal capitals of the Chou were located in the Weishui valley of Shensi, of which Hao, near Sian, was the best known and probably the most important. Eastern Chou refers to the period following the removal in 771 B.C. of the royal capital to Loyang in western Honan, under the reign of P'ing Wang. Eastern Chou is divisible into two minor periods, Ch'un-ch'iu, or Spring-and-Autumn, and Chan-kuo, or Warring-States. The dividing date between these two stages is variously set at 481, 478, 468, 453, and 403. For our purposes, round figures are sufficient: 1100 for the Conquest, 770 for the beginning of the Eastern Chou, and 450 for the beginning of the Warring-States period. These are all political events, and for cultural historical studies other subdivisions are often made, as will be made clear below.

CHOU BEFORE THE CONQUEST

The legendary ancestor of the Chou people is called Hou-chi or Ch'i. According to Ssu-ma Chien:

> Hou-chi's mother was a daughter of the Tribe Yu-yih and was called Chiang-yüan. Chiang-yüan was the first concubine of Emperor Kao. Once Chiang-yüan was out in the field and saw a footprint of a giant. She felt delighted and was desirous of fitting her own foot into it. She did so and felt her body moved like being pregnant. After the expected interval of time, she gave birth to a child, Ch'i. Shih Chi, vol. 4.)

The Book of Odes places the locality of Hou-chi at Yu-yih. Yu-yih has been variably identified with several places in the Middle Weishui valley of Shensi and the Lower Fenho valley of Shansi. It has been well established, in any case, that the Chou people

177

had been settled in the Weishui valley since the reign of T'ai-wang, who is said to have moved to Ch'i, near Pao-chi in the Middle Weishui. T'ai-wang was the great-grandfather of Wu Wang, under whose reign the Conquest was accomplished. Therefore it is without question that for at least four generations the seat of the state of Chou was located in the Weishui valley of Shensi, during a later part of the Shang Dynasty.

Archaeological excavations of the Lower Fenho and the Weishui valley have established that the ancient cultural sequence in these regions is a succession of Yangshao Neolithic, Langshanoid Neolithic, and Chou. Yin-Shang sites have been identified in the eastern extremity of Shensi; but these, pending detailed reports of the excavations, can only be regarded as indicating cultural influence of the Shang upon its contemporary Weishui valley inhabitants, whether they were still Neolithic or already Western Chou.

Western Chou remains in the Weishui valley were identified and excavated by Su Ping-chi and Shih Chang-ju during the thirties and forties,[3] but it was not until the early fifties that the Neolithic–Chou sequence began to be clearly defined and formulated. At K'ai-jui-chuang, near Sian, Su Ping-chi and Wu Ju-tso, as mentioned before, grouped the early cultural remains according to the stratigraphic evidence into three classes, Yangshao, Lungshanoid (K'ai-jui-chuang II in their terminology), and Chou, and characterized the Chou stratum as follows: [4]

> Gray pottery with relatively homogeneous color, wheel marks, angular rims, clearly defined, decorative cord marks confined to the body parts of vessels, *li* tripods with low feet, low collars, and nearly flat bottoms, basins, *tou*, and plain jugs with undecorated surfaces.

No less than nine localities in the neighborhood of Sian are assigned by Su and Wu to the Chou stratum; these are characterized as having deep cultural deposits, rectangular pits, graves containing human sacrifices, and relatively concentrated habitations.

The question we are interested in at the moment is not whether

---

3. Shih Chang-ju, *BIHP*, 27 (1956), 205–323; Su Ping-chi, *Tou-chi-t'ai Kou-tung-ch'ü mu-tsang*, Peiping, National Academy of Peiping, 1948.
4. Su Ping-chi and Wu Ju-tso, *KKTH*, 1956:2, 36.

Chou civilization has been established as later than the Neolithic stage in time, which is certainly the case, but whether in archaeological remains we can identify the period of the Western Chou before the Conquest of Yin. We need to know about this period in order to answer such questions as whether Chou had a well-developed state organization and advanced technology before taking over North China from the Shang and whether Western Chou had a distinctly different civilization of its own before taking over the Shang heritage, as distinguished from the contemporary Shang civilization to the east. We know for a fact that the Chou occupation in the Weishui valley continued after the Conquest, and that the Chou took over the cultural legacy of the Shang. Therefore, the problem of pre-Conquest Western Chou culture is extremely difficult to deal with in terms of archaeology.

Ritual bronzes and large tombs of the Chou period have been found in the Weishui valley, but all that have been found thus far seem to date within the latter parts of the Western Chou Dynasty.[5] Chou remains with Shang-Yin elements of Hsiao-t'un types have been found which are not necessarily contemporary with the Shang, and hence before the Conquest, (there is no reason to suppose these elements could *not* have been brought back to the west after the Conquest), such as those grouped by Shih Chang-ju in his Tou-men stage.[6] Remains of this kind are inadequately described, and afford no ground for speculation in cultural-societal terms. Cultural remains of Chou types with Yin-Shang elements of the Erh-li-kang phase have been identified at some of the Lower Weishui valley sites. These are the only remains that give any elucidation of the pre-Conquest periods of the Western Chou at all, aside from the reference to Chou in the Shang oracle texts as a powerful subordinate to be reckoned with. We know only that metal artifacts have been found here; the materials are far from sufficient for a precise definition of the Western Chou civilization.[7]

Until the pre-Conquest phases of the Western Chou civilization

5. The only existing inscribed bronze vessel that *could* date from the pre-Conquest period of Western Chou history is the so-called *T'ien-wang Kwei*; see: Sun Tso-yün, WWTKTL, 1958:1, 29–31; Chien Po-chüan, WWTKTL, 1958:12, 56–57; Sun Tso-yün, WW, 1960:5, 50–52; Yin Ti-fei, WW, 1960:5, 53–54.

6. Shih Chang-ju, BIHP, 27 (1956), 315.

7. Hsü Yih, WWTKTL, 1956:3, 65.

are better known, we are faced with two equally plausible alternative interpretations of this crucial historical stage. Either the Western Chou people were not much more than an advanced Neolithic Lungshanoid group, which conquered the Royal House of the Shang, adopted their Bronze Age cultural legacy and propagated the civilizational growth in North China; or they developed a distinctive Western Chou civilization on their Neolithic basis before the Conquest which was abandoned after the Conquest in favor of adopting and propagating the Shang civilization. No matter which of these theories eventually proves to be the case, the important point is that after the Conquest the Western Chou adopted the Shang civilization and made some changes without adding to it significant stylistic elements of a different strain. The Western Chou after the Conquest, therefore, was a linear descendant of the Shang civilization, and the Conquest involves no major discontinuity as far as the civilizational growth of the Yellow River valley is concerned.

The Royal Chou had a life span of approximately one thousand years. What happened during this long millennium in political history is described in many textbooks of ancient Chinese history and will not be dealt with in this volume. In order to show the pattern of civilizational growth and the forces of expansion which affected the rest of China, some topics in this cultural history of the Chou Dynasty will be selected for discussion. For the following presentation, primarily archaeological materials will be utilized.

DEVELOPMENT OF CITIES

In the last chapter the characteristics of the first cities in North China have been described; the Shang cities are shown to have consisted physically of an aristocratic center, in the shape of a walled enclosure of pounded earth, in which the aristocratic and ceremonial buildings and structures were located, and the area around this enclosure, where specialized industrial quarters and farming villages are found. When we trace these constituents of Shang cities down in time, a number of persistent traditions can be shown to have continued throughout the entire span of the Chou Dynasty, such as the wall of stamped earth, the ceremonial and palatial platform, and the aristocratic center. The basic pattern of urban organization, however, underwent some important changes with time.

In the history of city development, unfortunately, there is a considerable hiatus for the entire Western Chou period where archaeological materials are totally lacking. This hiatus is not fatal, however, for the culture during this interval of approximately four hundred years is known from other kinds of remains, to be discussed later in this chapter. Furthermore, as we shall see, the basic change in the pattern of urbanization seems to have come after the beginning of the Eastern Chou Dynasty.

There is no question that the Western Chou aristocracy were city builders. The poem *Wen Wang Yu Sheng* in the section of *Ta Ya* of the *Book of Odes* describes how Wen Wang built the city of Feng and Wu Wang the city of Hao. Lo-yang, an eastern capital during the Western Chou Dynasty, was, according to *Tso Lo Chieh* in *Yih Chou Shu*, situated between the River Lo in the south and Chia Mountain in the north, and consisted of two enclosures of considerable dimensions. This fragment of information about the double enclosures may or may not be reliable, as will be made clear below. The city enclosure was apparently again built of layers of stamped earth, the construction of which was described vividly in the poems of *Hung Yen Chih Shih* and *Mien P'ien* in the *Ya* sections of the *Book of Odes*, which are generally regarded as containing reliable data from the Western Chou Dynasty.

During the Eastern Chou Dynasty, when a series of local states came to age, the number of cities certainly increased greatly and their distribution expanded throughout North China. Oshima Riichi has been able, according to *Tso Chuan* and *Kung Yang Chuan*, to list no less than 78 cities that were recorded as having been built during the Ch'un-ch'iu period from 722–480 B.C. These include 27 cities in the state of Lu, 20 in Ch'u, 10 in Chin, 4 in Cheng, 3 in Ch'i, 2 in Sung, and 1 each in Chu, Ch'en, Wu, and Yüeh, extending in area throughout North China and the lower and middle Yangtze valley.[8] There were presumably other cities in these and other states that were not recorded in the two sources Oshima has consulted. Archaeological surveys and excavations have thus far located and explored the remains of the following cities of the Eastern Chou period (Fig. 14).

8. Oshima Riichi, *Tohogakuho*, 30 (1959), Kyoto, 53.

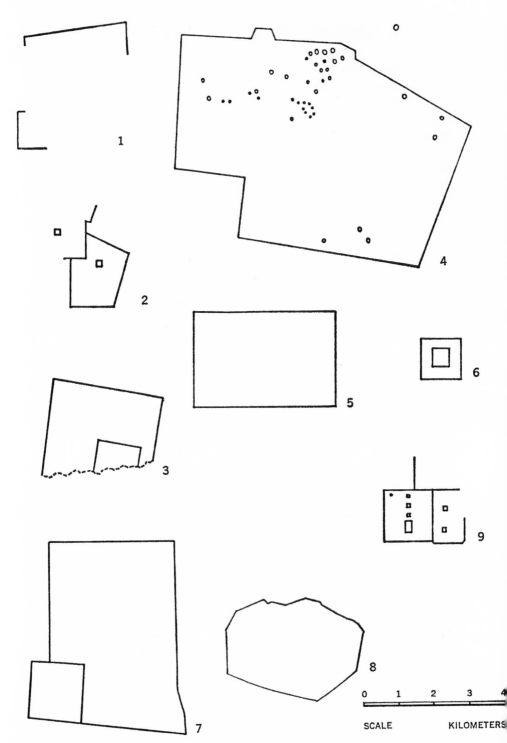

FIG. 14. Shapes and dimensions of known Eastern Chou cities. 1. Lo-yang; 2. Hsin-t'ien; 3. Wo-kuo; 4. Hsia-tu; 5. Hsüeh; 6. T'eng; 7. Lin-tzu; 8. Ch'ü-fu; 9. Han-tan.

Lo-yang (Royal Chou) The royal city of Lo-yang during the Eastern Chou Dynasty has only begun to be explored; the results published thus far are preliminary.[9] The city wall of the Eastern Chou period has been outlined, although only the northern wall, the northern sections of the western and eastern walls, a southern section of the western wall and a western section of the southern wall have been located. These walls made an enclosure approximately square in shape, with a length of 2890 meters on the northern side. The walls were built in stamped-earth layers, averaging about five meters wide at the base, with a surviving height of 1.5–4 meters. Excavations carried out within the enclosure tend to show that important buildings were located in the southern or central part of the enclosure, as indicated by a large amount of tiles (both flat and semicylindrical types) and eave tiles with *t'ao-t'ieh* and *yün* patterns. A pottery kiln area and one adjacent house foundation were located in the northwestern section of the enclosure; to the southeast of the kiln area there was a bone factory, and, further to the south, a factory for making stone ornaments. Water ditches have been identified at scattered spots within the city. Associated cultural remains show that the city was built prior to the middle of the Ch'un-ch'iu period and was continuously in use until the latter phases of the Western Han Dynasty, when a smaller enclosure within the former Lo-yang site was constructed. This Han Dynasty town is known as the seat of Honan county.[10]

Hsin-t'ien (State of Chin) The ruins of two old cities northwest of Hou-ma in southern Shansi were brought to light in 1957. Field work is still actively going on there, but a general idea about the setup of these cities can be obtained from a series of preliminary reports.[11] These ruins have been dated to a late phase of the Ch'un-ch'iu period, with one of the two probably succeeding the other, and are identified with the city of Hsin-t'ien, one of the capitals of the prince of Chin.

The two cities adjoined each other diagonally. One, in the northwest, has been called the Old City of P'ing-wang, named

9. Chen Kung-jou, *KKHP*, 1959:2, 15–34.
10. Kuo Pao-chün, *KKTH*, 1955:1, 9–21.
11. *KK*, 1959:5, 222–28; Chang Shou-chung, *WW*, 1960:8/9, 11–14; Yang Fu-tou, *WWTKTL*, 1957:10, 55–56; Chang Wen-chai, *WWTKTL*, 1958:12, 32–33; Chang Wen-chai, Chang Shou-chung, and Yang Fu-tou, *WW*, 1959:6, 42–44; *WW*, 1959:6, 43, 44–45; *WW*, 1962:4/5, 37–54.

after a village nearby, and the other, in the southeast, the Old City of Niu-ts'un, after a village of that name. Most of the walls of the Niu-ts'un city have been located in an enclosure 1340–1740 m. N–S and 1100–1400 m. W–E, forming a rough rectangle with an oblique northern wall. Only the southeastern corner of the P'ing-wang city has been found, which intruded into the northwestern corner of the Niu-ts'un city, and its general outline is still unknown. Both of the cities were built in stamped-earth layers by means of the pisé technique, but the surviving walls, completely covered under the ground, are only about one m. high. The earth making up the wall is fairly pure, and each stamped layer is about six cm. thick. The cities seem to have been built on top of a cemetery area of early Ch'un-ch'iu period, but were both intruded into by tombs of the Warring-States period and by vehicle roads constructed during the Warring-States and Western Han. It seems probable, therefore, that the two cities were built successively during a later period of the Ch'un-ch'iu.

The only remains found within the city enclosures are a road section within the Niu-ts'un city and two platforms, one in each city, on which relics of buildings were found. The platform of the P'ing-wang city is located in the southern part of the enclosure, but since the northern wall of this city has not been found the precise location is not clear. It was built on three levels. The bottom level is a square of 75 m. to a side, oriented according to the four cardinal directions. Only the top of this level has been excavated, which is of stamped-earth construction. A stamped-earth rectangle, 30 m. wide and over 20 m. long, adjoins the center of the southern side of the bottom level, and is attached to a sloping ramp, about 6 m. wide and over 20 m. long, extending toward the south. The second level is about 4 m. above the ground; the central portion of its southern side is sloping. The third level is situated atop the northern portion of the second level, making a rectangle 35 m. N–S and 45 m. E–W. Fragments of tiles and a stone block, possibly a pillar foundation, were found on the top level of the platform. The whole platform is 8.5 m. high, consisting entirely of compactly stamped pure earth. The Niu-ts'un platform, situated in the northern part of the center within the city enclosure, is a rectangle 52.5 by 52.5 m. and 6.5 m. high, composed of compactly stamped earth. Remains of buildings, such as fragments of tiles, are found on top of the platform, which has a

184

depth of over one meter. The northern side of the platform is vertical, and the southern side forms a slope. Investigators of the site call both of these platforms "palace foundations." Apparently the buildings atop the platforms were of considerable dimensions, facing south, and accessible by long ramps extending from the top of the platforms toward the bottom and the south.

A section of ditch 6 m. wide and 3–4 m. deep, possibly the remains of a defensive watercourse surrounding the city, was found outside of the south wall of the Niu-ts'un city.

Outside of the Hsin-t'ien cities, but in the immediate neighborhood, a variety of other remains of approximately the same age has been found. Two foundries were located to the south of the Niu-ts'un city, over 200 m. apart. Thousands of fragments of clay molds and remains of crucibles were found. At one of the two foundries, the molds were used exclusively for the manufacture of such implements as spades and chisels and *pu* coins, whereas at the other foundry only molds for the making of belt hooks and carriage fittings were uncovered. Three bone manufactories have been located in the Hou-ma group, two in the neighborhood of the foundries, the other one over 1000 m. to the southeast. Wastes and raw materials, mostly deer bones, constitute the bulk of recovered remains at these three spots. A pottery kiln area has been located 1000 m. to the southeast of the Niu-ts'un city; kilns are concentrated within an area of about half a square km., and some of them adjoin one another. The pots found in and near the kilns are of the same types as those found in the Niu-ts'un city area.

A residential village, also of the same age, was located approximately 5 km. to the east of the Niu-ts'un city. The dwellings were all semisubterranean, about 1.4–1.5 m. deep into the ground and 3 by 2.4 or 4 by 3 in dimensions. The doors always face the south, leading from the ground into the floor by stairways. Each house has a small cache on the wall, some of which are divided into two levels. The upper part of the house was apparently built with wooden beams and covered with tiles. These houses are always in clusters, and are accompanied by storage pits and sometimes by wells. Potsherds, shell saws, shell knives, bone hairpins, and bronze awls were found in and near the houses. Storage pits have been found at most of the sites in the Hsin-t'ien area. Some of them were apparently for the storage of grains and soybeans, remains of which have been found. Another residential village was found south of the Niu-ts'un city, where houses, storage pits, wells, and bronze foundries were identified.

Two groups of animal burials have been located, ½ km. south and the other 3 km. east of the Niu-ts'un city. These were oval pits, arranged regularly in groups, in which skeletons of horses (many), sheep (relatively few), and cattle (rare) were excavated. These animals seem to have been tied up and placed upside down alive in the pits. Associated with the skeletons were bronze ornaments and jade artifacts.

The Hsin-t'ien cities near Hou-ma, as described above, strongly recall the cities of the Shang Dynasty in their basic constitution. The city enclosures were probably the seats of aristocracy and state religion, and the farming and handicraft hamlets were located in the surrounding suburbs. The investigators have concluded, rightly I think, that these cities were no ordinary cities but the capitals of princes. They have attempted to identify these ruins as being the Hsin-t'ien city of Chin, capital of no less than thirteen Chin princes, on the basis that their geographic location matches the description given to this city in the historic records. Whether this identification is correct or not is of no great consequence for us. As far as the archaeological picture shows, the dating and basic pattern of these cities can be considered established.

Wo-kuo (*State of Chin*) A city site of the Eastern Chou period with a double enclosure was found in 1956 about 1 km. southwest of Ch'ü-wo in southern Shansi, approximately 8700–11,200 m. east of the city of Hsin-t'ien, described above. The inner enclosure is a square of about 1100 m. to a side, but the southern wall has been eroded by the River K'uai and only 600–1000 m. of the east and west walls are left. The walls have a remaining height of 1–3 m., are about 12 m. wide at the base, and are composed of stamped earth in layers 6 cm. thick. The outer enclosure now has only the northern and western walls left, the former over 3100 m. long and the latter 2600 m. The distance between the northern walls of these two enclosures is about 1400 m. Preliminary surveys at this site show that cultural remains are abundant within the inner enclosure, including some tiles and pottery of the Hsin-t'ien type, and also a large number of tiles which are probably Warring-States and Han Dynasty in date. The location of this site coincides with the description given in historic records for the Wo-kuo city, capital of the state of Chin before it was moved to Hsin-t'ien, although the ruins that have been found here seem to date from later periods.[12] To the west of the city site a Warring-States tomb containing human sacrificial victims has been found.[13]

Han-tan (State of Chao) Chin was divided up into three states during the Warring-States period, Han, Chao, and Wei. Except for a military stronghold town located in 1959 near Hua-yin Hsien, Shensi, which may have been Yin-chin of Wei in the historical books,[14] no archaeological ruins of Han or Wei states have been brought to light. Three city sites have been found, however, which are probably attributable to the State of Chao, namely, Han-tan, Wu-ch'eng and Wu-chi, all situated in the southern part of Hopei.

The name of Han-tan was first mentioned in *Tso Chuan,* the Tenth Year of Ting Kung (500 B.C.), and was the capital city of Chao from 386 B.C. (the first year of Ching Hou) to 228 B.C., when Ch'in conquered the city and terminated the state. This old city of Han-tan, known throughout Chinese history as located about 4 km. southwest of the present city of Han-tan in southern Hopei, was investigated by a group of Japanese and Chinese archaeologists in 1939.[15]

The ruins of Han-tan consist of two adjoining enclosures, with a possible third to the north. The city proper is roughly square-shaped, about 1400 m. to a side. An eastern annex, using the eastern wall of the city proper as its western wall, is about half the size. A section of a wall over 520 m. long, possibly the remains of a second annex, has been found, which extends from the northern wall of the city proper northward. The wall, of *hang-t'u* construction, is given a reconstructed height of over 15 m. and a reconstructed base width of over 20 m. Each of the walls of the city proper has from one to three openings, near which are scattered tiles and bricks. These were probably the gates of the city. Within and near the enclosures are remains of no less than sixteen earth

---

12. *KK,* 1959:5, 222–23.
13. Chang Wen-chai, *WW,* 1960:8/9, 15–18.
14. Li Yü-chun, *KK,* 1959:11, 604–05. See *KK,* 1961:1, 32, for a city site possibly of the state of Han.
15. Komai Kazuchika and Sekino Takeshi, "Han-tan," *Archaeologia Orientalis,* ser. B, 7, 1954.

platforms, ten of which are of considerable dimensions. At the middle of the city proper, four of these platforms are located along the N–S axis. The first one from the south, known among the natives as Lung T'ai, is the largest; it is 13.5 m. high, 210 m. (E–W) by 288 m. (N–S) at the base, and 105 (E–W) by 130–140 m. (N–S) at the top. On its flat surface no cultural remains of any significant amount have been found. The second platform, to the north of Lung-t'ai, is 4.5 m. high and 49 by 51 m. in size. On top of it were found two parallel rows of stone pillar foundations, lying N–S, and, outside of these, two more rows of bricks. These are considered to have been the remains of two corridors, on top of which was probably a second floor. The platform to its north, 3 m. high and 60 by 70 m. in size, has no stone foundations. On it were fragments of tiles, pottery, knife-coins, and a small number of other bronze and iron implements. The northernmost platform of this row is round, with a diameter of 62 m. and a height of 7.5 m. Two square platforms are located in the eastern annex, again along the N–S axis, slightly to the west of the middle. The other platforms, all rectangular or square except for one which is round, are scattered in and around the city. Bricks and tiles are found atop all the platforms; the eave tiles and pottery types date the city site to the Warring-States period.

A cemetery of this period was excavated in 1957 in an area west of the Chao city.[16]

Wu-ch'eng (State of Chao)   The ruins of Wu-ch'eng, found recently, form a rough square enclosure, about 1.1 km. to a side. The wall, with a remaining height of 6 m. and a base width of 12 m., is constructed of stamped earth layers, each 8–11 cm. thick. Five or six openings are located in the western and northern walls, which are intact. A long water ditch, 20–30 m. in length, was found along the northern wall. Cultural remains within the city, consisting of tiles, eave tiles, potsherds, *pu* coins, spindle whorls, and bronze arrowheads, are mostly of the Warring-States type, with some Han Dynasty forms. Urn-burials of infants have been excavated in an eastern part of the city.[17]

16. *KK*, 1959:10, 531–36.
17. Ao Cheng-lung, *KK*, 1959:7, 354–57.

Wu-chi (State of Chao)   Two ancient city ruins are known southwest of Wu-an Hsien, southern Hopei. The one in the west, near the town of Wu-chi, was investigated in 1956. The earthen walls, again of stamped earth, 8–13 m. wide and with a remaining height of 3–6 m., form a roughly rectangular enclosure, 889 m. E–W and 768 m. N–S. There was one gate in each wall, and paved roads extended in and out. Residential remains, wells, pottery kilns, and burials were found in the western part of the enclosure and indicate a dating of Eastern Chou through Western Han.[18]

Hsia-tu (State of Yen)   Excavated in 1930 and 1958, the ruined city of Hsia-tu, near Yih Hsien in Hopei, was an important city of the State of Yen, possibly occupied during the time interval between 697 B.C. and 226 B.C. It has a somewhat rectangular walled enclosure, approximately 8300 m. E–W and 3930 m. N–S. The southeastern third of the walled area was again divided by two internal walls into a smaller enclosure, about 4500 by 3200 m. in area. The wall is of pisé structure with an average remaining height of 5 m. Over fifty earthen platforms were seen outside the northern wall as well as inside the city, densely distributed along the two northern walls. Most of these platforms are believed to have been burial mounds, but several larger ones in the northeastern part of the city area (including both enclosures) may have been religious or palatial sites. The largest platform, Lao-lao-t'ai, lies outside the northern wall and is over 8 m. high. The southern side of the platform was cut into three levels. Architectural relics, pottery, bronze and iron implements, weapons, ornaments, and coins were found atop the Lao-lao-t'ai. At the center of the platform is a circular mound about 2 m. high.

Most of the cultural remains were collected and excavated within the inner enclosure, which was probably the center of gravity when Hsia-tu was a Yen capital. The northern part of the inner enclosure, where the larger platforms are situated, has yielded many stamped-earth foundations, constructed symmetrically in relation to the platforms, forming a row at the center perpendicular to the inner northern wall. According to the excavators, this was

18. Meng Hao, Chen Hui, and Liu Lai-cheng, *KKTH*, 1957:4, 43–47; Meng Hao, *KK*, 1959:7, 338–42; Chen Hui, *KK*, 1959:7, 343–45.

probably the palace region. Iron and bronze foundry remains are concentrated in an area immediately to the southwest of the palaces, and in the southern part of the inner enclosure were found residential remains, possibly indicating the location of the living quarters for the commoners.[19]

Lin-tzu (State of Ch'i)   The ruins of a Warring-States city, identified as the Ch'i capital of Lin-tzu, were investigated by Sekino in 1940 and 1941.[20] The city consists of two enclosures of stamped-earth walls. The larger one, rectangular in shape, is approximately 4 km. E–W and over 4 km. N–S. At the southwestern corner of the large enclosure was built a smaller one, about 1350 m. square. An oval-shaped earthen platform was located to the west of the center of the smaller enclosure, approximately 65 by 73 m. in size, atop which were found remains of tiles. Several other platforms were also found, one at the northeastern corner of the larger enclosure, and the others outside the city area. Cultural remains have been brought to light from all over the city, including tiles, eave tiles, bricks, potsherds, knife-coins, and bronze arrowheads. Cowry shells, a clay mold for mirror manufacture, and a clay seal were purchased from the natives and were reportedly found at various localities within the larger enclosure. According to Sekino,[21] the small enclosure was probably the seat of the Ch'i prince, where palaces and administrative offices were located, and the larger enclosure housed the markets and the residential area. According to Sekino's estimates, the dimensions of the city and the amount of cultural remains indicate a population of scores of thousands of households.

Summary   In assessing the significance of the data on Chou Dynasty cities in the development of the city in North China, the nature of our data must be constantly borne in mind. Among the scores of Eastern Chou cities we know from history, the above eight, together with a few others which have not been described because of the lack of relevant information, such as the T'eng,

19. Fu Chen-lun, *Kuo-Hsüeh Chi-k'an,* 3 (Peking Univ., 1932), 175–82; Fu Chen-lun, *KKTH,* 1955:4, 18–26; Hsieh Hsi-yih, *WWTKTL,* 1957:9, 61–63; Huang Ching-lueh, *KK,* 1962:1, 10–19, 54.
20. Sekino Takeshi, *Chugaku Kōkogaku Kenkyu* (Tokyo, Univ. of Tokyo, Institute for Oriental Culture, 1956), 241–94. For new investigations at this site in 1958, see *KK,* 1961:6, 289–97.
21. Ibid.

Hsüeh, and Ch'ü-fu cities in Shantung,[22] represent a mere fraction. Of those that have been described, not a single one has been intensively excavated, and the available information is very sketchy and uneven. Their chronological positions are not all sufficiently certain. Furthermore, these cities belonged to different states, which must have had somewhat distinctive cultural characteristics of their own within the general framework of the North China civilization of the Chou Dynasty. Some of these cities were probably royal or princely capitals, while others were presumably provincial towns. Undoubtedly their natures were not the same, and their basic constitutions not always comparable.

Even so, some broad general trends of city growth can be ascertained from the above data. There are, apparently, some constants observable in the city history from the Shang through the beginnings of the Han Dynasty. First, the cities tended to be walled. Second, the city wall was in all cases constructed of stamped earth. Third, the majority of the cities were rectangular or square in shape, though in some cases these shapes were of a rather irregular nature. Fourth, the orientation of the city enclosure and the ceremonial and palace structure was constantly guided by the four cardinal directions, with an emphasis upon the North–South axis. Fifth, earthen platforms or mounds always served as the foundation of structures which were politically and/or ceremonially important (Fig. 15). Sixth and last, the basic constitution of specialized quarters is constant to all of the cities. A city always consisted of a number of parts, no one of which could be considered totally independent in terms of economy, political system, and religion.

There are obviously also some profound differences. Some of these are in the area of architecture, such as the beginning of the use of tiles during the Western Chou Dynasty [23] and of bricks during the Warring-States. Others, however, are more reflective of socioeconomic changes. One of the most important changes of this nature has to do with the general layout of the city and its interior subdivisions.[24]

22. Ibid., pp. 303–25; Komai Kazuchika, *Archaeological Research Reports*, 2 (1951), Tokyo University, Faculty of Letters.
23. Lin Chih-ts'un, *KKTH*, 1958:9, 73.
24. Li Ya-nung, *Chung-kuo ti nu-li-chih yü feng-chien-chih* (Shanghai, Huatung Jenmin Press, 1954), pp. 138–46; Miyazaki Ichisada, *Asiatica, Studies in the Oriental History*, 1 (1957), 50–65; Oshima Riichi, *Tohogakuho*, 30, 1959; Miyazaki Ichisada, *Shirin*, 33, 1950.

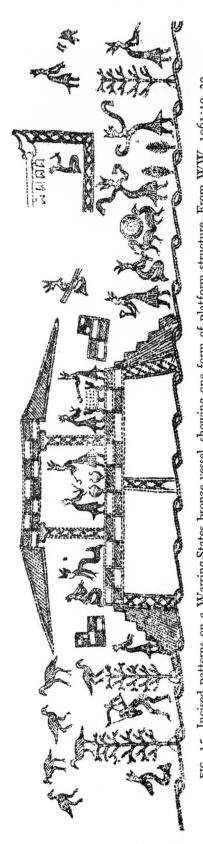

FIG. 15. Incised patterns on a Warring-States bronze vessel, showing one form of platform structure. From *WW*, 1961:10, 29.

The Shang city of Cheng-chou had a walled enclosure as its administrative and religious center; outside the enclosure there were specialized industrial quarters and residential and farming villages. The city at An-yang had the same arrangement, even though no walled enclosure has been brought to light. The essential contrasts within the city area, then, are those between the aristocratic center and the rest of the community. This basic pattern seems to be retained by the Chin State capital at Hsin-t'ien as late as the second half of the Ch'un-ch'iu period. In ancient literature pertaining to the Chou, this contrast appears to be reflected in several terms which are not, however, always clearly definable. The city as a whole seems to have been called "yih," a term which began to appear in the oracle bone inscriptions. The *yih* physically has two divisions, *tu* or *kuo*, where *chün-tzu* ("gentlemen") lived, and *pi*, occupied by *min* (folk) or *yieh-jen* ("people of the field").

A new layout of the city began to appear, in the case of Lin-tzu, for example, toward the end of the Ch'un-ch'iu period. In addition to a walled enclosure which housed the aristocratic center, a larger area was enclosed within another wall, which included the industrial quarters, along with residences and commercial streets. In the case of Lo-yang, as far as the available archaeological record goes, this change involves simply an enlargement of the city enclosure to include some residential and industrial quarters that were formerly outside the city. The Hsia-tu layout and functional specialization are not altogether clear; it has two walled enclosures, similar to Lin-tzu and Han-tan, but the inner enclosure includes industrial and residential quarters as well as the aristocrats' ceremonial and administrative quarters, and the functions of the outer enclosure are not clearly revealed by the excavated remains. In any case, in most of the Eastern Chou cities, there now were three contrasting spacial units within the city area: aristocracy in a small enclosure or at a special area; industrial and commercial quarters in a larger enclosure; and the farming fields outside the city wall. In *Mencius*, this triple division is made clear in the following quotation:

> [If so, then] the gentlemen scholars would be anxious to serve in Your Excellency's court, the farmers would be anxious to till Your Excellency's land, and the merchants would be anxious to store their goods in Your Excellency's market.

193

In the *Ch'i Yü* section of *Kuo Yü*, the same divisions are given as administration (*kuan-fu*), market (*shih-ching*), and fields (*t'ien-yieh*). In some of the lesser cities which were not capital seats of the princes, such as the Wu-chi city described above, the aristocratic center of the city may not have been a major center within the city, but the same principle, that of the walled enclosure including industries and residences as well as the aristocracy, still held. When there was a double enclosure, the outer wall was referred to as *kuo*, and the inner as *ch'eng*. Both of these terms can be applied to the wall when there is only a single enclosure.

This change in the city layout during the Chan-kuo stage, which archaeological materials have amply substantiated, is surely highly significant. In the first place, it is apparent that the more people there are enclosed within a walled area, engaging in specialized activities, the less people there are to participate directly in farming the fields outside the city enclosure. Such large Warring-States cities as Lo-yang (ca. 3000 m. square), Liu-tzu (ca. 4000 m. square), and Hsia-tu (ca. 8000 by 4000 m.) presumably housed a considerable population of remarkable density. This indicates, among other things, the existence of a highly developed technology, advanced cultivating techniques, and sophisticated administration.

Secondly, the new layout symbolizes the growing importance and increasing specialization of the handicrafts. Cheng-chou and Hou-ma cities have produced evidence to show that minute subdivisions within the manufacture of bronze artifacts alone were already developed. The new city layout further intensified this specialization by enclosing the industrial quarters within the control and protection of the walled city itself. In the third place, commercial streets, which had not been seen before, now form an important part of the city structure. Historic records show that jewelry, curios, furs and leathers, fabrics and clothing, salt, drugs, food, and wine were all purchased at stores in the Warring-States cities, where inns, restaurants, gambling houses, and brothels were also found. The widespread appearance of state currency and the construction of roads shown in the archaeological data further testify to the important role played by commerce in the cities. And finally, the enlarged enclosure and the water ditches surrounding the city indicate a growing need for defense against invasions. In *Tsa-shou-pien* of *Mo Tzu*, Mo Tzu listed five condi-

194

tions under which a city could not defend itself. These were (1) when a large city had a small population; (2) when a small city had a large population; (3) when a large population had insufficient food supply; (4) when the market area was too far from the administrative center; and (5) when the wealth and the wealthy were outside the city wall. Thus, a prevailing principle of urban planning during the latter part of the Eastern Chou was apparently to enclose the market, the industries, and the wealth within the city wall for defensive purposes.

The history of city development in North China cannot be understood without going into other aspects of the Chou cultural history; the following discussions may help to illustrate some of these aspects.

TECHNOLOGY

The archaeological evidence is ample and conclusive in showing that there were considerable and often revolutionary advances in technology during the latter half of the Eastern Chou Dynasty. The following are some of the major technological strides during the latter half of the Eastern Chou: highly developed iron metallurgy and extensive use of iron for implements; the use of iron plows, possibly drawn by cattle; and sophisticated and intensive irrigation systems.[25]

Umehara[26] suggested that the bronzesmiths of the Shang Dynasty had probably already mastered the chemical knowledge and practical control of the use of iron, as shown by the result of chemical analysis of some An-yang bronze artifacts. There is little question, however, that bronze was the only significant raw material for the making of artifacts throughout the Shang, Western Chou, and the early part of the Eastern Chou Dynasties. It is significant that during this long period (ca. 1700–500 B.C.) bronze was used primarily for making ceremonial vessels and weapons and thus was in the service, so to speak, of the aristocracy. Huang Chan-yüeh states in 1957[27] that:

25. For general discussions on some aspects of these problems, see Sekino Takeshi, *Chugaku Kōkogaku Kenkyu*; Joseph Needham, *The Development of Iron and Steel Technology in China*, London, Newcomen Society, 1958; Wang Chung-shu, KKTH, 1956:1, 57–76.

26. Umehara Sueji, *Shina Kōkogaku Runko* (Tokyo, 1929), pp. 179–80.

27. Huang Chan-yüeh, KKHP, 1957:3, 106.

bronze agricultural implements of Shang and Chou that have been excavated by archaeologists up to this date consist of only three Shang Dynasty spades (found from An-yang, Cheng-chou, and Lo-yang, respectively), and no more than ten adzes and axes . . . Extensive excavations undertaken by the Institute of Archaeology, Academia Sinica, in recent years in such regions as Feng, Hao, and Lo-yang, where there was intensive activity during the Western Chou Dynasty, have so far failed to turn out either a single piece of iron or agricultural implement made of bronze. On the other hand, the agricultural implements and handicrafts tools that have been found there consist of stones adzes, stone axes, stone knives, shell knives, shell sickles, bone needles, and bone chisels. Weapons, however, except for some bone and shell arrowheads, were all cast in bronze . . . We have, thus, reason to believe that the principal agricultural implements during the Western Chou Dynasty were basically wooden and stone; there were some that were made of bronze, but these are rare and of secondary importance and supplementary nature.

To my knowledge, this statement has thus far not been invalidated by more recent discoveries. Starting with the Warring-States period, however, both the wide use of iron and the use of metal (iron) implements are amply substantiated by archaeological discoveries of remains of this period from all over China.

Recent archaeological discoveries indicate a highly noteworthy phenomenon. Namely, tombs dated before the Warring-States, whenever and wherever the dating is certain, do not contain iron artifacts. Every cemetery of the Warring-States period and the Han Dynasty, on the other hand, yields some amount of iron artifacts, with almost no exceptions; in some cases the amount is even considerable. This is certainly not accidental . . . It is, therefore, our studied opinion that as a new and significant raw material of implement manufacture, the use of iron began toward the end of the Ch'un-ch'iu period and the beginning of the Chan-kuo period.[28]

28. Hua Chüeh-ming, Yang Ken, and Liu En-chu, *KKHP*, 1960:1, 82–83.

Moreover, as soon as iron implements began to appear in significant quantity in archaeological assemblages, both cast iron (pig iron) and wrought iron appeared at the same time. Sekino pointed out, some time ago, that many iron implements excavated prior to World War II in southern Manchuria and Korea which had been dated to the Warring-States period were, according to laboratory analysis, cast-iron implements; he speculated that the same technique must have been developed in North China.[29] The fact that a recent metallographical study of four iron implements from the Warring-States period (excavated from Hopei, Jehol, and Hunan) shows that they were all of the cast-iron variety, confirms Sekino's speculation.[30] It is therefore a remarkable fact that in China cast iron was developed at a much earlier date than elsewhere. Sekino has attempted to explain this by the following factors: the use of magnetite in North China, which requires and necessitates high temperatures to melt and thus tends to produce cast iron; the background knowledge and technique developed from a highly sophisticated bronze metallurgy; the previous high development of pottery making which required kilns capable of producing great heat; the desire of the common people to improve the effectiveness of their farming implements, hitherto made of wood and stone, by utilizing iron and improving upon the iron metallurgy; and, finally, the need for mass production of farming implements among the common people, who found a solution in the use of cast iron instead of wrought iron.[31]

The use of cast iron in making agricultural implements is undoubtedly a highly significant event in Chinese economic history. The common types of implements during the latter parts of the Eastern Chou Dynasty included axes, adzes, chisels, spades, sickles, and hoes; the plow was manufactured, but was relatively rare and does not seem to have been a highly effective implement to replace the spade and hoe as a principal cultivating tool. The earliest iron plows that are well documented archaeologically come from the Warring-States tombs at Ku-wei-ts'un, in Hui Hsien, northern Honan.[32] These are flat, V-shaped iron pieces which probably were mounted onto wooden blades and handles to serve as working

29. Sekino, *Chugaku Kōkogaku Kenkyu*, pp. 187–88.
30. Hua Chüeh-ming, Yang Ken, and Liu En-chu, *KKHP*, 1960:1.
31. Sekino, *Chugaku Kōkogaku Kenkyu*, pp. 189–91; see also Needham, *Iron and Steel Technology*.
32. Kuo Pao-chün, Hsia Nai, et al., *Hui Hsien fa-chüeh pao-kao*, p. 91.

edges (Fig. 16). The width of each of the two sides of the V-shape, measured from two complete specimens, averages 18 cm. In view of its relatively small size and its mounting device, which could not have been too secure, these plows seem to be highly primitive and not capable of turning up soil from any considerable depth.[33] There is no archaeological evidence as to whether cattle was utilized for drawing the plows. Cattle-drawn plows of considerable size, capable of deep plowing, did not appear in the archaeological record until the middle of the Western Han Dynasty.

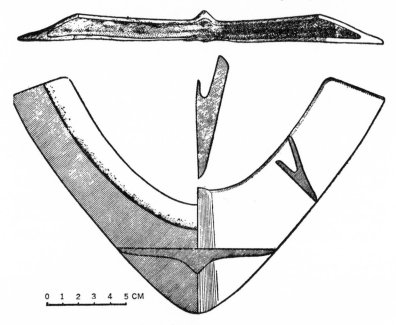

0 1 2 3 4 5 CM

FIG. 16. Iron edge blade of plow, excavated from a Warring-States tomb at Ku-wei-ts'un, in Hui Hsien, Honan. From Kuo Pao-chün, Hsia Nai, et al., *Hui-hsien fa-chüeh pao-kao* (Peiping, Science Press, 1956), Fig. 108.

However, with the advent of new iron implements, revolutionary changes must have occurred in the cultivation of farming fields. One of the most significant and consequential of these changes,

33. Huang Chan-yüeh, *KKHP*, 1957:3, 105.

FIG. 17. (*Opposite page and following two pages.*) Common bronze vessel forms in Shang and Chou Dynasties. From Okada Yoshisaburo, *A Taxonomy of Ancient Chinese Bronzes*, Kyoto Univ., Research Institute of Humanistic Sciences, 1953.

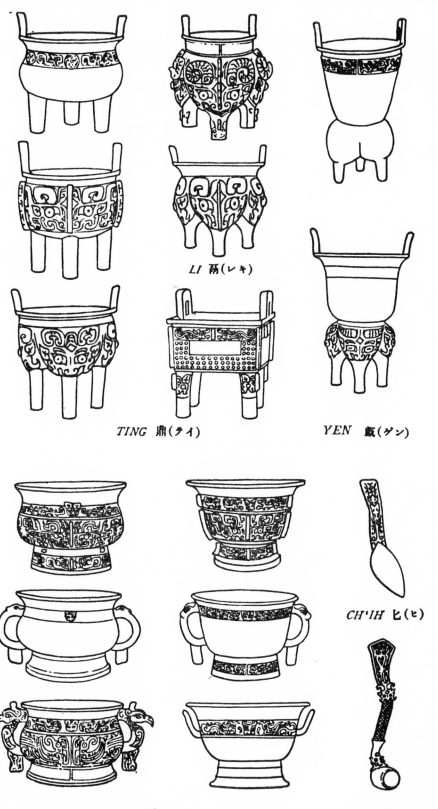

LI 鬲(レキ)

TING 鼎(テイ)　　　YEN 甗(ゲン)

KUEI 殷(キ)　　　SHUO 勺(シャク)

CH'IH 匕(ヒ)

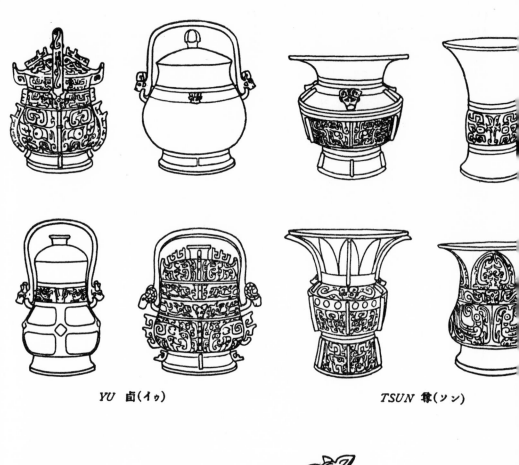

YU 卣(イゥ)　　　　　　　　　TSUN 尊(ソン)

HSIAO-TSUN 鴞尊(ケゥソン)　　P'EI 瓺(ホゥ)

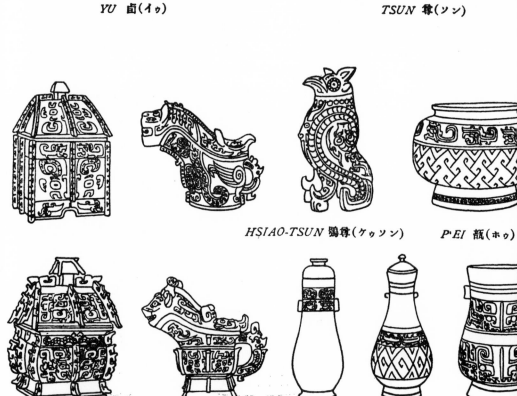

I 彝(イ)　　SSŬ-KUANG 兜觥(シクヮゥ)　　HU 壺(ニ)

KU 觚(コ)   CHIH 觶(シ)   CHIA 斝(カ)   P'AN 盤(バン)

CHÜEH 角(カク)

LEI 罍(ライ)   CHÜEH 爵(シャク)   HO 盉(クワ)

which may or may not be related to the use of iron implements, is that irrigation techniques were highly intensified and elaborated during the latter parts of the Eastern Chou Dynasty. Archaeological evidence on the construction of irrigating water ditches and canals is nonexistent until after the Han Dynasty, but reliable literary sources indicate that both Shang and Western Chou practiced irrigation to some extent. *Hsün-Tzu* recorded state officials who specialized in this phase of agriculture, and the deed of Li Ping of the State of Ch'in during the Warring-States period in the construction of irrigation works in Szechwan is well known.

In dealing with the development of artifacts and art styles during the Chou Dynasty, the data and topics presented must necessarily be highly restricted. I am going to discuss only those weapons, ceremonial vessels (Fig. 17), and decorative motifs that show profound changes during the period, and which may therefore serve both chronological and analytical purposes. Since most of the Chou bronzes (vessels and weapons) were found in tombs, and since some of the tombs have been accurately dated, let us first of all list some of the major tomb findings in chronological order (Table 9). These are all located in eastern Shensi, southern Shansi, and northern and western Honan, the heartland of the Chou (Map 11); burial groups in other areas will be discussed elsewhere. Most of these tombs have been excavated since the Communists took control of the Mainland. Former findings, either excavated or stray, are listed in a separate column.

The dating of the new sites, all of which were cemetery sites, has been made in the majority of cases on the basis of the inscriptions on the bronze vessels and, in some other cases, on the stylistic criteria that have been worked out from old findings for dating purposes. Since the dynastic dates cover relatively long time intervals, these datings are fairly safe for the present general discussion of cultural growth in North China. For more microscopic purposes, a more precise dating is often called for, for example, one that dates a find to the early or late phase of the Ch'un-ch'iu period. These discussions will not be covered in this chapter unless they are of absolute necessity.

A study of the typology and art style of the bronze vessels and weapons discovered in Chou Dynasty tombs arranged chronologi-

TABLE 9.

Old and New Discoveries of Shang and Chou Burial Sites

Dynastic Dating	New Sites		Old Sites	
Shang	Honan:	Erh-li-kang (Cheng-chou)	Honan:	Hsiao-t'un and Hou-chia-chuang (An-yang); Liu-li-ko (Hui)
Western Chou	Shensi:	Chang-chia-p'o (Sian); P'u-tu-ts'un (Sian); Li-ts'un (Mei)	Shensi: Honan:	Pao-chi Hsin-ts'un (Chün)
	Shansi:	Tung-pao and Fang-tui-ts'un (Hung-chao)		
Ch'un-ch'iu	Honan:	Shang-ts'un-ling (Shan); T'ai-p'u-hsiang (Hsia); Chung-chou-lu (Lo-yang)	Honan:	Hsin-ts'un (Chün); Hsin-cheng
Chan-kuo	Honan:	Pai-sha (Yü); Pi-sha-kang (Cheng-chou); Erh-li-kang (Cheng-chou); Shao-kou (Lo-yang)	Honan:	Shan-piao-chen (Chi); Liu-li-ko (Hui); Chin-ts'un (Lo-yang)
	Shensi:	Pan-p'o (Sian)	Shansi:	Li-yü-ts'un (Hun-yüan)
	Shansi:	Fen-shui-ling (Ch'ang-chih)		

cally makes it possible to establish a stylistic sequence which serves both as a dating criterion and as a tableau of the cultural evolution which took place in North China within the Chou Dynasty. Such studies were made in recent decades by a number of archaeologists and art historians, notably Kuo Mo-jo, Bernhard Karlgren, and Li Chi, on the basis of bronze artifacts unearthed in North China

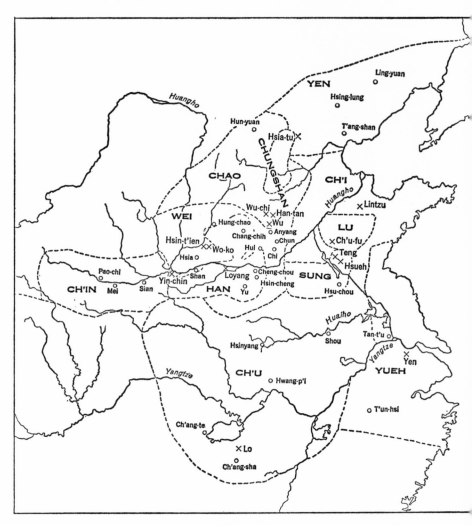

MAP 11. Location of some Shang and Chou city sites and tombs and the approximate boundaries of the Eastern Chou states around 350 B.C. Boundaries drawn after Yang Kuan, *Chan-Kuo-Shih*, Shanghai, Jenmin Press, 1957.

from past centuries through the early decades of the present century. New findings made since 1950 tend to confirm these early, now classic, studies, though certain modifications and clarifications are sometimes necessary. A full treatment of this topic will be made in another context; a summary of current understanding and problems is given below.

In the early thirties Kuo Mo-jo and Bernhard Karlgren, probably independently studying the bronze vessels of the Yin and Chou Dynasties, arrived at very similar methodologies and conclusions.[34] Their aims were to arrange the Yin and Chou bronzes into a chronological order and, from this, to study the problems of stylistic evolution. "We shall try first," Karlgren states, "to classify the inscriptions in their chronological order, without any sideglances at the types of the vessels; and once this literary chronology has been established we shall use it as a means for classifying the vessels, their types and decoration, in chronological groups." [35] Accordingly, Kuo Mo-jo has attempted to subdivide the Chinese Bronze Age into five stages: [36]

(a) *Stage of Beginnings:* a hypothetical stage in which bronzes first appeared in China. The time was possibly "late Hsia" Dynasty and early Shang Dynasty. The place was possibly the lower courses of the Yangtze and Huaiho, where copper mines were known in early historic periods. The bronze metallurgy in the Huangho valley, according to Kuo, may have been introduced from this area.

(b) *Stage of Florescence:* late Shang-Yin and early Chou Dynasty, including the reigns of Kings Ch'eng, K'ang, Chao, and Mu. The characteristic artifacts were *ting,* square *yih,* lidless *kuei, tsun, yu, chüeh, chia,* and *tuo. Li* and *chung* were present but rare. *Fu, hu, p'an,* and *yih* were absent. The artifacts were either completely decorated or not at all. The characteristic designs included *k'ui-lung, k'ui-feng, t'ao-t'ieh,* elephant, and *lei-wen;* the *t'ao-t'ieh* and the *lei-wen* being predominant. In general, the decorative patterns were "primitive" in character. In inscriptions, the composition was simple and succinct, and the calligraphy solemn and grave. The form of the vessels tended to be "heavy and solid," without any exhibition of "frivolity."

(c) *Stage of Decadence:* from the middle of the Western Chou Dynasty, including the reigns of Kings Kung, Yih, Hsiao, and Yih, through the middle of the Ch'un-ch'iu period. In bronze artifacts, *ting, li, kui, fu, chung* (bell), *fu,* and the like grew in quantity; the square *yih, yu, chüeh, chia, ku,* and the like became extinct; and *p'an, yih, hsü,* and *hu* began to appear. The decorations

34. Kuo Mo-jo, *Liang-chou chin-wen-tz'u ta-hsi,* Tokyo, 1932; *Ku-tai ming-k'ê ts'ung-k'ao,* 1933; *Liang-chou chin-wen-tz'u ta-hsi t'u-lu,* 1934; Bernhard Karlgren, BMFEA, 6 (1934); BMFEA, 8 (1936).
35. Karlgren, BMFEA, 8, 10.
36. Kuo Mo-jo, *Liang-chou chin-wen-tz'u ta-hsi t'u-lu;* Kuo Mo-jo, *Ch'ing-t'ung shih-tai,* Chungking, Wen-chih Press, 1945.

were made of shallow incisions and engravings, and were characterized by geometric patterns of thin lines. The *lei-wei* became rare, and the elephant pattern disappeared. The *ch'ieh-ch'ü* pattern replaced the *t'ao-t'ieh* as the leading decorative motif, whereas the *t'ao-t'ieh* was placed at such inconspicuous spots as the feet of *ting* and *kui* vessels. *K'ui-lung*, *k'ui-feng*, and *p'an-k'ui-wen* became deformed. In inscriptions, the characters became "relaxed" and random, including some cursory forms. The form of vessels was simple and crude, but was full of spirits of freedom and wilderness, emancipated from the "primitive" style and the mythological tradition.

(d) *Stage of Renaissance:* from the middle of Ch'un-ch'iu through the end of Chan-kuo. In artifact types, *tui* and *cheng* appeared, *pien-chung* became popular, *li* and *yen* became rare, and *hsü* was extinct. In decoration, the incisions and engravings became shallower and thinner. Repetitive motifs were widely applied with molds. The patterns included a great variety of motifs. Accessory ornaments were mostly realistic animals. In inscriptions, the composition tended to be rhyming, and the characters, a part of the total decor, were refined, regularly arranged, and placed in conspicuous places. In form, the artifacts were light, convenient, and fashion-conscious, indicating, according to Kuo, the commercialization of the bronzes during this period.

(e) *Stage of Decline:* after the end of the Chan-kuo period. Bronze vessels became simple and coarse, but practical and convenient. Decorative patterns became a rarity. Most of the inscriptions were incised rather than cast, and pertained to weight, volume, or names of the manufacturers rather than to history or morality. Bronze mirrors and coins prevailed, but otherwise iron served as the raw material for artifact making.

Karlgren's classification closely parallels this scheme of Kuo Mo-jo's. Omitting Kuo's *Stage of Beginnings* and *Stage of Decline*, which are beyond the temporal scope of the Yin and Chou anyway, Karlgren subdivides the Yin and Chou bronzes into three classes: [37]

(a) *Archaic*, further divisible into (1) Yin, prior to 1122 B.C.; and (2) Yin-Chou, 1122–ca. 950 B.C.

(b) *Middle Chou*, ca. 950 B.C.–ca. 650 B.C.

(c) *Huai*, ca. 650 B.C.–ca. 200 B.C.

37. Karlgren, BMFEA, 9 (1937), 5.

Thus, both in time and in definition, Karlgren's *Archaic* is identical to Kuo's *Florescence, Middle Chou* to *Decadence,* and *Huai* to *Renaissance.* In addition, Karlgren has painstakingly worked out a list of stylistic criteria which characterize each of his classes. These are listed as follows: *Archaic: Yin:* Square *ting; li-ting; yu; ku* and *tsun; yih; chüeh* and *chia; kuang;* cylinder legs; supporting animals; lid knobs; bottle horns; spikes; segmented flanges; free animal's head; *t'ao-t'ieh;* common bird; gaping dragon; vertical dragon; trunked dragon; winged dragon; feathered dragon; snake; cicada; rising blade; hanging blade; leg blade; animal triple band; scaled animal; spiral filling; spirals on figures; spiral band; compound lozenges; interlocked T's; circle band; whorl-circle; vertical ribs; T scores; square with crescents. *Archaic: Yin-Chou:* Most, if not all, of the above elements plus the following innovations: Bent ears; hook projections; tail-raising bird; and *p'an. Middle Chou:* The *Archaic-Yin* elements are completely abolished, whereas the following new stylistic elements occur: *chung;* arched *li; fu; yih; hsü;* shallow *ting;* carved legs; fin flanges; footed *kuei;* spiral horns; grooves; vertical stripes; scale band; vertical scales; wavy line; broad figures band; and back-to-back dragons. *Huai:* Marked by the revival of some of the Yin elements which were obsolete in the Middle Chou style: free animal's head; *t'ao-t'ieh* (in a modified form); snake; cicada; rising blades; hanging blades; scaled animals; spiral filling; interlocked T's; whorl-circle. New elements of the Huai include: squat *ting;* interlacery; hooks; plait; rope; rings on lid; warts; dots; spiral circle; and Huai geometric patterns.

Kuo and Karlgren, thus, have demonstrated quite independently that the political subdivisions of Chou into such categories as Western Chou, Ch'un-ch'iu, and Chan-kuo are not necessarily meaningful in the evolution of artifacts and art. Instead, three well-marked artistic and typological stages are discernible. The first is the early part of the Western Chou, up to the reign of King Kung, or roughly the year 950 B.C. The bronze art of this stage, called Yin-Chou by Karlgren, "in all essentials an epigonous art," [38] "was still essentially the same as that of the Yin, with but small innovations." [39]

The second stage, starting from the middle of Western Chou, (ca. 950) through the middle of the Ch'un-ch'iu period (ca. 650),

38. Karlgren, *BMFEA,* 8, 139.
39. Ibid., p. 89.

Kuo's stage of decadence or Karlgren's *Middle Chou style*, witnessed a

> sudden, complete and fundamental change in the art tradition in China. It is characterized on the one hand by a ruthless abolition of the whole array of Yin elements . . . on the other hand by the introduction of a series of new elements, most of which were entirely unknown in China before that time, and some of which had cropped up but sporadically, in exceptional cases, anterior to 947.[40]

Kuo characterizes the art of this stage as "degenerate," and Karlgren describes it as "poor and mediocre." [41] The latter author has further attempted to explain the sudden appearance of a whole series of new stylistic motifs as the "result of the widening of the sphere of Chinese civilization from the Shensi and Honan centers to large districts of China north of the Yangtze" [42] where contacts with alien peoples were made and new artistic inspirations were received.

On the basis of the Middle Chou style, an artistic renaissance occurred in the middle of the Ch'un-ch'iu period (ca. 650 B.C.) which gave rise to a new style, the Huai.[43] Karlgren characterizes this art style as a "self-conscious art, a "highly sophisticated one working with all the paraphernalia and tricks of a pompous baroque," and "keen on a brilliant impression of richness and variety." He states that "during the 7th–3d centuries B.C. the Chinese world was already sufficiently advanced in culture to allow a conscious artistic renaissance movement, which incorporated elements now already ancient and venerated in the new pompous baroque art," [44] and fresh artistic inspirations resulting from the expanding sphere of the North China civilization and increased contacts with the Ordos area in the North gave impetus to the development of the Huai style. The warring scene, for instance, is common to the Huai (Fig. 18) and the Ordos; both of these styles, furthermore, contained such curious and specific elements as pear-shaped cells or figures, comma-shaped figures, circles on

40. Ibid., p. 116.
41. Karlgren, *BMFEA*, 13 (1941), 4.
42. Karlgren, *BMFEA*, 8, 146.
43. Ibid., p. 90.
44. Karlgren, *BMFEA*, 13, 4.

208

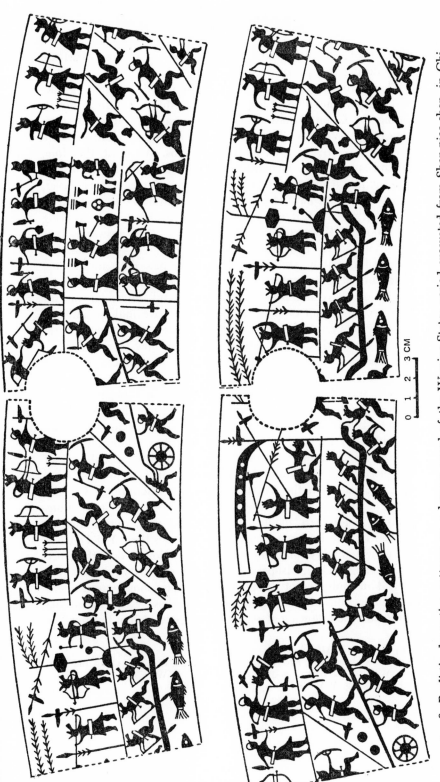

FIG. 18. Realistic decorative patterns on a bronze vessel of the Warring-States period excavated from Shan-piao-chen, in Chi Hsien, Honan province. From Kuo Pao-chün, *Shan-piao-chen yü Liu-li-ko* (Peiping, Science Press, 1959), Fig. 11.

the body of animals, and so forth, indicating an exchange of artistic ideas during this period.[45]

These studies of Kuo Mo-jo and Bernhard Karlgren, as described above, are of great importance to a study of cultural growth during the Chou Dynasty in North China. For the entire time span of the Western Chou Dynasty, archaeological discoveries are few and most frequently confined to tombs. We must, therefore, depend largely upon such studies of bronze vessels for an insight into the problems of cultural change during this period. However, over two decades have elapsed since these studies were published; we might ask what, if any, major strides have been made to bring the Kuo and Karlgren material up to date? The answer is that potentially useful data have been found in great quantities, but that, unfortunately, studies utilizing these new data are lacking. I am currently attempting to make such a study. Although final conclusions have not been reached and a full discussion of this topic would be out of place here, my tentative findings indicate that new data tend to confirm the basic framework of the classification of Kuo and Karlgren. Many details can now be added, however, and many others should be modified, sometimes quite drastically. I will give a few examples.

First, several graves have been excavated in the past decade, such as P'u-tu-ts'un (Sian) and Li-ts'un (Mei) in Shensi, and Fang-tui-ts'un and Tung-pao (Hung-chao) in Shansi, that are attributed to the early part of the Western Chou Dynasty.[46] Bronze vessels found in these tombs are indistinguishable from Yin pieces both in form and in decoration; in fact, in most cases these are dated to the Western Chou by inscriptions. On the other hand, two out of the four Yin-Chou style innovations claimed by Karlgren, namely, bent ear and *p'an*, were found, as pointed out by Karlgren himself, at An-yang; their Yin Dynasty dating, which was doubted by Karlgren, is no longer doubtful since the An-yang finds at Hsi-pei-kang are now well dated stratigraphically. Thus only two of Karlgren's Yin-Chou innovations are left, hook projections and tail-raising birds. To these, Chen Meng-chia would add the following as exclusively Western Chou but not Yin

45. Karlgren, BMFEA, 9, 102–11.
46. Shih Hsing-pang, KKHP, 8 (1954), 109–26; Li Chang-ching and Tien Yieh, WWTKTL, 1957:4, 5–9; Wang Chi-sheng, WWTKTL, 1955:4, 46–52; Hsieh Hsi-kung, WWTKTL, 1957:8, 42.

traits: *kui* with four ears; *kui* with square supports; independent square or rectangular vessel supports (the so-called *chin*); bent handle of *tou* (or *shao*); out-projecting flanges; some combinations of vessels that differ from the Yin pattern; and the absence of some Yin decorative patterns.[47] These traits, whether valid or not, do not occur universally among Western Chou vessels; among the early Western Chou tombs enumerated above, we find evidence of only one of these new elements, namely the bent handle of *tou*, which was found at an early Western Chou tomb at P'u-tu-ts'un.[48] I think we can positively say that the bronze art of early Western Chou was a continuation of the Yin bronze art. Karlgren justifies his separation of the Yin-Chou art from the Yin on the basis of the innovations.[49] But, as he himself points out, there were greater and more significant innovations within the Yin style. Karlgren attacks Tang Lan for making divisions of art history on the basis of political considerations only; what then are his own grounds (except for political considerations) for not subdividing the archaic style into more stages than Yin and Yin-Chou? The present evidence shows that the Archaic style of bronzes of the Florescence Stage (Yin and early Western Chou) is a continuous development; it can certainly be further subdivided, but the segment that is described as Yin-Chou by Karlgren is not stylistically significant enough to indicate either that the Chou art was different from the Shang art, or that the Chou people made any real contributions to their Shang heritage after the Conquest.

Another important fact concerning the Western Chou bronzes is their widespread geographic distribution. Not only have they been found in a wide area, ranging from Jehol in the north to Anhwei and Kiangsu in the south,[50] but we also find that funereal assemblages of typically early Western Chou types found at Yen-tun-shan in Tan-t'u, Kiangsu, can be dated to the reign of King Ch'eng or King K'ang at the latest.[51] The fact that during the early period of Western Chou the Chou sphere of cultural influence had already become so wide seems to be in strong support of Karlgren's contention that the emergence of the Middle Chou

---

47. Chen Meng-chia, *KKHP*, 9 (1955), 138; Chen Meng-chia, *WWTKTL*, 1955:5, 65.
48. Shih Hsing-pang, *KKHP*, 8 (1954), 120.
49. Karlgren, *BMFEA*, 9, 96.
50. Higuchi, *Toyoshi-Kenkyu*, 16 (1957), 40–61.
51. Chen Meng-chia, *WWTKTL*, 1955:5, 65.

style was the result of this widening of territory and consequently the greater extent of cultural contacts and exchange of new artistic ideas. This is, however, more apparent than real. Unless and until it can be demonstrated that the new Middle Chou elements pre-existed (either in bronzes or in some other media) in other regions in China, which archaeological data from regions outside the nuclear area of the Chou do not yet indicate, the basic dynamics of the emergence of this new style in North China must be sought for elsewhere. Cultures and civilizations in regions both north and south of North China contemporary with the Western Chou will be described in the following chapters. Both the Western Chou assemblages and the native cultural contexts show that the Middle Chou style is, in elements and in total, nowhere in sight in these areas before the cultural impacts rendered by the Chou civilization.

As far as North China is concerned, two of the most important discoveries of bronzes of the Middle Chou style are tombs at P'u-tu-ts'un, Sian, near those mentioned above of the early Western Chou stage,[52] and a large cemetery at Shang-ts'un-ling in Shan Hsien, western Honan, possibly of the state of Kuo.[53] The former assemblage is dated to be shortly after the reign of King Mu, whose name was mentioned in the inscriptions, and the latter is placed at the end of Western Chou and the beginning of the Ch'un-ch'iu period. Thus, these two discoveries chronologically mark both the beginning and the end of the Middle Chou style or of the stage of Decadence as defined by Karlgren and Kuo. Typologically, they do the same. The P'u-tu-ts'un find includes such Archaic elements as *ku*, *chüeh*, *yu*, and *ting* with vertical ears and cylindrical legs. But bells, *ting* with curved legs, and the so-called *ch'ieh-ch'ü* pattern (a variety of Karlgren's "broad band"), which are all diagnostic of Karlgren's Middle Chou style, had already appeared. It is indeed possible that some of the Archaic elements of this group may have been relics or antiquities at the time when the burial was made, and vessels that happened to be placed in one grave are not necessarily "contemporary" in the usual archaeological sense. However, this cannot explain the cases where both Archaic and Middle Chou elements are combined in

52. Ho Han-nan, *KKHP*, 1957:1, 75–85.
53. Lin Shou-chin, *Shang-ts'un-ling Kuo-kuo mu-ti*, Peiping, Science Press, 1959.

one and the same vessels. A *lei* and a *ho*, for instance, have both the hanging blades of Karlgren's Archaic style and the *ch'ieh-ch'ü* of his Middle Chou style. Such combinations lead us to conclude that the Middle Chou style did not replace the Archaic style suddenly and completely, as Karlgren has suggested. A transitional period, around the time of Kings Kung and Mu, perhaps, may have existed before the Middle Chou style became mature and well established. The Shang-ts'un-ling cemetery, on the other hand, shows a well-defined Middle Chou style of bronzes which had already foreshadowed the succeeding Huai style with such typical elements as the *t'ao-t'ieh* and the mirror. In many other aspects also, such as the type of weapons and modes of burial, the Shang-ts'un-ling find pushes back many of the Huai elements in time, as will be discussed later.

Our knowledge of the stylistic evolution of the Chou bronze vessels can be supplemented considerably by a study of the evolution of bronze weapons in North China. Such a study, taking into account all major findings to date, is still wanting, but published materials are available about some weapons that are often found in graves of the Chou Dynasty, such as the *ko* halberd, the arrowhead, and the sword.

The *ko* halberd, as Li Chi points out,[54] "is a weapon used for more than one thousand years by the Chinese fighting force in the classical period." Li Chi has examined 208 specimens of this weapon excavated prior to the Second World War in northern Honan from the following five localities: Hsiao-t'un, Hou-chia-chuang, Hsin-ts'un, Shan-piao-chen, and Liu-li-ko, belonging to Shang, Western Chou, and Warring-States periods. A typological development of the *ko* halberd through the Yin and Chou dynasties can thus be worked out. The *ko* of the Shang Dynasty "is frequently composed of an elongated tongue-shaped blade made of jade or other hard stone of fine grain, which may be hafted into a T-shaped bronze sleeve." "All bronze *ko* of this period were usually cast in imitation of the jade-with-bronze-sleeve type; the two projecting points on both edges of the socket were retained at the junction between the blade (*yüan*) and the hafting part (*nei*)." In the Western Chou period, as exemplified by the Hsin-ts'un finds, there is for the first time a definite sign of the development of *hu*, or neck, namely a downward projection at the hafting

54. Li Chi, *Chinese Civilization*, p. 54.

section of the blade, a device apparently invented to improve the efficiency of hafting. The typological development of the *ko* reached its zenith in the period of the Warring-States, when the *nei* was transformed from an ornamental into a functional part and when the *ko* and the *mao* (spearhead) were combined to make the efficient weapon known by the name of *chi*.[55] This typological sequence is confirmed by recent discoveries of tomb findings, particularly those of the early Western Chou period, a period not represented by Li Chi's data. Both the Western Chou tombs at Fang-tui-ts'un and those at Tung-pao in Hung-chao Hsien, southern Shansi, contain *ko* halberds with straight and ornamental *nei* and developed *hu* neck with one to three perforations.[56] Although evidence of the *chi* combination is still lacking, it appears that the Western Chou civilization had made some innovations in the Yin Dynasty prototypes in the design of bronze weapons.

In addition to *ko* halberds, arrowheads and swords (Fig. 19) have been utilized as chronological markers. It has been widely known that the three-winged arrowhead of bronze and the bronze sword were both innovations of the Chan-kuo period, probably indicating cultural contacts with alien peoples, presumably those in the Ordos area. New discoveries of Chou tombs, however, have pushed both types back considerably in time. Shang-ts'un-ling cemetery contains both bronze swords (four in number) and three-winged arrowheads, and the Chung-chou-lu at Lo-yang has yielded swords; both of these assemblages can be dated to the early part of Ch'un-ch'iu or the final Western Chou period.[57]

BURIAL CUSTOMS

Since the archaeological discoveries of the Chou period are in most cases derived from tombs, a typological sequence of the burial customs during this dynasty is fairly well documented. Some highly pertinent aspects may be mentioned at this juncture.

Throughout the entire span of both Yin and Chou Dynasties, cultural constants continually appeared in the burials. We encounter, for instance, in the tombs throughout this long epoch

55. Ibid., pp. 55–58.
56. Wang Chi-sheng, *WWTKTL*, 1955:4, 49; Hsieh Hsi-kung, *WWTKTL*, 1957:8, 42.
57. Lin Shou-chin, *Shang-ts'un-ling Kuo-kuo mu-ti; Lo-yang Chung-chou-lu Hsi kung-tuan*, 1959; Kuo Pao-chün, *KK*, 1961:2, 114–15.

such features as the following: interment; burial in open, vertical pits (the so-called *shu-hsüeh*); the use of wooden coffins and, in many cases, wooden chambers; an earthen platform in the pit (the so-called *erh-ts'eng-t'ai*); a pit at the center of the bottom of the chamber, in which a dog was buried (the so-called *yao-k'eng,*

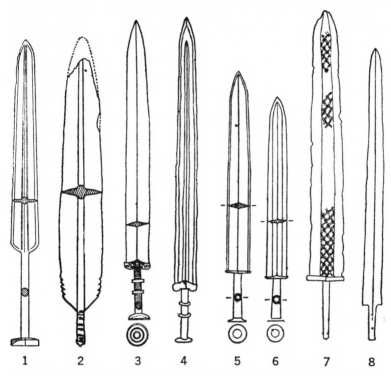

FIG. 19. Bronze swords of the Eastern Chou period excavated from North and South China. 1. Shang-ts'un-ling, Shan Hsien, Honan; 2, 3, 5, 6. Chung-chou-lu, Lo-yang, Honan; 4, 7. Ch'ang-sha; 8. Chao-hua, Szechwan. From WW, 1959:10, 28; *Shang-ts'un-ling Kuo-kuo mu ti* (Peiping, Science Press, 1959), Fig. 12.

or waistpit); the stretched-out posture; and the placement with the dead of mortuary goods, presumably as much as the family could afford, including artifacts, vessels, implements and, in some cases, horses and chariots, other animals (primarily dogs), and human victims. Some of these constants were apparently manifestations of a prevailing ancestor worship and a deep belief in the life

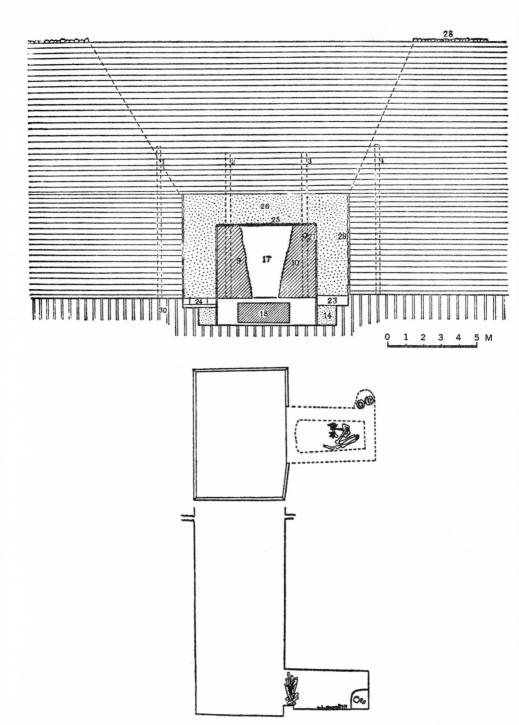

FIG. 20. Warring-States tombs of the Vertical Pit Type (*above*) and the Cave-chamber Type (*below*). Above: Ku-wei-ts'un, Hui Hsien, Honan, from *Hui-hsien fa-chüeh pao-kao*, Fig. 118; below: Pan-p'o-ts'un, Sian, Shensi, from *KKHP*, 1957:3, Fig. on p. 69.

of the afterworld during the Shang and Chou Dynasties, whereas some others, such as the details and features of the tomb construction, were presumably more significant of cultural traditions and styles.

Changes that took place during this long period did so in no less than five aspects of the burial customs, namely, tomb construction; the use of bricks; the burial mound; posture of the dead; and orientation. Extensive work remains to be done before details of the changes and their chronological placement can be worked out, but the general trends of change are evident.

In tomb construction, the basic vertical pit pattern prevailed throughout, although variations were plentiful. The pits could be large or small, the walls truly vertical or sloping, the ramps present or absent, and varying in number and length. The guiding principle, however, had always been that a rectangular pit was dug into the ground and that the dead was placed at the bottom of the pit (Fig. 20, above). This basic pattern is exemplified by the graves of Shang,[58] Western Chou,[59] and the early part of Eastern Chou.[60] At Pai-sha in Yü Hsien, and Pi-sha-kang in Cheng-chou, both in Honan, the tombs dated to the end of the Ch'un-ch'iu and the beginning of the Chan-kuo were still exclusively of this vertical pit pattern.[61] Later in the Chan-kuo period, however, another style of tomb construction began to appear, namely, the so-called *tung-shih-mu*, or cave-chamber graves. In such graves, a vertical pit was dug as usual, but a cave was further excavated sidewise into one of the pit walls and the corpse was then placed in a coffin in this cave-chamber instead of at the bottom of the vertical pit (Fig. 20, below). At the Warring-States cemetery near Shao-kou, in Lo-yang, there were sixteen cave-chamber graves as against forty-three vertical pit graves.[62] Of the one hundred and twelve Warring-States graves at the Pan-p'o cemetery near Sian, only eleven retained the old vertical pit pattern, and the rest were of the cave-chamber variety.[63] A tentative effort undertaken by the

58. Kao Chü-hsün, *Bull. Dept. Arch. Anth. Natl. Taiwan Univ.*, 13/14, 1959; Shih Chang-ju, BIHP, 23 (1953), 447–87.
59. Shih Hsing-pang, KKHP, 8, (1954), 110–13; Ho Han-nan, KKHP, 1957:1, 75–77; Wang Chi-sheng, WWTKTL, 1955:4, 49; Kuo Pao-chün, TYKKPK, 1 (1936), 167–200.
60. E.g., Lin Shou-chin, *Shang-ts'un-ling Kuo-kuo mu ti*, pp. 3–4.
61. Chen Kung-jou, KKHP, 7 (1954), 89.
62. Wang Chung-shu, KKHP, 8 (1954), 130.
63. Chin Hsüeh-shan, KKHP, 1957:3, 67–70.

present author to establish relationships between these two varieties of tomb construction and the posture and orientation of the dead during the Warring-States period failed to yield any correlation. The new mode of construction may merely represent a fashion of the times, which, in combination with bricks, completely replaced the vertical pits during the following Han Dynasty as the principal mode of tomb construction. Use of bricks of a hollow variety for the construction of the tomb chamber was also a fresh late Warring-States custom.[64]

Concerning the burial mound, archaeological information is singularly lacking. Historical records and local traditions both relate to burial mounds of the Eastern Chou period, but none of these identified mounds have been excavated. The question is, however, how far back the custom of mound building can be traced in time. Confucius, of the Ch'un-ch'iu period, is quoted as saying, "I hear that in ancient times the dead were interred but no mounds were built." The "ancient times" to Confucius was apparently Shang and Western Chou. The Hsi-pei-kang royal tombs of the Shang Dynasty were probably without mounds, and Kuo Pao-chün, who specifically looked for evidence of the mound at the Western Chou cemetery at Hsin-ts'un in Chün Hsien, found no mounds for that period.[65] Generalizations should probably not be made from these negative findings, but until definitive evidence is found to the contrary, it appears that the custom of building mounds atop a burial was not a wide general practice before the Eastern Chou period.

The posture and orientation of the corpse pose special and difficult problems. Throughout Yin and Chou, the stretched-out posture was predominant. Flexed posture, however, began to appear frequently during the Warring-States period, a fact which has led many authors to speculate that this represents a fresh idea in the burial custom and may have been introduced from the North during the Warring-States period.[66] Recent discoveries of Western Chou and early Eastern Chou tombs, however, do not seem to support this interpretation. The late Western Chou tomb at P'u-tu-ts'un contains three corpses, two of which had a contracted posture.[67] Among the eighteen early Western Chou tombs at

64. E.g., Honan Wehuachü, Cheng-chou Erh-li-kang (1959), pp. 80–81.
65. Kuo Pao-chün, TYKKPK, 1 (1936), 174.
66. E.g., Kao Chü-hsün, KKHP, 2 (1947), 121–66.
67. Ho Han-nan, KKHP, 1957:1, 76.

Fang-tui-ts'un in Hung-chao Hsien, Shansi, no less than four flexed burials are found.[68] At the late Western Chou and early Eastern Chou cemetery at Shang-ts'un-ling, two hundred and twenty-one graves contain recognizable skeletons, forty-four of which show a flexed posture.[69] It seems, therefore, that the flexed burial posture existed throughout the Chou Dynasty, although it may not have become numerically significant until the Chan-kuo period.

The problem of the orientation of the tomb and of the corpse is even more perplexing; one finds all sorts of variations but no clearcut regularities which change with time. All of the Yin tombs of the Hsi-pei-kang group were South–North oriented, but since all of them had been robbed during early historic times and no skeletons of the tomb masters were left at the time of excavations, the orientation of the corpses is a matter for speculation. During the Chou Dynasty, in all of its various subphases, both North–South and East–West orientations are found, and in the former case the head is sometimes oriented toward the north and sometimes toward the south. It is tempting to make a case here for a correlation of the orientation with the posture of the corpse or with the status of the dead, but generalizations should not yet be made.

GENERAL CONCLUSIONS

In the foregoing passages, information about the development of cities, technology, typology and art, and burial customs has been presented to fill in the pattern of cultural growth during the Chou Dynasty. In closing this chapter, we must ask: What is the summation of all these data?

In speaking of the cultural growth during the Chou Dynasty in North China literary records must be used for a complete picture. For the purposes of this volume, however, the archaeological data presented above have been sufficient to outline the high points in this picture as well as to bring forth the cultural relations of North China with the rest of the country.

The trends of cultural growth can be described in two ways. First, there was a constant territorial expansion of Chinese civilization. Second, there was an accelerated growth of the internal society, economy, and political organization. Furthermore, these

68. Wang Chi-sheng, *WWTKTL*, 1955:4, 49.
69. Lin Shou-chin, *Shang-ts'un-ling Kuo-kuo mu-ti*, p. 4.

two phenomena are probably interrelated and mutually conditioning.

In speaking of the territorial expansion of the Chou civilization, we again face the problem of cultural definitions. When archaeological assemblages of a certain type, that of Western Chou, for example, are found distributed in a certain area, we may or may not have at our fingertips the complete geographical distribution of the Western Chou civilization. Undoubtedly there was a nuclear region of this civilization which may be considered the center of radiation, whereas the other regions into which the civilization radiated may be regarded as marginal or peripheral. A variety of situations may be encountered in these marginal regions. Some of them may have been occupied by native cultures which received some cultural imports from the Western Chou civilization while maintaining their own ways of life and political autonomy. In such cases, in recovering artifacts of Western Chou types in these regions, archaeologists probably can only speak of the cultural influences of the Western Chou but not the geographical distribution of the dynasty. In some other regions, Western Chou military forces had accomplished a military conquest and established political control, while allowing the native cultures to continue. We may certainly include these regions in the political sphere of influence and/or control of the Western Chou government, but must not generalize to include these territories in the Western Chou economy and society. Still some other regions, while occupied by native, probably Neolithic, cultures during the Shang Dynasty, may have been thoroughly assimilated by the Western Chou civilization to the extent that in cultural style and socioeconomic situations alike the native cultures had become indistinguishable from the heartland of the Western Chou Dynasty. These may legitimately be called part of the expanded Western Chou territory of civilizational distribution. These distinctions, however, while easy to make on paper, are in most cases impossible to recognize in the archaeological material.

In the first section of this chapter, it was suggested that the "Western Chou people" during the Shang Dynasty may have been no more than a group of local inhabitants under Shang's rule who were within the expanse of the Shang civilization. In fact, it is difficult to recognize a separate Western Chou civilization which differs to any extent from the Shang. The "Conquest" in

220

1122 B.C., whereby the Chou replaced the Shang as China's masters, was, therefore, not a conquest by an alien people having an alien culture. It was, in fact, from all manifestations, no more than an internal struggle for power. The notion that the conquest of the Shang by the Chou represents the triumph of the Western Hsia over the Eastern Yih, as has been suggested by Fu Ssu-nien, is correct only if the Hsia and the Yin are considered no more than geographical variants of the same Chinese people.

Archaeological evidence shows no significant change in the basic pattern of Chinese civilization in North China immediately after the Conquest. The Western Chou took over the Shang culture in bronze metallurgy, burial rites, and decorative art in virtually unaltered forms. Karlgren's Yin-Chou elements plus Chen Meng-chia's new Western Chou innovation in the style of bronze vessels involved no basic changes in cultural beliefs and artistic fashion. Changes inevitably occurred, but are such that would take place over any period of time under normal incentives during the development of one and the same culture. Wang Kuo-wei in his *Yin Chou Chih-tu Lun* (*On Yin and Chou Institutions*) says that a major cultural and social change took place after the Conquest. This statement is amply refuted by archaeological evidence. Wang had in mind, apparently, the "feudalism" and *tsung-fa* system of kinship and ancestor cult which were considered to have been the inventions of Chou Kung's genius. Historical information derived from oracle bone inscriptions has begun to show convincingly that both of these institutions began, in a rudimentary form perhaps, during the later part of the Shang Dynasty. It is true that the Chou government consolidated and probably systematized the political institutions of the Shang rulers and tightened the political control over the vassal states, but I have yet to be shown that the beginning of the Western Chou Dynasty witnessed any major breakthroughs in the field of applied political and social sciences any more than in technology and art.

Nor, in the sense defined a few paragraphs back, did the Western Chou gain any real strides in territorial expansion during the first years of the dynasty. The sphere of cultural influence may have been expanded, compared to the Shang, as shown by the finding of Western Chou type of bronze vessels from a wider territory. But the Western Chou territory was wider than the Shang mainly because of the fact that the Western Chou had as a base in the first place Shensi and Shansi, where the Shang civilization is not significantly evidenced archaeologically. To the north, Chou assemblages have been found as far north as Jehol, but we know, as will be shown in the next chapter, that native cultures persisted in the northern frontiers in essentially unaltered forms until the Han Dynasty. A few Chou imports and isolated settlements in the north do not necessarily make the north a part of the Western Chou territory. In the south, we know from history that Huaiho valley natives considered themselves akin to the Shang rulers and were continuously rebellious under the Chou rule. A widespread rebellion shortly after the Conquest was soon subdued by the military expeditions of the King Ch'eng. Western Chou bronze assemblages found in Anhwei and Kiangsu, in the Huai region, bear out the historical records and indicate the fact that Western Chou powers became established in this region. But as will be shown in a later chapter, the Huai River valley cultures during both the Shang and the early Western Chou Dynasties were in the main Neolithic and maintained their own cultural integrity. A significant breakdown of the native cultural traditions and the establishment of typical North China kingdoms did not take place in the Huaiho valley and in the Yangtze Valley until after the beginning of the Western Chou Dynasty. Contacts with alien peoples surrounding the Royal Chou and a resulting fresh impetus in artistic inspirations may only partially account for the emergence of the Middle Chou style. A more impelling explanation must be sought for in Chou civilization's own development. The later parts of the Western Chou and the beginning of the Eastern Chou, the period covered by the Middle Chou style, was situated between the classical "Archaic" Yin and Chou civilization and the youthful and spirited Eastern Chou renaissance in style and revolution in technology and economy. The Middle Chou period thus represents a transitional stage wherein the classic systems began to give way to the new way of life in all Chinese territory.

In Eastern Chou was the beginning of a new era in the history of North China. In political history, ancient China had Yin and Chou Dynasties; but in cultural history, the subdivision may be placed at the middle of the Chou Dynasty, dividing the Yin-Chou periods into two stages, Yin and Early Chou, and Late Chou. Iron metallurgy was developed in the Eastern Chou, and industrial specialization was very much intensified. The old Yin and Western

Chou pattern of urban constitution lingered on for a while, but from the late Ch'un-ch'iu period on new cities emerged in all of North China which indicated the importance of industry and commerce by incorporating their quarters physically into the walled city. The new technology and economy undoubtedly intensified and consolidated the Chinese way of life and enabled the latter to expand, explosively, toward the rest of China. States of the Chou type which were established in the Huaiho valley and in much of the Yangtze will be described in the following chapters. Cultural contacts with foreign lands became very much more frequent, particularly in the North. During the Eastern Chou period, common cultural traits, including important elements of daily life, were shared more and more by North China and the steppe nomads. In art style, too, we have seen that the Huai style shared a number of characteristic traits with the Ordos and its adjacent cultures. The horse became a mounted animal as well as being used for drawing chariots, and swords came into use. Burial mounds were fashionable, belthooks were used, and flexed burials became important. These new cultural elements, and the old cultural traits that had gained in popularity at this time, are certainly indicative of the wider circle of cultural contact and communication between North China and the northern nomads, although the direction of the flow of these cultural traits cannot always be ascertained.[70]

The present chapter shows that what took place in North China, as a background for understanding the emergence of civilizations in other parts of China. It shows, moreover, that in most of China a single center of radiation conditioned the patterns of the local cultural growth, and that the road to the unification of Chinese territory under the Emperor Shih-huang of Ch'in in 221 B.C. was paved during the Eastern Chou period. Discussions in subsequent chapters will present additional material on the history of Chou development in relation to the North and the South.

70. Kao Chü-hsün, KKHP, 2 1947; Karlgren, BMFEA, 13; Kao Chü-hsün, BIHP, 23 (1951), 489–510.

Chapter Eight

Farmers

and Nomads

of the

Northern Frontier

During the late second and most of the first millennium B.C., various cultural transformations took place among the Neolithic farmers and sub-Neolithic hunter-fishers on the northern frontiers of the Yin and Chou civilizations. These cultural transformations apparently took place as a result of native cultural growth, but their processes and patterns were greatly conditioned by events in the adjacent regions, mainly North China and the steppe regions to the west. Literary records of the Eastern Chou and Han periods referred to these peoples in the various regions of the northern frontier by various names: the Wei-Mo people in southern Manchuria and the Pohai Bay coasts; the Northern Ti, Hu, or later, Hsiung-nu in the Yin Shan Mountains area between and including the Upper Liaoho and the Ordos; and the western Jung peoples to the northwest.[1] To what extent this ethnic classification of the Eastern Chou and Early Han periods for the northern frontier peoples was true and can be traced back in time is an ethno-historic problem. The archaeological material, however, tends to bear out this subdivision, in that no less than three regional cultural traditions can be distinguished for the Shang-Chou period in this area. These three archaeological traditions are: (1) the cist-grave builders of the Pohai Bay area and southern Manchuria; (2) the mounted nomads and farmers in the Yin Shan area; and (3) the "eneolithic"

1. E.g., Lin Hui-hsiang, *Chung-kuo min-tsu shih*, 2 vols. Shanghai, Commercial Press, 1936.

224

painted pottery traditions in Kansu and Chinghai. The geographical distribution of these various traditions (see Map 8), their different ecological situations and the diverse historical influences to which these cultural groups were exposed are problems of great theoretical interest.

THE POHAI CIST-GRAVE BUILDERS

This cultural tradition was centered in the area of the northern coasts of the Pohai, the Lower Liao-ho valley, and the Upper Sungari River. It was essentially a continuation of the old Neolithic cultures described in Chapter 5, but numerous cultural elements of North China origin or affinity have also been found from archaeological assemblages dated to this period. The peoples represented were farmers and pig-raisers, who made flat-bottomed pottery and polished slate and other stone implements, and buried their dead in cist-graves. Hunting was apparently still extremely important, as shown by the large number of arrowheads, mostly chipped in the old Microlithic tradition.[2]

Archaeologically speaking, definite Yin-Shang influences in this area are rare. Several "white sherds" of Shang type are reported to have been found at the Lao-t'ieh-shan site in the Port Arthur region at the tip of Liao-tung Peninsula,[3] and the historic records indicate that the peoples in this area were among the so-called Eastern Yih groups whose cultures were considered very close to the North Chinese. Chi Tzu, a brother of the last Yin monarch, is said to have led a group of Yin refugees into exile in northern Korea, where they established a civilization and taught the natives to raise silkworms and to farm. In the archaeological record, however, decisive evidence of significant North Chinese historical cultural penetration into the Pohai Bay area and southern Manchuria only began to show up during the Eastern Chou period. Metal objects such as axes, arrowheads, spearheads, and ornaments of Eastern Chou types were found east from Liao-tung Peninsula (at such sites as Kao-li-chai and Mu-yang-ch'eng),[4] and west to the Upper Liao-ho valley (at such sites as the Red Ware

2. Chang Kwang-chih, SJA, 17 (1961), 70–71.
3. Hamada Kosaku, JZ, 44 (1929), 319–26; Umehara Sueji, Toa Kōkogaku Kaikan (Kyoto, 1947), p. 63.
4. "Mu-yang-ch'eng," Archaeologia Orientalis, 2, 1931; "Pi-tzu-wuo," Archaeologia Orientalis, 1, 1929.

cemetery at Hung-shan-hou near Ch'ih-feng).[5] To the north, such metal objects reached as far as the Upper Sungari around the city of Kirin, and their influences upon areas further to the east can be seen in the stone imitations of metal swords and spearheads found in the Tumen valley, on the Pacific coast around Vladivostok, and in Korea and Japan.[6] Settlements of Eastern Chou style where the cultural influences extended from stylistic imports to the socioeconomic sphere are found at least as far away as northern Hopei. Stone molds, for instance, for making metal axes, knives, and spearheads (which were found at the Pao-shen-miao site near T'ang-shan), are dated to an earlier period than the Warring-States.[7] These molds undoubtedly indicate the local practice of metallurgy and point to a much more intensified acculturation of the natives by the oncoming North Chinese civilization than among the peoples to the north who apparently continued their old Neolithic way of life while adopting some cultural imports. However, by the end of the Han Dynasty at the latest, highly sophisticated civilizations were recorded in Chinese annals in a large part of southern Manchuria.[8]

During the Eastern Chou and the following Han period, the southern Manchurian farmers apparently were also intruded upon by alien peoples and cultures from the steppes to the west. Whereas the Chinese influences from the Huangho during the Eastern Chou period took the form of cultural infiltration and assimilation, the steppe nomads apparently took possession physically of territories in the lower Liao-ho valley, as shown by the cultural remains of steppe origin in whole assemblages discovered in isolated regions in Liaoning province. By the middle of the Western Han Dynasty, however, Wu Ti's military expeditions were successful enough to have incorporated the entire area of southern Manchuria and northern Korea into the vast empire of Han, though even the Han forces at times could not withstand the fierce penetration of the steppe nomads.[9]

5. "Ch'ih-feng Hung-shan-hou," *Archaeologia Orientalis*, ser. A, 6, 1938.
6. Chang Kwang-chih, *SJA*, 17 (1961), 70; G. I. Andreev, *KKHP*, 1958:4, 36; J. E. Kidder, *Japan* (New York, F. A. Praeger, 1959), p. 93.
7. An Chih-min, *KKHP*, 7 (1954), 85.
8. Wen Chung-yih, *BIE*, 5, 1958.
9. Tung Chu-chen, *KKHP*, 1956:1, 29–42; Chen Ta-wei, *KKTH*, 1956:2, 54–59; Li Wen-hsin, *KKHP*, 1957:1, 119–26.

FARMERS AND NOMADS, NORTH FRONTIER

The Yin Shan frontier of the Yin and Chou civilizations of North China, embracing the area known at the present time as Inner Mongolia, and the northern portions of Shensi, Shansi, and Hopei, was dominated in landscape by grasslands and plateaus. During early Recent times, as shown in a previous chapter, it was drained by a great number of small river valleys and large and small inland lakes and ponds. Today, many of these rivers and lakes are diminished in size or even completely dried up. It is, however, still not known when the dessication process began in this part of China. In the Huangho valley, we know that the dessication process did not begin extensively until after the Shang, and then only as a combined result of intensive deforestation and climatic change. In the steppe zone of the north, large sedentary farming settlements seem to have existed at some spots during the Eastern Chou period near water sources that are now dried up. It appears, therefore, that during the Shang-Chou period the northern frontier experienced no catastrophic dessication, which fact may have had a decisive effect upon the pattern of human settlement at that time.

Nevertheless, in many regions of the North where, as shown in Chapter 5, farming villages appeared during the Lungshanoid stage, a new way of life came into being during the period when the Shang and Chou civilizations thrived in the Huangho valley, a way of life in which the domestication of animals and the mobility of settlements became increasingly important. There were still farming settlements in the northeastern part of North China and in the Ordos, but animal herders had also appeared on the scene. We are not clear about the relationship between these farmers and herders. It is possible that farmers engaged in herding as a supplement or during some part of the year; it is also possible that farmers and herders were symbiotic occupants of the steppe and the oases. The possibility also exists that the northern farmers and herders were hostile toward each other and may have been of different cultural origins and traditions. Soon after the Yin-Chou period, nomads began to dominate the northern steppes. Farming lands shrank, and, in many places, disappeared altogether.

For the gradual replacement of farmers by herders in the north-

227

ern frontier, several probable causes can be discerned. First, the high grasslands of the northern frontier had never been as favorable to agriculture as the fertile plains and river valleys of the Huangho or the lower Liao-ho drainage systems. In the present day, it has an extremely continental climate, cold and arid, with long winters. During and after the climatic optimum of early post-Pleistocene times, the continentality of climate in this area may have been less severe, but the difference is probably one of degree. Secondly, and this may be the principal factor, during the first millennium B.C. a mobile and militant culture appeared in the steppe zone of the heartland of Asia, known to the west as that of the Scythians. By the end of the eighth century B.C., the Scythians and related complexes had replaced the Late Timber Culture in South Russia, the Late Andronovo Culture in Kazakhstan, and the Karasuk Culture in the Altai and Minusinsk Basin.[10] Karl Jettmar has pointed out that by the time the Maiemiric period appeared in the Altai to replace the Karasuk Culture, the whole steppe zone of Asia, from Pannonic steppes to China, had been unified culturally into a pattern characterized by mounted warfare.[11] This common Euro-Asiatic steppe culture, characterized by a mobile settlement pattern, a subsistence mode based principally upon the herding of sheep, cattle, and horses, mounted militancy, and an animal style of art, was apparently built upon a common ecological adjustment to the steppe environment, and in this common pattern a number and a variety of ethnic and cultural elements must have participated.[12] However, the widely seen cultural similarities must have resulted primarily from historical contacts among peoples, and the rapid and expansive cultural flow was greatly facilitated by the steppe environment and the mobile way of life.

10. James Gaul, *Papers of the Peabody Museum*, Cambridge, Harvard Univ., 20 (1943), 149–86; M. P. Griaznov, *Prähistorische Zeitschrift*, 15 (1928), 120–23; John F. Haskins, *Natural History*, 69 (1960), 8–17; Karl V. Jettmar, BMFEA, 23, 1951; M. Rostovtzeff, *The Animal Style in South Russia and China*, Princeton, Princeton Univ. Press, 1929; T. T. Rice, *The Scythians*, New York, F. A. Praeger, 1957; V. Tolmachev, *Eurasia Septentrionalis Antiqua*, 9 (1934), 256–58; S. P. Tolstov, *Antiquity* 20 (1946), 92–99; S. N. Kiselev, *Drevneishaia istoriia Yuzhnoi Sibiri*, Moscow, 1951; S. I. Rudenko, *Kultura naseleniia gornogo Altaia v skifskoe vremia*, Moscow, Akademia Nauk, 1953.

11. Jettmar, BMFEA, 23 (1951), 148.

12. Ralph M. Rowlette, *Early Phases of Horse Nomad Cultures of the Eastern Terminus of the Eurasiatic Steppe*, Report for Anthropology 111, Cambridge, Harvard Univ., 1960.

Seven hundred years B.C., the time when the so-called steppe nomads widely appeared in the vast steppe belt of Eurasia, was coincidentally the time when the Eastern Chou civilization began to radiate extensively toward the north as well as the south. Cultural exchange between the Huangho and the steppes and taigas in the north had been a constant phenomenon since Palaeolithic times. Around this time, however, such contacts took the form of cultural conflicts between the agrarian Huangho type of farmers and the steppe nomads. These conflicts often resulted in warfare and were amply recorded in the historical sources dated to the Eastern Chou and Han Dynasties. The Great Wall, sections of which were built by the various states in North China which joined borders with the steppe culture during the Eastern Chou period, symbolizes these conflicts and sharply demarcates the two basically different ways of life. Under such circumstances it is small wonder that herders' remains have been documented archaeologically on the northern frontier of Eastern Chou China and the Han Empire. Farmers, who found the new colonies not highly favorable for their settled way of life in the first place, were no match for the militant nomads in terms of bare physical strength, and gradually gave way to the new masters of the steppe. As far as the Chinese steppes are concerned, physical anthropological evidence is lacking to indicate whether the nomads, whose cultural remains have been widely found and clearly bear cultural affinities to the steppe cultures toward the west, were "intrusive" ethnic elements. We can, therefore, regard such cultural conflicts as those between two ways of life, although it is not unlikely that foreign ethnic elements were responsible for some of the cultural groups whose archaeological remains have been found.

The Neolithic farmers in Inner Mongolia and northern North China, among whom considerable hunting and fishing activity can be noted archaeologically, as discussed in Chapter 5, apparently continued their old way of life throughout the period during which Yin and Western Chou civilizations flourished in the Huangho valley. The northern limits of the Yin civilization, as defined at present, do not appear to have exceeded the southern parts of Hopei and the southern fringes of the Shansi Plateau. In what is now central and northern Hopei and southern Shansi, the Lungshanoid Neolithic culture must have persisted, and the occasional metal objects found from the Lungshanoid sites, as noted before, may have been the result of cultural contact with the Yin. Among the so-called Ordos bronzes, most of which can best be described as "stray finds," pieces occur that bear close similarities to the Yin bronzes.[13] In the Altai and the Minusinsk basin of the Upper Yenisie valley, the Karasuk Culture is usually considered a direct product of Yin-Shang stimulation.[14] Much archaeological evidence is needed before we can know exactly about the introduction of metallurgy into the western part of the Yin Shan area. As far as the eastern portion of this area is concerned, namely, the Upper Liao-ho valley, it is fairly certain that during the Yin Dynasty a farming culture based on a microlithic substratum continued in the northern part of the region, whereas the Lungshanoid culture persisted in the southern part.

The Western Chou civilization apparently had a deeper penetration into this region, as shown by a group of typically Western Chou bronze vessels discovered in Ling-yüan Hsien in Jehol province.[15] However, it was not until the Eastern Chou period that the Huangho River civilization pushed extensively into the northern frontier, as shown by widely found intensive settlements where Eastern Chou style objects remained, such as the so-called Red Ware settlement at Ch'ih-feng.[16] The intensity of Chou acculturation of this region is shown by the discovery of an iron worship site at Hsing-lung in Jehol. At this site, no less than eighty-seven pieces of iron molds for casting iron or bronze hoes, sickles, axes, chisels and cart fittings were excavated, indicating that during the Warring-States period, to which this site has been dated, not only Chinese stylistic imports were brought into Inner Mongolia but also iron foundries.[17] However, the frontier position of the Inner Mongolia province of the Eastern Chou civilization is clearly demonstrated by the presence of many cultural traits that point to either the microlithic substratum or to the contemporary northern cultures. Such traits include, for instance, slab graves, the red-brownish pottery with flat bottoms prevalent during the Neo-

13. Max Loehr, *Artibus Asiae*, 14 (1951), 1/2.
14. Karl V. Jettmar, *BMFEA* (22), 1950; Bernhard Karlgren, *BMFEA*, 17 (1945).
15. Li Ting-chien, *WWTKTL*, 1955:8, 16–27; for possible Western Chou influence in the western part of Inner Mongolia, see *WW*, 1961:9, 6.
16. Hamada Kosaku and Mizuno Seiichi, "Ch'ih-feng Hung-shan-hou," *Archaeologia Orientalis*, ser. A, 6.
17. Cheng Shao-tsung, *KKTH*, 1956:1, 29–35.

lithic period of the same area, stone battle axes, and microlithic implements which persisted even into the Han Dynasty sites.

At some of these Eastern Chou period settlements in the Yin Shan area, there is emphasis upon the domestication of animals. At Hung-shan-hou, Ch'ih-feng, for instance, a considerable number of cattle bones were found at the site, though the predominant mode of subsistence may still have been farming.[18] Some of the Ordos bronzes, many of which were presumably left by partial or full nomads with a culture similar to the steppe horsemen to the west, may also be dated to this period. During the last decade, at least three archaeological assemblages have been excavated which contain typical Ordos bronze elements and which can reasonably be dated to the Eastern Chou period.[19] None of these, however, are found in the Ordos region itself, but further to the east, one in the Upper Laoha River, a tributary of the Liao-ho, in Inner Mongolia, and the other two in Liaoning at the eastern fringes of the Mongolian Plateau, marking the intrusions of the steppe nomads into the southern Manchurian farming area. At these sites were found bronze weapons (swords, halberds, helmets, and arrowheads), horse fittings, implements, mirrors, and ornaments (animal styled pendants, buttons, and beads), together with stone artifacts (including microliths and rare agricultural implements) and pottery (Fig. 21). These remains apparently indicate a mounted culture, based for subsistence upon herding and hunting-fishing but little upon farming. It must have had a close cultural affiliation with the western part of the steppe belt rather than with the Huangho valley, even though many Eastern Chou types of artifacts, such as halberds, spearheads, and knives, have been found, by which these finds are dated. Similar cultural assemblages dated to the Han Dynasty have been found in much more widely scattered areas, indicating that the mounted nomads began to dominate the northern frontier at the expense of farmers.[20] A recent discovery of sixty-three graves dated to Western Han but apparently a continuation of the basic cultural tradition of the Eastern Chou nomads is abundant in cultural remains and particularly revealing as to the inhabitants' mode of subsistence.

18. Lü Tsun-eh, KKHP, 1958:3, 25–40.

19. Li Yih-yu, WW, 1959:6; Li Yih-yu, KK, 1959:6, 276–77; Chu Kui, KKHP, 1960:1, 63–70.

20. Li Yih-yu, WWTKTL, 1957:4, 29–32; Li Yih-yu, KKTH, 1956:2; 60–61.

This discovery is a cemetery found in 1956 at Hsi-ch'a-kou in Hsi-feng Hsien, in northeastern Liaoning. All of the sixty-three graves in the group were single burials, and each was accompanied by weapons, horse fittings, pottery, and ornaments. Horse teeth were collected from many of the graves, and three horse skulls

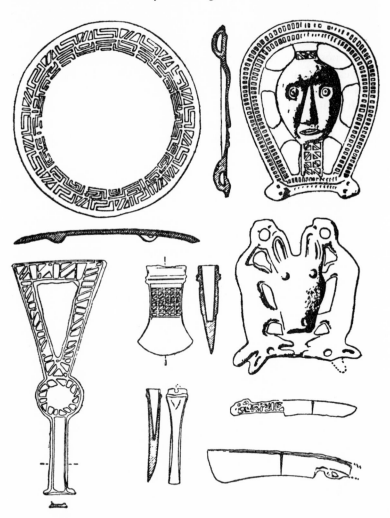

FIG. 21. Bronze artifacts discovered from an Eastern Chou tomb at Shih-erh-t'ai-ying-tzu, near Chao-yang, in Liaoning province. From KKHP, 1960:1, 67.

232

were found buried on top of a hill within the cemetery area. The human bones were entirely decomposed, but some remaining teeth show that aged people were rare among the dead. Many of the bronze ornaments depicted cattle, horses, sheep, dogs, and camels. These and other bits of evidence have led to the conclusion that

> this tribe [whose members were buried in this cemetery] belonged to a nomadic people, and pastoral nomadism occupied a principal position in the social economy. The bronze ornamental plates found from the graves indicate that horse, cattle, sheep, and camel were the major domestic animals in this society. The horse, particularly, was highly important both economically and militarily and was the basic means for transportation and warfare, as shown by the horse teeth and skulls. The large amount of hand-made, sand-tempered pottery, the persisting use of a small quantity of microliths, the appearance of hunting dogs and hunting falcons on the bronze ornamental plates, some microlithic arrowheads, a great variety of bronze and iron arrowheads and remains of fur clothes, all indicate that these northern peoples engaged in hunting and pastoral nomadism. It is noteworthy that from the cemetery not a single agricultural implement has been uncovered.[21]

Such a mode of life and such militant people are known to have appeared on the northern frontier at least as early as the Eastern Chou period of North China, marking the eastern extension of an Eurasian steppe culture pattern and apparently making the life of farmers in these regions increasingly difficult. The Great Wall marks the resistance of the agrarian residents to these nomads, but in spite of it, mounted warfare, certain burial customs, and many stylistic motifs in the decorative art were introduced into North China to enrich and provide variety to the Eastern Chou cultural life and artistic style. We need much more archaeological evidence to make any definite cultural delineations and to understand the process of these cultural contacts.

21. Sun Shou-tao, WW, 1960:8/9, 29.

The site of Yang-shao-ts'un in western Honan was discovered in 1920 by Liu Chang-shan, a field assistant of J. G. Andersson. In 1921 Andersson investigated the site himself, finding, among other things, some painted pottery which he considers to be related to the painted pottery cultures of Anau and Tripolye. From 1923–24, Andersson made an extensive survey in the area of eastern Kansu, presumed to be the area linking the East with the West. In the Huangho valley in eastern Kansu around the city of Lanchow and in the river valleys of T'ao and Huang-shui (Hsi-ning-ho), Andersson found a considerable number of early culture sites. Grouping these sites into six stages, Andersson considers them to be the linear succession of a "Painted Pottery Culture" tradition and gives a series of consecutive dates to each of the six stages.[22] Andersson's Kansu chronology, in its final, modified version, is as follows: [23]

Late Stone Age:	Ch'i Chia	(2500–2200 B.C.)
	Yang Shao (Pan-shan)	(2200–1700 B.C.)
	Ma Ch'ang	(1700–1300 B.C.)
Bronze Age:	Hsin Tien	(1300–1000 B.C.)
	Ssu Wa–Ch'ia Yao	(1000–700 B.C.)
	Sha Ching	(700–500 B.C.)

The Introduction to this volume might have been a more appropriate place for this chronological table, for such a succession of stages in Kansu is of little more than historical interest. I have cited it here, however, because this chronological scheme is still adopted by some writers of books and articles dealing with prehistory. Archaeological materials collected since Andersson offered his Six Stage Theory have proved this theory to be erroneous except for the facts that the "Late Stone Age" was earlier than the "Bronze Age," and that, within the Late Stone Age, Ma-ch'ang was probably later than Pan-shan. Otherwise there is no reason whatsoever to adhere to Andersson's scheme. The Ch'i-chia stage, as shown in a previous chapter, followed the Yangshao instead of preceding it. The chronologically linear succession of the three "Bronze Age" stages is not proven; rather, it has been demonstrated

22. Andersson, *GSuC, Mem.*, ser. A, 5 (1925).
23. Andersson, *BMFEA*, 15, 295.

that following the Ch'i-chia stage there were probably a small number of contemporary cultural assemblages such as Hsin-tien, Ssu-
wa, and Sha-ching, in the eastern Kansu area. Some of these may
be slightly earlier or later than the others, but all of them overlapped in time and cannot be considered successive "stages" of a
single culture. With these two major shifts of classification, Andersson's absolute dates are made completely meaningless. Andersson sees the whole sequence as ending around 500 B.C., which,
according to Andersson's authority, Bernhard Karlgren, is when
iron came into use in North China; however, iron was not found
in any of these sites, so that this evidence cannot be considered
conclusive.

We are not lost, however. Archaeological materials that have
accumulated since the early twenties in eastern Kansu show that
the first farmers who occupied eastern Kansu were the Yangshao
farmers of the Kansu subdivision, a derivative of the Yangshao
peoples in the Nuclear Area. These were followed by peoples of
the Ch'i-chia phase, corresponding in time to the Lungshanoid
horizon to the east but possibly of a different ethnic strain and
definitely of a distinctive cultural tradition. Between the Ch'i-chia
and the Ch'in civilization, which swept into this region and made
it a part of the Ch'in Empire, and contemporaneous with the Yin
and the Chou civilizations in the middle and lower Huangho
valley, the area in eastern Kansu was occupied by several contemporary or overlapping cultural traditions: Hsin-tien, Ssu-wa, and
Sha-ching (Map 12).

The Hsin-tien Tradition Archeological assemblages of the
Hsin-tien tradition have been recognized in the Lower T'ao-ho
valley north from the town of Lin-t'ao, the Huangho valley around
the city of Yüng-ching, and the lower Huangshui valley east of the
town of Lo-tu.[24] They consisted of some stone implements, copper
and bronze objects, and, above all, a distinctive ceramic tradition
characterized by coarse, red and gray fabrics, white and red slip,
and geometric patterns painted in black pigment. The pottery
was handmade by means of the coiling technique and a beater.
Both the coiled surface and the cord impressions produced by
the beater were then smoothed over with wet fingers. The black
paintings were simple and robust, executed free-hand in bands
around the shoulder and the middle circumference of the pot;

24. *KK* 1958:9, 47; *KK*, 1959:7, 379.

the designs were mostly curvilinear and round. The shape of the pottery is characterized by a distinctive demarcation of the body and the collar, with a large mouth and one or two large vertical handles, either attached to the middle part of the pot or with one end connected with the body and the other attached to the rim or below the rim.[25] Within this tradition, at least two phases

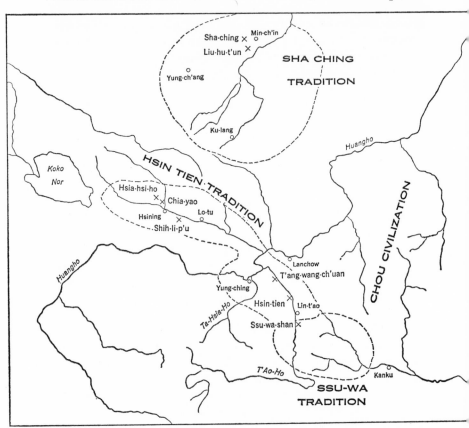

MAP 12. Eneolithic traditions in Kansu.

are distinguishable, namely, the Hsin-tien phase A, centering in the T'ao-ho valley, and the Hsin-tien phase B, concentrated in the Huangho valley near the city of Yüng-ching. Two other ceramic phases, T'ang-wang, near Yüng-ching and widespread in the Lower Huangshui, and Chia-yao (classified by Andersson with the Ssu-

25. Wu Chin-ting, *Prehistoric Pottery in China*, pp. 105–6.

236

wa Culture), also in the Lower Huangshui, may also be related to the Hsin-tien Culture.

The Hsin-tien Phase A, the classical Hsin-tien phase recognized by Andersson, is represented by a dwelling site at Hui-tsui and the cemetery at Hsin-tien (Hsin-tien locality A), both at T'ao-sha Hsien; burial sites of this phase have also been located in Lin-t'ao, Lin-hsia, and other localities in T'ao-sha.[26] The Hui-tsui dwelling site was located on a high terrace surrounded by deep ravines and was probably highly advantageous for defense purposes. Andersson believes that the natural topography of this site was essentially the same as it is today.[27] From this locality, pottery, stone and bone implements, beads, half a cowry shell, a bronze knife, and a bronze button were discovered by Andersson. The bronze knife has very similar counterparts among the Yin knives, and Wu Chin-ting finds some of the meander designs on the pottery reminiscent of North China bronze patterns.[28] A wu-shu coin of the Han Dynasty was found, but Andersson considers it intrusive. The pottery is coarse and highly porous, mostly of a gray or red color. The vessels were coiled, beaten, and then smoothed over with wet fingers. Two forms predominate, namely round-bottomed bowls and big-mouthed, high-collared jars with two handles. The handles are all vertical, either placed at the belly where they mark the maximum diameter of the pottery, or below the rim with one end attached to the rim or the upper part of the collar and the other end to the shoulder. The bottoms are predominantly concave. On the whole, the pots are relatively small, with an average height and diameter of 15 cm. The surface designs consist of the beaten cord marks that were not obliterated, incisions, scratched short parallel lines, and paintings in black pigment. The painting is largely confined to the shoulder and collar parts, consisting of simple geometric designs of forcefully but freely executed thick lines, such as horizontal black bands, narrow wavy lines, triangles, meander patterns, and N-shaped patterns. Some conventionalized anthropomorphic and animal-shaped patterns are also present.

The Hsin-tien Phase B is represented by three localities in Yüng-ching Hsien, namely Chang-chia-tsui, Han-chia-tsui, and Wa-cha-tsui.[29] In the same area assemblages of the Hsin-tien Phase

26. Andersson, BMFEA, 15, 167–79.
27. Andersson, BMFEA, 15, 168.
28. Wu Chin-ting, Prehistoric Pottery, p. 106.
29. An Chih-min, KKHP, 1957:2; KK, 1959:4.

A were also found. It is probable that these two phases were chronologically successive, with B the earlier of the two, although no stratigraphical evidence has been uncovered to confirm this view.[30] At the Chang-chia-tsui site, eighty-six round and rectangular pits were excavated, packed within a small area and yielding deep cultural debris. Chipped stone axes with ground edges, stone spades, knives (rectangular or notched), spindle whorls, perforated discs, and mortars and pestles were collected, along with bone spades, needles, awls, combs, ornaments, and two fragments of bronze or copper. Among the pottery remains, some red and gray pieces with a fine texture were noted, but most are of a kind of brick-red ware tempered with sand or powdered pottery. They were also coiled and smoothed over and burnished, like the pottery of Phase A, but on the whole they have a finer paste and a greater proportion of white slipped specimens. For surface decoration, cord marks, applied ridges, beaten checkers, and paintings are reported. The painting is again done in black pigment, but a few red patterns are found. The designs consist of parallel lines, deformed S-shapes, double spirals, N-shaped patterns, chevrons filled with parallel lines, sun patterns, crosses, and X-shaped patterns; most of these designs are common to both Phase A and Phase B, but others bear strong resemblances to the T'ang-wang phase. The forms of the vessels are more elongated, with larger handles than their Phase A counterparts, and the bottoms are uniformly flat rather than concave. In addition to jugs and bowls, pans, mugs, and *ting* and *li* tripods are also common [31] (Pl. VIII).

Closely related, if not practically identical, to the Hsin-tien Phase B is a ceramic phase that has been termed the T'ang-wang style.[32] The type site of this ceramic style is Shan-shen, near T'ang-wang-ch'uan, in Tung-hsiang Hsien, Kansu, in the Lower T'ao-ho valley, but pots and sherds of the same style have been collected at other sites near Yüng-ching, in Lin-t'ao Hsien in Lower T'ao-ho, and along the Lower Huangshui east of Lo-tu.[33] The site of Shih-li-p'u near Hsi-ning in Chinghai, found by Andersson, who classified it with the Ma-ch'ang phase of the Kansu Yangshao horizon, yielded pottery which shows no relation whatsoever to the Ma-

30. An Chih-min, *KKHP*, 1957:2, 30.
31. Ibid.; Hsieh Tuan-chü, *KK*, 1959:4, 182–83.
32. An Chih-min, *KKHP*, 1957:2, 23–27.
33. Ibid.; An Chih-min, *KK*, 1959:7, 379; Andersson, *BMFEA*, 15, 160–61.

ch'ang,[34] but unmistakable resemblance to the T'ang-wang style. The style is characterized by red ware of coarse paste, tempered with powdered pottery and occasionally with sand. Most of the sherds and pots are plain or corded cooking ware, but some of them were burnished and painted in black pigment. The surface was first smoothed over (thus obliterating the coil marks) and then, very often, slipped in red. Black patterns were executed on the slipped surface, mostly confined between two parallel lines around the belly, and consisting of spirals and whorls. Additional geometric patterns, such as S-shaped designs, parallel oblique lines, N-shaped designs, meanders, and chevrons filled with parallel lines, adorn parts of the rest of the pot on the collar, shoulder, or handle. The forms of the vessels include jars with two or four vertical handles, basins with two handles, single-handled mugs, *tou,* and *li* tripods. The most conspicuous feature in vessel forms is the very large loop handles, often higher than the mouths (Pl. IX).

Both in form and in decoration, the T'ang-wang style is very closely similar to the Hsin-tien phases, particularly Phase B, to which some investigators would assign this style altogether.[35]

In the same area of distribution as the T'ang-wang style is another ceramic phase typified by the site of Chia-yao, which was grouped by Andersson with the Ssu-wa culture but is considered by many other field workers as another independent culture.[36] I believe that it is neither, but that it should be regarded as a ceramic phase related to that of Hsin-tien, which we may call the Chia-yao phase. The type sites of this phase, Chia-yao and Hsia-hsi-ho, were first discovered during 1923–24 by Andersson in the valley of a tributary of the Huangshui in Hsi-ning Hsien, Chinghai.[37] The Chia-yao (Ch'ia-yao, K'a-yao) site, a cemetery, yielded no less than thirteen skeletons, which lie stretched on their backs, mostly heading west. Some of the burials were sprinkled with red ocher. Eight burials were found at Hsia-hsi-ho, another burial site across the river. The vessels found in the graves have flat or (more rarely) concave bases, big bellies, and collars of varying lengths. The saddle-shaped mouth occurs on some of the pots.

34. Chang Kwang-chih, BIHP, 30 (1959), 298.
35. Hsieh Tuan-chü, KK, 1959:4, 184.
36. Andersson, BMFEA, 15, 222; but see An Chih-min, KKTH, 1956:6; Chao Sheng-shen and Wu Ju-tso, WW, 1960:6, 36.
37. Andersson, BMFEA, 15, 185–97.

Most of the jars are equipped with two vertical handles, of the shoulder or collar types. Four-handled jars, with two large collar handles and two small shouldered loops, are also present. The surface of the pottery is brick-red or grayish, mostly plain; but corded specimens are also reported. Andersson reported no painted specimens. In addition to pottery, in the Chia-yao and Hsia-hsi-ho graves were found perforated stone discs, bone awls, plates, arrowheads, turquoise beads, clay spindle whorls, bronze buttons, folded buttons, links, openwork funnels, a knife, and some "rectangular objects." Andersson classifies these assemblages as Ssu-wa solely on the basis of some saddle-shaped mouth jars which are characteristic of the Ssu-wa Culture. This classification is dubious. It appears to me that the Chia-yao assemblages resemble the Hsin-tien phases more closely than the Ssu-wa Culture for the following reasons: (a) the saddle-shaped mouth occurs far from widely and is also found in the Hsin-tien phases, which may indicate cultural contacts with the Ssu-wa; (b) large collar handles, some of which are higher than the rim, are present; (c) four-handled jars are found; (d) concave bases are represented; and (e) geographically the Chia-yao phase is separated from the Ssu-wa area by a considerable area occupied by the Hsin-tien. This classification—with Hsin-tien instead of Ssu-wa—is strengthened by the result of new investigations in 1959 in Huang-chung Hsien and near the Hsi-ning city, which brought to light as many as thirty-one localities of the Chia-yao phase.[38] Among the pottery remains were found coarse, red sherds tempered with powdered pottery and occasionally with sand or mica. These were coiled, some slipped (in red or, rarely, grayish-white), and painted, corded, applied, incised, or combed. The painting was done in black pigment, consisting in design of zigzags, triangles, and spirals. In form, the pottery is characterized by a wide mouth and large and small vertical handles, mostly on the collar part of the jar. A few li tripods are found. Concave bottoms are found quite frequently. In addition, some stone, horn, and bronze artifacts were also found. Among the bronzes, the ko halberds, buttons, and two-winged arrowheads are said to resemble Chou types.[39] The close similarity of this Chia-yao assemblage to the T'ang-wang phase of the same region has been noted,[40] and

38. Chao Sheng-shen and Wu Ju-tso, WW, 1960:6, 35–36.
39. An Chih-min, KK, 1959:7, 380.
40. Ibid., p. 379.

it has been advanced that the T'ang-wang phase was probably the proto-Chia-yao, so to speak. At any rate, the Chia-yao phase is shown to be related to the Hsin-tien phases by the new finds in the following aspects: temper of powdered pottery, coiling, red slip, black pigment in painting, and spiral designs. It is thus possible that the Hsin-tien B phase and the T'ang-wang style represent an earlier phase or stage of the Hsin-tien culture, evolving into the Hsin-tien A in the T'aoho valley and into the Chia-yao phase in the Huangshui valley.

The Ssu-wa Tradition   The Ssu-wa tradition is now represented by over a dozen archaeological sites in the upper T'ao-ho valley, south of Lin-t'ao Hsien, and in the Upper Weishui tributaries in eastern Kansu.[41] The type locality of this tradition is the Ssu-wa-shan cemetery in Lin-t'ao Hsien, discovered by Andersson in 1924.[42] The pottery remains found in the eight burials here were plain, rather large, and brick-red or red in color. The shape of the vessels is characterized by jars with saddle-shaped mouths; some *li* tripods were found, and these had saddle-shaped mouths, too. The body of the vessels is essentially oval, which has led Wu Chin-ting to conclude that "these pots are so designed as to be easily portable." [43] Two vertical handles are attached to the upper part of the vessel. On the collar between the two handles there is, in some cases, an indented applied ridge. The average height of the vessels is 24 cm. They are coarse, sand-tempered, and hand-made and smoothed out while still wet. Wu also observes that "every characteristic of the pottery seems to testify that the Ssu-wa culture is not Chinese, though it might have been influenced by that culture." [44] In addition to pottery, Andersson found an armlet of bronze, a perforated axe, and two goat horns. According to Andersson the goats were probably domesticated.[45]

The Ssu-wa-shan site was again investigated by Hsia Nai in 1945, who excavated six additional burials. No less than three ways to dispose of the dead were distinguished by Hsia in his data: cremation and ash urns; interment of the dorsal and stretched

41. An Chih-min, *KKTH*, 1956:6, 15; Chang Hsüeh-cheng, *KKTH*, 1958:9, 47; An Chih-min, *KK*, 1959:7, 327, 380.
42. Andersson, *BMFEA*, 15, 179–85.
43. Wu Chin-ting, *Prehistoric pottery*, p. 107.
44. Ibid.
45. Andersson, *BMFEA*, 15, 185.

type; and probably secondary burials. These burial customs, Hsia contends, indicate that the Ssu-wa-shan people were not Chinese but were possibly the Ch'iang recorded in Chinese annals.[46] Pottery similar to Andersson's finds was uncovered by Hsia, who also recognized the use of the coiling technique and of powdered-pottery tempers. A stone and a clay ball were collected, possibly sling stones. On the surface of the potsherd, impressions of grains were noted.[47]

More sites of the Ssu-wa tradition were investigated in the T'ao-ho and Upper Weishui valleys in 1956,[48] 1957,[49] and 1958.[50] In 1957, some painted sherds were discovered in the Ssu-wa assemblages, with such patterns as concentric semicircles, meanders, and other geometric designs executed in black. Stone implements associated with the Ssu-wa pottery were mostly chipped, including edge-ground axes, knives with side notches, and shouldered axes.

The Sha-ching Tradition Approximately 200 km. to the north of Lanchow, in the arid land between the Huangho and the Ch'i-lien Mountains, lies the eastern segment of the so-called Ho-hsi Corridor, drained by the Pai-t'ing-ho River. Ecologically, this region is right on the border between the Huangho valley and the steppe, but is still on the south side of the Great Wall. During the final Neolithic period, the area contained the Shan-tan (or Ssu-pa) Tradition, described in Chapter 5. When the Ch'i-chia Tradition in the Huangho and T'aoho valleys to the south gave way to the eneolithic Hsin-tien and Ssu-wa phases described above, the arid land in the north was occupied by a different cultural tradition, the Sha-ching Tradition. Archaeological remains of this tradition have been located in Min-ch'in, Yüng-ch'ang, and Ku-lang counties.[51] It is typified by the archaeological sites at Sha-ching-ts'un, in Min-ch'in (Chen-fan) Hsien, which were discovered in 1923–24 by Andersson.[52] These sites consist of a fortified dwelling site, Liu-hu-t'un, and a cemetery. The former was a mud-walled fortress, 50 meters in diameter. Found inside were a *li*

46. Hsia Nai, KKHP, 4 (1949), 96.
47. Ibid., pp. 106–7.
48. An Chih-min, KKTH, 1956:6, 15.
49. Chang Hsüeh-cheng, KKTH, 1958:9, 45.
50. An Chih-min, KK, 1959:7, 327.
51. An Chih-min, KKTH, 1956:6, 16.
52. Andersson, BMFEA, 15, 197–215.

tripod, some handled high bowls, a steatite pan, some bone artifacts (needles, arrowheads, etc.), a bronze knife, a bronze prismatic
arrowhead, and a piece of golden string. The cemetery is situated
260 meters to the west, and in it over forty burials were excavated.
The skeletons lay on their backs, stretched or slightly flexed. The
pottery was reddish, containing sand or mica for tempers, beaten
and red-slipped. Some of the pots were painted in red pigment,
and the favorite designs were horizontal lines, triangles, and bird
figures. In form, two shapes are characteristic, handled mugs with
vertical walls and small jars with two small shoulder loops. The
bodies and the collars of the jars are not distinctively demarcated.
In addition to pottery, Andersson found in the burials stone and
turquoise beads, marble rings, perforated stone objects (similar
in shape to the banner stones of the eastern United States), cowry
shells (all ground flat and open at the back), and copper and
bronze artifacts, including a spearhead, an arrowhead (with square
cross-section), a ring, a knife tip, a flat 3-lobed piece with spiral
design on the front and a bridge on each of the end lobes on the
back (similar to an object found in a Warring-States grave in Luan-
p'ing, Jehol), tubes which were annulated at the ends and widened
and smooth in the center (identical to objects found in the Ordos),
and a button.

The chronological position of the above three traditions is
stratigraphically clear insofar as they can be shown to be earlier
than the Han Dynasty but later than the Ch'i-chia Tradition in
the same area. Stratigraphical evidence at Chang-chia-tsui and
Wu-chia in Yüng-ching Hsien shows that the Hsin-tien Tradition
was definitely later than the Ch'i-chia,[53] and that at Ssu-wa-shan
the Ssu-wa Tradition was subsequent to the Ma-chia-yao phase
of the Kansu Yangshao horizon.[54] Furthermore, the saddle-
mouthed jars sometimes found in the Hsin-tien assemblages indicate that the Hsin-tien and the Ssu-wa at least overlapped in
time.[55] Some idea of the absolute dating of these approximately
contemporary cultural traditions can be derived from the typology
of the *li* tripods found in these assemblages (most of which are
said to be of the Yin-Chou types), from the metal objects of Yin,

53. An Chih-min, *KKTH*, 1956:6, 15.
54. Hsia Nai, *KKHP*, 4 (1949), 74.
55. An Chih-min, *KKTH*, 1956:6, 15; Chang Hsüeh-cheng, *KKTH*, 1958:9,
47.

Chou, and Ordosian affinities, and from the fact that within the Ssu-wa, which adjoined the Western Chou civilization of the Weishui valley, cultural elements such as specific types of shouldered axes and side-notched stone knives have been found which indicate contacts with the Chou. It seems reasonable to place the Kansu eneolithic traditions at the end of the second millennium and during the first half of the first millennium B.C., an interval long enough for subdivisions to be made, such as the development of the Hsin-tien phases (Hsin-tien B and T'ang-wang to Hsin-tien A and Chia-yao).

If, as is shown, the Hsin-tien, Sha-ching, and Ssu-wa were approximately contemporary cultural traditions, what are they exactly in terms of archaeological nomenclature? In choosing the term "tradition," noted for its elasticity, I have revealed my uncertainty over this problem. Archaeologically all three traditions are known primarily by their ceramics. The following characteristics are common to the ceramics of all three: in shape, jars with vertical handles predominate, and the handles include both the small-belly and large-collar varieties, seeming, in these aspects, to carry on the basic ceramic forms of both the Pan-shan stage and the Ch'i-chia Tradition *in the same area*; pottery of all three traditions was coiled and beaten, with the roughened surface mostly smoothed out; ceramic painting is seen in all three traditions, although it occurs only rarely (as recorded thus far) in the Ssu-wa; the painted designs are geometric and conventionally realistic in all three traditions, and the lines are robust and the patterns succinct. In shape and in decorative painting, the minimum denominators common to all three traditions, still sufficiently specific in terms of style to make cultural historic connections, are of such a basic nature as to lead us to suspect that they may have been three different regional phases of the same cultural tradition, one that carries on the basic ceramic features of both the Kansu Yangshao phase and the Ch'i-chia Tradition in the area of eastern Kansu. It must also be noted that it is not at all impossible that some of the late Kansu Yangshao phases and the Ch'i-chia Tradition overlapped in time in the marginal regions of this area which may have resulted in a mutual influence or even a merging of styles.

On the other hand, many ceramic stylistic features set the Hsin-tien, the Ssu-wa, and the Sha-ching Traditions apart from one

244

another and from their local predecessors, a fact that also finds support from the little information available on their respective cultural contexts. In subsistence patterns, all three traditions appear to have been based on agriculture, but animal domestication may also have played an important role in the Ssu-wa, as indicated by remains of goat horns and the shape of pottery that may well have been designed for a mobile life, as Wu suggested. In burial customs, the Hsin-tien and Chia-yao used red ochers, the Ssu-wa had cremation, and the Sha-ching placed some of the dead in a somewhat flexed posture. In ceramics, the red pigment for paint-ing and the flat-bottomed mugs are distinctive of the Sha-ching Tradition, whereas both the Ssu-wa and the Hsin-tien stressed big-handled jars with well-defined bodies and collars, and used pow-dered pottery for tempering materials. To what extent these differ-ences in culture and technology indicate ethnic differences or diverse "origins" is an open question.

Chapter Nine

Early

Civilizations

in South China

During the late second and the first millennium B.C., cultural elements of the Yin and Chou civilizations penetrated deep into the northern part of eastern Asia, causing widespread cultural changes, but the Great Wall to a large extent marks the northern limits of the civilized states built upon the foundation of agriculture. No such limits in ecology were imposed upon the spread of civilization into subtropical South China, where the Yin and the Chou stimulated the formation of a number of early kingdoms. The introduction of North China civilizations into South China followed closely the paths used by the early Lungshanoid pioneer farmers: agricultural kingdoms emerged first in the Huaiho and the middle and lower Yangtze, and from there expanded to the Red basin and the Yünnan Plateau in the southwest.

THE GEOMETRIC HORIZON OF EASTERN SOUTH CHINA

In Chapter 4 it has been shown that the Lungshanoid farmers brought agriculture and a Lungshanoid cultural style with them into the eastern part of South China—the part that is drained by the middle and lower Yangtze, the Huaiho, and many small rivers along the southeastern coast, and consists of the present provinces of Anhwei, Kiangsu, Hupei, Kiangsi, Chekiang, Fukien, Taiwan, and the eastern part of Kwangtung. The Lungshanoid in South China is a bonafide horizon in the sense used by American archaeologists—a highly homogeneous style of artifacts brought into a large area by a rapid, or even explosive, expansion out of a center which was, in this case, the North China Nuclear Area. In eastern South China, the Lungshanoid was followed by another highly

246

homogeneous and even more widespread horizon, the Geometric.

The name "Geometric," used in archaeological literature to refer to the impressed designs on pottery in this area of this horizon, is used here to designate the horizon-style primarily characterized by the geometric-stamping tradition manifested in the pottery remains. Both pottery stamps and the geometric patterns (such as checkers, parallel lines, and wavy lines) appear in the Lungshanoid horizon, but in the Geometric horizon, geometric stamping dominated the ceramic decoration, was used far more extensively than before, and made use of greatly diversified design motifs. The color of the Geometric wares is predominantly red or grayish; the ware is handmade, beaten, and hard-fired. The beater also served as a stamp for decorative designs, which include a long list of such geometric basic patterns as checkers, chevrons, cross-hatches, meanders, spirals, triangles, quadrangles, and circles (Fig. 22). In shape, small-mouthed and flat- or round-bottomed urns predominate, though to some extent all Lungshanoid forms are continued. This new ceramic style of South China can certainly be linked with the "hard ware" of the Yin-Shang pottery, and the Geometric horizon in eastern South China was apparently a development of the local Lungshanoid substratum, under the continuous stimulation of the Shang and Chou cultural impacts.

In addition to the new ceramic style, the Geometric horizon carries over from the Lungshanoid Neolithic essentially the same cultural traditions of the area, such as the stone inventories (among which the stepped adze is the most characteristic),[1] agricultural crops (primarily rice), habitation patterns—dwellings on mounds or on wooden piles, apparently a feature which is environmentally oriented in the main—(Pl. VI), and other aspects of the material culture. However, at least one other significant addition was made to the Lungshanoid foundation during the Geometric period, namely, bronze metallurgy. Small pieces of bronze objects have been found at many Geometric sites dated to a pre-Han Dynasty period, and evidence of local bronze foundry has been discovered at many sites in southern Kiangsu.

The Geometric horizon spread over a wide area, largely the same as that outlined above for the Lungshanoid, but including Hunan and a wider area in Kwangtung. The Geometric horizon, however, occupied each of these regions far more intensively, and

1. Lin Hui-hsiang, *KKHP*, 1958:3, 1.

lasted for a long period of time. For the entire area, the Geometric horizon started with the first influence of the Shang civilization from the North, probably during the second half of the second millennium B.C., and ended toward the end of the first millennium B.C., although the Geometric Stamped pottery as a stylistic tradition of the area persisted throughout South China into the Han

FIG. 22. Geometric designs on pottery from the site at Pei-yin-yang-ying, near Nanking. From *KKHP*, 1958:1, 13.

Dynasty.[2] The Geometric horizon evolved in a number of different ways. At the beginning, the local communities in this area probably carried on the old Lungshanoid Neolithic ways of life, even though the new ceramic styling and some bronze metallurgy were introduced. In some regions, however, continuous Shang and Chou influences helped the local cultures to develop into states modeled

2. Yin Huan-chang, *KKHP*, 1958:1, 84.

248

on those of North China. To describe the contextual variations within the Geometric horizon during the different periods in the regions of eastern South China, we must try to trace the southern limits and extents of the historical cultural influences step by step.

THE ADVENT OF SHANG AND WESTERN CHOU CIVILIZATIONS IN EASTERN SOUTH CHINA

Centered in northern Honan, Shang Dynasty influences are discernible in the archaeological materials excavated from Kiangsu, Anhwei, Hupei, and Hunan. In the Huaiho valley of northern Kiangsu and Anhwei, and in the Hanshui valley of northern Hupei, the Shang cultural impact was so great that archaeologists have often been tempted to speak of Yin-Shang Culture sites in these regions, although in all probability these sites would be better described as "Yin-Shang-ized" Lungshanoid, or some such term.

In the neighborhood of Hsü-chou, a number of sites have been listed in current publications as "Yin-Shang sites," including: Kao-huang-miao II, Ch'iu-wan, Hsiao-hung-shan, Ku-t'u-tun, T'ai-shang, Hua-chia-ssu, Huang-lou, and Liang-wang-ch'eng.[3] Remains of stone, bone, and ceramics do occur at some of these sites, indicating cultural contacts with the Shang civilization to the northwest, in addition to a small number of bronze knives, arrowheads, and spearheads, as well as oracle turtle shells unearthed at Kao-huang-miao, and corded *li* tripods with nipple-shaped feet at some of the other sites. On the other hand, the field workers have not reported evidence of local metallurgy and urban settlement patterns from this area, and we cannot fail to take note of the fact that practically all of the implements and tools of these archaeological assemblages were made of stone, shell, and bone. It is my opinion that some of the archaeologists who reported on these sites have been too liberal in using such terms as "Yin-Shang Culture" and "Yin-Shang period." Identifications have sometimes been made positively upon very general and meager data. Take, for instance, the following reports:

> The Middle Stratum [of Kao-huang-miao] has relatively thick deposits, and represents a fairly long time duration. Among the remains that have been unearthed, stone, bone,

3. Hsieh Chun-chu, *KKHP*, 1958:4, 7–17; Yin Huan-chang and Chang Cheng-hsiang, *KK*, 1960:3, 28.

and shell tools and implements predominate in quantity. Some of these implements, such as stone sickles and shell knives, are more advanced than the Lower Stratum specimens . . . In addition, bronzes have been found, and oracle bones and turtle shells discovered. All such circumstances indicate that the cultural remains of the Middle Stratum belonged to the Yin-Shang period.[4]

The lower stratum [of the Liang-wang-ch'eng site] has yielded *li* tripods and urns of gray ware with corded surface, black pottery *tou* with string patterns, and, in addition, deer antlers, mollusc shells, and perforated flat axes, evidently showing characteristic features of Shang Dynasty remains.[5]

The Shang Dynasty sites [in the Hsu-chou area investigated in 1959] include Ch'iu-wan. . . . In the remains, such items as bronze arrowheads, bone hairpins, bone awls, bone arrowheads, corded *lei*, corded *li*, corded urns, pottery with *t'ao-t'ieh* patterns, and helmet-shaped pots, indicate Shang Dynasty characteristics.[6]

Some of these Shang Dynasty characteristics are, to be sure, of such specific and significant nature as to warrant the connection, but some others are so general and so widespread that they do not. In either event, the designation "Shang Dynasty sites" is unwarranted unless its meaning is made completely clear. These terminological jigglings may appear unnecessary in a general book like the present volume. But uncritical acceptance of such designations used by field workers in archaeological publications has resulted in the inclusion of such sites and regions into the circle of the Shang-Yin civilization in some recent discussions of the Shang[7] in such a way as to suggest that the cultural and societal changes which took place during the Shang Dynasty as evidenced by the archaeology of An-yang and Cheng-chow, also happened in such "Yin-Shang Dynasty" sites as, say, Kao-huang-miao of Hsü-chou in northern Kiangsu. This suggestion is certainly misleading, and to correct such erroneous impressions, it is necessary to start off by defining our terms.

At any rate, it is safe to say that the Yin-Shang cultural influ-

4. Hsieh Chun-chu, *KKHP*, 1958:4, 17.
5. Yin Huan-chang and Chang Cheng-hsiang, *KK*, 1960:3, 26.
6. Ibid., p. 28.
7. Cheng Te-kun, *Shang China*, p. 14.

ences were felt by the Lungshanoid farmers in the Hsü-chou area, and that the cultural remains these farmers left during the Shang-influenced period can be described as part of the Geometric horizon. The same can also be said for northern Anhwei in the Huaiho valley. Cultural elements similar to those of Yin-Shang have been found in Shou Hsien [8] and Fu-nan.[9] Wang Hsiang reported under the term "Hsiao-t'un Stage" many early cultural sites in Shou Hsien, including those where the following stylistic traits were present: short-footed *li* tripods; urns with cord marks and corded applied ridges; *tou* with thick rims; and deep dishes.[10] Li Chi [11] added what he calls the "Hsiao-t'un Stone Knife" from Yang-lin-chi to this list. In the district of Fu-nan, in the area of Anhwei closest to Honan, no less than twenty-six bronze vessels have been found since the nineteen-forties, but their provenance and cultural contexts are not known.[12] They have been described as Yin-Shang bronzes, but there is nothing to prevent them from being of the early Western Chou period. Western Chou bronzes have been found in well-documented circumstances as far south as the Lower Yangtze, as will be described below, and typology alone could not distinguish between Yin-Shang and early Western Chou.

Bronze vessels and weapons of Yin-Shang types were unearthed in at least two sites in Huang-p'i, near the confluence of the Han-shui and the Yangtze in central Hupei.[13] Some of these artifacts, such as a bronze *chüeh* tripod from Yang-chia-wan and three bronze *ko* halberds, are not only of the ordinary Shang types but are closer to varieties of the Erh-li-kang phase. These bronzes were all chance discoveries, but the exact spots of their origin are said to be known. In the neighborhood of these spots, in both cases, Geometric assemblages have been brought to light, although whether or not these were the cultural coexistents of the bronzes has not been determined. Much more work and many new materials will be needed before the extent of the Yin-Shang influence into the Hanshui valley can be clearly determined.

8. Wang Hsiang, *KKHP*, 2, 1947.
9. Kê Chieh-ping, *WW*, 1959:1.
10. Wang Hsiang, *KKHP*, 2 (1947), 250.
11. Li Chi, *BIHP*, 23 (1951), 612.
12. Kê Chieh-ping, *WW*, 1959:1.
13. Kuo Ping-lien, *KKTH*, 1958:1, 56–58; Kuo Ping-lien, *KKTH*, 1958:9, 72–73.

Further to the south, in the middle and lower Yangtze valley, Yin-Shang influence is indicated, though by no means demonstrated, by two bronze vessels of Shang type allegedly found in the province of Hunan,[14] and by some stylistic traits in the remains of the Geometric horizon in southern Kiangsu. Yin Huan-chang[15] has singled out the following traits of the Geometric horizon in southern Kiangsu which he considers to be derived from Yin or early Western Chou influences: (a) in ceramics, such forms as *p'o, lei, li, yen, kwei, yu, min,* and *tou,* such accessory parts as lugs, and such decorative designs as *yün* and *lei* patterns, cowry, bands of triangles, and strings, all similar to the bronzes of the late Yin and early Chou; (b) in stone typology, stone halberds and stone arrowheads similar in form to the bronze halberds of the Yin and Chou Dynasties and the bronze arrowheads excavated from Yin-hsü; and (c) bronze knives, arrowheads, and handles and feet of the *ting* tripods of the late Yin and early Chou styles. According to Jao Tsung-yih,[16] potsherds found in such regions to the far south as the Hanchiang River valley in eastern Kwangtung resemble the "white pottery" of the Shang Dynasty to such an extent in color and decorative designs as to suggest cultural influence.

Although conclusions regarding the extension of the Yin-Shang influence to the Yangtze valley or even further south might be regarded as far-fetched on the basis of the available archaeological evidence, there is no question that the Western Chou civilization extended to the Lower Yangtze. Groups of bronze vessels of probable Western Chou types have been discovered not only in the Lower Yangtze valley in Tan-t'u, Yih-cheng, and Nanking in southern Kiangsu but also from such southern localities as Ch'ang-hsing, on the western shore of T'ai-hu Lake in northern Chekiang, and T'un-hsi in southern Anhwei, in the upper reaches of the Chien-t'ang-chiang, or Chekiang River.[17] These bronzes exhibit either characteristic features that have been attributed to

14. Tsai Chi-hsiang, WW, 1960:3, 75. Pottery with the Yin style of forms and decorative designs has also been reported from Shih-men Hsien in Hunan; see Chou Shih-jung, KK, 1962:3, 144–46.
15. Tseng Chao-yü and Yin Huan-chang, KKHP, 1959:4, 54.
16. Jao Tsung-yih, Ta-lu-tsa-chih, 8 (1954), 65–67.
17. WWTKTL, 1955:5, 58–62; Wang Chih-min and Han Yih-chih, WWTKTL, 1956:12, 31; WW, 1960:7, 48; Li Wei-jan, KK, 1960:6, 41; Yin Ti-fei, KKHP, 1959:4, 59–87.

the Yin-Chou substage of the Archaic style according to North China criteria, or typical diagnostics of the Middle Chou style as defined by Bernhard Karlgren. Accordingly, these five sites can be grouped into two classes:

> (1) Early Western Chou: Tan-t'u and Yih-cheng finds, characterized by an Archaic style with features assumed to be Western Chou instead of Yin—four-eared *kwei*, *pan* with bent ears. These two sites are located in the Lower Yangtze in southern Kiangsu.
>
> (2) Late Western Chou or early Eastern Chou: Nanking, T'un-hsi, and Ch'ang-hsing finds, characterized by a typical Middle Chou style with local characteristics. The Nanking site is in the Yangtze valley of southern Kiangsu, but the other two sites are further south, in the Chekiang valley in southern Anhwei and northern Chekiang.

These findings are of considerable importance for the study of Western Chou bronzes, and in connection with the present discussions, their composition and geographical distribution are highly significant for the following reasons: (a) The distribution of the bronzes of different ages indicates that the southbound expansion of the North Chinese cultural influences extended toward the south from the Lower Yangtze to the Chekiang valley during the span of the Western Chou Dynasty; (b) In addition to some bronze types that are so similar to their North China counterparts as to suggest importation from the North,[18] a suggestion strengthened by the inscriptions of Western Chou characters on a *kwei* vessel from the Yen-tun-shan site of Tan-t'u, there are other forms of bronze and other decorative designs on the vessels that find no counterparts in North China, but must be considered as having been manufactured *in situ* and influenced stylistically by the local cultural tradition.

> Some of the vessels [from the Tan-t'u group] are not identical to North China bronzes stylistically. For instance, the lid-knob and *ting* ears in the shape of standing animals . . . are rarely seen on North China bronzes. The body shape and the foot form of two small *ting* tripods resemble the

18. Tseng Chao-yü and Yin Huan-chang, KKHP, 1959:4, 54.

pottery *ting* tripods of the [local Geometric horizon] cultures. The textile pattern on a pair of horn-shaped vessels and on several horse fittings are identical to the textile patterns on the local Geometric Stamped pottery. One can positively say that these bronzes were manufactured *in situ*, thus exhibiting some characteristic features of the local culture.[19]

At the T'un-hsi site, many ceramic remains found in association with the Western Chou type of bronzes are indistinguishable from the Geometric pottery discovered elsewhere in the same area in less glamorous contexts,[20] and the bronzes differ from North Chinese bronzes in decorative patterns, shapes, and sometimes even in type, as, for example, a special local kind of musical instrument. These distinctive local features, if indicative of the local manufacture of some bronzes, are significant indicators of the nature of the local communities which were responsible for the making, use, and burial of these bronzes.

(c) Another highly suggestive fact about these Western Chou bronzes is that, as they appear in the present archaeological record, they are isolated islands of high civilization surrounded by the sea of less advanced communities of the local Geometric horizon. In these communities, cultural elements indicative of Western Chou contacts, such as ceramic shapes, decorative designs, and the remains of bronze artifacts, are few and insignificant in comparison with the overwhelming majority of other remains found at the same sites, which consist of stone, bone, and shell implements of a local Neolithic tradition and ceramics of the Geometric Stamped style.

These facts suggest that the introduction of the Western Chou civilization into the Lower Yangtze may have been brought about by an elite class of Western Chou extraction who ruled the natives of the region, established a local technological and societal pattern after the North China model, and gradually acculturated the local Neolithic inhabitants in the farming villages. The region of southern Kiangsu was known in Western Chou as the state of Wu, and, according to local traditions, was the location of the burial place of two Western Chou princes, T'ai-po and Chung-yüng. These

19. Ibid.
20. Ibid., p. 78.

princes, according to Ssu-ma Chien's *Shih Chi* "escaped to the habitations of the Ching Man barbarians, tattooed and cut off their hair [according to the local customs] to indicate their decision of not returning . . . They called themselves Kou Wu. The Ching Man people considered them as righteous men, and more than a thousand families followed their leadership." To what extent the details of this story are valid is debatable, but the story in its broad outline and the archaeological facts have jointly established the process of acculturation in this region by the Western Chou civilization.

Such events were not confined to the Lower Yangtze and the Chekiang valleys. Eastern Chou historical documents have recorded that many civilized kingdoms in southeast China had communications, transactions, and warfare with the Royal Chou and other northern Chinese states. Of these kingdoms, Ts'ai of northern Anhwei, Wu of southern Kiangsu, Yüeh of Chekiang, Fukien, Kwangtung, Yen of southern Kiangsu, and Ch'u of southern Honan, Hupei, Hunan, and the Huaiho valley in northern Anhwei are the best known. It is evident that such kingdoms must have emerged during the Western Chou Dynasty, and the process described above may very well represent the initial phase of such an emergence. But in the archaeological record it was not until the Eastern Chou period that the remains of these early kingdoms in South China became widely found and substantially represented. In terms of society and cultural changes, Eastern Chou may be considered to be the period when these kingdoms, archaeologically speaking, were formed.

EASTERN CHOU KINGDOMS IN EASTERN SOUTH CHINA

Many of the Eastern Chou kingdoms as recorded in history were short-lived, and the expanse of their areas, which is often known only in a general way, frequently shifted from one century to the next. It is known archaeologically that the cultural remains in eastern South China of the Eastern Chou period belong either to the widespread Geometric horizon or to a time just after it, depending on the region. It is also known that the extent of civilization in terms of bronze and iron technology, stylistic sophistication, and political form varies widely from one region to another. But it is not always possible to identify archaeological phases with

255

historical states, since these historical states were not necessarily cultural areas at the same time, and since the archaeological assemblages can rarely be dated with the precision of decades, unless the remains were themselves dated by inscriptions (many of which are controversially interpreted) to meet the temporal specification of individual historic kingdoms. The cultural groups in eastern South China of the Eastern Chou period are thus defined below according to different criteria for different groups: stylistic criteria when ethnic and political identifications cannot be made, and ethnic and political criteria when such identifications are made possible by inscriptions and other relatively reliable evidence. This is done, instead of following stylistic criteria exclusively in accordance with the usual archaeological procedure, because of the rich literary records available for this period. If tentative ethnic and political identifications are first made, archaeologists can then use these literary records to very good advantage.

The "Hu-shu Culture" This is a term coined in 1959 by Tseng Chao-yü and Yin Huan-chang [21] to designate the culture of the Yangtze valley in southern Kiangsu and central Anhwei during the period between the Lungshanoid Neolithic and Han civilizations. The sites of this culture are on mounds or low hills and hill slopes, and the archaeological inventories are characterized by many common distinctive features in stone implements, ceramics, bone and antler artifacts, bronze metallurgy, house construction, scapulimancy, and burial customs. Among the pottery remains, red and black pottery of a Lungshanoid heritage still constitutes the majority, but Geometric wares are important elements also.

Whether this cultural grouping is justified or not, it underlines the continuity of a cultural tradition in this part of China during the Yin and Chou (both Western and Eastern) Dynasties which was the recipient of the North China historic influences described above, and which may represent the Ching Man ethnic group, or a part of it, mentioned in Ssu-ma Chien's Shih Chi. Pottery crucibles and fragments of bronze have been found, from a lower stratum of this cultural tradition, at Pei-yin-yang-ying, near Nan-

21. Ibid., p. 47. For further discussions on this cultural phase, see Chang Yüng-nien, KK, 1962:1, 32–37; Wu Ju-tso, KK, 1962:1, 38–40; Yin Huan-chang and Yüan Ying, KK, 1962:3, 125–28, 133.

king, indicating the practice of bronze metallurgy in the local village communities. A cemetery in the uppermost stratum of the same site, probably dating from the Eastern Chou period, yielded finely polished stone artifacts and jade and opal objects. The number of these burial objects varies widely from grave to grave, ranging from over forty items to a single piece, which suggests sharply differentiated social status.[22] Such indications undoubtedly support the historical records of Wu and Yüeh states in this and neighboring regions, although such states are yet to be identified precisely in the archaeological remains. Remains of stone plows, triangular in shape and closely similar to the iron plows of North China, have been unearthed in a Geometric horizon context at Yü-yao Hsien, Chekiang,[23] suggesting that the iron plow technology of the contemporary civilizations elsewhere had local imitations in the Hu-shu Culture and its related phases. The cultural and social implications of such influences cannot be overemphasized.

Yen Yen-ch'eng, the town of Yen, is a walled town site south of Wu-chin (Ch'ang-chou), to the south of the Yangtze valley in southern Kiangsu province. It has three concentric walls which are called, respectively, the outer wall, the inner wall, and the Tzu-lo or Royal Wall. The outer wall is an irregular circle, about 1500 m. across, surrounded by a defensive water ditch. Both the inner wall and the Royal Wall make approximately square enclosures, situated in the northeastern part of the outer enclosure, with another protective water ditch surrounding the inner wall. Between the outer and the inner walls, in the western part of the outer enclosure, is a row of three earthen mounds. The arrangement of this town is similar to some of the Eastern Chou cities in North China, as described above. Local traditions regard this town site as the remains of the capital of Yen, a Yüeh-related state in southern Kiangsu. Archaeological investigations were made at the site in 1935 and again in 1958, bringing to light a small amount of pottery, stone implements, bronze vessels, and wooden boats, but full-scale scientific excavations have yet to be carried out.

Pottery remains found at the Yen site belonged to the Geometric

22. Chao Ching-fang. *KKHP*, 1958:1. 7–18.
23. Chin Tsu-ming. *KKTH*, 1958:9, 71.

variety, including nearly twenty whole urns covered with impressed geometric designs, some of which apparently were imitations of bronze patterns.[24] The bronze vessels, discovered in 1958, consist of three *tsun* vessels, a *pan* with a handle, a spout, and three *ting*-like feet, a bronze *pan* with two wheel-feet and two animal-head-shaped handles, a set of seven portable bells, and an animal-shaped *yih* vessel.[25] One hundred and fifty meters to the south of the spot where the bronzes were found, in the water ditch surrounding the inner wall, three dugout canoes were uncovered, one of which is 11 m. long and 90 cm. wide at the top.[26]

The shape and decor of the bronze vessels find counterparts in the Huai style of North China, but many local characteristics are still highly conspicuous, such as the three-wheeled *pan*, the *yih* vessel with an animal-head-shaped spout, and the needle-shaped decorative designs on the *tsun* vessels. The associated Geometric pottery clearly indicates the basic cultural affiliation of this town site. In any case, this find gives an interesting example of the Yüeh civilization in the Eastern Chou period.

Ts'ai According to Ssu-ma Chien's *Shih Chi*, Ch'u invaded the state of Ts'ai and forced the Marquis Chao of Ts'ai to move his capital to Chou-lai in the year 493 B.C. Chou-lai is generally agreed to have been located in the neighborhood of Shou Hsien in the present province of northern Anhwei in the Huaiho valley. Ssu-ma Chien also reported that in 447 B.C. Ts'ai was finally overthrown by the Ch'u, who, in 241 B.C., under the reign of King K'ao-lieh, moved their capital to Shou-ch'un, southwest of the present Shou Hsien. An Eastern Chou tomb discovered in 1955 at Shou Hsien, in which over five hundred artifacts have been found, including bronze vessels with inscriptions mentioning the Marquis of Ts'ai, can thus be dated to the narrow temporal interval between 493 and 447 B.C., although exactly who this Marquis of Ts'ai might have been—five marquises had Chou-lai for their capital before the termination of the marquisdom under the Ch'u —is a controversial subject.[27]

The tomb is a rectangular earthen pit, oriented N–S, 8.45 m. long N–S, and 7.1 m. wide E–W. Remains of a lacquered wooden

24. Wei Chü-hsien, *Chung-kuo k'ao-ku-hsüeh shih*. p. 255; Tseng Chao-yü and Yin Huan-chang, *KKHP*, 1959:4, 54; WW, 1959:4, 5.
25. Ni Chen-kui, WW, 1959:4, 5.
26. Hsieh Chun-chu, WW, 1958:11, 80.
27. *Shou-hsien Ts'ai-hou mu ch'u-t'u yih-wu*, Peiping, Science Press, 1956.

coffin were found at the center of the tomb; the skeleton is completely gone, but according to the position of the jade ornaments and a bronze sword presumably worn at the side, the body was probably buried with its head to the north. A skeleton was found at the southeastern corner of the grave, probably a sacrificed victim. Pottery, lacquer, and bronze vessels, musical instruments, weapons, and horse and chariot fittings were buried in various places within the grave. Some of the vessels were inscribed, indicating that the tomb's master was probably a Ts'ai Marquis. Typologically, the decoration and the shape of the bronze artifacts present another example of the Huai style, and since they are precisely dated, they can also be taken as a type assemblage for the bronzes of the late Ch'un-ch'iu and early Chan-kuo periods.

For the purpose of the present discussion, this find shows that by the Eastern Chou period typical North China art, writing, and crafts had been implanted in the Huaiho valley. The political system of this area as indicated by such finds is probably comparable with the states in North China described in a previous chapter.

Ch'u During the Chou Dynasty, particularly the Eastern Chou period, the state of Ch'u was the most powerful country in South China, and probably also the most civilized. Furthermore, this state was not only a political but also a cultural and ethnic entity. In the poem *Pi-kung*, in the *Lu Sung* section of the *Book of Odes*, literature dating possibly from an early period of the Chou Dynasty, the peoples to the south are referred to as Ching and Shu. The inhabitants of the lower Hanshui valley in northern Hupei are known as Shu, and Ching, originally the name of a plant which was also known as Ch'u, refers to the people living around Mountain Ching, thought to be in the present Nan-chang Hsien, near Hsiang-yang, Hupei province. The names of Ch'u and Ching, therefore, were used interchangeably during the Chou period to designate the people in the Lower Hanshui and the Middle Yangtze valleys. The name of Ching seems to have appeared earlier than the Ch'u, although the name of Ch'u had since become widely used.[28]

The legendary beginnings of the Ch'u rulers were recorded in various literary records, but only around the time of Wen Wang of Western Chou did the genealogical record become historically established. Ssu-ma Chien's *Shih Chi* says that Ch'eng Wang of

28. Oyanagi Shigeta, *Tohogakuho*, 1 (1931), 196–228, Tokyo.

Western Chou made Hsiung Yih, the contemporary ruler of Ch'u, an earl to govern the people of Ch'u, and made Tan-yang his capital. The exact geographical location of Tan-yang is a disputed question. Four hypotheses have been advanced to identify Tan-yang as one of the following present-day locations: Tang-t'u, in central-eastern Anhwei on the Yangtze; Chih-chiang and Tzu-kui in western Hupei in the Yangtze valley; and the area between Shang Hsien in southeastern Shensi and Hsi-ch'uan in southwestern Honan, in the upper middle Hanshui valley.[29] Thus the majority of scholars believe that Tan-yang was somewhere in the Hanshui and Middle Yangtze valleys, but the Tang-t'u theory, advanced by the authoritative *Han Shu Ti Li Chih*, also deserves serious consideration. No matter where the original center of the political Ch'u may have been, by the beginning of the Eastern Chou period, under the reign of Earl Hsiung T'ung, the Ch'u state had already become a major power in central China. Hsiung T'ung went so far as to defy the Royal Chou's authority, and to call himself a king. From then on, throughout the Eastern Chou period, Ch'u was a major power to be reckoned with, not only in Central China but in North China as well. At the peak of their power, the territory of the Ch'u extended from eastern Shensi east to the Lower Yangtze valley, as far north as the heart of Honan, and as far south as the Tung-t'ing Lake area in southern Hupei and northern Hunan. This powerful state was overthrown by the Ch'in Dynasty in 223 B.C., but the people and the culture maintained their distinct identity into the Han Dynasty.

Archaeological remains within the Ch'u territory dating from the Eastern Chou period are abundant, most of them excavated during the last decade, but thus far sites dating from the Western Chou period and yielding bonafide Western Chou remains—such as those in Kiangsu and Anhwei described above—have not been found in South China west of the Huaiho and the Lower Yangtze.[30] Cultural remains lying beneath the Ch'u stratum and above the local Lungshanoid all belong to the Geometric horizon with the exception of the Yin style of bronzes found in Huang-p'i,

29. Hsüeh Ping-chang, *Chung-kuo ku-shih ti ch'uan-shuo shih-tai* (Shanghai, Chung-kuo Wen-hua Fu-wu Shê, 1946), p. 190.
30. Remains of timber structures, excavated in 1957 at the site of Mao-chia-tsui, northeast of Ch'i-ch'un Hsien, Hupei, together with stone, bone, and wooden implements, pottery, a bronze *chüeh* tripod, several bronze arrowheads, oracle bones and turtle shells, and remains of rice husks, have been dated to "early Western Chou, or earlier." See Chang Yün-peng, *KK*, 1962:1, 9.

Hupei. The total absence of Western Chou remains in the Hanshui and the Middle Yangtze valleys seems to indicate that the Ch'u civilization first emerged, under the influence of the Western Chou civilization, in the Huaiho and the Lower Yangtze, one of the regions to which the historical site of Tan-yang has been attributed and in which Western Chou remains have been found. Nevertheless, any statement pretending to certainty in this matter is entirely unwarranted at present, since a large area in the Middle Yangtze and the Hanshui valley remains unexplored.

It is no accident, however, that cultural remains of the Ch'u dated to the Eastern Chou period have been found in a very wide area of the eastern-central part of South China, covering the Huaiho valley in southeastern Honan and northern Anhwei and the Tung-t'ing Lake area of Hunan. The appearance of Ch'u remains over such a wide area bears out the literary tradition that the state of Ch'u expanded territorially around the turn of the two Chou's, which is also suggested by the relative homogeneity of the cultural style represented by the remains from within the entire area.

Under the state of Ch'u, town or city settlements must have been built comparable in the nature of their urbanization to the northern Chinese cities described earlier; in the language of Ch'u, which differed from the one or ones then spoken in the Nuclear Area, these were referred to as the *ch'eng* (modern mandarin pronunciation). None of these capital cities of the Ch'u, however, has thus far been identified. A small(490 by 400 m.) town site enclosed by pisé mud walls, 14 m. wide and 3 m. high, has been located near Hsiang-yin in Hunan, traditionally attributed to be the site of Lo, a small vassal state of the Ch'u. Cultural remains discovered in association with the town site probably belonged to an early phase within the Eastern Chou period, and another dwelling site of a comparable period was found at T'ai-tzu-ch'ung near Ch'ang-sha, Hunan province, where storage pits, pottery, and stone knives were collected.[31] Near the town of Wung-chiang in P'ing-chiang Hsien, also in Hunan, storage pits, pottery, iron axes, bronze vessels, weapons, and implements and evidence of bronze foundry have been found, indicating that this was probably the site of a local workshop.[32] These discoveries are, needless to say, insufficient representatives of the kind of urbanism and civic and public

31. Chou Shih-jung, *KKTH*, 1958:2, 10–14; *WW*, 1960:3, 66.
32. Chou Shih-jung, *WWTKTL*, 1958:1, 39–41.

structures that can surely be assumed to have existed in the state of Ch'u.

The Ch'u sites so far discovered consist mainly of tombs (see Map 11). Within the province of Hunan alone, a large number of Ch'u graves have been located in Ch'ang-sha, Ch'ang-tê, Heng-yang, Pin Hsien, Hsiang-t'an, Hsiang-hsiang, Lei-yang, Chu-chou, and Li-ling.[33] Of these sites, Ch'ang-sha is the most prolific, having so far yielded over one thousand two hundred individual graves dated to the Eastern Chou period.[34] Ch'ang-tê [35] and Heng-yang follow in number of graves produced, with approximately one hundred each. Outside of Hunan, highly important centers of Ch'u remains include Hsin-yang [36] in Honan and Shou Hsien [37] in Anhwei, both in the Huaiho valley. These three centers of Ch'u finds serve to outline the geographical extent of the Ch'u terri-tory represented by archaeological remains. The cultural influence of the Ch'u civilization surely went beyond its territories, and evidence of such influence is seen clearly in northern Kiangsu in the east [38] and Szechwan and Yünnan in the west.

These finds show that the Ch'u people built elaborate graves for their dead. The tombs in the Ch'ang-sha area were all earthen pits, rectangular in shape, with or without entrance ramps. Some of the pits were narrower than the others, and may have been earlier in date. The orientation of the tombs was somewhat irregu-lar, but North and East headings were relatively more common.

33. Kao Chih-hsi, WW, 1960:3, 33.
34. Hsia Nai, Chen Kung-jou, and Wang Chung-shu, Ch'ang-sha fa-chüeh pao-kao, Peiping, Science Press, 1957; Wen Tao-yih, KKHP, 1959:1, 41–58; Chang Chung-yih, KKTH, 1958:9, 57–61; Chang Hsin-ju, KKTH, 1958:12, 28–34; Kao Chih-hsi and Liu Lien-yin, KK, 1959:12, 649–52; Chou Shih-jung and Wen Tao-yih, WW, 1960:1, 63–64; Lo Chang, WW, 1960:3, 38–49; WW, 1960:3, 51–56; Chou Shih-jung, WW, 1960:3, 64–66; Jao Tsung-yih, Ch'ang-sha ch'u-t'u Chan-kuo tseng-shu, Hong Kong, 1958; Chiang Hsüan-yih, Ch'ang-sha Ch'u min-tsu chi ch'i yih-shu, Shanghai, Kunstarchäologie Society, 1949; Shang Cheng-tso, Ch'ang-sha ku-wu wen-chien-chi, Chengtu, Chinling Univ., 1939; Shih Shu-ching, Ch'ang-sha Yang-t'ien-hu ch'u-t'u Ch'u chien yen-chiu, Shanghai, Ch'ün-lien Press, 1955.
35. Wen Tao-yih, KK, 1959:12, 658.
36. Pei Ming-hsiang, Chang Chien-chung, and Chia Eh, WWTKTL, 1957:9, 21–22; Kuo Mo-jo, WWTKTL, 1958:1, 5; Ku Tieh-fu, WWTKTL, 1958:1, 6–8; Wang Shih-hsiang, WWTKTL, 1958:1, 15–23; Ho Kuan-pao and Huang Shih-pin, KKTH, 1958:11, 79–80.
37. Li Ching-tan, TYKKPK, 1, 1936; Liu Chieh, Ch'u ch'i t'u-shih, Peiping, National Library of Peiping, 1935; O. Karlbeck, BMFEA, 27, 1955; Yin Ti-fei, WW, 1959:4, 12; Pai Hsia, KK, 1959:7, 371–72.
38. Yin Huan-chang and Chang Cheng-hsiang, KK, 1960:3, 29.

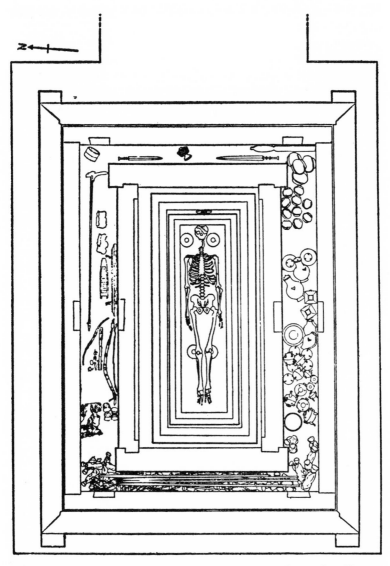

FIG. 23. A Ch'u Wooden-chambered tomb near Ch'ang-sha, Hunan.
From Hsia Nai, Chen Kung-jou, and Wang Chung-shu, *Ch'ang-sha
fa-chüch pao-kao* (Peiping, Science Press, 1957), Fig. 22.

The bottom of the pit was often plastered with a layer of limy white clay, and around the pit walls a platform was sometimes built, corresponding to the so-called *erh-ts'eng-t'ai*, or second-level platform, found in northern Chinese Bronze Age tombs. Caches or cavities perpendicular to the wall were excavated for the storage of grave goods. At the center of the tomb, a wooden chamber was built, inside which a wooden coffin was placed (Fig. 23). The coffin was often wrapped with cloths, probably to prevent moisture from penetrating. Grave goods were placed inside the coffin or outside in the pit, and the whole pit was then filled with earth, sometimes compacted by stamping.[39] Both the Shou Hsien and the Hsin-yang tombs were built in a similar manner, but the latter (two of which have so far been discovered) had a far more complicated wooden chamber structure, and were divided into several sections. Tomb structure of the kind just described apparently followed the common Eastern Chou pattern of North China, although local adjustments can be seen in the moisture-preventing devices of plaster and cloth-wrapping.

Such elaborate burials indicate a highly stratified society and an advanced technology and economy, but direct evidence of farming techniques is limited to the occasional discoveries of farming implements, including hoes and spades of iron.[40] There is no evidence of the use of the plow, which had begun both in contemporary North China and in the territory of Yüeh to the east. According to historical records, however, it is fairly certain that in the state of Ch'u as well as Yüeh, rice was cultivated and irrigated by both artificial and natural means. To the northerners of the Eastern Chou period as well as these of subsequent historical periods, the rich natural resources in and south of the Yangtze valley had been an object of constant envy. Ssu-ma Chien says in *Ho-chih Lieh-chuan*, *Shih Chi*, that the "territory of the Ch'u and the Yüeh is vast but the population sparse. Rice is the staple food, and fish the main dish. The people *keng* with fire, and *ju* with water." There are various interpretations of the last sentence,[41]

---

39. Hsia, Chen, and Wang, *Ch'ang-sha fa-chüeh pao-kao*, pp. 5–7; Wen Tao-yih, *KKHP*, 1959:1, 41–44.
40. Wen Tao-yih, *KKHP*, 1959:1, 43.
41. Nishijima Sadao, "The System of Rice Cultivation in Ancient China," in *Oriental Studies Presented to Sei (Kiyoshi) Wada* (Tokyo, Dainippon Yūbenkai Kōdansha, 1951), pp. 469–87; Amano Motonosuke, *Shigaku-Zasshi*, 61 (1952), 58–61; Yoneda, *Shirin*, 38 (1955), 1–18.

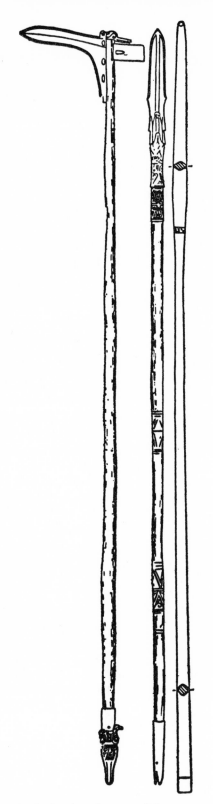

FIG. 24. Ch'u halberd and spears. The one at right was
made of wood. From ibid., Fig. 40.

but, whatever the interpretation, the use of water in an artificial way for the cultivation of rice is clear from Ssu-ma's words, which are also seen in *Shih Chi* on another occasion (*P'ing-chun-shu*).

In addition to agricultural implements, iron was employed to make axes, knives, adzes, weapons (swords, *chi* halberds, and arrowheads), and even ornaments (rings and belt hooks). Lead was another metal melted by the Ch'u smiths, who fashioned it into mortuary money and covers for wooden handles. But as far as the archaeological data show, bronze was still the basic raw material for artifact making. In the tombs, bronze vessels (*ting* tripods, *tui* tripods, *hu*, and dippers), weapons (swords, *ko* halberds, and spears—see Fig. 24), horse and chariot fittings, belthooks, mirrors, musical instruments (such as *pien* bells, portable bells, and kettle-drums), and even seals have been found in great numbers. A chemical analysis of some specimens of bronze [42] shows that the ratio of copper, tin, and various impurities was completely controlled. A large *ting* tripod unearthed from the Shou Hsien tomb is said to weigh nearly 400 kilogrammes,[43] indicating an advanced level of bronze metallurgy. The large number of bronze artifacts and their distinctive local features (such as the numerous stylistic motifs in the decoration and the distinctive inscriptions) rule out the possibility that these bronze artifacts were imports from North China, and the bronze foundry site in P'ing-chiang Hsien, Hunan, mentioned above, bears this out.

In addition to metallurgy of both bronze and iron, the Ch'u civilization was apparently highly developed in handicrafts, including ceramics, wood carving, carpentry, bamboo crafts, leatherwork, lacquer work, silk and hemp weaving, and stone and jade crafts. The pottery is predominantly grayish or brownish in color, either of fine texture or tempered with sand, depending upon the kind of vessel and its purpose. Glaze was applied in some cases. The basic technique of manufacture was by wheel, although handmade and molded pieces occur not infrequently. Most of the pots are plain, but there is also decorated pottery, which is corded, stringed, incised, or painted in red, yellow, blue, white, or black in spirals and geometric designs (Fig. 25). *Ting* and *li* tripods, *hu*, *tou*, bowls, cups, stoves, urns, and so forth are all represented, and the occurrence of particular shapes seems to have some chron-

42. Wen Tao-yih, *KKHP*, 1959:1, 48.
43. Liu Chieh, *Ch'u ch'i t'u-shih*, p. 3.

FIG. 25. Painted pottery of Ch'u from Ch'ang-sha. From *KKHP*, 1959:1, 46.

ological significance (Fig. 26). The lacquer objects of prewar finds from Ch'ang-sha have long been famous, and among more recent findings, a lacquer shield with painted patterns is of particular interest. Bamboo mats, bows, suitcases, wooden combs, spears (see Fig. 24), and leather remains are among the extraordi-

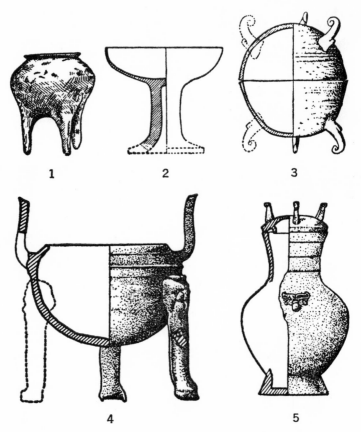

FIG. 26. Some Ch'u pottery of chronological significance. 1. *li*; 2. *tou*; 3. *tui*; 4. *ting*; 5. *hu*. From Ch'ang-sha fa-chüeh pao-kao.

nary discoveries made in recent years. Bamboo was also cut into elongated slips for writing; dozens of these inscribed slips have been found in tombs, along with remains of brushes and their containers. Wood carving is another noted craft of the Ch'u, and wooden human and animal figurines (Fig. 27; Pl. X), drums, animal tomb-guardians with antler horns (Pl. X), and carved boards have been found. Remains of wooden bases for the musical instrument, *sê*, have been collected from the tombs at Hsin-yang (Fig. 28). These remains vividly testify to the fact that industrial

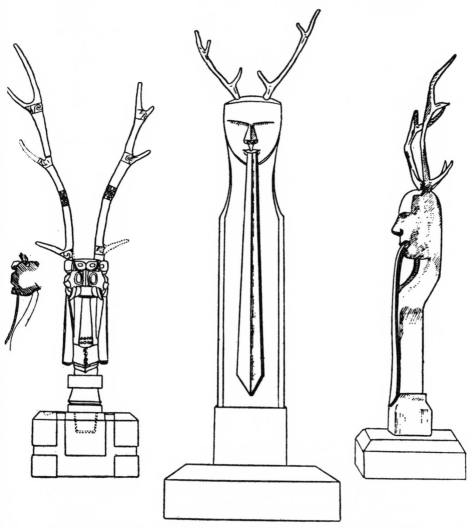

FIG. 27. Wood carvings from Ch'u tombs near Ch'ang-sha. From Chiang Hsüan-yih, *Ch'ang-sha Ch'u min-tzu chi ch'i yih-shu* (Shanghai, Mei-shu-k'ao-ku-hsüeh-shê, 1950) Pl. 34.

FIG. 28. Painted human and animal figures on a lacquered musical instrument discovered from the Ch'u tomb at Hsin-yang, Honan. From WW,1958:1, 27.

specialization must have developed to a very considerable extent in this part of China during the Eastern Chou period, a fact which is confirmed by the many names of handicraft products written on the bamboo tablets—probably lists of grave goods, many of which have since disappeared.

Supported by agriculture and industry of such high levels of complexity, the political and social organizations of the Chou were presumably also complex. No doubt the state of Ch'u deserves the designation of being a "state," and the titles of King and Earl must have been accompanied by corresponding political institutions. Archaeological evidence is lacking, but the remains of bronze coins (*yih-pi-ch'ien*, or "Ant-nose" coins) and bronze scales and weights show a good deal of social and economic sophistication. Moreover, the Ch'u was certainly a literary civilization, with writing still to be seen on bamboo tablets, weapons (Pl. XI), bronze vessels, and a silk clothing (Pl. XII). As in North China, the writing is composed of characters, many of which are identical to those used elsewhere in China. But unique characters, a distinctive calligraphy, and another distinctive system of character composition, mostly inscribed on weapons, indicate local characteristics. Kuo Mo-jo believes that during the Eastern Chou period, efforts were made to unify writing in the whole of China under the sovereignty of the Royal Chou, although various regional writing systems were still being used for certain specific purposes.[44]

Compared with contemporary North China, the Ch'u is also distinctive in being an especially religious-minded people. The Eastern Chou and Han saying, that the "Ch'u people are particularly superstitious," testifies to this fact. The elaborate burial customs indicate a highly complicated system of ancestor worship. In *Ch'u Tz'u*, a piece of genuine Ch'u literature handed down through subsequent historical periods, there is a long poem entitled *T'ien Wen*, in which Ch'ü Yüan, the alleged author and an officer of the King's Court, asks a series of questions concerning the creation of the cosmos, of man, the various deities, and the legendary history of the Ch'u kings. It has been suggested that this poem was probably composed in the ancestral temple of the Ch'u ruler, on the internal walls of which pictures depicting the various myths and legends were painted, and that Ch'ü Yüan asked questions on various topics as he looked at these pictures.[45]

44. Kuo Mo-jo, WWTKTL, 1958:1, 5.
45. Jen Shien-min, BIE, 6 (1958), 79.

This interpretation is quite stimulating, and considering that in *T'ien-wen* vivid descriptions of the interior of a certain building appear, and that in the ancestral temples of some modern Malaysian peoples such pictures are found,[46] it is even plausible. Unfortunately, however, ancestral temples of this nature have yet to be found. But among the Ch'u people there must have been beliefs concerning various spirits, deities, and possible "totems," as indicated by the text of a silk writing [47] (Pl. XII), by the remains of wooden animal tomb-guardians (Pl. X), wooden human figurines, and wooden human statues with protruding tongues and antler horns (Fig. 27). Snakes, phoenix, and dragons were favorite decorative motifs (Fig. 28), and musical instruments (wooden and bronze drums, bells, various kinds of wooden and bamboo wind and string instruments, and pottery whistles) must have had some ceremonial use.

The above descriptions of the Ch'u civilization suffice to show that this civilization was basically derivative of the Chou civilization of North China, but that distinctive characteristics are at the same time plentiful. In other words, here we probably have another case of acculturation, with a higher civilization introduced into a native Geometric base, rather than an example of pure and simple immigration of people and/or transplantation of culture. Legends of the Ch'u, as recorded by North Chinese historians, say that the founders of the Ch'u were descended from Tuan-hsü, a grandson of the Yellow Emperor. One may be tempted to regard the Ch'u rulers as North Chinese, whereas the ruled people were indigenous natives. This, however, was not necessarily so. Hsiung Ch'ü, an Earl of Ch'u and the near descendant of the First Earl, was quoted in *Shih Chi* as saying: "We are barbarians." The Ch'u system of government closely followed that of the Chou Dynasty, but according to the accounts in *Tso Chuan* (first year of Wen Kung and thirteenth year of Chao Kung), the succession to the monarch of the Earldom or, later, the Kingdom seems to have followed the rule of ultimogeniture rather than primogeniture as in the Chou Dynasty. The Ch'u language was decidedly different from the contemporary northern Chinese, as is shown by a few lexical elements recorded in North Chinese literature. In the archaeological remains, although the culture is shown to be basi-

46. Ibid., Ling Shun-sheng, *BIE*, 6, 1958.
47. Jao Tsung-yih, *Ch'ang-sha ch'u-t'u Chan-kuo tseng-shu.*

cally the same as the Eastern Chou of North China, many distinctive local features are discernible, such as the writing characteristics, the special deities and ceremonies, the highly developed wood carving and bamboo crafts, the tattooing of faces, the great abundance of mirrors and swords, the comparative scarcity of *tou* vessels, and the different system of currency.

On the other hand, the widely distributed Ch'u remains show remarkable homogeneity in style, although regional phases are discernible within this vast territory.[48] Ch'u remains began to appear at the beginning of the Ch'un-ch'iu period and, as far as we know from the available material, underwent a similar sequence of change and development throughout the entire area. In the region of Ch'ang-sha, no less than three well-defined stages can be distinguished both stratigraphically and typologically: [49]

(a) *Early:* Ch'un-ch'iu and the beginning of Chan-kuo. Approximately one hundred tombs (among the more than twelve hundred in the area) belong to this stage, and are characterized by: smaller and narrower tombs than the later ones; wall caches mostly at the head end; a scarcity of ramps; in ceramics, three combinations: *li*-bowl-*hu*-*tou*-jug, *lei*-bowl-*tou*, or *hu*-bowl-*tou*-urn; *li* tripods of pottery; certain types of bronze weapons and vessels; some iron implements.

(b) *Middle:* early Chan-kuo period. Over six hundred graves belong to this stage, characterized by: a growing number of wider grave pits, side caches, and ramps; pottery *ting* tripods taking the place of *li* tripods; the appearance of pottery *tui* tripods; bronze vessels and weapons of later types; more iron implements.

(c) *Late:* late Chan-kuo and the beginning of Western Han. Characterized by: predominance of rectangular grave pits of great width; a growing number of side caches; the appearance of cave chambers and multiple burials; the use of clay to seal off the wooden chamber; complex wooden chamber structures, much painted pottery, more complex bronze artifacts; more iron implements and even iron weapons; the occurrence of stone *pi* rings; decorative inscriptions on bronze weapons.

---

48. Shang Cheng-tso, *Ch'ang-sha ku-wu wen-chien-chi*, Chen Meng-chia's "Preface," p. 10.

49. Li Cheng-kwang and Peng Ching-yieh, *KKHP*, 1957:4, 47–48; Wen Tao-yih, *KKHP*, 1959:1, 55–56; Chang Chung-yih, *KKTH*, 1958:9, 60–61; Chang Hsin-ju, *KKTH*, 1958:12, 34; Kao Chih-hsi, *WW*, 1960:3, 33–34; Hsia, Chen, and Wang, *Ch'ang-sha fa-chüeh pao-kao*, p. 37.

A similar sequence can also be found in the burials of the Ch'ang-tê area.[50] Ch'u graves in the Huaiho valley are few, and thus not susceptible to such chronological treatment. However, it is noteworthy that the Hsin-yang tombs, while probably dated to an early period comparable to Ch'ang-sha's Early Stage,[51] contain many features that did not appear in Ch'ang-sha until a later stage. This may very well indicate that the cultural flow from North China to the Ch'u region was continuous throughout the Eastern Chou period, and reached such regions as Hsin-yang much earlier than the more distant Tung-t'ing area of Hunan.

These Eastern Chou states in eastern South China have been discussed in a group because of the fact that in this region the precivilization culture was characterized by the successive Lung-shanoid and Geometric horizons. We can, however, see distinctly from the above summary of data that the civilization of the Lower Yangtze and that of the Middle Yangtze are quite different. In the first place, the Ch'u civilization is much more advanced and complex than the civilizations in the Wu and Yüeh areas, at least insofar as the archaeological material goes. In the second place, in the Lower Yangtze civilizations there are a great many cultural continuities from the previous Neolithic and Geometric strata, whereas such continuities cannot be seen to any considerable extent in the Ch'u archaeological data. In the third place, the Ch'u culture, although it developed in the same general Geometric area, has a distinctive tradition of its own as manifested in its technology and religion, which is quite separate from the cultural form represented by the Wu and Yüeh materials. Such contrasts between the Ch'u and the Wu-Yüeh civilizations suggest three alternate explanations: (a) that a proto-phase of the Ch'u civilization, probably dated to Western Chou and presumably showing a greater continuity from the Geometric substratum, remains to be discovered; (b) that the Ch'u civilization that came into the area had been fully developed elsewhere, possibly in the Huaiho valley, where such a proto-Ch'u civilization can perhaps be found among the Western Chou assemblages; or (c) that the formation of the Ch'u and that of the Wu and Yüeh civilizations, although both due to the influence of a North China cultural impact, represent different processes and patterns

50. Wen Tao-yih, KK, 1959:12, 662.
51. Kuo Mo-jo, WWTKTL, 1958:1, 5.

274

of cultural assimilation. On the basis of the available archaeological data, it is impossible to say which of these interpretations is the right one, or even the most probable.

EARLY CIVILIZATIONS IN SZECHWAN

In the Upper Yangtze valley in the Red basin (Map 13), less is known about the beginning of civilization than in eastern South China, but the development must have been quite different. The

MAP 13. Early historic sites in Szechwan.

native cultural substratum in Szechwan differs from that of the Southeast in that neither the Lungshanoid nor the Geometric existed as a well-defined cultural horizon. Although agriculture and the domestication of animals were introduced into this area after stone polishing and ceramics, these innovations were made in an already established Mesolithic and sub-Neolithic population. The Neolithic culture, which, in contrast to the Lungshanoid to

275

the east, must have retained a considerable number of native elements, continued in Szechwan during the Bronze Age of North and Central China but received increasing influence from these civilizations, as the archaeological remains of this period show.

The late Yin and early Western Chou civilizations appear to have had some contact with the Szechwan Neolithic, as indicated by the remains of *li* tripods of gray and cord-marked ware, and sherds of *tou* of the Bronze Age style [52] found in the Yangtze valley in the extreme eastern end of Szechwan province, where it adjoins Hupei. The contacts probably resulted in no more than the introduction of these and perhaps a few other stylistic elements, whereas the native cultural context remains Neolithic, and even the few indications of influence are limited geographically. "The cord-marked *li* tripods extended westward no further than Wan Hsien, and the gray *li* tripods did not even reach Feng-chieh." [53] Some authors maintain that the Yin culture reached as far as the Min River valley, as shown by such sites as Shui-kuan-yin in Hsin-fan Hsien.[54] This is certainly an unwarranted conclusion, as we shall see. It would be even less warranted to state that western Szechwan was already within the territory of the Shang civilization.

The western part of Szechwan, nevertheless, was definitely reached by the influence of Western Chou civilization. Archaeological remains that can probably be dated to late Western Chou or early Eastern Chou have been discovered, thus far, in no less than four counties: Han-chow (Kwang-han), Hsin-fan, Ch'eng-tu, and Mien-yang, in the P'ei, T'o, and Min River valleys. The T'ai-p'ing-ch'ang site in Kwang-han was discovered in 1931 and investigated in 1933 by David C. Graham of the University Museum of West China Union University.[55] At this site, a habitation area was located, and a ceremonial pit was uncovered which contained over twenty stone discs of various sizes and a number of jade and stone ceremonial objects (circular *yüan*, square *tsung* tubes, *wuan-kui*, etc.). Some stone implements and a large number of potsherds were brought to light from the habitation layer. The pottery was red or grayish, with corded or plain surfaces, and in such forms as high-stem *tou*, urns, and tripods. No metal arti-

52. Yang Yu-jun, *KK*, 1959:8, 399–400.
53. Ibid., p. 401.
54. Ibid., Cheng Te-kun, *Shang China*, p. 16.
55. David C. Graham, *Journal of the West Border Research Society*, 6 (Cheng-tu, 1933/34), 114–31.

facts have been found, but a red iron nugget, a fragment of iron ore, and a small lump of copper ore were collected from the cultural debris.[56] Cheng Te-kun thinks that the ceremonial pit and the cultural debris were of different ages, the former probably dating from the Eastern Chou and representing the remains of a mountain-worship ceremony (possibly the worship of Mountain Min, as recorded in *Shan Hai Ching*), and the latter belonging to the so-called "eneolithic," dating from 1200–700 B.C.[57] Cheng's chronology is probably open to doubt. The stratigraphical relationship of the ceremonial pit and the habitation layers is not altogether clear, but they could very possibly be contemporary, since jade and stone rings and plates similar to those found in the ceremonial pit have been unearthed in the cultural layer, and perhaps should not be dismissed offhand as being "intrusive," as Cheng has called them.[58] Recent findings of cultural remains probably dating from a comparable stage seem to confirm this, since both stone and jade ceremonial objects and pottery that resemble the objects found at T'ai-p'ing-ch'ang from both the pit and the cultural layer have been shown to come from the same cultural stratum.

North of the city of Ch'eng-tu in the Min River valley is a low hill, known as Yang-tzu-shan. An earthen ceremonial platform was excavated on top of the hill in 1956. Since Warring-States tombs were built into it, the platform must have been built some time earlier than the Chan-kuo period.[59] The platform is square in shape and oriented Northwest–Southeast. It is constructed in three levels, measuring 31.6, 67.6, and 103.6 m. across, respectively, and has a total height exceeding 10 m. (Fig. 29). Within the platform, stone discs and pottery remains similar to those of T'ai-p'ing-ch'ang were found. Similar pottery sherds have also been unearthed at the Pien-tui-shan site in Mien-yang Hsien, on the Upper P'ei River.[60] High-stemmed *tou* vessels similar to those found in Kwang-han have been unearthed from the cultural strata at the site of Shui-kuan-yin in Hsin-fan Hsien, mentioned previously. At

56. Ibid., p. 123.
57. Cheng Te-kun, *Hsieh-ta Journal of Chinese Studies*, 1 (Foochow, 1949), 67–81.
58. Ibid., p. 75.
59. Yang Yu-jun, KKHP, 1957:4, 17–31.
60. Ibid., p. 30; also confirmed by new discoveries in Kwang-han, see WW, 1961:11, 27.

277

this site both habitation remains and burials have been found, but more than a single cultural stage is probably represented. Bronze arrowheads of the two-winged type, *ko* halberds of the Yin type, spearheads, axes, *yüeh* axes, and knives have been unearthed, but the overwhelming majority of the associated remains indicates a persisting Neolithic context.[61] This site has been given a Yin Dynasty date mainly on the basis of the Yin type of *ko* halberds; but the same type of weapon has been found in association with typical Warring-States inventories from the tomb at Yang-tzu-shan (intruded into the ceremonial platform described above), and this particular evidence is therefore of doubtful dating value.[62] Since

FIG. 29. Ceremonial platform at the Yang-tzu-shan site near Ch'eng-tu, western Szechwan. From *KKHP*, 1957:4, 20.

the arrowheads and some of the pottery and other bronze weapons do not show characteristic Chan-kuo features, the Shui-kuan-yin site can probably be dated to either late Western Chou or early Eastern Chou, broadly contemporary with the T'ai-p'ing-ch'ang and Yang-tzu-shan ceremonial assemblages.

These archaeological discoveries in the western part of Szechwan indicate a cultural tradition, essentially a continuation of the local Neolithic, which was heavily influenced by the Western or early Eastern Chou civilizations of North China, and in which ceremonial structures and stone and jade ceremonial objects played significant roles, though metallurgy may not have developed locally to any considerable extent. In this part of Szechwan, megalithic structures have been noted in historical literature and investigated

61. Yang Yu-jun, *KK*, 1959:8, 401.
62. *KKHP*, 1956:4, 6; *ko* halberds of Yin style and *t'ao-t'ieh* designs on bronzes are seen also at Chu-wa-chieh, P'eng Hsien, see *WW*, 1961:11, 30.

by archaeologists; their correlation with archaeological remains is still not clear. Cheng Te-kun [63] is inclined to correlate the megalithic monuments with the ceremonial pit at T'ai-p'ing-ch'ang, and this seems to be supported by the ceremonial platform discovery at Ch'eng-tu. Such ceremonial structures and objects certainly invite inferences regarding the religion and political authority of the people who left such remains, but further characterizations in culturo-social terms are impossible to make at the present time.

Whatever the nature of the civilizations in Szechwan during the Western Chou and early Eastern Chou periods of North China, by the beginning of the Warring-States period, intensified civilizations appeared in many parts of the province, as indicated by archaeological remains abundant in bronze and iron artifacts, evidence of tightened political control, and writing. Three groups of metal culture sites in Szechwan in the Warring-States period can be discerned in the archaeological material: one represented by burials in the Chialingkiang valley of eastern and central Szechwan; one centering in the valley of Minkiang near the plains of Ch'eng-tu; and one confined to the extreme northwestern portion of the province, in the foothills and river valleys of the eastern Tibetan plateau. The former two groups, while exhibiting certain distinctive features, seem to have formed a single cultural tradition; whereas the third constitutes a separate culture of its own.

Two sites of the Chialingkiang burials have been discovered so far, namely, the Pao-lun-yüan cemetery in Chao-hua in north central Szechwan, and the Tung-sun-pa cemetery in Pa Hsien, near the confluence of the Chialingkiang and the Yangtze, close to the city of Chungking.[64] At least thirteen individual burials, four of which are intact, have been brought to light at the Pao-lun-yüan site, and no less than eighteen, with one completely preserved, at the site of Tung-sun-pa. Both of these cemeteries were situated on river terraces. The individual graves, arranged in regular rows crowded into small areas, were rectangular earthen pits, perpendicular to the river banks. In size, the pits were only just big enough to contain individual dugout canoes, which served as coffins. Each canoe was about 5 m. long and 1 m. wide, with a flattened bottom, two beveled ends, each with a big hole, and a dugout cavity

63. Cheng Te-kun, *Archaeological Studies in Szechwan*, p. xiv.
64. Feng Han-chi, Yang Yu-jun, and Wang Chia-yu, *KKHP*, 1958:2, 77–95.

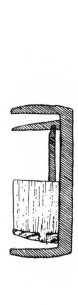
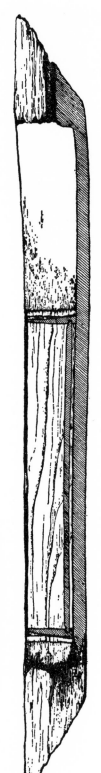
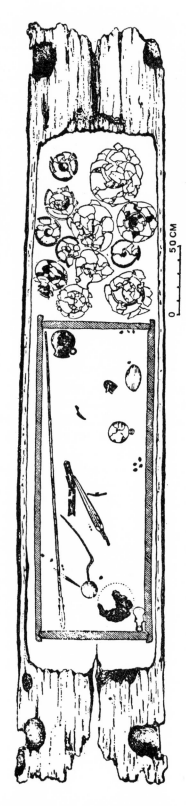

FIG. 30. A boat coffin in the Eastern Chou and Han cemetery at Pao-lun-yüan, in Chao-hua Hsien, northern Szechwan. From KKHP, 1958:2, 81.

50 CM

0

at the top, which contained the dead as well as grave goods (Fig. 30). In several cases the canoe and the cavity were so large that they served as wooden chambers into which a smaller coffin containing the human body was placed, together with grave goods, but these are believed to be of a later type. Bronze, iron, stone, bamboo, wooden artifacts, pottery, lacquer, silk and hemp clothes, and clay and glass beads were uncovered from the graves. Among the bronze artifacts are axes, spears, *ko* halberds, arrowheads, vessels, mirrors, belt hooks, knives, seals, and scale-weights, mostly of the Warring-States varieties, but the most characteristic bronzes are a sort of willow-shaped sword and a socketed axe with a circular blade. The blade of the sword tapers toward the handle end to become a handle, which was then lengthened with the addition of wooden splints, and was decorated with many kinds of unusual designs, such as tiger heads, tiger-skin patterns, "hand-and-heart" patterns, and writings (Fig. 31). The "hand-and-heart" pattern is seen only on the bronze swords, not only in these boat burials but throughout the Szechwan area, and is never used for other kinds of weapons or vessels with the single exception of one spearhead. The other decorative patterns are found on other kinds of implements and weapons. Metallurgical analysis has shown that the bronzes found in the boat burials contain a lower quantity of tin than usually found in Chinese bronzes, and that the artifacts of bronze are therefore relatively soft. In several burials, bronze *pan-liang* coins of the Ch'in Dynasty were found, but these burials are thought to be of a later phase than the rest. Iron artifacts are few, and consist only of knives and axes. The pottery is predominantly brownish in color and sand-tempered; in form it is characterized by flat or round bottoms and the use of ring feet. It is mainly wheel-made, and painted decorations are rare.

The Warring-States period sites in the Ch'eng-tu area include a cemetery site in P'eng-shan, a group of bronzes from Lu-shan,[65] and several groups of burials and habitation remains in the neighborhood of the city of Ch'eng-tu, such as Ch'ing-yang-kung, Yang-tzu-shan, Pai-ma-ssu, and one outside the southern city gate. Of these, the P'eng-shan site and the site at Pai-ma-ssu were discovered before and during the Second World War, and it has been reported that the heart-and-hand patterned bronze sword is characteristic of the Pai-ma-ssu burials[66] (Fig. 32). Sand-tempered

65. Lu Te-liang, *KK*, 1959:8, 439.
66. Wei Chü-hsien, *Shuo-wen Yüeh-k'an*, 3 (1941), 1–29.

FIG. 31. Designs on spearheads (*above*) and halberds (*below*) discovered from the Eastern Chou and Han burials in the Chialingkiang region of Szechwan. From *KKHP* 1958:2, 89.

brown pottery similar to that of the Chialingkiang sites is found
at the Ch'ing-yang-kung site in Ch'eng-tu, where a bronze knife,
oracle bones, and turtle shells were also reported.[67] Generally
speaking, however, the Warring-States period cultural remains at
Ch'ing-yang-kung indicate certain similarities to—or more probably
continuities from—the period represented by the Shui-kuan-yin
locality. The site outside the southern city gate of Ch'eng-tu was
a secondary burial, in association with which were pottery, and

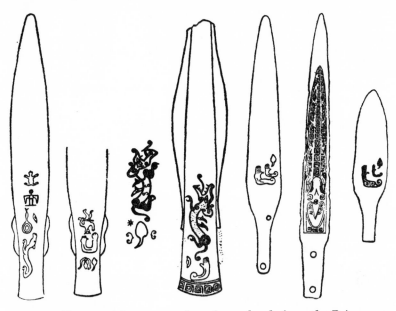

FIG. 32. Decorated bronze swords and spearheads from the Pai-ma-ssu
site, near Ch'eng-tu, western Szechwan. From *Shuo-wen*, 3, Shanghai,
1941.

some bronze vessels, weapons, and implements. Among the weapons is a type of *ko*, triangular in shape and having a tiger-head
decoration, which is one of the most characteristic types of artifacts in the Ch'eng-tu area.[68] The Warring-States burials at Yang-
tzu-shan, north of the Ch'eng-tu city, were intrusive into, and
hence subsequent in time to, the ceremonial square platform described above. A tomb, No. 172, that has been described in

67. Chiang Hsüeh-li and Lu Te-liang, *KK*, 1959:8, 411–14.
68. Lai Yu-tê, *KK*, 1959:8, 449–50.

published reports, is of the usual Warring-States type, with rectangular pit, wooden chamber, and wooden coffin graves. The grave goods include gray pottery, bronze vessels, weapons, implements, mirrors, belt hooks, seals, and horse and chariot fittings, lacquers, jades, precious ornaments, glass beads, and an iron tripod. Most of these are of the typical Warring-States types seen in North China. It is, nevertheless, of particular interest that among the findings many characteristic features recall the Ch'u civilization to the east, such as the "bronze sword with jade-decorated handles, the *t'ao-t'ieh* pattern of the feet of the big *ting* tripods, the *yen* steamers divided into two parts, the shape and decors of the bronze *lei*, the decorative patterns of bronze spearheads and lacquer boxes, and the gold- and silver-inlaid decorative designs." [69] Furthermore, some features of this assemblage have been enumerated as having local characteristics: the shape of the pottery urns, the bronze vessel handles with stranded-cord designs, the white glue used to adhere the gold and silver pieces of the inlay designs, the lack of any attempt to achieve symmetry in the decor, the bas relief animals on the belt hooks, and the distinctive writing system. On the other hand, some decorative motifs, such as the moth-brow pattern, find close relatives in the Dongson Culture to the south. On the whole, the Yang-tzu-shan burial exhibits its Szechwan characteristics, but an increasingly strong influence of North China traditions upon the native civilization is indicated toward the end of the Warring-States period.

To the west of both of these two groups—Chialingkiang and Ch'eng-tu—there was another cultural tradition, beginning no later than the final phases of the Chan-kuo period. This is represented by the finds at Li-fan (or Fan) and Kan-tzu in westernmost Szechwan, the region that begins to climb uphill toward the Tibetan plateau. At Li-fan, a large group of slab tombs (cists of slates) were excavated during the Second World War, and from the burials pottery, bronzes, iron, glass beads, and a wooden container were brought to light. The interesting and instructive point concerning the Li-fan slab tombs is that from among the grave goods cultural influences from more than a single direction are discernible. Contacts with the Chinese civilization of late Eastern Chou and Ch'in and Han Dynasties are indicated by Chinese inscriptions (of the styles of the various stages) and many types of pottery and bronze artifacts,

69. *KKHP*, 1956:4, 19.

including *pan-liang* and *wu-shu* coins. On the other hand, cultural contacts with Kansu, directly to the north, are shown by some ceramic features, particularly the flat-bottomed jars with two large vertical loop handles and the concave bottom of several jars "which [were hollowed out] with a sharp implement, probably of bamboo, when the paste was still wet," [70] both of which recall the Hsin-tien ceramics described in the previous chapter. Moreover, the so-called "Ordos" bronze features are very strongly represented in (a) the large number of weapons and armors which indicate the prevalence of close combat; (b) the small artifacts such as bells, buttons, tubes, rings, and plates; (c) the bronze kettles; (d) the dotted designs; and (e) the animal style represented by a bronze ring with three birds in relief. Glass beads, according to Cheng, suggest indirect contacts with Western Asia via the steppe nomads. A group of similar bronze artifacts, among which the horse fittings are outstanding, has been found further to the west, in the area of Kan-tzu.[71] This area of Li-fan and Kan-tzu is now inhabited by the Chiang people, whose legends relate that a slate-tomb building people, called the Ko, occupied the region before the Chiang came.[72] These Ko may have been farmers, as Cheng suggests, but apparently their settlements were mobile and mounted warfare prevailed. This region is separated from the steppe nomads by a great expanse of land which was occupied by the farming peoples of Kansu during its "eneolithic" stage. Whether there were direct connections between the Li-fan region and the steppe, or whether any such connections were by way of the Chinese civilization, cannot be certainly determined until the intervening regions are better known archaeologically.

It is evident that the above three groups of Warring-States period cultures in Szechwan represent two principal cultural traditions. With the Li-fan and Kan-tzu finds being placed in a separate category, the Warring-States period civilizations of both the Chialingkiang and the Ch'eng-tu groups were probably the development of a single local culture, with intensive influences from North China and from the Ch'u of the Middle Yangtze. Cheng Te-kun points out that "Szechwan is fundamentally a marginal area, and the culture of this province had never been a result

70. Cheng Te-kun, *Harvard Journal of Asiatic Studies*, 9 (1946), 67.
71. An Chih-min, *KKTH*, 1958:1, 62–63.
72. Cheng Te-kun, *Harvard Journal of Asiatic Studies*, 9, 77.

of independent development. It has always been under the influence of some neighboring culture." [73] Applied to the Warring-
States period, this statement must not be taken literally, for the
many distinctively local stylistic characteristics make it hard to
believe that all of the Szechwan civilizations were nothing but imports from North and Central China. Although the bronze and
iron implements and weapons in this region closely follow North
Chinese prototypes, they were apparently modified to conform to
local beliefs, usages, and traditions. The hand-and-heart design,
the characteristic writing and other decorative symbols on weapons,
the tiger as a favorite decorative motif, the distinctive types of the
willow-shaped bronze swords and the circular socketed yüeh axes,
the triangular ko halberds, the bridge-shaped bronze "coins," the
bronze seals with undeciphered signs,[74] and the boat burials and
cliff burials (which have been found dating to the Han Dynasty,
but must have had a pre-Han background), all testify to the fact
that the civilization of Szechwan had a distinctive and original spirit
that is more than a pure imitation of North China prototypes, let
alone a full-scale importation. Eastern Chou and Han literature
refers to the ancient peoples dwelling in the Red basin as the Pa
and the Shu peoples; according to Hua-yang-kuo Chih, compiled
during the Chin Dynasty, the Pa territory was in the eastern part
of Szechwan, and the Shu territory in the western, coinciding with
the division made above into the Chialingkiang and the Ch'eng-tu
subareas, although a positive identification must await further
findings and more precisely dated discoveries. To be sure, the
Chialingkiang and the Ch'eng-tu groups were probably only slightly
different phases of the same cultural tradition, but nevertheless
some differences can be enumerated between these two subareas.
For instance, the circular-socket yüeh axe is relatively rare in the
Ch'eng-tu area, but the same area is abundant in the triangular
shaped ko halberds and in bird designs as decorative motifs, which
are scarcely represented at all in the Chialingkiang boat burials.[75]
Feng Han-chi has convincingly shown that the Chialing and the
Ch'eng-tu ko and swords can be distinguished by some minute
and distinctive differences.[76] (Pl. XIII.) As a cultural complex,

73. Cheng Te-kun, Archaeological Studies in Szechwan, p. xix.
74. Lu Tê-liang, KK, 1959:8, 439.
75. Feng Han-chi, Yang Yu-jun, and Wang Chia-yu, KKHP, 1958:2, 94.
76. WW, 1961:11, 33.

boat burials have so far not been found west of the Chialing valley. Moreover, the eastern division of the Szechwan civilization appears to continue into the area of Hunan, and its relations with the Ch'u must have been highly intimate. Boat burials, for instance, have been recorded widely in the historical documents of South China, particularly the Ch'u and the Yüeh areas.[77] On the other hand, the western division of the Szechwan civilization shares with the contemporary civilization of Yünnan (Tien and the Dongsonian) many decorative motifs and implement types, as well as the kettle drum. This does not mean that the East–West subdivision of the Szechwan civilizations of the Chan-kuo period was clearly demarcated. Szechwan civilization as a whole shared with both the Ch'u and the Tien many stylistic characteristics. This civilization, furthermore, must have had a complex political organization and a sophisticated social stratification approaching the levels of a state structure. Throughout this civilization, the tiger played prominent ritualistic roles. In *Hou Han Shu*, in the "Biography of the Southern Man," a story relates that when the paramount chief of the Pa died, his soul was reincarnated as a white tiger, and that the people made offerings of human victims to him, believing that tigers ate human blood. If this story was indeed that of the Szechwan people of that time, which is likely in view of the prevalence of tiger motifs in their civilization, it gives us an idea of many political and religious institutions existing among them at that time. Historical books say that the Pa-Shu civilization came under the control of the state of Ch'in in 329 B.C., over a century before the Emperor of Ch'in conquered the whole of China, but the distinctive civilization of Szechwan apparently persisted, in quite undisturbed form, into the Ch'in and early Han Dynasties until the time when the Han style of brick tombs appeared widely in the province.

EARLY CIVILIZATIONS IN YÜNNAN

Further upstream along the Yangtze from the Red basin is the high hilly plateau country of the Chin-sha-kiang valley, drained by the upper reaches of the Yangtze, the Red, and the Mekong Rivers, where the modern provinces of Szechwan, Sikang, and Yünnan meet (Map 14). This country, inhabited by the Neolithic

77. Ling Shun-sheng, *BIHP*, 23 (1951), 639–64.

peoples during the first millennium B.C., was open to cultural influences from at least three sources: the Yüeh and the Ch'u civilizations to the east, which could make access to this area via the Pearl River; the Pa-Shu civilization of Szechwan, a little way down the Yangtze; and the Li-fan and Kan-tzu hilly country to the north, which connects this area with the steppe zone to the far north. Since these latter regions had no highly developed civilizations themselves until the Eastern Chou period, Yünnan was not

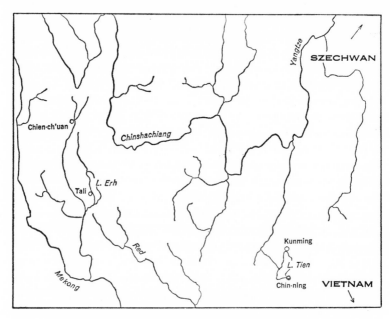

MAP 14. Yünnan and important cities.

exposed to the influence of the Yin and early Chou cultures. Archaeological evidence of any such influences, direct or indirect, is completely lacking.

The available archaeological record in Yünnan shows that civilization apparently came to Yünnan during the latter part of the Eastern Chou period, simultaneously with irrigated farming and the use of iron implements. In this connection, Wu Chin-ting's investigations during 1938–40 in Ta-li Hsien, in Lake Erh, and the Tien-ts'ang Mountain area of western Yünnan a little way below

288

the Chin-sha-kiang, are highly important.[78] At the site of Ma-lung, a protracted occupation by prehistoric inhabitants has been brought to light. During the period when the site was continually inhabited by the people of the same cultural tradition, a major change occurred which divides the culture of this site into two stages. The first stage is that of the Neolithic culture of this area described in Chapter 5. The second stage, although a continuation of the same cultural tradition, is marked by the simultaneous appearance of (a) terraced fields; (b) construction of water ditches probably for irrigation purposes; (c) construction of mud village walls; (d) growing use of potter's wheels; and (e) use of both bronze and iron, as shown by remains of fragments of bronze objects, an iron fragment, and an iron sickle. This discovery, which has never received the wide attention and recognition it rightfully deserves, is important in that it gives a basis for dating the appearance of metallurgy and irrigation in the area of Yünnan, and that it suggests that societal changes (such as the beginning of fortification and the intensification of industrial specialization) were concurrent with the appearance of metallurgy and irrigation in this area. The full implication of the latter innovations can be realized in the sites located further to the east, where a full-fledged civilization took the form of the so-called Dongson Culture.

Before giving a description of the Dongson Culture in Yünnan, mention must first be made of a habitation site at Chien-ch'uan, between the Chin-sha-kiang valley and Lake Erh in northwestern Yünnan, discovered in 1957. It is a pile-dwelling village, built lengthwise alongside the Hai-wei River, half on the bank and the other half submerged under water. Remains of agricultural implements and grains of rice, wheat, and millet were found, together with a large number of mollusc shells, animal bones, and fish hooks. Implements were mainly made of stone, including axes, adzes, sickles, chisels, scrapers, arrowheads, awls, spindle whorls, and grinding stones. Pottery is of the local Neolithic tradition, but the percentage of strikingly Lungshanoid types, such as black and lustrous pottery, ring-footed vessels, high stemmed *tou*, and perforated ring feet, is remarkably large for this area. Fourteen copper artifacts were found at the site, including axes, knives,

78. Wu Chin-ting, Tseng Chao-Yü, and Wang Chieh-chen, *Yünnan Ts'ang-Erh ching k'ao-ku pao-kao.*

chisels, rings, fish hooks, and ornaments, all hammered except for the axes, which were cast.[79] This site can be classified as essentially Neolithic in character, but whether or not it represents the first step taken by the Dongson civilization to achieve a full-fledged metal culture depends upon which route Chinese Eastern Chou influence took to Yünnan, and whether the Chien-ch'uan region was directly on this route or only on the periphery.

The Dongson Culture in Yünnan, remains of which have been collected from various localities in the province in past decades,[80] is typified by the cemetery at Shih-chai-shan, a small, low hill (about 20 meters high) situated between Lake Tien to the west and the city of Chin-ning to the east. A Dongsonian cemetery was found in the eastern part of the hill top, and four seasons of excavation were carried out between 1955 and 1960 by the Yünnan Provincial Museum. No less than thirty-four individual tombs were opened, and over four thousand pieces of artifacts have been brought to light.[81] A summary of the findings and the culture and society reconstructed thereby is given in Table 10.

TABLE 10.

Reconstruction of the Shih-chai-shan Culture

Tombs Mostly oriented E–W, with the head pointing to the east. The pits were simple earthen pits, without a regular plane, sometimes outlined by naturally placed rocks. When the dead body and grave goods were placed in the pit, the pit was filled with the dug-out earth or sandy earth mixed with pebbles. There is one tomb which has fire-hardened walls, a wooden chamber, and an *erh-ts'eng-t'ai*. Remains of wooden coffins covered with lacquer and wrapped with clothes have been found in some graves.

Implements Of the 706 implements reported in May 1959, 558 are bronzes, 92 iron, 43 stone, and 13 clay (spindle whorls). The bronze implements include 21 plows, 23 spades, 1 saw, 108 axes, 11 adzes, 23 chisels, 5 sickles, 26 knives, and a cylindrical object probably used for collecting molluscs. According to some of the pictures on the

79. KKTH, 1958:6, 5–12.
80. Komai Kazuchika, "On Stone Implements and Bronze Artifacts of South China," *Lectures on Anthropological and Prehistoric Topics*, 19 (1940), Tokyo.
81. *Yün-nan Chin-ning Shih-chai-shan ku mu ch'ün fa-chüeh pao-kao*, Pei-ping, Wenwu Press, 1959; WW, 1959:5, 59–61; KK, 1959:9, 459–561, 490.

bronzes which depicted the plow (Pl. XIV; Fig. 33) it was probably hafted onto a bent wooden handle, at the far end of which was a small crossbar. One or two men pulled the plow with a rope, and another pushed from behind. The biggest plow found weighs 750 grammes, and is 29 cm. long by 20 cm. wide. Iron implements include adzes, axes (iron-edged), and knives.

Subsistence and Handicrafts Apparently agriculture was practiced. Cattle, sheep, dogs, horses, chickens, and pigs are depicted in the decorative and plastic art; horses were used for riding and warfare, and cattle probably only for meat and ceremonial use. Hunting was carried on with the help of hunting dogs. Handicrafts were highly developed, as shown by the wineware, finely made bronzes, iron metallurgy, opal work, and leather work.

Trade and Currency Hundreds of thousands of cowry shells were found in drum-shaped containers. Plastic scenes of markets depicted the exchange of cattle and food (Pl. XV). Some of the coins, mirrors, lacquers, crossbows, *ko* halberds, arrowheads, and *chi* halberds were identical to North China types of Eastern Chou and Han periods, and were probably imports.

Weaving A plastic bronze model shows a type of horizontal loom now widely seen in Southeast Asia. Hemp was probably cultivated.

Utensils Sophisticated sets of daily utensils, of pottery or bronze.

Habitation Pile dwellings, depicted by plastic bronze models, have two stories (upper level for men, and lower level for domestic animals) and thatched roofs (Pl. XVII; Fig. 33).

Social Stratification Three social classes are distinguished by the excavators according to the hairstyles and dresses of the human figurines in the plastic bronze models:

(a) Aristocracy and the rich, the "owner of the cowry shells." One of the tomb masters was particularly wealthy, being accompanied by a *pien* bell set, jade objects, bronze *ting* tripod, four cowry-shell containers, and a gold seal with four Chinese characters inscribed: *Tien Wang Chih Yin* or "the Seal of the King of Tien." Women apparently enjoyed higher status than men, or at least had special deference shown them, such as being carried sitting in stools, as is seen in the plastic bronze models (Fig. 33).

(b) Freemen, the people of the same group, serving as managers.
(c) Slaves.

Warfare A large number of weapons is found, including both bronze and iron types. Most of these were of bronze, including 214 bronze

291

swords, 299 spearheads, 14 crossbows, and 266 arrowheads. Iron was used only to make swords, and these were protected in gold sheaths. Warfare is also depicted in plastic models, which show mounted horsemen and headhunters (Pl. XVI). Horse-and-chariot fittings of bronze are also abundantly represented.

Luxuries Gold objects, opal ornaments, silver, jade, lacquers, and turquoise objects.

Rituals Many ritual scenes are depicted with bronze plastic models, e.g., one in which a pillar, with a snake coiling around it and a tiger at the top, is surrounded by people killing human victims. Several others show the ceremonial killing of cattle. Bronze kettle drums, many of which were found, figured importantly in rituals, as shown by another model (Pl. XVII). Some ritual participants wore feathered plumes, such as the cattle killer and the dancers. Priests and/or shamans played musical instruments, made gestures, and danced. The wooden boat was another important element of the rituals. Cattle and peacocks apparently had some special ritualistic significance.

Art The bronzes show an extremely sophisticated decorative art, in plane or plastic forms. Dancing was probably part of the rituals. Musical instruments included bronze kettle drums, *sheng*-pan-pipes, flutes, and *pien* bells.

The characterization of the Shih-chai-shan culture in Table 10 approaches an ethnographic account, but there really is no call for skepticism on the part of the reader. The finds of representative art are abundant, and archaeologists *read* rather than *reconstruct* the life of a people depicted in the bronze art. This picture represents a lengthy period of occupation during which cultural changes occurred. The excavators have been able to distinguish four classes of tombs which can be grouped into three stages. The first stage, probably dated to the late Chan-kuo period and the beginning of the Western Han, has relatively few iron implements, and no Chinese coins or other imported artifacts such as the mirrors, belt hooks, and bronze utensils which came later. The second stage, probably dated by the Chinese coins as being between 175 B.C. and 118 B.C., witnessed a growing occurrence of mirrors, iron axes and swords, and bronze implements made in China. The third stage is dated by Chinese coins to late Western Han and early Eastern Han.[82]

82. *Yün-nan Chin-ning Shih-chai-shan ku mu ch'ün fa-chüeh pao-kao*, p. 133.

FIG. 33. An incised decorative band on a bronze vessel excavated from the Tien cemetery at Chin-ning, Yünnan. From *WW*, 1959:5, inside cover.

The importance of the Shih-chai-shan discovery can hardly be exaggerated. The proximity to the classical site of Dong Son in the Gulf of Tonkin [83] and the many stylistic similarities which these two sites share indicate without question that they represent one and the same culture, characterized by the following stylistic elements: bronze kettle drums; fan-shaped and boot-shaped bronze axes; plastic bronze art as a decorative adjunct to ceremonial objects, artifacts of high prestige value (e.g., heads for sticks and tops of cowry-shell containers), and similar weapons forms; cattle and peacocks as favorite decorative motifs, with ceremonial implications; and certain other distinctive decorative motifs such as connected concentric circles, whorls, moth-brow designs, and S-shaped patterns.[84] In terms of society and economy, there is no question that the Dongson Culture had a highly sophisticated and stratified society and intensive industrial specialization. On the other hand, it seems to have had no writing, and the dwelling sites that have been found show no evidence of mature urbanization. Typologically, the civilization represented by the sites of Dongson and Shih-chai-shan appears to be comparable with the Yayoi Culture of Japan and the Circum-Caribbean Culture of South America, in both of which socially stratified villages were the prevalent unit of social interaction and economic self-sufficiency, but in none of which is evidenced an urban-rural interdependence, such as that achieved by the Shang and probably the Ch'u and Yüeh civilizations.[85]

This highly developed civilization apparently centered in Yünnan and the northern part of Indo-China, but its influence had been widely felt. Bronze drums have been found or recorded in most of South China,[86] including the regions of the Ch'u and the Pa-Shu civilizations, and Dongsonian elements have been enumerated from a large part of Southeast Asia.[87] The discovery at Shih-chai-shan, furthermore, shows that the initial stimulation which brought

83. O. R. T. Janse, *Archaeological Research in Indo-China III: The Ancient Dwelling-site of Dong-Son (Thanh-Hoa, Annam)*, Bruges, Institut Belge des Hautes Études Chinoises, 1958.

84. Chang Kwang-chih, *BIE*, 7 (1959), 56; Kobayashi Tomowo, *Kōkogaku-Zasshi*, 26 (1936), 701–18.

85. Chang Kwang-chih, *BIE*, 13, 1962.

86. Ling Shun-sheng, *Bull. College of Arts, National Taiwan Univ.*, 1, 1950.

87. H. R. van Heekeren, *The Bronze-Iron Age of Indonesia*, 'S-Gravenhage, Martinus Nijhoff, 1958.

about the emergence of this civilization in Yünnan was introduced mainly from the areas of Ch'u and Szechwan toward the
end of the Eastern Chou Dynasty, approximately the fourth and
the fifth centuries B.C. Many bronze elements in the Shih-chai-shan
cemetery also indicate direct influence from the Li-fan and Kan-
tzu group of Eastern Chou and early Han bronzes, such as the
vivid animal style of art depicted in small, single-motif art objects.
Heine-Geldern believes that the Dongson owed its impetus directly
to the Western Asiatic and European Bronze Age and Iron Age
cultures.[88] This view is no longer tenable, however, since the cultural affinities of the Shih-chai-shan cemetery clearly lie in the area
of China. The Li-fan and Kan-tzu group of Szechwan civilizations
certainly provided the immediate sources for any Western Asiatic
elements in the Dongson Culture.

GENERAL CONCLUSIONS

South China's prehistory and early history are full of intriguing
problems; within the cultural framework outlined in Chapter 5
and in the present chapter, many specific questions remain to be
answered and a good many details of tremendous historical significance deserve more extensive treatment than the space here
can possibly afford. In concluding the discussion on the emergence
of civilizations in South China, a few paragraphs should now be
devoted to this area as a whole, pulling together the fragmentary
pieces of information given above to show the general tendency
of its cultural development during the Yin and Chou periods of
North China and the patterns involved in the process.

Attention must once more be directed to the native cultures
of South China, which in the main played recipient roles under
the tremendous impact of the everexpanding Bronze Age and Early
Iron Age civilizations of the Huangho valley. Two main cultural
traditions played important parts in South China, namely, the
Lungshanoid farmers in eastern South China, and the Southwestern Neolithic in Szechwan and Yünnan. The former culture was
essentially an extension of the Lungshanoid in North China and
was composed of immigrant farmers who brought along a North

88. Robert von Heine-Geldern, *Saeculum*, 2 (1951), 225–55; and *Paideuma*,
5 (1954), 347–423.

China heritage, although many adjustments were necessary for them to tackle the new problems that arose in the change of habitat. The latter, the Southwestern Neolithic, probably grew out of the Southwestern Mesolithic and sub-Neolithic basis, under the Lungshanoid influences seen in the introduction of agriculture and the domestication of animals.

The civilizations of the Shang Dynasty and of the Western Chou apparently had continuous contacts with the aboriginal peoples of South China, but archaeological data indicate that their cultural influences were largely confined to the middle and lower Yangtze valley and the Huaiho valley. State organizations came into being toward the end of this stage in the Huaiho valley and probably in the Lower Yangtze, and late Western Chou and early Eastern Chou impacts probably reached as far south as the Chekiang valley. Elsewhere in eastern South China the introduction of metallurgy and the bronze and pottery arts of the Shang and Chou styles brought about the formation of the Geometric horizon. It can be clearly seen, however, that the native Lungshanoid tradition persisted into this period, and even in the Huaiho states where sinicization was the most extensive, native pottery styles continued.

Archaeological evidence indicates two major sweeping waves of North Chinese civilizations into South China, the first dated to the Eastern Chou period, probably closer to the Warring-States period than to the Ch'un-ch'iu, and the second, the political and military expansion of the Ch'in and the Han Empires. Various southern states emerged, probably as a result of the Eastern Chou expansion, but they were subsequently incorporated, one after another, into the Ch'in and Han.

The Eastern Chou expansion into South China was closely linked to the internal changes taking place in North China itself. Archaeological materials from the Eastern Chou states of South China indicate that iron implements were found from the beginning of their civilizations along with bronze implements, although the latter were far more abundant in most regions. The evidence from Ch'u and from Ta-li in Yünnan further suggests that the Eastern Chou expansion was probably also linked with the increased use of irrigation. It is thus apparent that with the use of iron and the expanded role of irrigation in field cultivation, the

Eastern Chou civilization of North China not only changed its own structures in its homeland but expanded geographically toward the north and the south.

The South China Neolithic cultures, already infiltrated by Yin and Early Chou cultural elements, and presumably already stimulated toward an intensive internal growth in some regions, swiftly grew into a Metal Age culture under the suddenly accelerated impacts of the Eastern Chou North China. In some regions where previous contacts with Yin and Western Chou were frequent and considerable, such as the regions of the Ch'u and the Yüeh, there were probably transitional stages between village and state, and upon this basis state organizations and a literate civilization came into being during the Eastern Chou period. In some other regions, such as Yünnan, the Eastern Chou civilization found a pure and simple Neolithic basis. With the sudden burst of metal culture and sophisticated art, these cultures were apparently boosted onto a level approaching that of the great civilizations, but at a societal level these civilizations lacked urbanism and writing. The precise form of the Pa-Shu civilizations in terms of such typological classifications is not clear at the moment.

In addition to such typological differences among the southern civilizations in the Eastern Chou period, there are also stylistic differences which may serve among other things in making cultural groupings. There are many common characteristics that are found throughout South China as a cultural sphere, in contrast to the North, which may indicate that the southern civilizations contained some unifying factors, many of which were apparently the result of similar ecological adjustments to a similar natural environment, but some of which probably indicate a certain degree of historical connection. These common features of South China include, for instance, pile dwellings, rice cultivation, the tubular borer, burial in boats and on cliffs, and the use of bronze kettle drums. Distribution of these and other traits, however, suggests that there were actually parallel cultural traditions rather than a single cultural area in South China during this time interval, and that the widespread occurrence of certain characteristic features was the result of cultural contacts or similar ecological conditions. At least the following different cultural traditions can be distinguished among the Eastern Chou civilizations in South China:

(1) Yüeh: in the eastern and southern coastal areas.
(2) Ch'u: in the Middle Yangtze and the western Huaiho valley.
(3) Pa-Shu: in the Red basin of Szechwan.
(4) The Li-fan and Kan-tzu assemblages of westernmost Szechwan.
(5) The Tien of Yünnan.

The stylistic characteristics of these traditions have been enumerated above, and repetition is not necessary. The powerful expansion of the Ch'in and Han Empires brought all of these cultural traditions under the same political system and civilization, but in different areas the actual process of assimilation, as well as its rate and tempo, apparently differed. These different traditions also had dissimilar relations with cultures and civilizations in areas outside of China. Historical and modern non-Han Chinese ethnic groups have claimed different descents from the various cultural traditions of the Eastern Chou period. Discussions of these problems must be left out of the present volume, but there is material here for many future studies which could make significant contributions to our knowledge of the culture history of Southeast Asia.

Conclusions

and

Prospect

The year 221 B.C. has been chosen as a terminal date for the present study of ancient Chinese archaeology for two reasons. First, the year marked the unification of China under Shih Huang Ti, the first emperor of the Ch'in Dynasty, and the consolidation of the Chinese as a single people with a single culture and a sense of common nationality. The various local cultures which flourished in different parts of China up to this time were cultures of the formative stage of Chinese civilization. Second, we find that for the various cultures before the Ch'in and the Han Dynasties, either no historical record was kept at all or else the historical documents that survive are fragmentary and far from complete. The basic data for a study of the culture, society, and history of prehistoric and early historic China are provided by archaeology. It is true that for the preparation of a complete history of the Yin and Chou Dynasties, literary records would have to be utilized to a far greater extent than has been done in this book, in which they are included only when they render archaeological data more meaningful. These historical documents are largely neglected for considered reasons. In the first place, the data for the same periods from literary sources is readily available in many good books already in existence. The writing of a book which uses both historical and archaeological materials to the full may be highly desirable, but it cannot be undertaken at a time when the archaeological data, much of which has only been made available in very recent years, still need processing and interpretation. In the second place, archaeology and history, by virtue of their different source materials, tend to stress different aspects of the same culture history.

299

In historical studies political events are generally given paramount attention at the expense of cultural and social changes and information about the origins and development of cultural traditions. Archaeological data happily fill such vacuums, and the present book supplements rather than overlaps the works on ancient Chinese history which have made use of literary sources.

A cultural historical framework has thus been presented in this book, within which most of the available archaeological data from the area of China can be interpreted. We have seen that this area has been occupied since the beginning of the Middle Pleistocene period at the latest, and that industrial diversification and innovation and the evolution of man himself occurred within the area of China during the Pleistocene period. During the early post-Pleistocene period, Mesolithic cultures of two major types were distributed in the northern and the southern parts of China, respectively. Subsequently the food-producing way of life developed in the north, which ignited an explosive cultural growth leading to the formation of a Chinese civilization. This civilization has been carried down uninterruptedly to the present time and has helped to shape the course of civilizational development in the entire Far East.

Agriculture and the domestication of animals in China probably emerged first in the north in what we have called the Nuclear Area. The exact time at which this important event took place, gradually or abruptly, is unknown, and its relation to the Neolithic revolution in the distant Near East is not clear. But however the initial appearance of the new subsistence and technological patterns came about, the Neolithic culture of the Huangho valley possessed a distinctive and highly original character which characterizes a North China cultural tradition and which was carried over into the historical civilizations of this area. These early farmers underwent at least two major stages of cultural and social development—the Yangshao stage of primary village efficiency and the Lungshanoid stage of expanding village farmers—before the first civilization, the Shang, eventually appeared in the plains of the Lower Huangho. The Shang civilization was taken over by the Western Chou Dynasty, but by the middle of the Eastern Chou period a series of interrelated events and factors appeared, among which the highly developed iron metallurgy and intensified communications throughout the country were paramount, which

300

made the Huangho tradition expand toward both the north and the south, thus paving the way for the unification of China under the Ch'in and Han Empires.

In the northern parts of China, primarily because of ecological limitations, the Mesolithic hunting-fishing cultures lingered on for a considerable length of time during the same period in which farming and, subsequently, civilization developed in the Huangho valley to the south. Agriculture and the domestication of animals were introduced to the southern fringes of this area, and neolithic technology penetrated even deeper. But on the whole, the northern frontiers remained a province of the Northeast Asia culture area throughout the Neolithic, sub-Neolithic, and early Metal Age periods. By the middle of the first millennium B.C. two major historical waves radiated into this area, one from the expanding Eastern Chou civilization, and the other from the Central Asiatic steppes which were dominated by mounted nomads of a variety of cultural extractions and affiliations. The Great Wall symbolizes the conflicts of these two ways of life, agricultural and pastoral nomadic. The zigzag back and forth movements of the borders between China and the nomad territory result from the seesawing of sovereignty rights over the small strip of arable land along the borders of the Eastern Chou territories.

North China peoples and cultures continually poured into South China after the beginning of agriculture in the North. First there were the Yangshao farmers, who were themselves largely confined to the Nuclear Area, but whose cultural influences were at least partially responsible for the introduction of neolithic technology—pottery and polished stone implements—into the Southwest and even further down in Southeast Asia. Then there were the Lungshanoid immigrants who brought both their Neolithic culture and the concept of farming villages into the eastern part of South China, an area then probably sparsely inhabited by Mesolithic hunter-fishers, and probably first introduced agriculture among the Southwestern sub-Neolithic population. The Neolithic cultures in South China continued into the Shang and Early Chou periods, although the North China Bronze Age civilizations incorporated the Huaiho and the Lower Yangtze into their sphere of influence and made significant and even consequential changes in some of the other areas where certain elements of civilization were adopted as a result of increased contact. By the middle of the Eastern Chou, incentives for expansion once more increased enough to cause another explosive expansion of the Huangho civilization into South China, resulting in the formation of a number of contemporary states and regional cultural traditions. These states and cultural traditions were incorporated into the succeeding Ch'in and Han Empires.

This brief outline of South China prehistory and early history shows that three major waves of cultural influence reached South China from the North, namely, the Lungshanoid, the Eastern Chou, and the Ch'in and Han, before South China became an integral part of the cultural China. In speaking of "Chinese influences" in South China and Southeast Asia, it is thus necessary to specify which of these major waves of influence is referred to.

These cultural events finally led to the unification of China, the history of which concludes this volume. It can clearly be seen that by the end of the Warring-States period much of China was already unified culturally, as indicated by the cultural tradition and style which is encountered in almost all of China, from southern Manchuria to the coasts of Kwangtung. We encounter variations of the same civilizational form and spirit, exemplified in the tomb construction patterns, in the remains of a bronze mirror and an iron sword, in the decorative patterns of pottery and bronzes, or in the forms of writing. The unification of China by the Ch'in and the Han empires was not a conquest accomplished by a single, powerful state and culture over a miscellaneous assortment of political groups and cultural traditions. Essentially this unification was a political followup of the cultural unification and the emergence of the Chinese national spirit which were already in force toward the end of the Eastern Chou, and which probably not only stimulated but also enabled—or at least facilitated—the political conquest which marked the year 221 B.C.

In 221 B.C. the state of Ch'i, in Shantung, the last remaining power of the Warring-States, was officially dissolved by General Wang P'en of the Ch'in. But the actual political unification of China was more or less continuous, for several centuries. The state of Ch'in claimed the status of kingdom in 325 B.C. Four years before, it had already taken over Szechwan, as previously mentioned. Many historians are of the opinion that the rich resources and the high civilization of Szechwan which came under Ch'in's control were largely responsible for the phenomenal rise of the

Ch'in state and its overwhelming power. In 256 B.C., Ch'in overthrew the Royal Chou. By 221 B.C., all of the major states in North and Central China, including Ch'u, Yen, Chao, Wei, Han, and Ch'i, bowed to the military might of the Ch'in. However, the incorporation of southern Manchuria [1] and the southern Yüeh [2] came later. By the time of Han, what is now southern Manchuria, Inner Mongolia, and all of China proper were completely and directly dominated by the Han civilization. Sugimoto and Kano [3] have listed the Han Dynasty remains brought to light during the last decade in the area of China. Three things are made clear by that list: (a) Han remains have been found from every province of China proper and many regions in Southern Manchuria, indicating the extent of the Han civilization within China; (b) in each province the number of Han Dynasty sites is considerable, suggesting the intensity of the Han acculturation in some of the marginal provinces; (c) it is clear that the Han remains from all China represented a single major cultural tradition.

I have mentioned that the Ch'in and Han political unification was essentially a political followup of a cultural unification which had been developing for some centuries before 221 B.C. I did not mean to say, however, that the total cultural unification of China was completed in every region of the area by 221 B.C. Native civilizational elements persisted into the Han and subsequent historical periods in many of the regions, particularly in the southwest.[4] But the political control of these regions under the Han Empire certainly accelerated and intensified their cultural assimilation into the Han civilization.

Whether the above interpretation is valid, and how many of the hypotheses proposed here will stand, remains to be seen—only time will tell. In any event, this interpretation and the basic data I have presented can probably be made use of by archaeologists working in other areas of the world and by cultural historians at large. Some possible conclusions reaching beyond the confines of China have been hinted at here and there in my discussions, some of which might now be made more explicit.

In the first place, the early development of Chinese civilization

1. Tung Chu-chen, *KKHP*, 1956:1, 29–43.
2. L. Aurouseau, *Bulletin de l'École Française d'Extrême-Orient*, 23 (1923), 127–265.
3. Sugimoto and Kano, *Toyoshi-Kenkyu*, 16, 1957.
4. Chang Kwang-chih, *COWA Survey*, Area 17, No. 1, 1959, p. 6.

and the contemporary cultural traditions in the area of China are topics essential to students of prehistory and early history of other parts of the Far East, just as their contributions in their own fields are in many cases indispensable to a specialist working in China. It is superfluous to stress that ancient cultures were not limited

TABLE 11.

Early Cultural Levels in China: East-West Section

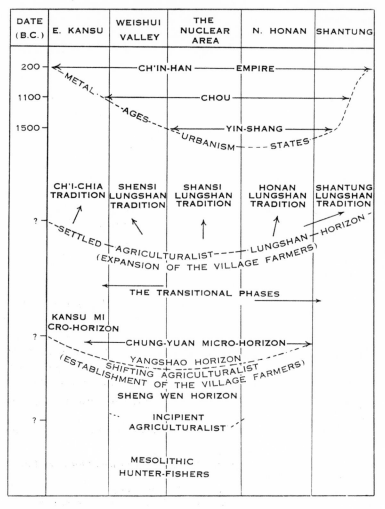

by present boundaries of sovereignty. Regional archaeological studies may be handicapped, however, if the cultures they deal with extended into another region which may not be known archaeologically, or whose archaeology may not be of ready use be-

TABLE 12.

Early Cultural Levels in China: North-South Section

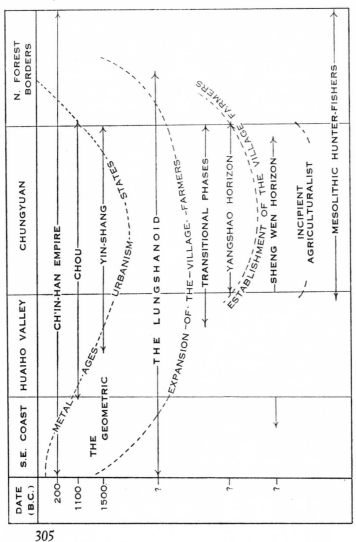

cause of linguistic and political difficulties or because its data have been differently interpreted and are not subject to immediate reference. For instance, few students in the Palaeolithic and Meso-lithic cultures of Siberia and Japan [5] have fully utilized the Chinese data of the Fenho, the Ordosian, and the Sha-yüan assemblages, which are certainly relevant. The current data on the Mesolithic, sub-Neolithic, and Neolithic cultures of Manchuria, Inner Mongolia, and North China, may prove useful to the studies of cultural areas of Neolithic Northern Asia, such as those made by Okladnikov [6] and Chard.[7] The Chinese Southwest has yielded much indispensable data pertaining to the problems of the Hoabin-hian, the Dongsonian, and the origin of agriculture in Southeast Asia. South China is still considered by many archaeologists to be a terra incognita where the supposed homeland of the so-called proto-Malayo-Polynesians is often located.[8] Furthermore, if the field archaeologists in China had been better acquainted with the data on the Shell Mound Culture of the Pacific coast of Siberia and Korea, or on the Dongsonian materials from Indo-China, they would have discussed their own data from Manchuria and Yünnan in a much wider perspective, and would not have left many of the essential questions unanswered. It is indeed unfor-tunate that the archaeological data of China have been difficult for scholars in other fields to use because of language difficulties, and vice versa.

In the second place, the archaeological data from China afford a good deal of raw material for studies in the classification of cul-ture. Taking the Eastern Chou civilizations in the area of China as an example, it is clear that a number of regional traditions can be distinguished, which pose different problems pertaining to the cultural development. One particularly pressing problem is the distinction between nuclear and marginal areas, such as can be made between the Huangho valley and the Yünnan and northern Indo-China regions. Cultural sequences, the progression in which various cultural elements appeared, and the incentives behind the development and the appearance of new elements must be dealt with quite separately in the nuclear and the marginal areas. In

5. E.g., John Maringer, *Kōkogaku-Zasshi*, 42 (1957), 1–8.
6. A. P. Okladnikov, *Cahiers d'Histoire mondiale*, 6 (1960), 476–502.
7. Chester S. Chard, *Anthropologica*, n.s. 2 (1960), No. 2, pp. 1–9.
8. E.g., Chen Chi-lu, *Bull. Ethnol. Soc. China*, 2 (1958), 9.

making a "developmental classification," therefore, it is often necessary to distinguish between the different roles played by the
cultures of the nuclear areas and those of the marginal phases.
For the Nuclear Area in North China, the formative sequence
from the terminal Mesolithic to the emergence of the Empire is
both interesting and instructive; reference might be made to this
sequence in formulating "stages" of cultural growth of universal
validity and applicability.[9] The technological models of the Stone,
Bronze, and Iron Ages must also be differently applied to North
China and the Middle Yangtze, for example.

Finally, the problems concerning the dynamics and processes of
cultural growth in this part of the world are certainly of wide
interest. It is evident that many factors are known to have played
a part in bringing about cultural and social change and growth
in China, but that a monolithic deterministic cause cannot account for what we have seen happen in the whole area of China.
Ecology is certainly highly significant in shaping the courses of
cultural development, as shown by the cultural and natural groupings made in this volume, and the importance of technology is
most clearly revealed by the development of cities and the expansion of North China civilization during the Eastern Chou period
when iron metallurgy made significant strides. Irrigation, which
to some authors is the single factor in bringing about the emergence of civilization,[10] played considerable roles in the development of North China Bronze Age civilizations and in the expansion of the Eastern Chou, but archaeological data has failed to
prove that irrigation was the leading and decisive factor. The evolution of the Neolithic culture in North China from the Yangshao
to the Lungshan and the emergence of the Shang civilization,
on the other hand, cannot be accounted for entirely in terms of
technological advances, as, it has been shown, the agricultural
techniques did not undergo decisive and major changes until the
Eastern Chou. These advances must additionally be explained in
terms of a tightened social organization and an intensified political control, phenomena which are amply demonstrated by the

9. E.g., Robert J. Braidwood, "Levels in Prehistory," in Sol Tax, ed., *Evolution of Man after Darwin*, 2; Julian H. Steward, *Theory of Culture Change*,
Urbana, University of Illinois Press, 1955.

10. E.g., J. H. Steward, ed., *Irrigation Civilizations: A Comparative Study*,
Washington, D.C., Pan American Union, 1955.

archaeological data in such spheres as industrial specialization and social stratification. Moreover, cultural contacts are shown to have played decisive roles in some regions of China, as with the emergence of the sub-Neolithic cultures in the northern frontiers and in the Southwest, the beginning of agriculture in South China, and the appearance of civilizations in the Yangtze valley. Patterns of diffusion and acculturation are not only revealed by such events as the expansion of the Huangho civilizations, but are also exemplified by the internal development of the Huangho cultural tradition itself in such significant phenomena as the formation of the different horizon styles and the various local traditions.[11] Unless and until the mechanisms and patterns involved in the formation of such horizons and traditions of, for example, the Lungshanoid stage in northern and eastern China are made demonstrably clear, the cultural growth of the Huangho civilization itself cannot be said to be sufficiently understood.

So much for the possibilities. After all, Chinese archaeology is still young, and I look forward to seeing the day when new data and research will compel me to rewrite this volume completely anew.

11. E.g., Lee A. Parsons, *Anthropology Tomorrow*, 5, 1957.

PLATE I. Two bowls painted with fish figures discovered from the Yangshao stage settlement at Pan-p'o, near Sian, Shensi province. From *Wu-sheng ch'u-t'u chung-yao wen-wu chan-lan t'u-lu* (Peiping, Wen-wu Press, 1958), Pls. I and II.

PLATE II. *Above:* Potsherd with relief of human face, collected from a Yangshao stage site at Chiang-hsi Ts'un, in Fu-feng Hsien, Shensi. From *KK*, 1959:11, Pl. VIII, no. 1. *Below:* Two painted jars (left one 12 cm. high, the other 17 cm.) excavated from the Lungshanoid site at Pao-t'ou-ts'un in Ning-yang Hsien, Shantung. From *WW*, 1960:2, inside cover.

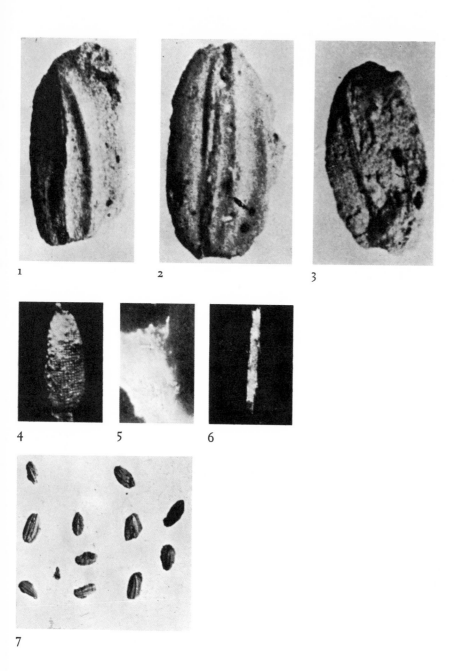

PLATE III. Rice husks found from Lungshanoid sites in Hupei. 1. Fang-ying-t'ai, near Wu-ch'ang; 2. Ch'ü-chia-ling, near Ching-shan; 3. Fang-ying-t'ai; 4–6. microscopic photographs; 7. Fang-ying-t'ai (right two rows), and Ch'ü-chia-ling (left two rows). From *KKHP*, 1959:4, plate facing p. 35.

PLATE IV. Pottery of the Weishui phase of the Lungshanoid Neolithic. 1. *ting* tripod; 2,3. *chia* tripods; 4,5. *li* tripods; 6. *kui* tripod; 7–9. pots; 10. lid. From *KK*, 1959:10, Pl. II.

PLATE v. The Lungshanoid sites at Ta-ch'eng-shan, in Hopei (*above*), and Yang-t'ou-wa, in Liaoning (*below*). Upper picture from *KKHP*, 1959:3, plate facing p. 36; lower picture from Kanazeki et al., "Yang-t'ou-wa," *Archaeologia Orientalis*, ser. B, no. 3, 1942, Pl. I, no. 1.

1

2

3

4

5

6

PLATE VI. Habitation mounds of the Lungshanoid and Geometric stages in Kiangsu.
1. Shen-tun, in Mo-ling; 2. T'uan-shan, in Chen-chiang; 3. Yen-tai-shan, in Tan-t'u;
4. Ta-fen-t'ou, in Kou-jung; 5. Yao-kang-shan, in Li-shui; 6. Ch'ien-t'ou-shan, near
Nanking. From *KKHP*, 1959:1, plate facing p. 40.

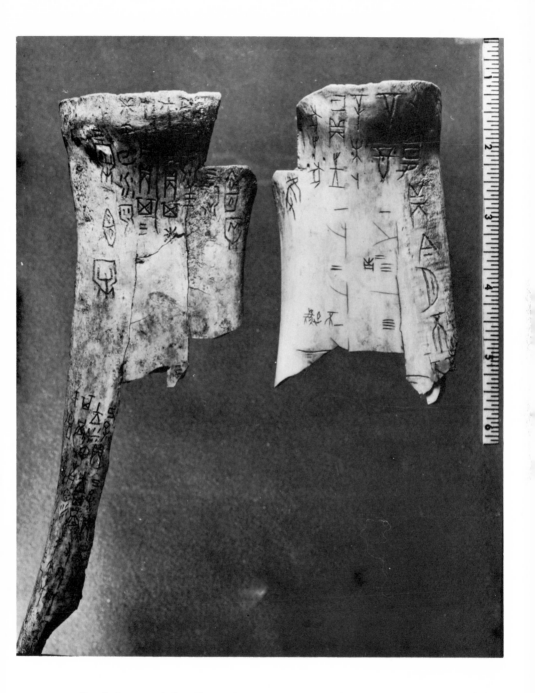

PLATE VII. Oracle bones of the Shang Dynasty, excavated from Hsiao-t'un. Collection of Academia Sinica; photo courtesy of *Life* magazine.

PLATE VIII. Pottery of the Hsin-tien B phase. From *KKHP*, 1957:2, plate facing p. 33.

PLATE IX. Pottery of the T'ang-wang style. From *KKHP*, 1957:2, Pls. I, II, III, following p. 32.

PLATE X. Painted wooden animal figures, excavated from the Ch'u tomb at Hsin-yang, southern Honan. From WW, 1957:9, frontispiece.

PLATE XI. Decorated bronze halberds excavated from the Ch'u tombs near Ch'ang-sha. From *KKHP*, 1959:1, Pl. XI following p. 60.

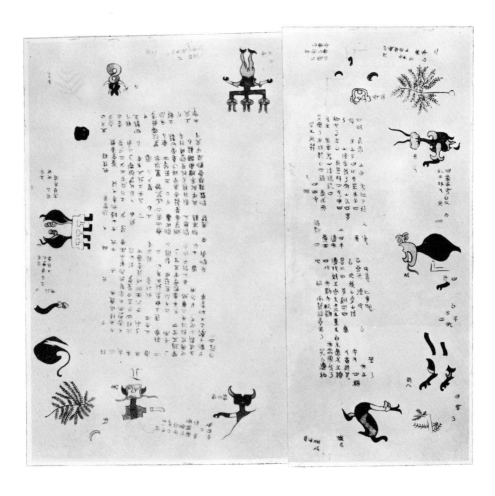

PLATE XII. Painted and inscribed silk from a Ch'u tomb near Ch'ang-sha. From Chiang Hsüan-yih, *Ch'ang-sha Ch'u min-tsu chi ch'i yih-shu* (Shanghai, Mei-shu-k'ao-ku Hsüeh-shê, 1950), Pl. 27.

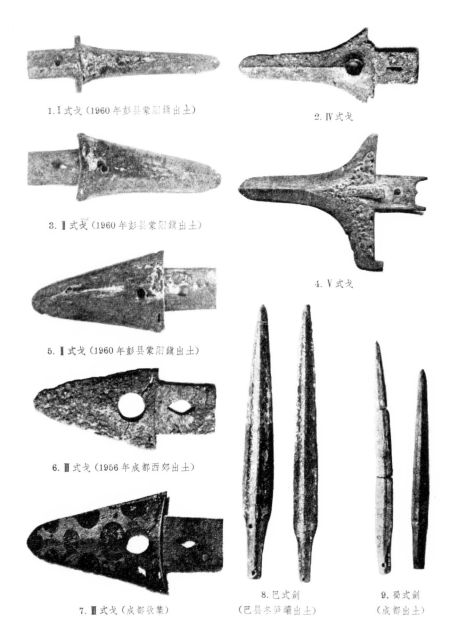

1. I 式戈（1960年彭县蒙阳镇出土）

2. IV 式戈

3. II 式戈（1960年彭县蒙阳镇出土）

4. V 式戈

5. II 式戈（1960年彭县蒙阳镇出土）

6. III 式戈（1956年成都西郊出土）

7. III 式戈（成都收集）

8. 巴式剑
（巴县冬笋坝出土）

9. 蜀式剑
（成都出土）

PLATE XIII. Bronze weapons from Pa and Shu tombs of Szechwan. 1–7. halberds, found in Ch'eng-tu and P'eng Hsien; 8. swords of the Pa type, found in Pa Hsien; 9. swords of the Shu type, found in Ch'eng-tu. From WW, 1961:11, Pl. II.

PLATE XIV. Bronze plow with a section of wooden handle in socket, excavated from a Tien tomb in Yünnan. From *Yün-nan Chin-ning Shih-chai-shan ku mu ch'ün fa-chüeh pao-kao* (Peiping, Wen-wu Press, 1959), Pl. V.

PLATE XV. Market scenes cast in the round on the top of a bronze vessel, excavated from a Tien tomb in Yünnan. From ibid., Pl. XLVII.

PLATE XVI. Scene of a battle cast in the round on the top of a bronze vessel, excavated from a Tien tomb in Yünnan. From ibid., Pl. L.

PLATE XVII. A ritual scene cast in the round on the top of a bronze vessel, excavated from a Tien tomb in Yünnan. From ibid., Pl. LII.

Appendix.

Chinese Characters

for Proper Names

and Technical Terms

This appendix lists the Chinese characters of which transliterations appear in the text. Characters for materials used in the footnotes and for such common geographical and historical names as Huangho, Yangtze, the provincial names, and the dynastic names and subdivisions (e.g., Shang, Ch'in, Chan-kuo, etc.), are not included.

A-ti-ts'un 阿底村

Aksu 阿克蘇

Amano Motonosuke 天野元之助

An Chin-huai 安金槐

An-yang 安陽

Ang-ang-hsi 昂昂溪

Ao 敖

Balin 巴林

Ch'an (R.) 滻

Chang-chia 張家

Chang-chia-p'o 張家坡

Chang-chia-tsui 張家嘴

Ch'ang-chih 長治

Ch'ang-chou 常州

Ch'ang-ch'un 長春

Ch'ang-hsing 長興

Ch'ang-sha 長沙

Ch'ang-tê 常德·

Ch'ang-yang 長陽

Chao-hua 昭化

Chao-ko 朝歌

Chao-yang 朝陽

Chao-yih 朝邑

Chen Meng-chia 陳夢家

Chen-chiang 鎮江

Chen-fan 鎮番

cheng 盠

ch'eng 城 . 郢

Cheng Te-kun 鄭德坤

Cheng-chou 鄭州

Ch'eng-tu 成都

Ch'eng-tzu-yai 城子崖

chi 戟

Ch'i 岐 . 祁 契 棄

Chi Hsien 薊縣 汲縣

Chi Tzu 箕子

Chi Yen-pei 祁延霈

Ch'i-chia-p'ing 齊家坪

309

Ch'i-li-p'u　七里舖
Ch'i-lien-shan　祁連山
Ch'i-lin-shan　麒麟山
Chi-nan　濟南
chia　斝
Chia-yao　甲窰、卡約
Chiang-hsi-ts'un　姜西村
Chiang-yüan　姜嫄
ch'ieh-ch'ü　竊曲
Chien-ch'uan　劍川
Chien-ti　簡狄
Ch'ien-t'ou-shan　前頭山
Chih-chiang　枝江
Ch'ih-feng　赤峯
chin　禁
Chin Shih Hsüeh　金石學
Chin-ch'eng　晉城
Chin-ning　晉寧
Chin-ts'un　金村
Ch'in-wang-chai　秦王寨
Ch'in-wei-chia　秦魏家
Ching　涇、荊
Ch'ing-lien-kang　青蓮崗
Ching-shan　京山
Ch'ing-shui-ho　清水河
Ch'ing-t'ai　青台
Ching-ts'un　荊村
Ch'ing-yang　慶陽
Ch'ing-yang-kung　青羊宮
Chiu-ch'üan　酒泉
Ch'iu-pei　邱北
Ch'iu-wan　丘灣

Chou　紂
Chou Kung　周公
Chou Shu　周書
Chou-k'ou-tien　周口店
Chou-lai　州來
Ch'ü Yüan　屈原
Chu-chia-chai　朱家寨
Ch'ü-chia-ling　屈家嶺
Ch'ü-chiang　曲江
Chu-chou　株州
Ch'ü-fu　曲阜
Ch'u-tz'u　楚辭
Ch'ü-wo　曲沃
Ch'ü-yang　曲陽
Chuang Tzu　莊子
chüeh　爵
Chün Hsien　濬縣
chün-tzu　君子
Chün-wang-ch'i　郡王旗
chung　鐘
Chung Hsien　忠縣
Chung Yüan　中原
Chung-chou-lu　中州路
Chung-wei　中衛
Chung-yüng　仲雍

Djalai-nor　札賚諾爾

Erh-hai (L.)　洱海
Erh-lang-kang　二郎崗
Erh-li-kang　二里崗
erh-ts'eng-t'ai　二層台

Fan-chuang 范莊

Fang-tui-ts'un 枋堆村

Fang-ying-t'ai 放鷹台

Fen-shui-ling 分水嶺

Feng 豐

Feng Han-chi 馮漢驥

Feng Hu Tzu 風胡子

Feng-chia-an 馮家岸

Feng-chieh 奉節

Feng-hao-ts'un 豐鎬村

Feng-huang-t'ai 鳳凰台

Fo-ting 佛頂

fu 父、婦、簠、鎛

Fu Ssu-nien 傅斯年

Fu-feng 扶風

Fu-nan 阜南

Fu-niu-shan 伏牛山

Hai-feng (Hoifong) 海豐

Hai-wei-ho (R.) 海尾河

Han Shu Ti Li Chih 漢書地理志

Han-chia-tsui 韓家嘴

Han-ching-kou 竇井溝

Han-chou 漢州

Han-tan 邯鄲

Hang Hsien 杭縣

hang-t'u 夯土

Hao 鎬

Hê-hsü 赫胥

Hei-ching-lung 黑景隆

Hei-liu-t'u-ho 黑流兔河

Heng-chen-ts'un 橫陳村

Heng-shan 橫山

Heng-yang 衡陽

ho 盉

Ho Hsi 河西

Hou Chi 后稷

Hou Han Shu 後漢書

Hou-chia-chuang 侯家莊

Hou-chia-chuang-nan-ti 侯家莊南地

Hou-kang 後岡

Hou-ma 侯馬

Hsi-ch'a-kou 西岔溝

Hsi-ch'eng-chuang 西成莊

Hsi-chiao-shan 西樵山

Hsi-chiao-ts'un 西樵村

Hsi-feng 西豐

Hsi-hou-tu 西侯度

Hsi-liao-ho (R.) 西遼河

Hsi-ning 西寧

Hsi-pei-kang 西北岡

Hsi-tz'u 繫辭

Hsi-yin-ts'un 西陰村

Hsia 夏

Hsia Hsien 夏縣

Hsia Nai 夏鼐

Hsia-hsi-ho 下西河

Hsia-tu 下都

Hsiang-fen 襄汾

Hsiang-jih-tê 香日德

Hsiang-hsiang 湘鄉

Hsiang-t'an 湘潭

Hsiang-yang 襄陽

Hsiang-yin 湘陰

311

Hsiao 囂

Hsiao-chuang 小莊

Hsiao-hung-shan 小洪山

Hsiao-ssu-k'ung-ts'un 小司空村

Hsiao-t'un 小屯

hsien (= *yen*)

Hsin-cheng 新鄭

Hsin-fan 新繁

Hsin-hsiang 新鄉

Hsin-min 新民

Hsin-tien 辛店

Hsin-t'ien 新田

Hsin-ts'un 辛村

Hsin-yang 信陽

Hsin-yih 新沂

Hsing-lung 興隆

Hsing-t'ai 邢台

Hsiung Ch'ü 熊渠

Hsiung T'ung 熊通

Hsiung Yih 熊繹

hsü 盨

Hsü Ping-chang 徐炳昶

Hsü-chou 徐州

Hsüan-yüan 軒轅

Hsüeh 薛

Hsüeh-chia-chuang 薛家莊

hu 壺 胡

Hu-hsi 滸西

Hu-shu 湖熟

Hua Hsien 華縣

Hua-chia-ssu 花家寺

Hua-t'ing-ts'un 花廳村

Hua-ts'e 畫策

Hua-yang-kuo Chih 華陽國志

Hua-yin 華陰

Huai-an 淮安

Huan (R.) 洹

Huang Chan-yüeh 黃展岳

Huang-chung 湟中

Huang-lou 黃樓

Huang-niang-t'ai 黃娘台

Huang-p'i 黃陂

Huang-shui 湟水

Huang-ti 黃帝

Hui Hsien 輝縣

Hui-tsui 灰嘴

Hun-yüan 渾源

Hung Yen Chih Shih 鴻雁之什

Hung-chao 洪趙

Hung-chia-lou 洪家樓

Hung-shan-hou 紅山後

Huo Ch'ih Lieh Chuan 貨殖列傳

Jao Tsung-yih 饒宗頤

Jen-min 人民

Jih-chao 日照、

ju 耰

Jui-ch'eng 芮城

Jui Yih-fu (Ruey Yih-fu) 芮逸夫

K'ai-jui-chuang 開瑞莊

Kan-ku 甘谷

Kan-tzu 甘孜

Kang-shang-ts'un 崗上村

Kao 謈

Kao Chü-hsün 高去尋

Kao-ching-t'ai-tzu 高井台子

Kao-huang-miao 高皇廟

K'ao-ku 考古

K'ao-ku-hsüeh-pao 考古學報

K'ao-ku-t'u 考古圖

Kao-ku-t'ung-hsün 考古通訊

Kao-li-chai 高麗寨

K'ao-lieh 考烈,

Kao-tu 高都

Kao-tui 高堆

keng 耕

ko 戈

K'o-hsing-chuang 客省莊

K'o-shih-k'o-t'eng 克什克騰

Ko-ta-ts'un 屹墖村

Ko-ta-wang 旭笛王、屹墖王

Kou Wu 句吳

Kou-jung 句容

ku 瓠

Ku Hsieh-kang 顧頡剛

Ku Shih Pien 古史辨

Ku-hsiang-t'un 顧鄉屯

Ku-lang 古浪

Ku-t'u-tun 古土墩

Ku-wei-ts'un 固圍村

kuan-fu 官府

kuang 觥

Kuang-han 廣漢

Kuang-shê 光社

Kuang-wu 廣武

313

kui (kuei, kwei) 鬹、毇

Kui-chou 歸州

k'ui-feng 夔鳳

k'ui-lung 夔龍

Kui-tê 貴德

Kung Yang Chuan 公羊傳

kuo 國、郭

Kuo 虢

Kuo Mo-jo 郭沫若

Kuo Pao-chün 郭寶鈞

Kuo Yü 國語

Lai-pin 來賓

Lao-ha-ho (R.) 老哈河

Lao-ho-shan 老和山

Lao-lao-t'ai 老姥台

Lao-t'ieh-shan 老鐵山

lei 耒、罍

lei-wen 雷文

Lei-yang 耒陽

li 鬲

Li Chi 李濟

Li Ching-tan 李景聃

Li Hsüeh-chin 李學勤

Li Ping 李氷

Li-ch'eng 歷城

Li-fan 理番

Li-ling 醴陵

Li-shui 溧水

Li-ts'un 李村

Li-yü-ts'un 李峪村

Liang Ssu-yung 梁思永

Liang-ch'eng-chen 兩城鎮
Lung-shan-chen 龍山鎮

Liang-chu 良渚
Lung-tung 龍洞

Liang-ts'un 梁村

Liang-wang-ch'eng 梁王城
Ma-ch'ang-yen 馬廠沿

Lin-fen 臨汾
Ma-chia-yao 馬家窰

Lin-hsi 林西
Ma-lang-chi-shan 馬郎磯山

Lin-hsia 臨夏
Ma-lang-ch'uan-shan 馬郎船山

Lin-shan-chai 林山砦
Ma-lung 馬龍

Lin-t'ao 臨洮
Ma-pa 馬壩

Lin-tzu 臨淄
Ma-yü-kou 麻峪溝

Ling Shun-sheng 凌純聲
Man 蠻

Ling-yüan 凌源
Mei Hsien 湄縣

Liu-chiang 柳江
Mi-chia-yai 米家崖

Liu-ch'üan 柳泉
Miao-ti-kou 廟底溝

Liu-chuang 劉莊
Mien P'ien 緜篇

Liu-hu-t'un 留胡屯
Mien-ch'ih 澠池

Liu-li-ko 琉璃閣
Mien-yang 綿陽

Liu-tzu-chen 柳子鎮
min 民、皿

Lo 羅
Min-ch'in 民勤

Lo-han-t'ang 羅漢堂
Min-lo 民樂

Lo-ning 洛寧
Ming-kung-lu 銘功路

Lo-ta-miao 洛達廟
Ming-yü 鳴玉

Lo-tu 樂都
Mo-ling 秣陵

Lo-yang 洛陽
mu 母

Lu Sung 魯頌
Mu-tan-kiang (R.) 牡丹江

Lü Ta-lin 呂大臨
Mu-yang-ch'eng 牧羊城

Lu-shan 蘆山

Lu-t'ai 蘆台
Nan-chang 南漳

Lu-wang-fen 潞王墳
Nan-chao 南召

Luan-p'ing 灤平
Nan-hai 南海

Lung-hsi 隴西
Nan-kuan-wai 南關外

Lung-ma 龍馬
Nan-pa-t'ai 南霸台

Nan-ta-kuo-ts'un 南大郭村

Nan-yang 南陽

nei 內

Ning-ting 寧定

Ning-yang 寧陽

Niu-chai 牛砦

Niu-kou-yü 牛溝峪

Niu-ts'un 牛村

No-mu-hung 諾木洪

Oshima Riichi 大島利一

Pa Hsien 巴縣

Pa-lung 巴隆

Pai Hu T'ung 白虎通

Pai-chia-chuang 白家莊

Pai-ho (R.) 白河

Pai-ma-ssu 白馬寺

Pai-sha 白沙

Pai-tao-kou-p'ing 白道溝坪

Pai-t'ing-ho (R.) 白亭河

p'an 盤

P'an-keng 盤庚

p'an-k'ui-wen 蟠蠆紋

pan-liang 半兩

Pan-p'o-ts'un 半坡村

Pan-shan (-ch'ü) 半山區

Pao-chi 寶鷄

Pao-lun-yüan 寶輪院

Pao-shen-miao 電神廟

Pao-tê 保德

Pao-t'ou 包頭

Pao-t'ou-ts'un 堡頭村

Pei Wen-chung 裴文中

Pei-ch'iu. 北丘

Pei-kao-ts'un 北高村

Pei-yin-yang-ying 北陰陽營

P'eng Hsien 彭縣

P'eng-shan 彭山

pi 鄙

p'i 妣

Pi Kung 閟宮

Pi-sha-kang 碧沙岡

Pi-tzu-wo 貔子窩

Pien-chia-kou 邊家溝

pien-chung 編鐘

P'ien-kuan 偏關

Pien-tui-shan 邊堆山

Pin Hsien 彬縣

P'ing Chun Shu 平準書

P'ing Wang 平王

P'ing-chiang 平江

P'ing-lu 平陸

P'ing-wang 平望

p'o 瓿

Po Hsien 亳縣

pu 布

Pu-chao-chai 不召寨

P'u-tu-ts'un 普渡村

San-ho 三河

San-li-ch'iao 三里橋

sê 瑟

Sekino Takeshi 關野雄

Sha-ching (-ts'un) 沙井村

Sha-kang 沙崗

Sha-kuo-t'un 砂鍋屯

Sha-yüan 沙苑

Shan Hai Ching 山海經

Shan Hsien 陝縣

Shan-piao-chen 山彪鎮

Shan-tan 山丹

Shang Chün Shu 商君書

Shang-chieh 上街

Shang-tien 上店

Shang-ts'un-ling 上村嶺

shao 杓

Shao-hu-ying-tzu-shan 燒戶營子山

Shao-kou 燒溝

Shen-nung 神農

Shen-tun 神墩

sheng-wen 繩紋

Shih Chang-ju 石璋如

Shih Chi 史記

Shih Kuo 十過

Shih Yih Chi 拾遺記

Shih-chai-shan 石寨山

Shih-chia-ho 石家河

shih-ching 市井

Shih-li-p'u 十里舖

Shou Hsien 壽縣

Shou-ch'un 壽春

Shu 舒蜀

Shui-kuan-yin 水觀音

Shui-tung-kou 水洞溝

shu-hsüeh 豎穴

Sjara-osso-gol 薩拉烏蘇河

ssu 邦

Ssu-ma Chien 司馬遷

Ssu-mien-pei 四面碑

Ssu-pa-t'an 四壩灘

Ssu-p'an-mo 四盤磨

Ssu-wa-shan 寺窪山

Su Ping-chi 蘇秉琦

Sun-ch'i-t'un 孫旗屯

Ta Ya 大雅

Ta-ch'eng-shan 大城山

Ta-fen-t'ou 大墳頭

Ta-ho-chuang 大何莊

Ta-hsi 大溪

Ta-hsin-chuang 大辛莊

Ta-kou 大溝

Ta-lai-tien 大賚店

Ta-li 大荔. 大理

Ta-ssu-k'ung-ts'un 大司空村

T'ai P'ing Yü Lan 太平御覽

T'ai Po 太伯

T'ai Wang 太王

T'ai-hu (L.) 太湖

Tai-hsi 代溪

T'ai-p'ing-ch'ang 太平場

T'ai-p'u-hsiang 太僕鄉

T'ai-shang 台上

T'ai-tzu-ch'ung 太子冲

T'ai-yüan 太原

Tan-t'u 丹徒

Tan-yang 丹陽

T'ang 湯

Tang Lan 唐蘭

Tang Yün-ming 唐雲明

T'ang-shan 唐山

Tang-t'u 當塗

T'ang-wang-ch'uan 唐江川

T'ang-yin 湯陰

T'ao (R.) 洮

Tao T'uo 盜跖

T'ao-sha 洮沙

t'ao-t'ieh 饕餮

T'eng 滕

T'eng Hsien 滕縣

Ti Hsin 帝辛

Tiao-yü-t'ai 釣魚台

Tien 滇

T'ien Wen 天問

Tien-ch'ih (L.) 滇池

Tien-chün-t'ai 點軍台

T'ien-men 天門

T'ien-shui 天水

Tien-ts'ang-shan (Mt.) 點蒼山

t'ien-yieh 田野

ting 鼎

Ting-ts'un 丁村

Torri Ryozo 鳥居龍藏

tou 豆,斗

Tou-chi-t'ai 鬥鷄台

Tou-men-chen 斗門鎮

Tsa Shou P'ien 雜守篇

Ts'ai 蔡

Ts'ao-tien 草店

Ts'ao-yen-chuang 曹演莊

Tseng Chao-yü 曾昭燏

tseng 甑

Tso Chuan 左傳

Tso Lo Chieh 作洛解

Tsou Heng 鄒衡

tsu 祖,族

tsun 尊

tsung 琮

tsung-fa 宗法

tu 都

T'uan-shan 團山

tui 敦

T'u-men (R.) 圖們

T'un-hsi 屯溪

Tung Tso-pin 董作賓

Tung-chai 董砦

Tung-hsiang 東鄉

Tung-hsing 東興

Tung-hu 東滸

Tung-kan-kou 東乾溝

T'ung-lo-chai 同樂寨

Tung-pa-chia 東八家

Tung-pai-chung 東白塚

Tung-pao 東堡

tung-shih-mu 洞室墓

Tung-sun-pa 冬筍壩

tuo 鐸

Tzu 子

Tzu-ching-shan 紫荆山

Tzu-kui 秭歸

Tzu-lo 子羅

317

Tz'u-ts'un 時村
Tzu-yang 資陽

Umehara Sueji 梅原末治

Wa-cha-tsui 瓦碴嘴
Wa-kuan-tsui 瓦罐嘴
Wan Hsien 萬縣
Wan-ch'üan 萬泉
Wang Chia 王嘉
Wang Hsiang 王湘
Wang Kuo-wei 王國維
Wang P'en 王賁
Wang-chia-kou 王家溝
Wang-chia-wan 王家灣
Wang-yü-k'ou 王峪口
Wei Chü-hsien 衛聚賢
Wei Mo 濊貊
Wen Wang Yu Sheng 文王有聲
Wen-hsi 聞喜
Wen-wu 文物
Wen-wu ts'an-k'ao
    tzu-liao 文物參考資料
Wo-kuo 沃國
Wu Gin-ding (Wu
    Chin-ting) 吳金鼎
Wu Ju-kang (Woo
    Ju-kang) 吳汝康
Wu Ju-tso 吳汝祚
Wu Wang 武王
Wu-an 武安
Wu-ch'ang 武昌

Wu-ch'eng 武城
Wu-chi 午汲
Wu-chia 吳家
Wu-chin 武進
Wu-kuan-ts'un 武官村
Wu-shan 武山、巫山
wu-shu (wu-chu) 五銖
Wu-wei 武威
wuan-kui 琬圭
Wung-chiang 瓮江

Ya 雅
Ya-an 雅安
Ya-p'u-shan 鴨蹼山
Yang Chung-chien (Young
    Chung-chien)
Yang Lien-sheng 楊聯陞
Yang-chia-wan 楊家灣
Yang-lin-chi 楊林集
Yang-shao-ts'un 仰韶村
Yang-t'ou-wa 羊頭窪
Yang-tzu-shan 羊子山
Yao 堯
Yao-kang-shan 窯岡山
yao-k'eng 腰坑
yen (= hsien) 甗
Yen 燕 奄
Yen-ch'eng 奄城
Yen-shih 偃師
Yen-tai-shan 烟袋山
Yen-tun-shan 烟墩山

yieh-jen 野人

Yih 夷、易

yih 邑、鬻 匜

Yih Chou Shu 逸周書

Yih Hsien 易縣

Yih Shih 逸史

Yih-ch'ang 宜昌

Yih-cheng 儀徵

Yih-ching 義井

yih-pi-ch'ien 蟻鼻錢

Yih-tu 宜都

Yih-yang 伊陽

Yin Huan-chang 尹煥章

Yin Shan 陰山

Yin Ta 尹達

Yin-chin 陰晉

Yin-hsü 殷墟

Yin-kuo-ts'un 尹郭村

Ying-tsê 滎澤

Young Chung-chien 楊鍾健

yu 卣

Yü Hsien 禹縣

Yü-chia-lin 于家林

Yü-chung 榆中

Yu-jung 有娀

Yü-yao 餘姚

Yu-yih 有侁、有駜

yüan 援

Yüan K'ang 袁康

yüeh 鉞

Yüeh Chüeh Shu 越絕書

yün-wen 雲文

Yün-meng 雲夢

Yüng (R.) 雝

Yüng-ch'ang 永昌

Yüng-ching 永靖

Recommendations

for

Further Reading

The references cited in this volume are given in full in the footnotes, which constitute an intensive bibliography for the field of ancient Chinese archaeology up to mid-1962. The following list comprises a highly selected minimum of titles that are recommended for their wide coverage and general significance. It can also be used as a reading list for a graduate course in the archaeology of ancient China.

General works and bibliographies

An Chih-min, comp., *Chung-kuo shih-ch'ien k'ao-ku-hsüeh shu-mu*, Peiping, 1951.

Chang Kwang-chih, "China," in Robert J. Braidwood and Gordon R. Willey, eds., "Courses Toward Urban Life," *Viking Fund Publications in Anthropology*, 32, 1962.

Chang Kwang-chih, "Chinese Prehistory in Pacific Perspective: Some Hypotheses and Problems," *Harvard Journal of Asiatic Studies*, 22 (1959), 100–149.

Chang Kwang-chih, "Chung-kuo hsin-shih-ch'i-shih-tai wen-hua tuan-tai," *BIHP*, 30 (1959), 259–309.

Chang Kwang-chih, *COWA Survey and Bibliography, Area 17 Far East (China and Formosa)*, No. 1 (1959), and No. 2 (1961).

Chang Kwang-chih, "Hua-nan shih-ch'ien min-tsu wen-hua shih t'i-kang," *BIE*, 7 (1959), 43–103.

Chang Kwang-chih, "Prehistoric Archaeology in China: 1920–60," *Arctic Anthropology*, no. 2 (in press).

Cheng Te-kun, *Archaeology in China* (Vol. 1, *Prehistoric China*; Vol. 2, *Shang China*), Cambridge, W. Heffer & Sons, 1959 and 1961.

Chung-kuo-ko-hsüeh-yüan K'ao-ku-yen-chiu-suo, *Hsin Chung-kuo ti K'ao-ku Shou-huo*, Peiping, Wen-wu Press, 1961.

Hsia Nai, "Shih-nien lai ti Chung-kuo k'ao-ku hsin fa-hsien," *KK*, 1959:10, 505–12.

K'ao-ku-hsüeh Yen-chiu-suo, *K'ao-ku-hsüeh chi-ch'u*, Peiping, Science Press, 1958.

321

Li Chi, *The Beginnings of Chinese Civilization*, Seattle, University of Washington Press, 1957.

Liang Ssu-yüng, "Hsiao-t'un, Lung-shan, yü Yangshao," *Chi-nien Ts'ai Yüan-p'ei hsien-sheng liu-shih-wu-sui lun-wen chi*, Pt. 2 (1933), pp. 555–68, Academia Sinica, Nanking.

Mizuno Seiichi, "Chugaku senshijidai kenkyu no tenbo," *Toyoshi-Kenkyu*, 16 (1957), 1–39.

Sekai Kōkogaku Taikei (*Vol. 5, Eastern Asia: Prehistoric Period; Vol. 6, Eastern Asia: Shang and Chou Periods*), Tokyo, Heibonshya, 1958 and 1960.

Sekino Takeshi, *Chugaku Kōkogaku Kenkyu*, Tokyo, Univ. Tokyo, Institute for Oriental Culture, 1956.

Teilhard de Chardin, Pierre, and Pei Wen-chung, *Le Néolithique de la Chine*, Peiping, Institut de Géo-Biologie, 1944.

Watson, William, *Archaeology in China*, London, Max Parrish, 1960.

Watson, William, *China Before the Han Dynasty*, New York, F. A. Praeger, 1961.

Wei Chü-hsien, *Chung-kuo k'ao-ku-hsüeh shih*, Shanghai, Commercial Press, 1937.

Wu, Chin-ting, *Prehistoric Pottery in China*, London, Kegan Paul, Trench, and Trubner, 1938.

The Palaeolithic Period and Early Man

Black, Davidson, P. Teilhard de Chardin, C. C. Young, and W. C. Pei, "Fossil Man in China," *GSuC, Memoirs* Ser. A, No. 11, 1933.

Boule, M., H. Breuil, E. Licent, and P. Teilhard de Chardin, "Le Paléolithique de la Chine," *Archives de l'Institut de Paléontologie Humaine, Mémoire 4* (1928).

Chang Kwang-chih, "New Evidence on Fossil Man in China," *Science*, 136 (1962), 749–60.

Chang Kwang-chih, "New Light on Early Man in China," *AP*, 2 (1958), 41–61.

Kuo Mo-jo, Young Chung-chien, Pei Wen-chung, Chou Ming-chen, Woo Ju-kang, and Chia Lan-po, *Chung-kuo jen-lei hua-shih ti fa-hsien yü yen-chiu*, Peiping, Science Press, 1955.

Movius, Hallam L., Jr., "Early Man and Pleistocene Stratigraphy in Southern and Eastern Asia," *Papers of the Peabody Museum*, Cambridge, 19, 1944.

Movius, Hallam L., Jr., "The Lower Paleolithic Cultures of Southern and Eastern Asia," *TAPS*, n.s. 38 (1949), Pt. 4.

Movius, Hallam L., Jr., "Palaeolithic Archaeology in Southern and Eastern Asia, Exclusive of India," *Cahiers d'Histoire Mondiale*, 2 (1955), 257–82, 520–53.

Teilhard de Chardin, P., *Early Man in China*, Peiping, Institut de Géo-Biologie, 1941.

Woo Ju-kang and N. N. Cheboksarov, "O neprevynosti razvitiia fizi-

cheskogo tipa, khoziaistvennoi deiatel'nosti i kultury liudei drev-
nogo kamennogo veka na territorii Kitaia," *Sovetskaia Etnografiia*,
1959:4, 3–24.

The Mesolithic Cultures

An Chih-min, "Kuan-yü wo-kuo chung-shih-ch'i-shih-tai ti chi-ko
yih-chih," *KKTH*, 1956:2, 72–78.
An Chih-min and Wu Ju-tso, "Shan-hsi Chao-yih Ta-li Sha-yüan
ti-chi'ü ti shih-ch'i shih-tai yih-ts'un," *KKHP*, 1957:3, 1–12.
Chia Lan-po and Chiu Chung-lang, "On the Age of the Chipped
Stone Artifacts in Kwangsi Caves," *VP*, 4, 1960.
Pei Wen-chung, "The Upper Cave Industry," *PS*, n.s. D, No. 9, 1939.

The Neolithic Stage of the Middle and Lower Huangho and Yangtze

An Chih-min, "Chung-kuo shih-ch'ien shih-ch'i chih nung-yieh," *Yen-
ching Social Studies*, 2 (1949), 37–58.
An Chih-min, "Shih lun Huang-ho liu-yü hsin-shih-ch'i shih-tai wen-
hua," *KK*, 1959:10, 559–65.
An Chih-min, Cheng Nai-wu, and Hsieh Tuan-chü, *Miao-ti-kou yü
San-li-ch'iao*, Peiping, Science Press, 1959. (See also a review of and
comments on this volume in *KK*, 1961:1, 22–28; 4, 222–26.)
Andersson, J. G., "Researches into the Prehistory of the Chinese,"
BMFEA, 15, 1943.
Chang Kwang-chih, "Chung-kuo yüan-ku-shih-tai yih-shih sheng-huo
ti jo-kan tzu-liao," *BIE*, 9 (1960), 253–70.
Chiang Tsuan-chu, "Kuan-yü Chiang-su ti yüan-shih wen-hua yih-
chih," *KKHP*, 1959:4, 35–43.
Hsü Shun-chen, "Kuan-yü Chung-yüan hsin-shih-ch'i-shih-tai wen-hua
chi ko wen-t'i," *WW*, 1960:5, 36–39.
Li Chi, et al, *Ch'eng-tzu-yai*, Nanking, Academia Sinica, 1934.
Liang Ssu-yüng, "The Lungshan Culture," *Proceedings of the 6th
Pacific Science Congress*, 4 (1939), 69–79.
Liu Tun-yüan, "Lung-shan wen-hua jo-kan wen-t'i chih yih," *Wen-
shih-chê*, 1958:1, 45–50.
Liu Yao, "Yang-shao wen-hua yü Lung-shan wen-hua chih fen-hsi,"
KKHP, 2 (1947), 251–82.
Shih Hsing-pang, "Huang-ho liu-yü yüan-shih shê-hui k'ao-ku yen-
chiu shang ti jo-kan wen-t'i," *KK*, 1959:10, 566–70.
Su Ping-chi and Wu Ju-tso, "Hsi-an fu-chin ku wen-hua yih-chih ti
lei-hsing ho fen-pu," *KKTH*, 1956:2, 32–38.
Ting Yih, "Chiang Han p'ing-yüan hsin-shih-ch'i-shih-tai hung-shao-
t'u chung ti tao-ku k'ao-ch'a," *KKHP*, 1959:4, 31–33.
Tung Chu-chen, "Chung-kuo yüan-shih shih-tai wan-ch'i li-shih ti chi
ko t'o-cheng," *KK*, 1960:5, 27–32.
Tung Chu-chen, "Huang-ho Ch'ang-chiang chung-hsia-yu hsin-shih-

ch'i-shih-tai wen-hua ti fen-pu yü fen-ch'i," *KKHP*, 1957:2, 7–21.

Yin Huan-chang and Chang Cheng-hsiang, "Tui Chiang-su T'ai-hu ti-ch'ü hsin-shih-ch'i wen-hua ti yih-hsieh jen-shih," *KK*, 1962:3, 147–57.

Shang and Chou Civilizations in North China

Amano Motonosuke, "Chugaku kodai nogyo no tenkai—kahoku nogyu no keiseikatei," *Tohogakuho*, 39, Kyoto, 1959.

Amano Motonosuke, "Yintai no nogyo to shakai kozo," *Shigaku Kenkyu*, 62 (1956), 1–16.

An Chin-huai, "Shih lun Cheng-chou Shang-tai ch'eng chih—Ao tu," *WW*, 1961: 4/5, 73–80.

Barnard, Noel, "Bronze Casting and Bronze Alloys in Ancient China," *Monumenta Serica Monograph*, 14, 1961. Australian National University and Monumenta Serica.

Chao Chuan-ku, et al, "Cheng-chou Shang-tai yih-chih ti fa-chüeh," *KKHP*, 1957:1, 53–73.

Chen Meng-chia, "Hsi-Chou t'ung-ch'i tuan-tai," *KKHP*, 9 (1955), 137–75; 10 (1955), 69–142; 1956:1, 65–114; 1956:2, 85–94; 1956:3, 105–27; 1956:4, 85–122.

Chen Meng-chia, *Yin-hsü p'u-tz'u tsung-shu*, Peiping, Science Press, 1956.

Cheng Te-kun, "The Origin and Development of Shang Culture," *Asia Major*, n.s. 6 (1957), 80–98.

Chou Yung-chen, "Yin-tai mu-tsang hsing-chih," *KKTH*, 1955:6, 42–48.

Higuchi, T., "Shin hakken no Seishu dokigun to sono mondai," *Toyoshi-Kenkyu*, 16 (1957), 40–61.

Honan Wenhuachü, *Cheng-chou Erh-li-kang*, Peiping, Science Press, 1959.

Hu Hou-hsüan, *Chia-ku-hsüeh Shang-shih lun ts'ung*, 2 vols. Chinan, Ch'i-lu Univ., 1944 and 1945.

Hu Hou-hsüan, *Yin-hsü fa-chüeh*, Shanghai, Hsüeh-hsi-sheng-huo Press, 1955.

Hua Chüeh-ming, Yang Ken, and Liu En-chu, "Chan-kuo Liang-Han t'ieh-ch'i ti chin-hsiang-hsüeh k'ao-ch'a ch'u-pu pao-kao," *KKHP*, 1960:1, 73–87.

Huang Chan-yüeh, "Chin-nien ch'u-t'u ti Chan-kuo Liang-han t'ieh-ch'i," *KKHP*, 1957:3, 93–108.

Jung Keng, *Shang-Chou yih-ch'i t'ung-k'ao*, Peiping, Yenching University, 1941.

Jung Keng and Chang Wei-chih, *Yin-Chou ch'ing-t'ung-ch'i t'ung-lun*, Peiping, Science Press, 1958.

Kao Chü-hsün, "Chan-kuo mu nei tai-kou yüng-t'u ti t'ui-tz'u," *BIHP*, 23 (1951), Pt. 2, 489–510.

Kao Chü-hsün, "Huang-ho hsia-yu ti ch'ü-chih-tsang wen-t'i," *KKHP*, 2 (1947), 121–66.

Kao Ming, "Chien-kuo yih-lai Shang Chou ch'ing-t'ung-ch'i ti fa-hsien chi yen-chiu," WW, 1959:10, 24–31.

Karlgren, Bernhard, "Yin and Chou in Chinese Bronzes," BMFEA, 8, 1936.

Karlgren, Bernhard, "New Studies on Chinese Bronzes," BMFEA, 9, 1937.

Karlgren, Bernhard, "Huai and Han," BMFEA, 13, 1941.

Li Chi, Hsiao-t'un T'ao-ch'i, Taipei, Academia Sinica, 1956.

Loehr, Max, Chinese Bronze Age Weapons, Ann Arbor, University of Michigan Press, 1956.

Needham, Joseph, The Development of Iron and Steel Technology in China, London, Newcomen Society, 1958.

Oshima Riichi, "Chugaku kodai no shiro no tsuite," Tohogakuho, 30 (1959), 39–66.

"Shan-hsi-sheng Wen-kuan-hui Hou-ma kung-tsuo-chan kung-tsuo ti tsung shou-hu," KK 1959:5, 222–28.

Tsou Heng, "Shih lun Cheng-chou hsin fa-hsien ti Yin-Shang wen-hua yih-chih," KKHP, 1956:3, 77–103.

Wang Po-hung, Chung Shao-lin, and Chang Chang-shou, "1955–57 nien Shan-hsi Ch'ang-an Feng-hsi fa-chüeh chien pao," KK, 1959:10, 516–30.

Yu Chieh, "Chan-kuo shih-tai ti mu-tsang hsing-chih," KKTH, 1957:4, 93–101.

Ancient Cultures of the Northern Frontiers

KANSU AND CHINGHAI:

An Chih-min, "Ch'ing-hai ti ku-tai wen-hua," KK, 1959:7, 375–83.

An Chih-min, "Kan-su yüan-ku wen-hua chi ch'i yu-kuan ti chi-ko wen-t'i," KKTH, 1956:6, 9–19.

An Chih-min, "Lüeh chi Kan-su Tung-hsiang tzu-chih-hsien T'ang-wang-ch'uan ti t'ao-ch'i," KKHP, 1957:2, 23–31.

Andersson, J. G., "Preliminary Report on Archaeological Research in Kansu," GSuC, Memoirs, ser. A, 5, 1925.

Chang Hsüeh-Cheng, "Kan-su ku wen-hua yih-ts'un," KKHP, 1960:2, 11–52.

Wu Ju-tso, "Kan Ch'ing ti-chü yüan-shih wen-hua ti kai-mao chi ch'i hsiang-hu kuan hsi," KK, 1961:1, 12–19.

INNER MONGOLIA AND THE ORDOS:

An Chih-min, "Hsi-shih-ch'i wen-hua," KKTH, 1957:2, 36–48.

Andersson, J. G., "Selected Ordos Bronzes," BMFEA, 5 (1933), 143–54.

Egami Namio and Mizuno Seiichi, "Inner Mongolia and the Region of the Great Wall," Archaeologia Orientalis, ser. B, 1, 1935.

Loehr, Max, "Ordos Daggers and Knives," Artibus Asiae, 14 (1951), 77–162.

Maringer, John, *Contribution to the Prehistory of Mongolia*, Stockholm, 1950.

MANCHURIA:

Chang Kwang-chih, "Neolithic Cultures of the Sungari Valley, Manchuria," *SJA*, 17 (1961), 56–74.

Chu Kui, "Liao-ning Chao-yang Shih-erh-t'ai-ying-tzu ch'ing-t'ung-tuan-chien mu," *KKHP*, 1960:1, 63–70.

Tung Chu-chen, "Chi-lin hsin-shih-ch'i wen-hua ti san-chung lei-hsing," *KKHP*, 1957:3, 31–39.

Tung Chu-chen, "K'ao-ku-hsüeh shang Han-tai chi Han-tai yih-ch'ien ti Tung-pei chiang-yü," *KKHP*, 1956:1, 29–42.

South China Civilizations

SOUTHEAST COAST:

Tseng Chao-yü and Yin Huan-chang, "Shih lun Hu-shu wen-hua," *KKHP*, 1959:4, 47–56.

Yin Huan-chang, "Kuan-yü tung-nan ti-ch'ü Chi-ho-yin-wen-t'ao shih-tai ti ch'u-pu t'an-ts'e," *KKHP*, 1958:1, 75–85.

Yin Ti-fei, "An-hui T'un-hsi Hsi-Chou mu-tsang fa-chüeh pao-kao," *KKHP*, 1959:4, 59–88.

CH'U:

Hsia Nai, Chen Kung-jou, and Wang Chung-shu, *Ch'ang-sha fa-chüeh pao-kao*, Peiping, Science Press, 1957.

Wen Tao-yih, "Ch'ang-sha Ch'u mu," *KKHP*, 1959:1, 41–58.

SZECHWAN:

Cheng Te-kun, *Archaeological Studies in Szechwan*, Cambridge, Univ. Press, 1957.

Cheng Te-kun, "Ssu-ch'uan ku-tai wen-hua shih," *West China Union University Museum, Monograph Ser. No. 1*, 1946.

Feng Han-chi, Yang Yu-jun, and Wang Chia-yu, "Ssu-ch'uan ku-tai ti ch'uan-kuan tsang," *KKHP*, 1958:2, 77–95.

YUNNAN:

"Chin-ning Shih-chai-shan ch'u-t'u yu-kuan nu-li shê-hui ti wen-wu," *WW*, 1959:5, 59–61.

Wu, C. T., Tseng, C. Y., and Wang, C. C., *Yünnan Ts'ang Erh ching k'ao-ku pao-kao*, Lichuang, National Museum, 1942.

Yün-nan Chin-ning Shih-chai-shan ku mu ch'ün fa-chüeh pao-kao, Peiping, Wenwu Press, 1959.

Index

A-ti-ts'un, 99

agricultural implement: legendary invention of, 131; raw materials of, 195–96; Yangshao, 60; Lungshan, 93; Inner Mongolia, 114; Ch'u, 264. *See also* digging stick; hoe; stone sickle; plow; spade

agriculture: legends of, 130, 131–33; beginning in the Near East, 52; beginning in North China, 51–57; Yangshao, 59–60, 92; Lungshan, 92–93; spread from Nuclear Area, 110–29; beginning in South China, 50, 106–08; in Inner Mongolia, 115–16; Manchuria, 116–17; Kansu, 119; Southwest, 123, 126; of Shang, 172

Aksu, 118

Altai, 228, 230

Amano Motonosuke, 140, 174, 323

Amur (R.), 24, 127

An Chih-min, 320, 322, 324

An Chin-huai, 146, 150, 323

An-yang, 12, 14, 156, 172, 210, 250; importance in Chinese archaeology, 12, 130–31, 155–56, 164; as Shang capital, 135, 139, 143, 146, 166, 169; stratigraphy and cultural remains, 78, 89, 154–62, 164–65; ancient climate, 38; dates, 135–36; significance in the development of metallurgy and writing, 139–40

Anau, 128, 234

ancestor cult: in Neolithic, 56; Yangshao, 64–65; Lungshan, 65, 93, 95; Shang, 167, 169; Chou, 215, 221; Ch'u, 271

Andersson, J. G., 5, 6–8, 10, 45, 57, 64, 66, 69, 74–76, 99, 119, 122, 234–43 passim, 322, 324

Andronovo Culture, 228

Ang-ang-hsi, 11, 37, 117

Anhwei: Lungshan, 87, 93, 95, 106–09 passim, 246; Hushu Culture, 256; Shang, 12, 145, 164, 175, 249, 251; Western Chou, 211,

252–53, 260; Ts'ai, 258–59; Ch'u, 12, 261, 262

animal domestication: beginning in North China, 50, 51–57; Yangshao, 60; Proto-Lungshan, 80; Lungshan, 94; spread from Nuclear Area, 110–29 passim; in Inner Mongolia, 114, 233; Manchuria, 117; Kansu and Chinghai, 120, 121; Shang, 137, 173

animal herders, 227–28

animal sacrifice: Ch'i-chia Culture, 120; Shang, 143, 153, 169, 173; Chou, 186, 215

animal style of art: Shang, 173; steppe, 228, 231, 233; Szechwan, 285

antler implements: in Mesolithic, 41, 43; Yangshao, 66; Proto-Lungshan, 85; Lungshan, 92, 96; Microlithic cultures, 114

Anyathian, 46

Ao, 149, 153

Archaic (style of Shang and Chou art), 206, 207, 211, 212, 253

architecture: Shang, 143; Eastern Chou, 191

aridity, 36, 113

aristocracy: Shang, 143, 166–70

arrowhead (metal): Shang and Chou, 173, 214; steppe, 231; Ch'u, 266

arrowhead (stone): Mesolithic, 44, 45, 111; Yangshao, 60, 66; Lungshan, 96, 105; Microlithic, 111, 225; Southwest, 123; Shang, 173; prismatic, 45

art: Yangshao, 68, 93; Lungshan, 91, 93, 95; Shang, 144, 145, 173; Chou, 202–213; Yünnan, 292

Ashkabad, 128

australopithecines, 29

Baber, C. E., 11

Bacsonian, 129

Baikal (L.), 127

Balin, 115

bamboo tablets (for writing), 271
Barnard, Noel, 140, 323
basket patterns of pottery decoration:
in Neolithic North China, 55, 81,
102; Southwest, 124
battle-axe, 231
Beaten Pottery Culture. *See* Gray
Pottery Culture
belt hook, 185, 223, 266, 284
Bergman, Folke, 11
bird, 60, 105; legends of, 132, 167
Bishop, Carl, 75
Black, Davidson, 9, 321
Black Earth Horizon, 37
black pottery, 10–11, 78, 82–84, 91,
102–07 passim, 114, 116, 124
Black Pottery Culture, 10, 15, 51.
See also Lungshan Culture
Black Sea, 118
blade: in Middle Palaeolithic, 32;
Upper Palaeolithic, 32, 33, 46;
Mesolithic, 44; Microlithic, 111
bone industry: Palaeolithic, 28; Meso-
lithic, 39, 41–43; Yangshao, 66;
Proto-Lungshan, 85; Lungshan, 96;
Shang, 137, 152, 171 ff.; Eastern
Chou, 183, 185; Microlithic, 114,
117; in Northeast Asia, 129
Boule, M., 321
bow and arrow, 60
Braidwood, R. J., 17, 51, 54
Breuil, Henri, 28, 321
brick, 187, 188, 190, 191, 217, 218
Bronze Age: history of research, 12–
13, 16; climate during, 38; cultural
continuities from Neolithic, 137;
differences from Neolithic, 137;
Pre-Shang stage, 134; subdivisions
and sequence, 205–06; nature of
bronze artifacts, 195–96; in Kansu,
234
bronze inscriptions, 139, 176, 202,
205, 206, 210, 253
bronze metallurgy, 136, 137, 139–41,
151–52, 157, 159, 165, 171, 172,
185, 247, 256, 266, 281, 291
bronze-smith, 171
bronzes: studies of, 2, 3, 13; Shang,
144; Shang and Chou, 205 ff.; importance for Western Chou studies, 210; Ch'u, 266
brush (for writing), 268

burial: Mesolithic, 41, 42; Yangshao,
63, 64–66, 92; Lungshan, 92, 95,
105; Shang, 137, 143, 153, 157,
160, 161, 203; Chou, 187–89, 203,
214–19; Southern Manchuria, 225;
steppe, 232–33; Hsin-tien Culture,
237; Ssu-wa Culture, 241–42; Sha-
ching Culture, 243; Geometric,
257; Ts'ai, 258–59; Ch'u, 262–64;
Chia-ling-kiang, 279–81; Ch'eng-tu,
281–84; Li-fan, 284; Yünnan, 290
burial mound, 189, 217, 218, 223
burin, 33
Burma, 46

camel, 233
canoe, 257, 258, 279–81
Caspian Sea, 118, 128
cattle: in Neolithic North China, 55;
Yangshao, 60; Proto-Lungshan, 85;
Lungshan, 94, 103, 105; Shang,
137, 152, 153, 173; Eastern Chou,
186; Microlithic cultures, 114;
steppe, 228, 233; Ch'i-chia Culture, 120; Inner Mongolia, 231;
Yünnan, 291
cemetery: of Neolithic villages, 63–
65; of Shang, 160
Central Asia, 127
Central China: Lungshan expansion,
92. *See also* South China, and
names of constituent provinces
Central Plains. *See* Chung-yüan
ceramics, 50, 80–85 passim, 93. *See
also* pottery
ceremonial altar: Shang, 143, 151,
157
ceremonial vessels: Neolithic North
China, 55, 85, 90, 91, 93, 95;
Shang, 137, 144, 169; Chou, 202–
213 passim
Ch'an (R.), 62
Chan-kuo. *See* Warring-States Period
Chang Chang-shou, 324
Chang Cheng-hsiang, 323
Chang Hsüeh-cheng, 324
Chang Kwang-chih, 320–22, 325
Chang Wei-chih, 323
Chang-chia, 99
Chang-chia-p'o, 203
Chang-chia-tsui, 237, 243
Ch'ang-ch'un, 117

Ch'ang-hsing, 252, 253
Ch'ang-sha: Ch'u tombs, 12, 262–
  64; living sites, 261; chronology,
  273
Ch'ang-tê, 262, 274
Chao, 187–89
Chao Chüan-ku, 323
Chao-ko, 163
Chard, Chester S., 306
Cheboksarov, N. N., 321
checker impression on pottery, 101–
  09 passim, 116, 124, 148
Chekiang: Neolithic, 11, 87, 107,
  246; Western Chou, 252, 253;
  Geometric, 257
Chekiang Lungshan Culture, 107
Ch'en, 181
Chen Kung-jou, 325
Chen Meng-chia, 210, 221, 323
Cheng, 181
cheng, 206
ch'eng (term for city in Ch'u), 261
ch'eng (term for city in North
  China), 194
Cheng Te-kun, 18, 164, 165, 277,
  279, 285, 320, 323, 325
Cheng-chou, 145, 147, 171, 172,
  250; relations with Lungshan,
  141–42; pre-An-yang bronzes, 140;
  as a Shang city, 146–54, 165, 166,
  173, 193, 203; chronological sig-
  nificance, 164–65; Chou tombs,
  203
Ch'eng-tu, 276, 277
Ch'eng-tzu-yai, 10, 38, 77, 90, 94,
  97, 98, 108, 109
chi, 214, 266
Ch'i (ancestor of Chou), 177
Ch'i (ancester of Shang), 167
Ch'i (place in Shensi), 178
Ch'i (state under Chou), 181, 190,
  302
Chi Hsien (Honan), 12
Chi Hsien (Hopei), 37
Chi Tzu, 225
Chi Yen-pei, 12
Ch'i-chia Culture, 102, 119–21, 234,
  235
Ch'i-chia-p'ing, 74, 119
Ch'i-li-p'u, 96, 163, 165
Ch'i-lien (Mts.), 242
Ch'i-lin-shan, 47

chia: pottery, 83, 85–87, 91, 100,
  104; bronze, 205–07 passim
Chia (Mt.), 181
Chia Lan-po, 321, 322
Chia-ling-kiang (R.), 123, 279, 284
Ch'ia-yao, 234, 239–41
Chiang, 285
Chiang Tsuan-chu, 322
Chiang-yüan, 177
chicken: in Neolithic North China,
  55, 85; Shang, 137, 173; Yünnan,
  291
ch'ieh-ch'ü, 206, 212
Chien-ch'uan, 289
Chien-ti, 167
Ch'ien-shan-yang, 93
Ch'ien-t'ang-chiang (R.), 252
Chih-chiang, 260
Ch'ih-feng, 11, 230. See also Hung-
  shan-hou, Tung-pa-chia
Childe, V. G., 17
chin, 211
Chin, 181, 183, 186, 187
Chin Shih Hsüeh, 3
Ch'in Dynasty, 106, 135, 176, 187,
  223, 235, 299, 302–03
Chin-ch'eng, 113
Chin-sha-kiang (R.), 287
Chin-ts'un, 203
Ch'in-wei-chia, 120
China: geology, 25; geography, 21–
  25; earliest man, 26–28; continuous
  development of man and culture,
  30, 31, 33–34, 45–46; Mesolithic
  culture traditions, 50; first village
  farmers, 87; first civilization, 130
  ff.; early cultures: a summary, 299–
  305
Chinese archaeology: history of, 1–
  16, 155–56; importance in Old
  World archaeology, 303, 304, 306
Chinese civilization: prehistoric back-
  ground, 5, 93, 137–38; formative
  stages, 6; history of research, 1–16.
  See also Shang, Chou
Chinese Culture tradition: beginning
  in the Neolithic, 53, 55–56; continuation in Bronze Age, 142
Chinese Turkestan. See Sinkiang
Ching, 259
Ching (R.), 89, 98
Ch'ing-lien-kang, 107

Ch'ing-lien-kang Culture, 107

Ch'ing-shui erosion, 26, 32

Ch'ing-shui-ho, 40, 111

Ch'ing-t'ai, 89

Ching-ts'un, 59, 60, 79, 102

Ch'ing-yang, 6

Ch'ing-yang-kung, 281

Chinghai: Yangshao, 69; Tsaidam Culture, 118, 119, 121; Hsin-tien Culture, 238–39

Chiu Chung-lang, 322

Chiu-ch'üan, 119, 121

Ch'iu-wan, 249, 250

chopper and chopping-tool, 29, 32, 41, 46, 48–50. See also pebble tool

chopsticks, 55

Chou (name of Shang king), 135

Chou (dynasty/civilization): stratigraphic relation with Neolithic, 89; mythological origins, 177–78; before the Conquest, 177–80; conquest of Shang, 135, 175; historic records, 176; chronology, 176–77; territorial definition, 221–22; trends of cultural growth, 219–23. See also Western Chou, Eastern Chou, Spring-Autumn Period, Warring-States Period

Chou Ming-chen, 321

Chou Yung-chen, 323

Choukoutien, 6, 8–9, 27; localities 1, 5, and 13, 9, 29; Upper Cave, 9, 37, 40, 41–43

Choukoutienian, 15, 30, 32

Chou-lai, 258

chronology: Painted Pottery Culture by Andersson, 234; beginning of absolute dates, 135; Shang, 135–36; Chou, 176

Chu, 181

Ch'u, 255, 258, 259–75; origin, 259–61, 272, 274–75; expanse, 261–62; chronology, 273–74; characteristic features, 273; town sites, 181, 261; tombs, 12, 262–64; metallurgy, 261, 266; handicrafts, 266; subsistence, 264; pottery, 266, 268; social institutions, 271; religion, 271–72; language, 272; comparison with Yüeh, 274; comparison with Szechwan, 284

Chu Kui, 325

Ch'u Tz'u, 271

Ch'ü Yüan, 271

Chu-chia-chai, 58, 61, 70, 74

Chu-chou, 262

Ch'ü-chia-ling Culture, 105

Ch'ü-fu, 191

chüeh, 202, 205, 207, 212, 251

Chün Hsien, 12

Chün-wang-ch'i, 111

Ch'un-ch'iu. See Spring-Autumn Period

chung, 205, 207, 212. See also pien-chung

Chung Hsien, 124

Chung Shao-lin, 324

Chung-chou-lu, 203, 214

Chung-king, 11

Chung-wei, 27, 118

Chung-yüan, 69; subhorizon of Yangshao, 70–74, 76

Circum-Caribbean cultures, 294

cist-grave, 224, 225, 284

city: Shang, 146–64 passim, 165–66, 170, 180, 193; Western Chou, 181; Eastern Chou, 166, 180–95 passim, 223; history of development in North China, 180–95; Yen, 257; Ch'u, 261

city-wall, 150, 159–60, 180–90 passim, 191, 257

clactonian, 32

classes. See social stratification

climate: early Post-Glacial Period, 35–39; effects on Mesolithic cultures, 39, 50

coiled pottery: Neolithic North China, 56; Yangshao, 66, 81, 82; Lungshan, 81, 82, 100, 105; Hsin-tien Culture, 237, 240, 241; Ssu-wa Culture, 242

coinage, 185, 189, 271

collecting: in Yangshao, 60

combed pottery, 114, 120, 128, 240

communal house: Yangshao, 62, 64; Lungshan, 95

community patterns: Neolithic North China, 56; Yangshao, 62–64, 93; Lungshan, 93, 94–95, 137; Shang, 137, 143, 149–53, 157, 161, 165; Microlithic cultures, 115

composite tools, 39

continuity: from Palaeolithic to Neolithic, 30, 31; within Palaeolithic, 33–34; from Mesolithic to Neolithic, 45–46, 51, 52; from Mesolithic to Sub-Neolithic in Southwest, 50, 122; from Yangshao to Proto-Lungshan, 85; from Neolithic to Bronze Age, 136–37; from Shang to Western Chou, 180, 211, 220

copper: Ch'i-chia Culture, 120; Nomuhung Culture, 121; Hsintien Culture, 235, 238

cord-marked pottery: Neolithic North China, 55; as first ceramic horizon in North China, 56–57; as first ceramic horizon in South China, 57; in Yangshao and Lungshan, 81, 101–05; Shang, 137, 144, 148, 155; Ch'i-chia Culture, 120; Southwest, 122–24, 126

cord-mat-basket pottery patterns, 55, 104

core, 28, 32, 44, 49

cowry-shell, 144, 190, 237, 243, 291

cultural contact, 108, 120, 141, 220, 223, 228–29

cultures: definition in archaeology, 17–18

currency: Shang, 137, 144, 168; Eastern Chou, 194; Ch'u, 273

Darwin, Charles, 5

de Morgan, Jacques, 5

de Terra, Helmut, 9

"death pattern," 65

deer burial, 66

developmental classification, 17, 307

digging stick, 60, 172

Djalai-nor, 9, 36, 40, 43

dog, 55; Yangshao, 60; Proto-Lungshan, 85; Lungshan, 94, 105; Shang, 137, 153, 172; Chou, 215; steppe, 233

Dong Son, 294

Dongsonian Culture, 289, 290, 294–95, 306

Dye, D. S., 11

East-West cultural relations: in general, 18–19, 118–19, 128; beginning of agriculture, 52–53; painted pottery, 10, 75–76; beginning of civilization, 136 ff.; Kansu's role, 234

Eastern Chou, 177; archaeological studies during, 1–2; myths, 131; historical records, 176; urbanization, 16, 166, 180–95 passim; cultural development, 222–23; cultural groupings, 16, 255 ff.; relation with the northern frontier, 114, 116, 224–26 passim, 230–33 passim. *See also* Spring-Autumn Period, Warring-States Period

Eastern Manchurian Uplands, 23, 24

Eastern South China: history of archaeological research, 11–12; geography, 22–24; lack of Mesolithic evidence, 77; Lungshanoid, 87, 106–08; Geometric, 13, 124, 246–49; Shang and Western Chou, 249–55; Eastern Chou, 255 ff.

eave tile, 183, 188, 190

ecological adaptation of prehistoric cultures, 21, 26; Mesolithic, 39, 45, 50; Microlithic, 127; steppe nomads, 228; agriculture in Northeast Asia, 128; Lungshanoid in South China, 39, 45, 50

Edgar, J. H., 9, 11

Egami Namio, 324

end-scraper, 33

eneolithic: in Kansu, 234 ff.

Erh-hai (L.), 126, 288

Erh-lang-kang, 104

Erh-li-kang, 146, 148, 149–53, 155, 161, 164, 179, 203, 251

erh-ts'eng-t'ai, 215, 264, 290

Eskimo, 42

fabrics, 60, 94, 121

Fairservis, Walter A., Jr., 75

falcon (hunting), 233

Fan-chuang, 154

Fang-tui-ts'un, 203, 210, 214, 219

farmers: first farmers in the Huangho, 52; Yangshao, 57 ff.; Shang, 172–74; converted from hunter-fishers, 110; in the northern frontiers, 225, 229

fecundity cult, 95

Fen-shui-ling, 203

Feng, 181

Feng Han-chi, 325
Feng-chia-an, 163
Feng-chieh, 276
Feng-hao-ts'un, 89, 99
Feng-huang-t'ai (in Cheng-chou), 146
Feng-huang-t'ai (in Kwang-wu Hsien), 89
Fenho (R.), 54; Palaeolithic, 30, 32; Yangshao, 59; Lungshan, 102–03, 109; Western Chou, 177
Fenho Complex, 15
Fenho erosion, 25, 26
fertility cult, 66, 93
fertilizer: Lungshan, 92, 94; Shang, 172
Finn, D. J., 11
fire: use by Peking Man, 29; legend of invention, 130
Firth, Raymond, 169
fishing, 54, 61, 94, 105, 110, 122, 128, 173
flake: Palaeolithic, 28–33 passim; Mesolithic, 41, 44, 46–49; Micro-lithic, 111
flat-bottomed pottery, 117, 128, 225, 230
Fo-ting, 126
food-production: beginning in North China, 50, 51 ff.; spread from Nu-clear Area, 77
Formosa, 107. See also Taiwan
Formozov, A. A., 127
fortification, 92
Fried, Morton H., 169
fu: bronze vessel type, 205; another bronze vessel type, 205, 207
Fu Ssu-nien, 78, 221
Fu-nan, 251
Fu-niu (Mts.), 104
Fukien, 87, 246

Geometric Horizon, 246–49, 252, 254
Geometric Pottery Culture, 11, 13, 106, 108, 175. See also Geometric Horizon
Gigantopithecus blacki, 28, 29
Glacial stage. See Himalayas
glazed pottery, 144, 145, 266
"Gobi Culture," 128
"Golden Age," 3, 4, 8

Graham, D. C., 11, 276
gray pottery: Neolithic, 81–84, 91, 96, 98 ff.; Chou, 178
Gray Pottery Culture, 15, 99
Great Wall, 229, 233, 242, 246
Gulf of Tonkin, 294
Grunai, 40

Hai-feng, 107
Hai-wei-ho (R.), 289
Hainan (I.), 123
hairpin: Proto-Lungshan, 85; Shang, 149, 151, 155, 162
Hami, 118
Han, 187
Han Dynasty, 1–2, 106, 116, 117, 130, 150, 183, 184, 226, 299, 302
Han Fei Tzu, 1
Han-chia-tsui, 237
Han-ching-kou (R.), 124
Hanchiang (R.), 252
hand-and-heart pattern, 281
hand-axe, 30, 46, 48
hang-t'u, 191; Neolithic North China, 10, 55; Lungshan, 78, 92; Shang, 137, 143, 150, 152, 157, 164; Chou, 181 ff., 191
Hangchow Bay, 98
Hanshui (R.), 123; Lungshan, 94, 104–06, 109; Shang, 142, 249, 251; probable origins of Ch'u, 360
Hantan: Lungshan, 94; Eastern Chou, 187–88
Hao, 177, 181
Harbin, 43, 117
Hê-hsü, 2
Heanley, C. M., 11
Hei-ching-lung, 48
Hei-liu-t'u-ho (R.), 111
Heilungchiang, 37
Heine-Geldern, Robert [von], 139, 295
helmet, 231
Hemanthropus peii, 28
hemp: Neolithic North China, 55; Yangshao, 60; Ch'i-chia Culture, 120; Shang, 173; Ch'u, 266
Heng-chen-ts'un, 58, 79, 85
Heng-yang, 262
herbalist: role in invention of agri-culture, 132–33

Higuchi, T., 323
Himalayas: glacial sequence, 9, 25, 26, 32, 33, 35
Hipparion fauna, 25
history: beginning in North China, 130–33
ho, 100, 213
Ho-hsi Corridor, 242
Ho-pao-hsi, 125
Ho-yin Hsien, 7
Hoabinhian, 46, 49, 50, 77, 129
hoe: stone, 60, 66, 93, 96, 103, 105, 113–15, 124, 137, 172; iron, 197, 264
Holocene, 35–39 passim, 43. *See also* Post-Glacial Period, Recent
Homo sapiens, 32, 41, 48
Honan, 54, 87, 89, 94, 95, 103, 106, 107, 109; Neolithic in Northern Honan, 59, 60, 69, 87, 97, 98, 103–04; early stratigraphy in N. Honan, 78; Neolithic in Western Honan, 5, 8, 10, 15, 59, 61, 63, 66, 69, 76; Neolithic in Southern Honan, 104, 106, 107; Shang, 16, 130, 140, 141, 142, 145, 146, 154, 163, 164, 203, 213; Chou, 12, 197, 202, 203, 212, 213, 217; Ch'u, 260
Hong Kong, 11, 47, 48, 123
Hooton, E. A., 42
Hopei: Palaeolithic, 26; Mesolithic, 40; Neolithic, 69, 87, 94; Shang, 16, 145, 162, 163; Eastern Chou, 187, 188, 226; northern cultures, 111, 227; ancient peats, 37
horizon: definition, 246. *See also* pottery horizon, horizon-style
horizon-style: Yangshao, 68; Lungshan, 91; Shang, 143–45; Geometric, 246–47
horse: in Neolithic North China, 55; Lungshan, 94, 103, 138–39; Shang, 137, 138–39, 173; Chou, 186, 215, 223; Microlithic, 114; steppe, 228, 232–33; Southwest, 124, 291
horse-and-chariot fittings: Shang, 144; Ch'u, 266; Szechwan, 284
horse-chariot: legends of, 133; Shang, 137, 139, 144, 168; Chou, 215
horse-riding, 139, 223, 227 ff.
Hou-chi, 177

Hou-chia-chuang, 160, 203, 213. *See also* Hsi-pei-kang
Hou-chia-chuang-nan-ti, 154, 160
Hou-kang, 10, 11, 58, 61, 78, 89, 94, 154, 160, 161
Hou-ma. *See* Hsin-t'ien
house: Yangshao, 62–64; Proto-Lungshan, 80; Lungshan, 95, 100, 101, 105; Shang, 137, 143, 149–61 passim, 171; Eastern Chou, 183, 185; Microlithic, 115
Hsi-ch'a-kou, 232
Hsi-ch'eng-chuang, 146
Hsi-chiao-shan, 47, 48, 122
Hsi-ch'uan, 260
Hsi-han-shui (R.), 120
Hsi-hou-tu, 28
Hsi-liao (R.), 113
Hsi-ning-ho (R.), 75. *See also* Huang-shui
Hsi-pei-kang, 154, 160, 203, 210, 218, 219. *See also* Hou-chia-chuang
Hsi-yin-ts'un, 11, 58, 60, 102
Hsia: Western Hsia as ethnic division, 10, 78, 221
Hsia dynasty, 9, 15, 130, 131, 134, 205
Hsia Nai, 12, 14, 241, 320, 325
Hsia-hsi-ho, 239, 240
Hsia-tu, 12, 189–90
Hsiang-hsiang, 262
Hsiang-jih-tê, 121
Hsiang-t'an, 262
Hsiang-yin, 261
Hsiao, 149
Hsiao-chuang, 154
Hsiao-hung-shan, 249
Hsiao-ssu-k'ung-ts'un, 154
Hsiao-t'un, 12, 99, 151, 154, 157–60, 164, 169, 172, 173, 179, 203, 213, 251
Hsiao-t'un Stone Knife, 251
hsien, 55, 97, 102, 155. *See also* yen
Hsin-cheng, 6, 203
Hsin-tien, 69
Hsin-tien Culture (Tradition), 122, 235–41; dates, 234–35; Phase A, 237; Phase B, 237–38; Tang-wang Phase, 238–39; Ch'ia-yao Phase, 239–41
Hsin-t'ien, 183 ff.

Hsin-ts'un, 203, 213, 218
Hsin-yang: Lungshan, 107; Ch'u, 262, 264, 269, 274
Hsing-lung, 230
Hsing-t'ai, 145, 146, 162–63, 172
Hsiung Ch'ü, 272
Hsiung T'ung, 260
Hsiung Yih, 260
Hsiung-nu, 224
hsü, 205–07
Hsü Ping-chang, 8
Hsü Shun-chen, 322
Hsü-chou, 249
Hsüan-yüan, 2
Hsüeh, 191
Hsüeh-chia-chuang, 154, 160, 161
hu, 205
Hu, 224
Hu Hou-hsüan, 323
Hu-hsi, 99
Hu-shu Culture, 256
Hua Chüeh-ming, 323
Hua Hsien: Yangshao sites, 63
Hua-chia-ssu, 249
Hua-t'ing-ts'un, 107
Huai style, 206–08, 213, 258, 259
Huaiho (Huai R.), 22, 23, 46, 77, 98, 106, 108, 145, 175, 205, 249, 261, 274
Huan (R.), 154
Huang Chan-yüeh, 195, 323
Huang-lou, 249
Huang-niang-t'ai, 120
Huang-p'i, 251, 260
Huangho (R.): geology, 25; geography, 21–23; beginning of Neolithic, 51 ff., 54; development of Neolithic cultures, 51–52; Yangshao remains, 59; Lungshan remains, 87; cultural influence on the North, 117, 127
Huangshui (R.), 70, 74, 119, 236, 238, 239, 241. See also Hsi-ning-ho
Huang-ti, 2, 131, 133
Hui Hsien (Huei Hsien, Hwei Hsien), 12, 145, 163, 203
Hui-tsui (in Honan), 89
Hui-tsui (in Kansu), 237
human figurine, 68, 268
human remains: Palaeolithic, 28–32; Mesolithic, 41–42, 48; Neolithic North China, 52; Shang, 152, 173;

Neolithic in Szechwan, 124; in Southeast Asia, 129
human sacrifice, 136, 137, 143, 153, 155, 157, 159, 161, 169, 173, 178, 187, 215, 259, 292
Hunan: Shang influence, 145, 249; Geometric, 247; Ch'u, 12, 261, 262
Hung-shan-hou, 114, 226, 231
Hung-tzê (L.), 24
hunting: Yangshao, 60; Lungshan, 94; Shang, 173; Southwest, 122; Manchuria, 225
Hupei, 113; geography, 22; Palaeolithic, 26; Neolithic, 87, 104, 105, 113, 123, 246; Shang, 142, 249, 251

Ikhen-kung, 40
Indochina, 46, 122, 129
Indus Valley, 166
Inner Mongolia, 24, 40, 111–13, 227, 229, 231
Institute of Archaeology, 14, 44, 79, 99
Institute of History and Philology, 8, 12, 14, 78, 154
Institute of Vertebrate Palaeontology and Palaeoanthropology, 14
Interglacial stage, 26, 32. See also Himalayas
Iran, 128
iron implements: Eastern Chou, 195–98; Ch'u, 266; Szechwan, 284; Yünnan, 290, 291
iron metallurgy: Eastern Chou, 195–98; northern frontier, 230
Irrawaddy (R.), 46, 122
irrigation: Lungshan, 92, 94; Shang, 172; Eastern Chou, 195, 202; Yüeh and Ch'u, 265; Yünnan, 289

jade: Neolithic North China, 55; Yangshao, 66; Lungshan, 93; Shang, 137, 144, 151; Ch'u, 266; Szechwan, 284
Jao Tsung-yih, 252
Japan, 226, 294, 306
Jehol, 23, 24, 37, 113, 211, 230
Jeitun Culture, 128
Jeitun-Tepe, 128
Jen-min Park, 148, 153, 154

Jettmar, Karl, 228
Jih-chao, 97
Jung, 224
Jung Keng, 323

K'ai-jui-chuang, 89, 99, 100, 178
K'ai-jui-chuang Culture, 99–100
Kan-ku Hsien, 72
Kan-tzu, 284, 285
Kang-shang-ts'un, 107
Kansu, 5, 6, 7, 11; Yangshao, 59,
   64–66, 69–76; Post-Yangshao Neo-
   lithic, 118 ff.; Eneolithic, 234 ff.
Kao, 167
Kao Chü-hsün, 12, 323
Kao Ming, 324
Kao-ching-t'ai-tzu, 89, 154
Kao-huang-miao, 249
Kao-li-chai, 225
Kao-tu, 113
Kao-tui, 60, 89, 102
K'ao-ku-t'u, 3
kaoliang, 55, 59, 137
Karasuk Culture, 228, 230
Karlgren, Bernhard, 13, 205–13 pas-
   sim, 221, 235, 253, 324
Kelteminar Culture, 127, 128
kettle-drum, 266, 292, 294
Khazakstan, 128
Khingan (Mts.), 23, 24, 127
Kiangsi: geography, 24; Lungshan,
   246; Shang influence, 145
Kiangsu: Lungshan, 87, 93, 95, 107,
   109, 246; Geometric, 247; Shang
   influence, 175, 249, 250, 252;
   Western Chou, 222, 252–54; Hu-
   shu Culture, 256; Yen, 257; Ch'u
   influence, 262
Kiangsu Lungshan Culture, 107
kinship: Neolithic, 56, 65; Shang,
   168, 169; ties with industry, 170–
   71; ties with political status, 169;
   Chou, 221
Kirin, 117, 226
kitchen-middens, 126
ko halberd: Shang, 137, 213–14;
   steppe, 231; Hupei, 251; Szechwan,
   283
Ko-ta-ts'un, 102
Ko-ta-wang, 141, 148, 149
K'o-hsing-chuang, 99, 101
K'o-shih-k'o-t'eng, 115

Korea, 127, 128, 226
ku, 205, 207, 212
Ku Hsieh-kang, 4, 130
Ku-hsiang-t'un, 9, 40, 43
Ku-lang Hsien, 242
Ku-t'u-tun, 249
Ku-wei-ts'un, 197, 216
K'uai (R.), 186
kuang, 207
Kuang-shê, 103
kui (*kuei, kwei*; bronze vessel type),
   205, 207, 211, 252, 253
kui (*kuei, kwei*; pottery tripod type),
   78, 83, 85, 91, 97, 100, 104, 106,
   109
Kui-chou, 124
Kui-tê, 70, 74
Kung-kung, 130
kuo (aristocratic quarters of town),
   193
kuo (city-wall, especially outer wall),
   194
Kuo Mo-jo, 13, 203–10 passim, 271,
   321
Kuo Pao-chün, 8, 218
Kwang-han, 12
Kwang-wu, 60, 89
Kwangsi: Mesolithic, 9, 46, 47; Sub-
   Neolithic and Neolithic, 122, 123
Kwangtung: Palaeolithic, 30; Mesolithic, 46–48 passim; Sub-Neolithic
   and Neolithic, 123; Lungshan, 87,
   107, 246; Geometric, 247; Shang
   influence, 252
Kweichou, 122, 123

lacquer, 266, 268, 292
Lanchow, 72–74, 234
Lao-ha (R.), 113, 231
Lao-ho-shan, 107
Lao-lao-t'ai, 189
Lao-t'ieh-shan, 225
Laufer, Berthold, 5
lead, 266
legend: North China, 130 ff.; Ch'u,
   259
lei (agricultural implement), 131
lei (vessel type): Shang, 144; Chou,
   213; Geometric, 250
Lei-yang, 262
Lena (R.), 127
Levalloisian flake, 30

li tripod: as horizon marker, 8; North China Neolithic, 55, 83, 85, 91–109 passim; Shang, 148, 155; Inner Mongolia, 111, 115, 116; Northwest, 128; Hsin-tien Culture, 238; Ssu-wa Culture, 241; Sha-ching Culture, 243; Szechwan, 124; Geometric, 249, 250; of bronze, 205–06

Li Chi, 4, 8, 9, 12, 19, 160, 173, 203, 213, 214, 251, 321, 322, 324

Li Ching-tan, 12

Li Hsüeh-chin, 167

Li Ping, 202

Li-fan, 284–85

Li-ling, 262

li-ting, 207

Li-ts'un, 203, 210

Li-yü-ts'un, 6, 203

Liang Ssu-yung, 8, 78, 97, 98, 104, 321, 322

Liang-ch'eng-chen, 90, 108, 109

Liang-chu, 107

Liang-chu Culture, 107

Liang-ts'un, 66

Liang-wang-ch'eng, 249, 250

Liaoho (R.), 24, 25, 113 ff., 224–26

Liaoning: Black Earth Horizon, 37; Neolithic, 5, 87, 95; nomads, 226, 232

Liaotung Peninsula, 94, 116, 175, 225

Licent, Emile, 6, 26, 321

Lin-hsi, 11, 37, 115

Lin-shan-chai: Yangshao, 58, 64, 65, 146; Lungshan, 79, 146

Lin-t'ao, 235, 238, 241

Lin-tzu, 190

Ling-yüan Hsien, 230

Liu Chang-shan, 234

Liu En-chu, 323

Liu Tun-yüan, 322

Liu Yao, 322. *See also* Yin Ta

Liu-chiang, 27, 32, 33, 43

Liu-ch'üan, 102

Liu-chuang, 89

Liu-hu-t'un, 242

Liu-li-ko, 203, 213

Liu-tzu-chen, 38, 58, 59, 64, 65, 71, 80, 89, 100

Lo, 261

Lo (R.), 181

Lo-han-t'ang, 58, 60, 61, 66, 70, 74

Lo-ning Hsien, 61, 89, 94

Lo-ta-miao, 141, 148, 149, 155

Lo-tu, 235, 238

Lo-yang: Shang, 145, 163; Eastern Chou, 177, 181, 183

Loehr, Max, 139, 324

loess, 26, 32, 37

Loessic stage, 26, 32, 33, 35, 37

Lu, 181

Lü Ta-lin, 3

Lu-shan, 281

Lu-t'ai, 89

Lu-wang-fen, 163

Luan-p'ing, 243

Lung T'ai, 188

Lung-hsi Hsien, 72

Lung-ma, 99

Lung-tung, 30

Lungshan Culture, 10, 11, 51, 77; characteristics, 10; distribution, 78; subdivisions, 97; relations with the Yangshao Culture, 10, 11; relations with the Shang, 10. *See also* Lungshan Horizon, Lungshan stage

Lungshan Horizon, 89, 91

Lungshan stage, 58, 78, 89; characteristic features, 10, 91–93; stratigraphic position, 89; chronology, 109–10; distribution, 87; eastward and southward expansion, 59, 77, 87, 89, 106, 129, 246; regional traditions, 15, 88, 92, 97 ff., 141; compared with Yangshao, 92–93; relations with Yangshao, 10, 11, 55, 77 ff.; relations with Hsia dynasty, 134–35; relations with Shang, 10, 135 ff.; Proto-Lungshan Complex, *see* Proto-Lungshan Complex; settlement patterns, 92, 94, 100; agriculture, 92, 93; rice in South China, 59, 93, 105, 107, 108; animal domestication, 85, 94, 105; hunting-fishing, 94; industry, 85, 92, 95–96; pottery, 80–85, 91–109 passim; pottery kiln, 80; metal, 91, 96, 108; house, 80, 95, 100, 103, 104; community patterns, 94–95; social features, 95; war, 94; art, 95; religion, 90, 91, 93, 95; burial, 95, 105

Lungshanoid, 87

Ma-ch'ang (stage), 70, 234
Ma-ch'ang-yen, 58, 70–72, 74
Ma-chia-yao, 38, 58, 61, 69, 71–74
Ma-lang-ch'uan-shan, 48
Ma-lung, 126, 289
Ma-pa, 27, 30
Ma-yü-kou, 72
Maglioni, R., 11
Malan Loess, 35, 36. *See also* loess, Loessic stage
Malaysia, 129
Manchuria, 5, 9, 11, 77, 112, 127, 224; geography, 21, 23, 24; early climate, 37; Mesolithic, 40, 41, 43–45; Lungshan, 92; Neolithic and Sub-Neolithic in southern Manchuria, 113 ff.; in central Manchuria, 116 ff.; cist-grave builders, 225 ff.; Han dynasty, 226
marine shell, 42
Maringer, John, 325
Maritime Province, Siberia, 128
market: in legend, 131; Eastern Chou, 190, 193, 194, 195; Tien, 291
mat patterns of pottery decoration, 55
megalith, 278
Mekong (R.), 122, 287
Melanesoid, 42. *See also* Oceanic Negroid
Menam (R.), 122
Mesolithic, 9, 13; natural environment, 35, 45; subdivisions, 45, 50; North China, Manchuria, and Mongolia, 39 ff., 54, 111; South China, 46 ff., 122, 126; survivals in Neolithic stage, 45, 52, 77; introduction of Neolithic technology, 77, 126
Mesopotamia, 139, 166
metal implements and metallurgy: legend of beginnings, 133; in North China Neolithic, 51, 91, 108, 109, 120, 134, 137; pre-An-yang stage in Cheng-chou, 139–41; northern frontiers, 226
Mexico, 166
Mi-chia-yai, 100
Miao-ti-kou, 58, 89; Miao-ti-kou I, 8, 61, 63, 64, 67, 76; Miao-ti-kou II, 8, 15, 80, 86; distribution of type II sites, 79–80; ceramic

change from type I to type II, 80–87
micro-blade, 33, 39, 40, 45, 50, 111
micro-core, 33, 40
micro-flake, 33, 40
microlith, 43, 44, 113–16, 128
Microlithic cultures and industries, 11, 13; influence from North China, 11, 113–14; occurrence in North China, 44; absence in South China, 46; in northern frontier, 113, 114, 116, 225, 231; Sinkiang, 118, 119, 127
Middle Chou style, 206–08, 211–13, 222, 253
millet, 24; in Neolithic North China, 55; Yangshao, 59; Lungshan, 93, 107, 137; Shang, 137, 172; legends of, 132; Manchuria, 117; Ch'i-chia Culture, 120; Yünnan, 289
min, 252
Min (R.), 276, 279
Min-ch'in Hsien, 242
Min-lo, 121
Ming-kung-lu, 152
Ming-yü, 99
Minusinsk Basin, 228, 230
Mizuno Seiichi, 321, 324
Mohenjo Daro, 166
Mongolia, 7, 11, 23, 25, 36, 77, 127; Mesolithic, 40, 41, 44, 45; Sub-Neolithic and Neolithic, 113 ff. *See also* Outer Mongolia, Inner Mongolia
Mongoloid race, 30, 33, 42–52 passim
mound-dwelling: Lungshan, 107; Geometric, 247, 256
mounted nomads, 227 ff.
"Mousterian" flake, 33, 44, 46, 111
Movius, Hallam L., Jr., 9, 25, 26, 321
Mu-yang-ch'eng, 225
Mutankiang (R.), 117
mythology: basis in Neolithic, 56; in ancient China, 130 ff.; Shang origins, 167; Chou origins, 177

Nan-chang Hsien, 259
Nan-kuan-wai, 141, 148, 151, 153
Nan-pa-t'ai, 154
Nan-ta-kuo-ts'un, 162
Nanking, 252, 253
neanderthaloid, 30, 32, 33

Near East: developmental classification, 17; first farmers, 52; suggested origin of first Chinese farmers, 53; suggested origin of Yangshao Culture, 7; routes of cultural contacts, 118; first civilizations, 136

Needham, Joseph, 324

needle-case, 117, 129

Negroid. *See* Oceanic Negroid

Nelson, N. C., 11

Neolithic: definition, 51; history of research, 9–11, 15–16; natural environment, 36, 38; theory of Two or Three Cultures, 13, 15, 51, 78–79; theory of sequential development, 51–52, 79, 91; as a tradition in North China, 55; stratigraphy, 78, 89; beginning in North China, 50, 51 ff.; continuities from Mesolithic, 45; pre-Yangshao stage, 54, 56–57; first ceramic horizon in North China, 56–57; Yangshao stage, 57–68; ceramic changes from Yangshao to Lungshan, 82, 85; Lungshan stage, 108 ff.; as basis for civilization, 93, 135 ff.; continuities into Bronze Age, 137; diffusion from Nuclear Area, 77; South China, 50; Southwest, 122 ff.; Manchuria, 113 ff.; Northeast Asia, 128; Sinkiang, 119

neolithic technology: diffusion of, 110–29 passim

New World: developmental classifications, 17

Nihowan, 26, 28

Ninghsia, 33, 118

Niu-chai, 146

Niu-ts'un, 184 ff.

No-mu-hung, 121

nomads, 113, 114, 121, 223, 224, 227 ff.

Nomuhung Culture (Phase), 119, 121–22

Nonni (R.), 117

North China: geography, 21, 22; early climate, 21, 22, 35 ff.; first Mongoloid occupation, 43; Mesolithic, 39 ff.; Nuclear Area, 50, 53, 54–55; beginning of food production, 51 ff.; Neolithic cultures and development, 51–52, 77–78; civi-

lizations, 130–223 passim; stratigraphy of early cultures, 78, 80, 89

North China Nuclear Area, 50, 53, 54–55. *See also* Nuclear Area: North China

Northeast Asia, 127, 128

Northwest, 118 ff., 127. *See also* names of constituent provinces

Nü-wa (Nü-kua), 130

Nuclear Area: North China, 50, 53, 54–55, 58, 59, 64, 75, 76, 79, 87, 89, 92, 93, 94, 106, 108, 119, 123, 142, 246; Iraq-Iran, 128

Oceania, 129

Oceanic Negroid, 33, 43, 46, 50, 129

Okhotsk (Sea), 127

Okladnikov, A. P., 306

oracle bone: Lungshan, 6, 91, 100, 136; Shang, 135–37, 144, 153, 155, 159, 160, 167; Ch'i-chia Culture, 120

Ordos, 6, 9, 111; Palaeolithic, 32, 33; Eastern Chou, 208, 214, 223; Ordos bronzes, 231

Ordos Tooth, 31

Ordosian, 15, 45, 118

Oshima Riichi, 181, 324

ostrich egg shell ring, 41, 45

Outer Mongolia, 40. *See also* Mongolia

Pa, 286, 287, 298

Pa-lung, 121

Pacific coast of Northeast Asia, 117, 127, 128, 226

Pacific seaboard, 77, 106 ff.

paddle-and-anvil: technique of pottery manufacture, 56, 82, 96, 97, 101, 109

Pai-chia-chuang, 148, 153

Pai-ma-ssu, 281

Pai-sha, 203, 217

Pai-tao-kou-p'ing, 66

Pai-t'ing-ho (R.), 242

Paiho (R.), 104

painted pottery, 5, 9; Yangshao, 57, 68, 81, 82, 99, 102; Proto-Lungshan and Lungshan, 81, 82, 85, 91, 95, 105, 106, 109; Inner Mongolia, 111, 114; Sinkiang, 118, 119; Ch'i-chia Culture, 120; Ssu-pa Culture,

121; Hsin-tien Culture, 237–41 passim; Ssu-wa Culture, 242; Southwest, 124, 125; Ch'u, 266
Painted Pottery Culture: Neolithic, 5, 9, 10, 11, 15, 51; Eneolithic, 234 ff. *See also* Yangshao Culture
palace: in legend, 133; Shang, 159, 160; Eastern Chou, 185, 190
Palaeolithic: first discovery in China, 5; history of research, 8–9, 13, 15; cultural remains, 26–33 passim; as foundation for civilizational beginnings, 18, 34, 45; in Ninghsia, 118; survivals in Northwest, 128
pan, 205, 207, 209, 258
Pan-ch'iao Erosion, 33, 36
Pan-p'o-ts'un, 8, 58, 65, 66; remains of millet, 59; settlement patterns, 61; village layout, 62–63; type site of substage, 76; Eastern Chou burials, 203, 217
Pan-shan, 58, 64, 70–74, 234
P'an-keng, 135, 160, 161
P'an-ku, 130
P'an-nan-ts'un, 58, 79
Pao-chi: Pre-Yangshao Neolithic, 54, 57, 58; Yangshao, 63, 64; Western Chou, 178, 203
Pao-lun-yüan, 279
Pao-shen-miao, 226
Pao-t'ou, 111
Paranthropus, 28
peacock: ceremonial significance, 292
Pearl (R.), 22, 47, 48, 122
pebble tool, 29, 32, 46, 49, 129. *See also* chopper and chopping-tool
pedestal: of pottery, 84; with cut-out patterns, 81, 106. *See also* ring-footed pottery
P'ei (R.), 276
Pei Wen-chung, 6, 8, 9, 29, 41, 42, 321, 322
Pei-ch'iu, 107
Pei-kao-ts'un, 102
Pei-yin-yang-ying, 107, 248, 256
Peiping, 38
Peking Man, 29, 30, 32. *See also* Sinanthropus pekinensis
P'eng-shan, 281
phallus: stone models, 121
Phillips, Philip, 17
pi, 193

Pi-sha-kang, 203, 217
Pi-tzu-wo, 11
Pien-chia-kou, 64
pien-chung, 206
Pien-tui-shan, 277
P'ien-kuan, 40, 111
pig: Neolithic North China, 55; Yangshao, 60; Proto-Lungshan, 85; Lungshan, 94, 103, 105; Shang, 137, 148, 152, 153, 173; Microlithic, 114; Manchuria, 117; northern frontier, 225; Ch'i-chia Culture, 120; Szechwan, 124; Yünnan, 291
pile-dwelling: Geometric, 247; Yünnan, 289, 291
Pin Hsien (Hunan), 262
Pin Hsien (Shensi), 99
P'ing Wang, 177
P'ing-wang, 183, 184
pithecanthropoid, 30
Pithecanthropus: as a group, 28; Java, 9; Peking. *See* Peking Man, *Sinanthropus*
plant cultivation: legendary beginnings, 131–32; beginning in North China, 50, 51 ff.; Yangshao, 59–60. *See also* agriculture
platform, 180, 184, 188, 190–92, 277
Pleistocene: prehistoric research, 8, 9, 15; geology and palaeontology, 25–26, 35 ff., 46; human and cultural remains, 26–33, 46; cultural traditions, 39
Pliocene, 25, 36
Pliocene-Pleistocene boundary, 25
plow: Shang, 172; Eastern Chou, 197–98; Geometric, 257; Yünnan, 290–91
p'o: Lungshan, 91; Shang, 144, 155; Geometric, 252
Po-yang (L.), 24
Pohai Bay, 111, 113, 224; Lungshan, 87, 106, 108, 109; cist-grave builders, 225 ff.
point: Palaeolithic, 32, 33; Mesolithic, 43, 44, 111. *See also* projectile point
pointed-bottomed pottery, 56; Yangshao, 68; Lungshan, 85, 102, 105
polished stone implement: Sub-Neolithic, 50; Neolithic, 51

Pontian flora, 25

population: Yangshao, 92; Lungshan, 92; Shang, 153, 166; Eastern Chou, 190, 194

Post-Glacial Period: climatic change, 35–39; hunting-fishing cultures of North China, 39–46; of South China, 46–49

Post-Neolithic, 50. See also Bronze Age, Shang, Chou

Post-Pleistocene, 33, 35 ff., 43, 44. See also Post-Glacial Period, Recent

potter: Shang, 171

pottery: legend of invention, 131; Neolithic North China, 51, 55; first horizon, 56; Yangshao, 66–68, 92; changes from Yangshao to Lungshan, 80 ff.; Lungshan, 85, 91, 92, 95–96, 97–108 passim; Shang, 136, 137, 144–45, 148–55 passim; Western Chou, 178; various types in steppe region, 127; Inner Mongolia, 111, 114; Manchuria, 117; Sinkiang, 118–19; Ch'i-chia Culture, 120; Shan-tan Culture, 121; Nomuhung Culture, 121; Hsin-tien Culture, 235–41 passim; Ssu-wa Culture, 241, 242; Sha-ching Culture, 242, 243; South China Sub-Neolithic, 48; Geometric, 247 ff., 256; Yen, 257–58; Ch'u, 266; Southwest, 122–25 passim, 129

pottery horizon: corded ware, 57; changes from Yangshao to Lungshan, 79 ff. See also horizon

pottery kiln: location in Neolithic village, 56; Yangshao, 63; Proto-Lungshan, 80; Lungshan, 100, 105; Shang, 149, 152, 159, 162; Eastern Chou, 183, 185, 189

pottery tradition: corded ware, 56, 57; in Yangshao, 69; changes from Yangshao to Lungshan, 82, 85; Geometric, 247

poultry: Lungshan, 94, 105. See also chicken

pounded earth. See hang-t'u

Pre-Yangshao Neolithic, 56–57

pressure-flaking, 39, 44, 45

priest: Shang, 169

primary village-farming efficiency:

North China, 51, 59, 91–93, 106, 133

projectile point, 39, 45

prone burial, 95, 137

Proto-Lungshan Complex, 79 ff., 86, 87, 102, 103, 105, 106, 109; stratigraphic position of, 80

proto-neolith, 122

P'u-tu-ts'un, 203, 210–12, 218

races: Palaeolithic, 33; Mesolithic, 46

Recent, 36 ff., 129. See also Post-Glacial Period, Post-Pleistocene

rectangular stone knife, 45, 55, 60, 66, 92

Red Basin. See Szechwan

Reddish Clay, 25, 26, 28–30, 32

religion: Yangshao, 65; Lungshan, 95; Shang, 169; Ch'i-chia Culture, 120; Ch'u, 271; Yünnan, 292

rice: North China Neolithic, 38, 55, 59; Lungshan, 93, 105, 107, 108, 137; Shang, 137; Geometric, 247; Ch'u, 264; Southwest, 126; Yünnan, 289

ring-footed pottery, 56, 91, 96, 98, 101, 104, 105, 126. See also pedestal

road: Eastern Chou and Han, 184, 189, 194

rocker-stamping, 114

Russian Turkestan, 127

Sahlins, Marshall, 169

San Huang (Three Sovereigns), 130

San-li-ch'iao, 80 ff.

Sangkan (R.), 26

Sanho, 37, 38

Sauer, Carl, 54

scapulimancy, 10; North China Neolithic, 55; Lungshan, 78, 91, 95, 100, 102, 103; Shang, 137, 144. See also oracle bone, turtle shell

Schofield, W., 12

scraper: Palaeolithic, 28, 32; Mesolithic, 41, 43, 44, 46, 111; Microlithic, 111

Scythian, 228

sea-mammal hunting, 128

Sekino Takeshi, 190, 197, 321

Selenga (R.), 127

semilunar stone knife, 45, 55, 60, 85, 137
semisubterranean dwelling, 45, 62, 80, 95, 100, 137, 152, 159, 185
settlement patterns: Yangshao, 61–62, 92; Lungshan, 92, 94, 101; Shang, 136; steppe, 228
Sha-ching Culture (Tradition), 122, 234, 242 ff.
Sha-ching-ts'un, 242
Sha-kang, 37
Sha-kuo-t'un, 5, 11, 116
Sha-yüan, 40, 43 ff., 54, 111
Shabarakh-usu, 40
Shan Hsien: Neolithic, *see* Miao-ti-kou, San-li-ch'iao; Shang, 145, *see also* Ch'i-li-p'u; Chou, *see* Shang-ts'un-ling
Shan-piao-chen, 203, 209, 213
Shan-shen, 238
Shan-tan, 121
Shan-tan Culture (Phase), 119, 121
Shang (Dynasty/civilization), 10, 13, 99, 108, 130, 133; definition, 142–45; expanse, 145, 163–64, 175; stratigraphy, 78, 89; history of development, 164 ff.; subdivisions, 164–65; origins, 51, 135 ff.; sphere of influence, 175; influence to the north, 225, 229–30; to the south, 249–52; to Szechwan, 276; written records, 6, 137, 176; city, 146–64 passim, 166, 181, 191; An-yang, 12, 130, 154 ff.; Cheng-chou, 16, 146 ff., 193; other sites, 16, 162–64; urbanism, 137, 165–66; agriculture, 137, 172; animal domestication, 137, 173; hunting and fishing, 173; stone, bone, shell industries, 137, 144; jade, 137, 144, 151; silk, 137; handicrafts, 137, 152, 159, 170 ff.; pottery, 137, 148–49, 155; bronze metallurgy, 137, 171–72, 195; knowledge of iron, 195; house and architecture, 137, 147 ff.; community patterns, 137, 143, 151 ff., 157 ff., 163, 166, 193; social stratification, 166; war and weapons, 137, 213 ff.; government, 137, 143, 166 ff.; trade, 137, 144; religion, 137, 144, 169; burial, 137, 143, 153, 160, 203, 217; art,

137, 144, 145; conquest by Chou, 135
Shang Hsien, 260
Shang-chieh, 141, 148, 165
Shang-tien, 89
Shang-ts'un-ling, 203, 212–14, 219
Shansi, 54, 89; ancient landscape, 37; Palaeolithic, 15, 28, 30, 32; Neolithic in Southern Shansi, 9, 59, 60, 66, 69, 79, 87, 89, 95, 102; Neolithic in Central Shansi, 59; Neolithic and Sub-Neolithic in Northern Shansi, 111 ff.; Shang, 142, 145; Western Chou, 177, 203, 210, 214; Eastern Chou, 6, 183, 186, 202, 203, 229
Shansi Lungshan Culture, 102–03
Shantung, 77; geography, 22, 23; Neolithic, 10, 11, 77, 87, 95, 97, 98, 107, 109; lack of painted pottery before the war, 78; Shang, 12, 145, 163; Eastern Chou, 190
shao, 211
Shao-hu-ying-tzu-shan, 116
Shao-kou, 203, 217
Sharamurun (R.), 115
sheep-goat: Neolithic North China, 55; Yangshao, 60; Proto-Lungshan, 85; Lungshan, 94, 100, 103, 105; Shang, 137, 173; Eastern Chou, 186; Microlithic, 114; steppe, 228, 233; Ch'i-chia Culture, 120; Ssu-wa Culture, 241; Szechwan, 124; Yünnan, 291
shell artifacts: Proto-Lungshan, 85; Lungshan, 92, 96, 105; Shang, 137, 141, 149; Microlithic, 114
Shen-nung, 2, 131–33
Sheng-wen Horizon, 57
Shensi, 54, 89; ancient "nors," 37; Palaeolithic, 33; Mesolithic, 40, 43; Neolithic in Central-Eastern, 59, 61, 63, 66, 69, 76, 80, 87, 88, 93, 99; Neolithic and Sub-Neolithic in Northern, 111 ff.; Shang influence, 145, 164, 175, 179; Western Chou, 175, 177, 203; Eastern Chou, 187, 202, 203, 210; nomads, 227
Shensi Lungshan Culture, 99
Shih Chang-ju, 12, 15, 98, 99, 140, 157, 178, 179

Shih Chi, 2, 131, 154, 167, 176, 255, 256, 258, 259, 264, 266, 272
Shih Ching, 177, 181, 259
Shih Hsing-pang, 322
Shih Huang Ti, 175–76, 223, 299
Shih-chai-shan, 290 ff.
Shih-chia-ho, 105
Shih-erh-t'ai-ying-tzu, 232
Shih-li-p'u (Chinghai), 238
Shih-li-p'u (Honan), 163
Shou Hsien: Lungshan, 107; Shang influence, 251; Ts'ai, 258; Ch'u tombs, 12, 262, 264, 266
Shou-ch'un, 258
shouldered axe, 123, 125, 129
shovel-shaped incisors, 30–32
Shu (in Hanshui), 259
Shu (in Szechwan), 286, 298
shu-hsüeh (tomb type), 215
Shui-kuan-yin, 276, 278
Shui-tung-kou, 27, 33
Shun, 4
Sian, 61, 66. *See also* Pan-p'o-ts'un, Mi-chia-yai, P'u-tu-ts'un
Siberia, 44, 45, 127, 306
sickle. *See* stone sickle
Sikang, 123
silk: Neolithic, 55, 60; Shang, 137, 173; Ch'u, 266
silkworm, 60, 225
Sinanthropus officinalis, 32
Sinanthropus pekinensis, 29–31, 33. *See also* Peking Man
Sinkiang, 5, 11, 21, 23, 25, 77, 112, 118 ff., 127, 175
"Six Stage Theory," 234
Sjara-osso-gol, 27, 33, 36
slash-and-burn cultivation, 61, 92, 94
slate, 225
slaves: Shang, 137, 173; Yünnan, 291
social stratification, 92, 95, 137, 291
Sogho-nor, 40
South China: history of prehistoric research, 11; Palaeolithic, 28, 30, 32, 46; Mesolithic, 46 ff.; first ceramic horizon, 57; Neolithic and Sub-Neolithic in general, 129; Lungshanoid expansion, 87, 92, 106 ff.; rice cultivation, 59, 93; early civilizations, 246–95; relations with North China, 12, 129, 302

Southeast. *See* Eastern South China
Southeast Asia, 298; Upper Palaeolithic, 46, 49; early Post-Glacial cultures, 49; Mesolithic population, 50, 129; origin of agriculture, 93, 129; Dongsonian, 294; relation with South China, 12
Southwest: history of prehistoric research, 11; geography, 21, 24; Early Man, 28, 32; ancient races, 46; Mesolithic, 77; Sub-Neolithic and Neolithic, 49, 122 ff.; civilizations, 275–95. *See also* names of the constituent provinces
soy bean, 55, 185
spade: stone, 60, 93, 96, 103, 114, 115, 137, 172; iron, 197, 264
spear, 60
specialization: of crafts, 92, 95, 137, 171, 194, 271; of occupation, 92, 95; of settlement, 143, 166
spindle-whorl, 60, 68, 94, 105, 114
Spring-Autumn Period, 177, 183, 203
ssu, 131
Ssu-ma Chien, 2, 131, 154, 167, 176, 255, 256, 258, 259, 264, 266
Ssu-mien-pei, 154
Ssu-pa Culture (Phase), 119, 121. *See also* Shan-tan Culture
Ssu-pa-t'an, 121
Ssu-p'an-mo, 154
Ssu-wa Culture (Tradition), 122, 234, 241–42
Ssu-wa-shan, 241
stamped earth. *See* hang-t'u
state: legendary beginning, 133; basis in Lungshan stage, 137
steamer: pottery in North China, 55, 83. *See also* hsien, yen, tseng
steppe, 21, 111, 118–21, 127, 128, 224, 226 ff., 285
stepped adze, 124, 129, 247
stone axe and adze: Yangshao, 60, 66; Lungshan, 78, 92, 96, 100, 103, 105; Proto-Lungshan, 85; Shang, 137; Microlithic, 113, 116; Southwest, 124
stone ball, 32, 60
stone chisel: Yangshao, 66; Lungshan, 92, 96, 103; Southwest, 124
stone implement: studies of, 3; Yangshao, 66, 92; Proto-Lungshan, 85; Lungshan, 92, 96, 103, 105; Shang,

137, 144; Inner Mongolia, 114; Southwest, 124, 125

stone knife, 45; Neolithic North China, 55; Yangshao, 60, 92; Proto-Lungshan, 85; Lungshan, 92, 96, 103; Shang, 148; Microlithic, 113, 116; Manchuria, 117. *See also* rectangular stone knife, semilunar stone knife

stone sculpture: Shang, 137, 143, 144

stone sickle: Proto-Lungshan, 85; Lungshan, 92, 93, 100, 103; Shang, 137, 144, 172, 173; Microlithic, 113, 116; Manchuria, 117; Southwest, 126

stratified village farmers, 52, 133

Su Ping-chi, 178, 322

Sub-Neolithic, 110, 127; in Northeast Asia, 127; Manchuria, 116, 117; Mongolia, 41, 114, 116; Northwest, 119; Southwest, 49, 123

Suiyüan, 111

Sun-ch'i-t'un, 58, 65, 79, 89

Sung, 181

Sungari (R.), 24, 25, 36, 116, 127, 129, 225

sword, 214, 215, 223, 231, 266, 281; stone imitation of bronze and iron prototype, 226

Szechwan, 132; geography, 23, 24; Palaeolithic, 9, 32, 46; Mesolithic, 46, 47; Neolithic and Sub-Neolithic, 122 ff., 275; Shang influence, 145, 276; Western Chou influence, 12, 276; Ch'u influence, 262; relation with steppe, 285; civilizations, 275 ff., 298

Ta-ch'eng-shan, 108, 113

Ta-ho-chuang, 120

Ta-hsin-chuang, 163

Ta-kou, 43

Ta-lai-tien, 89, 94

Ta-li, 126, 288

Ta-ssu-k'ung-ts'un, 154, 160, 161

T'ai (L.), 24, 252

Tai-hsi, 47

T'ai-p'ing-ch'ang, 277

T'ai-p'u-hsiang, 203

T'ai-shang, 249

T'ai-tzu-ch'ung, 261

T'ai-wang, 178

taiga, 127

tailored garment, 55

Taiwan, 87, 123, 246. *See also* Formosa

Taiyüan, 36

Tan-t'u, 252, 253

Tan-yang, 260

T'ang, 135

Tang Lan, 211

Tang Yün-ming, 164

Tang-t'u, 260

T'ang-wang Culture (Phase), 122, 238–39

T'ao (R.), 64, 72, 73, 75, 119, 120, 234–36, 238, 241

t'ao-t'ieh, 144, 205–07, 213

technology. *See* stone, bone, shell, metal implement and/or industry, Neolithic technology, metallurgy, bronze metallurgy, iron metallurgy

Teilhard de Chardin, Pierre, 6, 8, 9, 26–28, 36, 321

temple: Shang, 157; Ch'u, 271–72

T'eng, 190

Teotihuacan, 166

terrace field, 126

Three Age System, 2

Three Culture Theory, 15

Three Dynasties, 2, 5, 130

Ti, 224

Ti-hsin, 135, 160

Ti-yih, 160

Tiao-yü-t'ai, 93

Tibet, 7, 21, 46, 284

Tien, 291, 298

Tien-ch'ih (L.), 125, 126

Tien-chün-t'ai, 89

Tien-ts'ang (Mts.), 126, 288

Tien-tsin muds, 38

T'ien-shui Hsien, 72

tiger, 37, 281, 287

tile: Western Chou, 191; Eastern Chou, 183–90 passim

Timber Culture, 228

ting tripod (bronze), 205, 207, 212

ting tripod (pottery): Neolithic North China, 55, 83, 85, 86, 91, 104–06, 109, 126, 128, 155, 238

Ting Yih, 322

Ting-ts'un, 27, 31, 32

T'o (R.), 276

Torri Ryuzo, 5, 114

tou (bronze ladle), 211
tou (fruit-stand), 84, 85, 91, 100, 103, 105, 106, 148, 155, 251, 266, 273
Tou-chi-t'ai, 59
Tou-men, 99, 179
trade: Mesolithic, 42; Yangshao, 68; Shang, 137
tradition: pottery, *see* pottery tradition; North China Neolithic Culture, *see* Chinese Culture Tradition
tripods: Neolithic North China, 55, 56; Lungshan, 78, 85, 91, 96, 97, 101–09 passim; Shang, 144, 148, 155; Microlithic, 111, 114, 116; Manchuria, 117; Northwest, 128; Hsin-tien Culture, 238; Southwest, 124, 126
Tripolye, 234
Ts'ai, 258–59
Tsaidam Culture (Phase), 119, 121
Ts'ao-tien, 89
Ts'ao-yen-chuang, 162
tseng, 55
Tseng Chao-yü, 256, 325
Tsinling (Mts.), 22, 46, 54
Tso Chuan, 170, 176, 181, 187, 272
Tsou Heng, 164, 165, 324
tsun: Lungshan, 91; Shang, 155; bronze, 205, 207, 258
tsung-fa, 169, 221
tu, 193
T'u-men (R.), 24, 117, 129, 226
Tuan-hsü, 272
tui, 206, 273
T'un-hsi, 252, 253
Tung Chu-chen, 322, 325
Tung Tso-pin, 8, 135, 159, 161
Tung-chai, 141, 148
Tung-hu, 102
Tung-kan-kou, 165
Tung-pa-chia, 114–15
Tung-pai-chung, 102
Tung-pao, 203, 210, 214
tung-shih-mu, 217
Tung-sun-pa, 279
Tung-t'ing (L.), 24
T'ung-lo-chai, 89, 154
tuo, 205
turtle shell, 144, 155, 250
Two Culture Theory, 10, 13, 78, 91

Tzu-ching-shan, 146, 151–53, 171
Tzu-kui, 260
Tzu-yang, 27, 32, 33, 43
Tz'u-ts'un, 107

Umehara Sueji, 195
Upper Cave. *See* Choukoutien: Upper Cave
Ur, 166
urbanization: in legend, 133; basis in Lungshan stage, 137; Shang, 138, 143–44, 165–66; Chou, 16, 180 ff. *See also* city
urn burial, 63, 105, 188

Villafranchian, 25, 26, 28
village: of first farmers, 51–52; Yangshao, 61 ff.; Lungshan, 92, 94, 95, 103, 105; Shang, 143; Eastern Chou, 185; general layout in Neolithic, 55; cemetery, 63 ff.; wall, 63, 92, 94, 95, 114; fortification, 92, 137
Vladivostok, 226
von Koenigswald, G. H. R., 9, 28, 30

Wa-cha-tsui, 237
Wa-kuan-tsui, 64
Wan Hsien, 276
Wang, C. C., 325
Wang Chia-yu, 325
Wang Chung-shu, 325
Wang Hsiang, 251
Wang Kuo-wei, 221
Wang Po-hung, 324
Wang-chia-kou, 64
Wang-chia-wan, 59
Wang-yü-k'ou, 154
war: Lungshan, 94, 137; Shang, 137, 168; Yünnan, 291–92
Warring-States Period, 2, 177; cities, 184, 186, 188; implements, 196, 197; burials, 12, 203
water-buffalo, 137, 173
water-ditch: Shang, 153, 157, 172; Eastern Chou, 183, 185, 188; Yen, 257
Watson, William, 321
wattle-and-daub: North China Neolithic, 55; Yangshao, 62; Proto-Lungshan, 80; Lungshan, 103, 105; Shang, 159

weapon: Lungshan, 92; Shang, 137, 168; Chou, 213–14; steppe nomads, 231; Szechwan, 283
weaving, 55, 291. See also fabrics
Wei, 187
Wei (R.): ancient cultural sequence, 178; Mesolithic, 111; Yangshao Neolithic, 59, 61, 62, 72, 76; Lungshan, 98–102, 109; Shang, 145, 175, 179; Western Chou, 177, 178; Ch'i-chia Culture, 120; Ssu-wa Culture, 242
Wei Chü-hsien, 2, 321
Wei-Mo, 224
Weidenreich, Franz, 9, 28–30, 42, 43
well: Lungshan, 94; Eastern Chou, 186, 189
Wen Tao-yih, 325
Wen Wang, 181
Wen-chia-t'un, 116
Western Asia, 10, 78, 285
Western Chou, 99, 120, 177–81 passim, 191, 195, 196, 203, 205, 207, 210–14 passim, 217–22 passim, 230, 252–55 passim, 259–61 passim, 276 ff
wheat, 24; Yangshao, 59; Lungshan, 93; Shang, 137, 172; Yünnan, 289
wheel-made pottery, 10, 91, 92, 95, 100, 102, 104, 105, 126, 137
white limy house floor (pai-hui-mien): Neolithic North China, 55; Proto-Lungshan, 80; Lungshan, 95, 100, 103, 104; Shang, 137
white pottery: Shang, 144, 145; Lao-t'ieh-shan, 225; Hanchiang River, 252
Willey, Gordon R., 17
Wo-kuo, 186
Woo Ju-kang, 29, 321
wood-carving: North China Neolithic, 55, 66; Ch'u, 268–69
woodland cultures, 45
wool, 121
writing, 56, 135; legends of invention, 130, 133; early history of, 139; Shang, 137, 144, 153, 156, 160, 168; Ch'u, 271, 273; Szechwan, 284
Wu, 181, 254, 255, 257
Wu Chin-ting (Wu Gin-ding), 12, 77, 126, 241, 245, 288, 321, 325

Wu Hsin-chih, 43
Wu Ju-tso, 178, 322, 324
Wu Ti (Five Emperors), 130
Wu Wang, 178, 181
Wu-ch'eng, 188
Wu-chi, 189
Wu-chia, 243
Wu-kuan-ts'un, 154, 160
Wu-shan Hsien (Eastern Kansu), 72
Wu-shan Hsien (Szechwan), 124
Wung-chiang, 261

Ya-an, 123
Ya-p'u-shan, 48
Yalu (R.), 24
Yang Chung-chien (Young Chung-chien), 6, 9, 118, 321
Yang Ken, 323
Yang Yu-jun, 325
Yang-chia-wan, 251
Yang-lin-chi, 251
Yang-shao-ts'un, 5, 7, 8, 11, 38, 58, 59, 62, 66, 69, 79, 85, 89, 234
Yang-t'ou-wa, 11, 94, 108, 116
Yang-tzu-shan, 277, 281, 283
Yangshao Culture, 10, 51, 78; relation with Lungshan Culture, 10, 11, 78; distribution, 78, 79; dates, 234. See also Yangshao Horizon, Yangshao stage
Yangshao Horizon, 68–69; sub-horizons, 69 ff., 119
Yangshao stage: climate, 38; origins, 75–76; subsistence, 59–60; importance of fishing, 60; settlement patterns, 61, 62; stone and bone industries, 55, 66; pottery, 66–68; house, 62 ff.; community patterns, 62–63; kinship, 65; burial, 65; religion, 65–66; distribution, 54; regional styles, 69–70; contemporary cultures, 77; influences among above, 77, 113 ff.; ceramic horizons, 70 ff.; chronology, 54, 70–76, 234; relations with Lungshan, 10–11, 51–52, 77 ff.; compared with Lungshan, 91–93
Yangtze (R.), 9, 11, 22, 24, 87, 93, 205
Yao, 1, 4
yao-k'eng ("waist-pit"), 161, 215
Yayoi Culture, 294

INDEX

Yellow Emperor. *See* Huang-ti
Yellow River. *See* Huangho
yen, 55, 206, 252. *See also hsien*, steamer
Yen (state in Lower Yangtze), 257
Yen (state in North China), 12, 189
Yen-ch'eng, 257
Yen-erh-wan, 73
Yen-tun-shan, 211, 253
Yenisie (R.), 230
yih (bronze vessel type), 144, 205, 207, 258
yih (another bronze vessel type, of later date), 205, 207
Yih (Eastern Yih), 10, 78, 221, 225
yih (term for city), 193
Yih-ch'ang, 123
Yih-cheng, 252, 253
Yih-ching, 103
yih-pi-ch'ien, 271
Yih-tu, 124
Yin, 2, 3, 13, 135, 154; as art style, 206, 207, 211
Yin Huan-chang, 12, 252, 256, 323, 325
Yin Shan (Mts.), 224, 227 ff.
Yin Ta, 12. *See also* Liu Yao

Yin Ti-fei, 325
Yin-chin, 187
Yin-Chou: art style, 206, 207, 211, 253
Yin-kuo-ts'un, 162
Ying-tsê, 149, 150
yu: Shang, 144, 155; Chou, 205, 207, 212; Geometric, 252
yü, 155
Yü, 1, 2, 4
Yü Chieh, 324
Yü-chia-lin, 107
Yu-jung, 167
Yü-yao Hsien, 257
Yu-yih, 177
Yüan Kang, 2
Yüeh, 2, 181, 255, 257, 258, 264, 274, 298
Yüeh Chüeh Shu, 2
Yün-meng (L.), 24
Yüng (R.), 98
Yüng-ch'ang, 121, 242
Yüng-ching, 236–38
Yünnan: Palaeolithic, 46; Mesolithic, 46–48; Sub-Neolithic and Neolithic, 122–24, 126; civilizations, 12, 287–95; Ch'u influence, 262

346